RED TORY BLUES

HEATH MACQUARRIE

Red Tory Blues
A Political Memoir

UNIVERSITY OF TORONTO PRESS
Toronto Buffalo London

© University of Toronto Press 1992
Toronto Buffalo London
Printed in Canada
ISBN 0-8020-5958-9

Printed on acid-free paper

All photographs are used courtesy of Senator Heath Macquarrie, with the
exception of the cartoon on page 68 (courtesy of the *Winnipeg Free Press*);
'At the Vatican, March 1968' (courtesy of Pontificia Fotographia); and
'Roman in the Gloamin'' (courtesy of Wayne Wright).

Canadian Cataloguing in Publication Data

Macquarrie, Heath, 1919–
Red Tory blues

Includes index.
ISBN 0-8020-5958-9

1. Macquarrie, Heath, 1919–   . 2. Progressive
Conservative Party of Canada — History — 20th
century. 3. Canada — Politics and government —
1935–   .* 4. Canada — Politics and government —
1930–1935.* 5. Politicians — Canada — Biography.
I. Title.

FC601.M32A3 1992   324.27104'092   C92-093219-3
F1034.3.M32A3 1992

This book has been published with the help of grants from the Canada
Council and the Ontario Arts Council under their block grant programs.

Contents

Preface

Although there was never any great lobby urging that I write this book, a number of kind and possibly misguided friends have suggested I record my recollections of the gathering years. I usually replied that I was neither old enough nor famous enough for autobiographical exercises. Now at least, or at last, I'm old enough.

I hope my timing is reasonably good. A septuagenarian should be pardoned for a tendency to reminiscence, but he must remember that anecdotage is often the phase that precedes dotage. So far too, I have not even been tempted into that antiquarians' perspective which sometimes sees the days of yore as unending glory and contemporary times as something less than satisfactory.

Much has happened in the more than sixty years I have tried to relive in these pages. From the beginning I was diffident about producing a volume of memoirs. Such a project seemed presumptuous. Rather had I envisaged an informal history of the Conservative party as seen through my aging eyes. Even though my own preference has been abandoned, this is in large part a chronicle of my party as well as a personal recollection.

In that portion of Canadian history covering the years 1930 to 1991 my party had nine full-time leaders, all of them known to me. We had electoral triumphs and disasters, great days and some terrible times. Many of my colleagues have quit the course long ago, most of them involuntarily. Because, as I can testify, political life can be irksome, frustrating, sometimes heartbreaking, but it is never dull.

I am enormously thankful for my thirty-four years on Parliament Hill representing my beloved native province. Although never an ardent partisan, I have long been convinced of the value of broadly based national parties in a country as diverse as Canada. The ecumenical party created under the pragmatic leadership of John A. Macdonald was, in itself, a major factor in the creation of a united Dominion of the North, as historian Donald Creighton proudly called it. In today's age of the pollsters, we have forebodings about the rise of splinter or sectional protest groups and the consequent fracturing of national parties. Such a development could be a vital threat to Canadian unity, which must remain our dearest goal.

God knows, these are not the best of times for the Progressive Conservative party. I used to think we had seen our worst days in the Depression-ridden thirties. But in 1935 with a highly unlikeable leader and a prominent Conservative leading a populist party, we nevertheless won 29.6 per cent of the vote in the election.

Now for months we have moved between 12 and 17 per cent in the polls.

I have no major elixir for my party but I will presume to offer advice. Over the years, in our better days, we were perceived as a party of the centre, not of the right. In 1854 John A. Macdonald opened the party to all desirous of calling themselves progressive Conservative. In 1942 the party chose John Bracken as leader and officially became Progressive Conservative. John Diefenbaker's first brief government in 1957–8 probably brought in more progressive and socially beneficial legislation than any preceding or succeeding government. To become more right-wing than the Reform party, to become a devotee of Reaganism (or Thatcherism), after that creed has been exposed as wanting in its place of origin, is pitifully self-defeating.

The Progressive Conservative Party of Canada will not regain public approval by a neoconservative posture. Rather it must recall that government should do most for those who most need help. Because I worry about our current sense of values, I've called these candid memoirs *Red Tory Blues*.

I've spent more than sixty years living this book and an overly long time writing it. Although flaws, errors, and any other demerits may be charged to me, I still wish to thank those who helped me along the way. The Library of Parliament has served me with efficiency and sensitivity for years. Its staff were always helpful in this project. Deborah Brazeau, chef de cabinet, has been helpful all the way. Research assistants Alan Riddell, Chris Kent, Kathleen Csaba, Bruce Campbell, and Nevio Christante have vindicated my judgment in asking them to join my staff. Anne Harris was in the forefront of those who provided practical assistance and inspiration, as were Bhupinder Liddar, Gordon Cullingham, and Tom Sloan. I appreciate the guidance of people at the University of Toronto Press like Gerald Hallowell and Mary McDougall Maude. My wife, Isabel, who might well be dubbed editor in chief of the whole operation, demonstrated her great skill in composition and, as in all other things, has been my most devoted supporter and counsel.

Heath Macquarrie
September 1991

The carefree author aged four at home base, Victoria, PEI

My parents, Wilfred Macquarrie and Mary Mallard. I was lucky in my
parentage.

With three of my favourite Canadians, Dalton Camp, Bob Stanfield, and Eugene Forsey, at the PC Thinkers' Conference at UNB in 1964

A Highlander on the Hill, 1966

For a campaign pamphlet in 1968, my four best supporters: Isabel, Iain 10, Heather 16, and Flora 14

Daughter Flora, wearing a Stanfield hat, joyously welcomes Bob Stanfield at Ottawa airport following the great 1967 convention.

Son Iain Heath's graduation photo from St Andrew's College, 1978

Daughter Heather Jean with her husband, Colin Ritchie, and our five lovely, lively grandchildren: (clockwise from top) Jamie, Emily, Nicholas, Pamela, and Andrew

At the Vatican, March 1986, with the Canadian Branch of the
Canada-Europe Parliamentary Association

Being greeted by Prime Minister Indira Ghandi, Delhi, 1971

With President Anwar Sadat at Marmora Palace, Alexandria, in 1978.
We talked mainly about the Palestinians, and I thought him one of
the great statesmen of our time.

HRH Crown Prince Hassan of Jordan, a wise and constructive statesman

With Yasser Arafat in Beirut 1978: 'a much maligned man who in a sea of difficulties has sought to pilot his people'

Isabel and I with John and Cate Fraser, celebrating Mr Speaker's
birthday, 15 December 1989

With Honourable James M. Lee, former PC premier of PEI, at the Confederation Chamber of the Provincial Building, Charlottetown, 1991. The men who met in that room in 1864 were our best constitution makers.

The cartoonist of the Summerside *Journal-Pioneer* depicts one of my best days.

RED TORY BLUES

... if you believe that in Big Business, that in capitalism, there are abuses which work hardship upon the people of this country, if you believe that the faults of capitalism have brought about injustices in our social state, if you believe that these injustices manifest themselves in lower wages and too high costs of living and unemployment, – then support my Party. For my Party has already undertaken and will pursue to the end, a program of reform which will rid the system of these disabilities. It stands for the freedom of the individual and private initiative and sound business, but it stands with equal certainty for permanent and better relationships between the people and those instruments of commerce and finance which are set up to serve them ... My Party stands simply for the greatest good of the greatest number of the people. And it shapes and will continue to shape its policy of reform, to make that sure.

R.B. BENNETT
Radio broadcast, 11 January 1935,
on the 110th anniversary of the
birth of Sir John A. Macdonald

1

The Beginning of It All

In the vain world in which politicians flourish I have encountered many who claim they staked out their destiny and way of life shortly after being weaned. Many presidents, prime ministers, and other greats have testified that they knew all along where they wanted to go and what they wished to be. Sometimes I have wondered whether there was a highly retroactive element about these declarations of strength of purpose.

Personally I don't recall such clear youthful visions, but I can remember vividly my first exposure to political life. The year 1930 was a big one for me. I had won my school leaving certificate in June, 'having passed courses in arithmetic, English, drawing, writing, hygiene, geography, history and rural science.' This cherished document, as I recall, signified full compliance with the compulsory schooling law and opened the way to grade 9. Those who went on after grade 8 became high school students, although I can't remember anyone at the time making this distinction in nomenclature. Since I was about three months shy of my eleventh birthday I probably didn't feel or look like a typical high schooler, and it would be a decade before I had the right to vote.

But while it would be a long time before I could approach the ballot box, it was a short distance to Victoria Hall, where a big political event was scheduled for the night of 10 July 1930. Victoria is the name of the village I grew up in on the south shore of Prince Edward Island, west of the capital, Charlottetown, and then located in the constituency of Queens, one of two dual constituencies in Canada electing two members to the House of Commons. The event was to be a 'joint meeting' at which opposing candidates exposed their political style and arguments before the electors. Prince Edward Islanders were noted for a deep interest in the political process. They were ready to hear their politicians plead their cases and causes, and the confrontational aspect added interest. Some people declared they wouldn't miss such shows for anything. At our joint meetings, as a dual constituency, we had two orators from each party. This fact might make for more excitement, but it also made for longer meetings.

My father was an active member of the Victoria poll committee on the Conservative side. My mother had voted in the 1917 election in which women with family in the military were given the right to vote. She also was a hardshell Tory. In any case they were quite agreeable to my going along to the meeting. I can't remember whether I went in the hope of being entertained or with a desire to be informed. As a pre–high school student, surely I didn't go for any light or shallow reasons!

In some informal exercise of democracy, Jabez Lea, an impressive town patriarch, was chosen chairman. Since the Liberals were in power in both Ottawa and Charlottetown there was probably some unwritten law which dictated that, like deputy returning officers on election day, the chairmanship of joint meetings should go to the 'ins.' In any case, Mr Lea had the voice and the appearance suited to the occasion. He called the meeting to order, announced the sequence of speakers and, after placing his splendid gold watch on the table, had the debate begin.

Public meetings of this kind seem to encourage a slow start and a gradual increase of oratorical momentum to ensure the major impact in the finale. I doubt that this was consciously planned for the Victoria meeting but it happened.

The first Liberal speaker, Robert Harold Jenkins, a former mayor of Charlottetown and Queens MP since 1925, seemed low-key and his delivery was not spectacular. Chester McLure for the Conservatives handled things with competence. He had served in the provincial legislature since 1923 but was making his first try for the federal constituency of Queens. I had never seen him before but was delighted when he noted with approval the presence in the audience of one who was very young. Since I was the only child there, I took it as a personal and welcome greeting.

A new and exciting element in the election was the candidacy of Dr Cyrus Macmillan, dean of arts and science at McGill University and a distinguished Islander. Prime Minister Mackenzie King had just made him minister of fisheries. In those days, Prince Edward Island didn't often rate a federal cabinet minister with portfolio and the Honourable Cyrus was therefore a major attraction.

Dr Macmillan was a son of the Island, but the Conservatives were not averse to representing him as a parachuted candidate. Chester McLure, always gentlemanly in his presentations, carefully referred to Macmillan as 'the honourable gentleman from Montreal' every time he mentioned him, which was quite often that night.

Although by far the most highly educated man on the platform, Dr Macmillan was obviously uncomfortable. He seemed tense and fidgety, blushed a great deal, and was discomfited by even the gentlest heckling. As he began rebutting McLure's criticisms, he groped in his pocket for some notes and statistics, and the other Tory candidate, John Myers, observed loudly from his seat: 'The honourable gentleman seems to have more in his pocket than he has in his head.' Needless to say, this little intrusion did nothing to help the unfortunate Macmillan get under way.

While the meeting was well conducted and orderly and everyone received a good hearing, it was apparent that the two Grits faced the heavier challenge. They had lots of cheering supporters, as did the Tories, but it was the Liberals who were on the defensive. Candidates supporting a government always are defensive, but there were grave economic problems during the Mackenzie King administration then in office. Unemployment stalked the land; commodity prices were grievously low. A Victoria farmer, Park Rogerson, delivered milk in our village for seven cents a quart. That was also the price per pound that my father and his fellow fishermen received for market lobsters, while canners fetched a nickel.

It is hard to believe that the supercautious King would ever make an utterance that would cause his party to lose votes, but, at the Victoria meeting on that far-off July night and in hosts of other political gatherings elsewhere, King was excoriated for his callous statement that he wouldn't give a five-cent piece in employment aid to any province with a Tory government.

The Liberals that night had more than Mackenzie King and the Depression and his five-cent speech to contend with. Conservative candidate John Myers was in his home poll; a veteran politician, he had run in Queens before and had been dubbed Jack the Giant Killer when, in a provincial election, he had lost the nomination in his own riding of 1st Queens and had to run against incumbent Walter M. Lea in 4th Prince. Mr Lea, also from Victoria and a leading light in the provincial Liberal party, was the loser in that contest. Mr Myers was therefore a heavyweight whom the Victoria audience expected to deliver a rousing speech.

And deliver he did. These joint meetings required special platform skills. Neither the arts of the courtroom practitioner nor the learned declarations of the lecture podium would suffice. John Myers was a farmer and, although he was a graduate of a good business college, he came across as one of the folks. Not for him the written speech or the prosy discourse. Few public speakers on or off the Island could match the brilliance of his wit or the rapier sharpness of his repartee. He chided, scolded, and mocked the honourable gentleman from Montreal. Myers didn't dwell on Dr Macmillan's notable achievements, but made much of his unfitness for the portfolio of fisheries. According to the Tory candidate, the minister knew absolutely nothing about fish or fishing. He made one exception. Macmillan knew something about red herrings since his appointment was itself a red herring to draw across the trail of Liberal neglect of Queens County and PEI.

Any participation by a heckler served but to spur on the big burly farmer from the local area. John Myers was a ruggedly handsome man with the easy manner which many politicians develop. The star of that evening, he must have delighted in the response on his home turf. But, as sometimes happens, cheers don't always translate into votes. Dr Macmillan was the most popular man in the Victoria poll on the vital day of election, but in the constituency the two Conservatives topped the Liberals. In the previous election, in 1926, the Liberals had elected both their candidates in Queens.

In those days in the dual riding of Queens, one of the candidates was invariably a Charlottetown man. Chester McLure was a successful businessman in the capital city. He had attended Prince of Wales College and had taught school for six years. He was always extremely well dressed and a bit formal in manner. At this time and thereafter he was a paunchy man but, unlike some, he never sought to minimize his girth. In fact, he seemed rather proud of it. Despite this, some nasty Grits used to whisper that he wore a corset, a common garment among the women of that era. Or at least I gathered this from the Eaton's catalogue as I tried to learn the facts of life from its pages. Chester also sported a magnificent and well-waxed moustache. My father, despite his own more modest moustache, said he would never vote for Chester McLure until he shaved off that waxed monstrosity. For once my father was not as good as his word and he was proud to vote for McLure until the end of his life. Of course by that time Chester had disposed of the controversial waxed tips.

After the oratory came the inevitable pressing of the flesh which politicians of any kind and in any age must do. I had the pleasure of meeting Mrs McLure who was devoted to her husband's success and a practised campaigner in her own right. She made a bit of a fuss over me, which was appreciated. She had an interesting way of introducing herself: 'I belong to Chester McLure.'

On the way out of the hall, John Myers greeted my mother with a friendly, 'Ah, there's my favourite white-haired girl.' Having developed a certain realism about the political breed she replied that she was most certainly white-headed but could not vouch for the rest.

I don't remember meeting the Liberal candidates. This is perhaps not surprising since I belonged to a committed Tory family. In those days, as election day neared partisan sentiments strengthened. Jim Knox, a prominent Tory and family friend, used to note with some interest that the audience was likely to be more intense about their political differences than were the candidates. He often told that when some Victoria folk went to joint meetings in nearby Crapaud they would be so keyed up that on the way home there was danger of fisticuffs. The next day he would hear that, while the Victoria men were still fighting the issues, the candidates were drinking out of the same bottle in Crapaud.

Those interesting political institutions, joint meetings, did not totally disappear from PEI politics with their demise in Queens in 1935. The neighbouring constituency of Kings clung to them for some time and in many provincial contests they were a part of electoral campaigns for a good many years. In today's television age all-candidate meetings are being revived.

These direct confrontations of office-seekers with their constituents were useful, if not essential, elements of election campaigns in the pre-radio and pre-television age. And newspapers could not serve as an ample vehicle of communication. In those days newspapers in Prince Edward Island, like most elsewhere in Canada, were notoriously partisan. According to the *Patriot*, the Victoria meeting of 10 July 1930 was a walkaway for the Liberal stalwarts. The *Guardian* reported that the Liberals had been routed by the noble Tories.

But I believe that these minuscule manifestations of political democracy were more than a mere convenient electioneering device. They gave depth to the political process. Of course there was a degree of oneupmanship and perhaps an occasional resort to 'dirty tricks' at the Victoria meeting. The candidates were neither angels nor Milquetoasts. They didn't always resist the temptation to take advantage of the other person's slip of the tongue, and they were not above trying to distort his meaning if the opening was there. But to see it as a mere game, an empty charade, would be to misread and underrate the whole thing.

Prince Edward Island was beautifully described by one of my favourite history professors, W. Menzies Whitelaw: 'In no other province is the population so dense; in no other is it so small.

Diminutive and proud, dour and lovable, Prince Edward Island still remains among the provinces unique and a paradox.'[1]

It is also uniquely fitted to be a political laboratory. Its small population, its compactness, and in this age its excellent transportation links make it something like an enlarged and continuous New England town meeting. With all the oratorical feints, partisan jabs, and eager thrust and parry of political gladiators, that meeting in Victoria had much of real value to those who cherish the view that an enlightened electorate and sensitive representatives are the *sine qua non* of a decent democracy. I was not quite eleven at the time and more than half a century has flooded my memories since, but I do recall the pith and substance of that confrontation of four decent Island men seeking to represent their province in the Parliament of the Dominion of Canada, as our country was then so appropriately called.

There was much discussion of Maritime rights in Confederation. Reference was made to the Duncan and White royal commissions, which had studied the problems of the economic disparity of our region.[2] In the 1980s, I used to hear contemporary politicians talk about regional disparity as if they had discovered the issue. One of the 1930 candidates, Dr Macmillan, had been a member of the Duncan Commission, which sat from April to September of 1926. Our tariff and transportation problems were talked about. Analyses of the American Hawley-Smoot and Fordney-McCumber tariffs were offered. It was the first time I had heard of countervailing duties. A big issue in 1930, they were still a hot item in the nineties. The imperial preference was another topic. Agriculture problems and commodity prices were major subjects of debate and, of course, the blight of unemployment and the economic blizzard buffeting the world came in for careful and concerned attention. In fact, the Canadians sitting in the community hall of the beautiful little village of Victoria, in Canada's smallest province, heard a real discussion of the real issues facing their country, and they listened and cared.

Local issues were not neglected. Ingratitude is a prevalent malady among electorates and requires a frequent antidote of stimulated remembrance provided at election time by vote-seeking politicians. There were recollections of favours bestowed during that evening in Victoria. Cyrus Macmillan pointed out that eighty carloads of produce had been shipped from Victoria last year on an ocean-going steamship which was loaded at all three hatches simultaneously. He noted that they could not have taken advantage of such improved technology a few years earlier. A regular caller at Victoria's busy port, the ss *Harland*, had received a subsidy from the Liberals.

On 28 July, a fortnight after the Victoria meeting, the election took place and the Conservatives won both in Queens and in Canada. On election night I learned that while I might have been old enough to go to the joint meeting, I wasn't old enough to go to the victory celebration at John Myers's place. My parents were delighted that my sister and brothers from the Boston area were home and able to join in the jollification. I don't think I really expected to go, and I did not feel any great sense of deprivation.

I didn't know it then, but that night in July 1930 would be my dear father's last opportunity to celebrate the election of a Conservative government in Canada. There would be no other until 1957, ten years after his death.

I still remember the euphoria of that day. The results which the deputy returning officer, Jabez Lea, had read out from the steps of Victoria Hall did not bring much joy to a Conservative in our village. Macmillan 88, Jenkins 81, Myers 73, and McLure 57 couldn't prompt any Tory to dance on Victoria wharf. But the constituency returns coming in on the radio were better. When it was over the results showed McLure 9310, Myers 9178, Macmillan 8482, and Jenkins 8767.

Although I was certainly not involved in or even a witness to any such celebratory rituals, I am confident that the tonic effect of these figures was buttressed by the spirited support of a few drinks of rum, as the 'good old Tories' shared the delight of the good news.

In later years when I myself had become a party candidate, I appreciated even more the emotional and sentimental satisfaction of winning an election. In 1956 a dear octogenarian in North

Rustico told me that although his health was poor he hoped and prayed he would live to see his party win once more. He was to be doubly blessed. He was able to help bring the Conservatives to office in 1957, and he also saw the triumphant result of 1958. Without skirting irreverence I think the old chap died a happy man.

People like my mother and father were partisan die-hards; so were Jabez Lea and others on the Liberal side. It would be easy to say that if all voters were similarly rigid there would be little point in having elections, seeking good candidates, or holding intelligent discussions of issues. Unless people are capable of changing their minds, the electoral parliamentary process can't work. Indeed. But without the hardshell types, the unregenerate Grits and Tories, the party system wouldn't and couldn't work. A story is told of a man who came up to John A. Macdonald and said: 'John A, I'll always be behind you so long as you are right.' That wise old man replied: 'Yes, but in my business I need to have some people who'll stand behind me even when I'm wrong.'

Possibly I may be perceived as atavistic and unrealistic to make so much of these far-off political debates. In these days of handlers, spin doctors and image makers, and the twenty-second television clip, isn't it archaic to suggest that a discussion of real issues is germane to the vote-influencing process?

Lest I suggest that either I or my fellow Islanders go for the sedate or over-serious in discussions of politics or any other subject, the joint meetings could be, and often were, fun. One of my political friends and a long-time poll chairman, Jack Doyle, told me of the repartee of a Tory speaker at a joint meeting in Kings County, the home ground of many colourful Islanders to this day. The type of meeting he described was a joint nominating meeting. The stalwart Liberal who nominated his candidate dwelt at great length on the fact that his nominee was a self-made man, normally, then as now, a fairly good gambit. But when the Tory nominator rose he was by no means cowed. While noting the frequent references to the self-made man, he said that God made his nominee and added: 'Ladies and gentlemen, there is as much difference between the two men as there is between the two makers.'

At another meeting a Liberal candidate had fun recalling an event when he and his running mate had called on a farmer in the area and found him shearing sheep. It was, and I suppose still is, the invariable custom to begin this process at the sheep's head. This farmer started at the other extreme. The Liberal candidate won great applause when he explained that he had learned that the farmer had voted Conservative in the last election and was presumably ashamed to look even a sheep in the eye. When the Tory candidate rose, he didn't skirt the issue but said that, if he had been a member of the House of Commons for four years and had nothing to show for it but the appointment of his brother to the Senate, he wouldn't be able to look either end of a sheep 'in the eye.'

As I ponder those days now being enveloped in the mists of antiquity, I wonder whether the deeper, more deliberative interplay between electors and elected made for a more substantial political process and more solid judgments than the instant appraisals of our more tinselly age. Did the voters, exposed as they were to their politicians in the flesh and given a chance to see them do their stuff before their eyes, make more perceptive judgments? Any man who passed the rugged test of in-depth confrontation with his opponents was bound to be pretty well known. In those days before the glib analysts and the slick political salesmen, there was not much specialist assistance. The persuading had to be done by the candidate himself.

While skilful hucksterism may make for a better or at least a quicker sale, it may contribute to an accelerated devaluation. Today's shining hero can become tomorrow's fallen idol much more easily if the earlier appraisal had nothing for its basis but the slick salesmanship of a professional hawker of political wares.

Along with the organized debates which the joint meetings provided, the Island political process had another less admirable feature. This was the general practice of using booze as a sort of hidden persuader on election day. Liquor as a weapon in political warfare had a long if not honourable history in Prince Edward Island politics. In our sister Maritime provinces it was also a part of the electioneering process. When I became a resident of Manitoba, people there seemed genuinely unfamiliar with such practices.

I suppose to some members of the poll committees the booze added a dimension of power and sharpened the competitive edge. Not only did both sides have a supply, but each group had to make strategic and tactical judgments as to how to use the firewater most effectively. There would be little use in sending good liquor after a bad vote. I never sat in on the sessions at which the allocations were made, being first too young even to hear about it, and later totally repelled by the idea. Presumably the doubtful voters, the 'loose fish' as John A. Macdonald called them, would get first priority. Of course, if he were really skilled, a finagler could convince both sides to invest a bottle in his vote. At elections there were sometimes a number of ballots on which the elector had voted for both party's candidates. Some of these spoiled ballots were said to be the work of the doubly bribed who sustained their honour by showing their gratitude for each of their benefactors. My father once said it would probably be more effective to use inducements to keep those characters away from the polls. At least that way you could be sure they could not vote against the hand that bribed them.

But the liquor wasn't just for the swing voters. Would not the old faithful reliable Grits or Tories deserve their reward? And so the process of calculation became more complicated.

Although I thought then and think now that bribing by booze is a reprehensible and self-defeating practice, it had its interesting aspects. My father, who loved a drink of rum, thought that the hard-core party workers should stand aside and use the stuff to help the party and derive their satisfaction from such service. My mother had a different view. If it was being passed out to all and sundry, the old reliables should get their share. Because she liked her drink best in the form of a carefully measured bedtime tot, her bottle probably outlasted all the other election largesse.

In the days of my youth on Prince Edward Island, liquor was very much involved in the social and political patterns of the province. The provincial Tories had lost an election in 1927 largely, it was alleged, because they had opted for government control of liquor, that is, the sale of alcoholic beverages through government-run stores (which is now the norm in Canada). The shrewder Grits had declared for a plebiscite on the matter. The strength of the temperance lobby was made apparent in the subsequent plebiscite, and for many years, while Islanders drank in secret, the political parties stood in fear of the temperance forces.

In their efforts to make the province as dry as the Sahara Desert, the provincial authorities did some interesting things. For years in Prince Edward Island, liquor was available to the citizens only on production of a doctor's prescription. After paying the physician for the legitimizing piece of paper and also paying for the right to purchase, the thirsty Islander paid a good price for his medicine. This he did at a high security outlet run by the Prince Edward Island Temperance Commission; no nasty word like 'liquor' was allowed to appear in our pristine province's dispensing authority for fire-water. This foolishness lasted a long time. In 1949, when bringing about the end of prohibition, a courageous Liberal premier, J. Walter Jones, spoke straight words on the issue, pointing out that prohibition's strongest supporters had been the preachers and the bootleggers.

So in those days, apart from the Dominion Election Act's penalties about corrupt practices, the poll workers had some pretty stringent provincial restrictions with which to contend as they sought to apply the lubrication of liquor to the electoral machinery.

Within the poll there was the problem of deciding who should handle the stuff. Naturally it wouldn't go to the biggest lush. Nor would it be safe to put it in the hands or the cellar of the biggest blabbermouth. The Victoria Conservative Committee once prevailed upon Charles Rogers to 'do the honours.' He was a man of unquestioned probity, a Church of Scotland elder, as close to a saint as we had in our village. He abominated liquor. Canny members of the committee thought a stern teetotaller the best custodian of the precious stuff. So Mr Rogers allowed his fidelity to his party to overcome his hatred of liquor. I don't know whether the Tories bettered themselves in Victoria poll, but I understand the old elder did not give a second performance as keeper of the booze.

To me, in 1930, Ottawa seemed a remote place. The only big urban area I knew was Boston. Like many Maritimers it was the first large metropolis I had ever seen and is still a special place to me. Because of a temporary family move, I had been a little Bostonian for a year in 1926. The culture shock of moving from my Victoria two-room schoolhouse to a 1200-pupil school had been traumatic but not fatal. Many years would pass before I walked the streets of Canada's capital.

But our newly elected members for Queens were soon Ottawa-bound. Prime Minister R.B. Bennett called the new Parliament into session with all possible speed. Messrs Myers and McLure, using their railway passes for the first time, travelled by CNR from PEI to Ottawa on 6 September and were assigned office space in the Centre Block, as were all members of the House and Senate in those less commodious days on Parliament Hill. Myers and McLure shared an office and a secretary. They were fortunate to secure the services of Hazel Kennedy, daughter of the legendary Conservative, Murdock Kennedy, who had run for Queens constituency in 1926. They were sworn in as members of the House of Commons and attended the ceremonies opening the 17th Parliament. Mrs Myers and Mrs McLure came to Ottawa with their husbands for the opening and, like them, were doubtless impressed and thrilled by the ceremonial activities which on such occasions add glitter to parliamentary life.

Neither Queens member made it to the cabinet nor did they expect such exalted status. Their Kings County colleague, John Alexander Macdonald ('Cardigan Jack'), had been sworn in as minister without portfolio in Arthur Meighen's short-lived government (29 June–25 September 1926) and would be again. Prince Edward Island still would not have a minister with portfolio. As MPS from such a small province Myers and McLure were shut off from early advancement, since to have two ministers from PEI was unthinkable! It is unlikely it troubled them overmuch. They liked the wise old Macdonald who helped them acclimatize to the national capital, and he was a good friend. He and John Myers had been colleagues in the PEI cabinet and had been known to share a social glass on occasion.

In forming his cabinet in 1930, R.B. Bennett fell back on the old pattern of half-hearted recognition of Prince Edward Island's place in the top echelon. Until Cyrus Macmillan's brief hour of glory as fisheries minister, there had been no portfolio holder since the resignation of Louis Davies as minister of marine and fisheries in 1901. Cardigan Jack Macdonald was a proven politician quite capable of handling a department, but he entered Bennett's cabinet as minister without portfolio.

When political parties take office after a long absence from the corridors of power, much is expected of them. Although the 1917 election was won by a great Conservative prime minister, Sir Robert Borden, it was not essentially a party triumph. The wartime prime minister had shown great skill in attracting the support of many pro-conscription Liberals for his Union government. Borden's articulate and brilliant successor, Arthur Meighen, won a plurality but not a majority in 1925. It could be said that Bennett's triumph was the first real Tory win since 1911. Not surprisingly, Canadians, and especially Conservative Canadians, saw 28 July 1930 as ushering in a new era.

I didn't attend any joint meetings during the provincial campaign of 1931. This was not because of lack of interest on my part; no meeting was scheduled for Victoria Hall. But I followed the campaign through the columns of the newspapers and on radio. Of course there was much political talk in my home, sometimes meetings of the poll committees, and visits from the Conservative candidates.

In the late summer of 1931, I met my first governor general. In addressing a group from the steps of Victoria Hall, the Earl of Bessborough, as was the custom, declared a school holiday for the Victoria kids on his birthday, 27 October. As the vice-regal party left, he stopped and asked me: 'Now when is that holiday?' I was able to tell him, but of course I didn't call him 'your Excellency.' In Victoria, we didn't see governors general or British peers everyday!

Whether consciously or not, Prince Edward Island voters often followed the national pattern in federal elections. During the long Laurier era, it was called 'Little Quebec.' Not surprisingly then, there was a general feeling in 1931 that the provincial Tories would topple the Liberal government of Walter M. Lea. This proved to be the case, and 6 August brought another celebratory occasion for the Tories. At a jubilant election rally in Charlottetown's Capital Theatre, Dr W.J.P. MacMillan was the star performer. A devout, hard-line politician with a fine vocabulary and a sonorous voice, he regaled the happy Tory crowd. In those days speakers at public meetings didn't have microphones and, in any case, Dr MacMillan didn't need one. Prince Edward Island is not given to many electrical storms but it certainly had one that night. As the thunder roared and lightning flashed, Dr MacMillan's proud oratory filled the crowded theatre. Once he was drowned out by a mighty thunder clap, but the jubilant doctor was not even slightly put off. When the thunder faded away, he said: 'See, even the Heavens rejoice in the downfall of the Lea government.'

I can recall a pitifully short honeymoon for the Conservative governments elected in 1930 and 1931. There was a fearful uproar about Bennett's tax on sugar. To hear some of the Grits in PEI, one might think it was our basic or sole food source!

In the government of Premier J.D. Stewart, Dr MacMillan became minister of health and education, a portfolio to which his talents and interests were ideally suited. While he was minister, two serious fires destroyed Falconwood Mental Hospital and Prince of Wales College and Provincial Normal School. Naturally they were rebuilt and, under his leadership, arose from their ashes nobly and better than ever before. The exterior of the attractive Prince of Wales College (now Holland College) looks today just as it did when I first entered its doors in 1933, fifty-eight years ago. Prince of Wales college did not grant degrees. Before the fire it offered three years of instruction, the first two being the equivalent of grades 11 and 12 in most of the provinces. Under Dr MacMillan's leadership a fourth year was added. It was with the greatest difficulty and sacrifice that my parents were able to finance the two years let alone four. It was also the provincial Normal School and I qualified for a first class teachers' licence.

At the opening of the new college in 1933, to which another year's instruction had been added, Dr W.J.P. MacMillan shared the speaking honours with Dr Cyrus Macmillan. Much later, another platform participant, Dr Carleton Stanley, then head of the Canadian Universities Association, told me that Dr Cyrus was nervous, uncertain, and asked Stanley what he should say and how to say it. But the other MacMillan needed no guidance. He was in full force all the way. His upbeat performance prompted my brother Clifford to observe: 'Dr Macmillan won't go behind their backs to tell them how good he is.'

After the death of Premier Stewart, Dr MacMillan succeeded him and put his distinct mark on provincial politics. He obviously relished slugging it out with the fearful Grits. Audiences loved him, but some of the party bigwigs were sometimes a bit uneasy at his lack of tact. He had said of Walter Lea: 'He's the first farmer premier and I hope he's the last.' This was quite a smart crack but perhaps not too helpful politically in a province where the rural vote was all important. As an impressionable youth, I found Dr MacMillan highly interesting and entertaining. He was an impressive orator and was extremely well versed on Island-Dominion relations. He was an eloquent and persuasive advocate of the Island's cause at Ottawa. But even some of his own said that, while he was a good premier, he was a poor politician. Internal critics said the same thing about Bennett.

Although I was precociously interested in both federal and provincial politics, I did not confine myself to political interests. I read widely, borrowing books from Victoria ladies. Mrs Murchison lent me Shakespeare plays, while Mrs Jabez Lea lent me many of the books from her Harvard graduate son's library. Later, at Prince of Wales College, I was sharply criticized by the English instructor, G.D. Steel, for 'not writing a single note during the whole lecture.' So respectful was I, that I did not point out that Lorne Lea had neatly entered all his points in the *Paradise Lost* volume that his mother had given me. Steel was not one to waste or vary his ancient lecture notes. Mrs Miner MacNevin had all the L.M. Montgomery books and I read every one. I was convinced even then that her books were not just for children. Mrs Edward Boswell gave me a boxed set of great orations. The opener was Pericles' funeral oration. She had good training in elocution and seemed to have me often doing readings or recitations at church and community functions. Such success as I later had in public speaking derives in considerable part from her interest and help. She was the sister of Walter M. Lea, the leader of the Liberal party in PEI. Her husband was a strong Tory, but I tended to believe that in politics she was her brother's backer.

Schoolwork was enormously important and I had been proud to attain perfect attendance year after year. While I had trouble with arithmetic, I had no problems with most other courses. I was delighted to make 99 per cent in a geography exam in a grade higher than my own. In Victoria school, the senior room had grades 6 to 10 and I did some auditing of the higher grades. Perhaps my scholastic gifts were not all that helpful. I sometimes think I was promoted too soon and ended up at Prince of Wales College before I was old enough to derive the fullest benefit from it.

Victoria was a hockey town and I followed its success, but I was no hockey player myself. I don't think I was ever a serious possibility even for the school team. I learned to swim early and was competent. When I was six, my father taught me to skate in one lesson and I became a good skater. In those more gracious days, young men tended to skate with young girls and I had no difficulty getting partners. But that didn't bring me very close to being the athlete of the year in any year.

By 1935 I was a teenager with two years at Prince of Wales College behind me, and although I was interested in all federal ridings in PEI and indeed in the Dominion, my greatest concern was for the constituency of Queens. In the five years since I had first become a political buff, I had deepened and broadened my contacts. At Prince of Wales College in my time, they didn't go in for extras, and there were no such diversions as campus political clubs. But they did have debates in which, despite the reticence incumbent upon being the youngest student in the college, I participated.

I did get to know John Myers much better. In my years at Prince of Wales College 1933–5, he was helpful to me in my information-seeking on current events, my favourite part of the school program. I remember his kindness in copying out longhand the names and full titles of all the cabinet ministers. In all my years in the House of Commons, I never had writing paper of the quality of the three or four vellum sheets which Mr Myers used. I can also say that I never filled a sheet with the splendid copperplate penmanship which he displayed. Sharp of tongue and mind always, he told me that the minister with the most initials behind his name was the one with the fewest brains in his head. That pride of place he gave to New Brunswick's contribution to the ministry, the Honourable Murray MacLaren.

During my years at Prince of Wales College, I had the good fortune to board with Norman and Lulu Nicholson, to whom I shall be ever grateful for hospitality, friendship, help, and guidance far beyond the deserts of a mere boarder. Lulu was John Myers's oldest daughter and had been a friend of my only sister. To Lulu's lovely new home her father often came when he was in Charlottetown.

He was the first politician I ever saw in full morning suit. This he wore when he came to Charlottetown to attend the funeral of the able and distinguished Island premier, J.D. Stewart, who died in October 1933. I also attended that funeral which was held in the historic and beautiful Kirk of St James. I had never been to such an impressive and elaborate religious service. Never before had I seen a clergyman in Geneva gown and academic hood. At Victoria United Church, which I regularly attended, the clergy wore Roman collars and often formal suits – frock coats or Prince Alberts – but never gowns or hoods. Even less likely to appear so garbed were the preachers in the austere Church of Scotland in nearby DeSable. My father was a devoted adherent of this church and I often went with him to hear most excellent expository sermons, which I found too long. The devout Scots elders were dead set against worldliness or ostentation. Since they could not (and their successors still don't) tolerate an organ, they would probably have viewed a begowned preacher with a negative attitude similar to that of Prime Minister Brian Mulroney, when one of his ministers, Thomas Siddon, appeared in the House of Commons in his academic gown and PHD hood.

In this connection Mr Myers, who was a born tease, used to try to get under my skin by making references to some affiliation anxieties through which the Church of Scotland was then passing. He claimed that he heard the only solution for them was to join the Church of England. He asked me how I thought Johnny Colin MacNevin (an ancient who looked like an old testament prophet) and the other church leaders would like to see the Anglican rector at Crapaud, Mr Bridgewater, with his cassock, surplice, and stole holding down the lofty pulpit. Although not high in the council of the church, I knew the answer. In any case, the Church of Scotland people, having been cast off from the home church in the old country, joined a smaller group, the 'Wee Frees,' and became the Free Church of Scotland.

Mr Myers was a great talker and used to tell me of his experiences in Ottawa and his observations of that scene. He loved politics and because of his platform gifts became a popular figure on Parliament Hill. One denizen of the place apparently didn't care for him and the favour was returned. Agnes MacPhail, elected in 1921 as the first woman MP in Canada, was not one of John H.'s favourites. She had a tendency to draw on her nine years' experience and make such condescending remarks as 'When the Honourable Member is here a little longer he will learn that ...' I suppose Agnes MacPhail and John Myers were a contradiction of textures. He was humorous, gregarious, witty, and charming. in a candid, earthy way. I have never heard that the courageous and able lady from Grey-Bruce was much given to gaiety, fun, or laughter. Whether she was, in fact, an old battleaxe I don't know, but my member of Parliament, John Myers, called her that.

Myers, like Chester McLure, performed his parliamentary duties well and conscientiously. A look at the House of Commons Hansard for the 17th Parliament shows that. In the grim depression of the years they served as Bennett back-benchers, they must have found their time in Ottawa strenuous enough, but it would have been less demanding than the months at home in their constituencies. In those days, sessions were much shorter than they are now. John Myers told my father that, while he hated to do it, he had to take his home telephone out because of the incessant demands for jobs, assistance, or other services. At the time, he was on a party line which would add technical complications to the political realities. Because so many people were without, almost everyone wanted something, and in those dire straits you turn to your MP. Both men were deluged with requests which they could not fill.

Like all Tory MPs in those tough years, the two were reviled and denigrated. Angus MacPhee, Liberal MLA for 2nd Queens, told an audience: 'We might just as well have sent two old women to Ottawa as Myers and McLure.' With his heavy Scots accent, it sounded like 'weemen.' In those days, neither the senior citizens nor the feminists were as well organized as they are now, and MacPhee's sarcasm brought no backlash.

As I reflect upon those far-off days, I wonder whether anyone who defended the Bennett government didn't deserve a medal for sheer bravery if nothing else. At the time, I fear we didn't give marks for courage to John Myers and Chester McLure. It was a difficult government to defend from day to day. Even among the polite and civilized Islanders, the hard times in PEI could encourage discourtesy and even nastiness.

I took a special interest in the Empire Conference held in Ottawa in 1932. This was Bennett's initiative and many Tories thought he had upstaged the British, some of whom had scorned his suggestion for such a meeting at the 1930 Imperial Conference. John Myers sent me a copy of an Ottawa newspaper's feature edition on the gala gathering. I didn't articulate it in such terms then, but I suppose I was pleased that a Canadian was not kowtowing to the lofty lords of empire at Westminster. Somehow, too, it was something of a venture in internationalism.

More important still was the impact of a politician from the other side of Canada. H.H. Stevens, Bennett's trade and commerce minister, was exposing shocking 'sweatshop' conditions in Canadian business establishments. The painfully low wages and the heavy mark-up in prices stirred me. I knew what the primary producers were being paid on PEI. The fishermen were getting a pittance for their product. Through my church and Sunday school exposure, I was developing a social awareness. In those days, there was a strong community conscience. I remember my father and mother sitting up all night with sick neighbours. In my teens, I regularly visited the elderly folk in our village. Once Mrs Ab Clark told me: 'We used to have a little money but sickness has taken it all.' Mrs Jabez Lea, our next-door neighbour, a gracious and intelligent schoolteacher, became excessively, perhaps obsessively frugal. She seemed to fear an old age of penurious dependence. Some of my father's friends had to go on relief and that was a traumatic experience. I didn't have in my vocabulary such terms as social justice or social welfare, but that's what I obviously had in mind.

So I was impressed by Stevens. Often I was bewildered whether he was in or out of the Conservative party. Early in 1935, I thought my anxiety on that score was at an end. R.B. Bennett launched a series of five radio broadcasts to which I listened with rapt attention and sympathetic vibrations. It was the dynamic Bennett of 1930, once again a confident fighter with a clear vision for his country. I had heard Franklin Roosevelt's 'fireside chats' in 1932 and I thought of him as a political hero. The word was that W.D. Herridge, Bennett's brother-in-law and Canada's minister to Washington, had inspired and even written Bennett's speeches. If so, he did a fine job and the message was a good one.

I can still hear Bennett's sonorous cadences bursting from the de Forrest Crossley radio in our Victoria home. Today, after the passage of fifty-six years, as I reread those addresses, I find them still impressive and stirring.

In one of the passages I liked best, he said:

... in my mind, reform means Government intervention. It means Government control and regulation. It means the end of laissez-faire. Reform heralds certain recovery. Reform or no reform! I raise that issue squarely. I nail the flag of progress to the masthead. I summon the power of the state to its support.[3]

In his remarkable quintet of radio addresses, Bennett propounded many programs, analyzed many serious national issues, and vigorously asserted a new political alignment in the country. Some critics at the time saw the speeches as socialist utterances. I don't find socialism in these addresses. As I see it, Bennett did not come to bury capitalism but to control it and correct such egregious social ills and inequalities as those revealed by Stevens's Price Spreads Inquiry.

But there were some who, regarding themselves as the stalwarts and princes of the party, turned against their leader for his seeming apostasy. Not many denizens of the boardrooms on St James or Bay Street were enthusiastic. Even Arthur Meighen found the talks frightening. Ever the master of the colourful phrase, historian Arthur Lower spoke of Bennett's performance as 'the Bennett Bull in the Capitalist China Shop' and 'Satan rebuking sin.'[4]

The comprehensive economic and social program promulgated by Bennett in the first few days of January 1935 was soon dubbed the Canadian New Deal, although Bennett himself never used the expression in his speeches. His opponent said that the prime minister, after nearly five years as Herbert Hoover, was trying to become a Franklin Roosevelt. Such an accusation was clever rather than precise. Some of the promised program was under way and other items had been forecast. What the program indicated, of course, was a renewed determination and dedication to fight the Depression-borne ills afflicting the people of Canada. The national headquarters of the Conservative party, so long moribund, published the five speeches and I ordered them.

The pamphlets were modestly dubbed: *The Premier Speaks to the People*. On the cover was an outline map of Canada. Unfortunately, PEI was not shown. Jubilant Grits in PEI constantly declared: 'The Island was left off the map by the Tories and R.B. Bennett.'

In each pamphlet, there was an excellent photo of Bennett. In one of them he was actually beaming; in all he was, if not quite handsome, certainly a striking man, personifying brains, prosperity, sincerity, and power. In all the photos, the bachelor prime minister was, as usual, immaculately dressed. Not one of the five shows him without the wing-collar and stickpin in his necktie.

As I look today at these pictures, I reflect upon the differences in electioneering techniques in his age and ours. It seems to me that Mackenzie King's campaign picture never varied. I saw him as a sedate forty-year-old, even in his later elections when he was over sixty. Today our advertising men convince seekers of office to do many irrelevant things to present the right image. You should be seen with a loving spouse and a cluster of children around you. (This would have been hard on the two bachelors King and Bennett.) Or you should be seen riding a horse, patting a dog or cat, greeting the multitudes, pretending to be interested in athletics, munching a hamburg, or, better still, cooking one at your own barbecue. In other words, don't waste time being seen as your usual self or, God help us, talking issues. Pierre Trudeau probably gained many votes because of a photograph showing him doing a splendid high dive. Robert Stanfield doubtless lost votes because he was seen failing to catch a football the tenth time it was thrown at him. But in neither case was the federal electorate choosing an athlete.

Each of Bennett's pamphlets had a foreword by a distinguished Canadian. I thought the first of these the best. It was written by Stephen Leacock, who is well known as Canada's best humorist. Not so widely known is the fact that he was a highly respected economist. Other forewords were written by H.R. MacMillan, president of the H.R. MacMillan Export Company of Vancouver, and Henry Wise Wood, former president of the United Farmers of Alberta and one of the wisest prairie leaders ever. Another famed contributor was Lionel Conacher, one of Canada's great athletes. Although not an enthusiast for athletic heroes (the only sports picture I ever hung was one of my favourite NHL hockey teams, the Montreal Maroons), I admired Lionel Conacher.

Although some people were perplexed by the ideas put forward and some Conservatives were critical – and the Grits talked about death-bed conversions – the 'New Deal' speeches were essentially well received by the Canadian voters. Bennett's enemies of course responded by attacking his sincerity.

My euphoria over Bennett's reform posture was not long sustained. The Grits claimed it was a phoney stance; old guard Tories thought it was heretic. The election which many expected in early 1935 did not materialize. Bennett was off to Britain, where he became ill. In all of this, the momentum was lost. But worse still, so was Stevens.

The depression-ridden electorate might have rallied to the born-again chieftain of the Conservative party. In such a brave attempt to win favour, a major role for H.H. Stevens, the poor man's champion, was essential. But instead of re-establishing Stevens as a supportive colleague, the arrogant and haughty Bennett made the breach wider. Stevens, persuaded to return to the party caucus, was totally ignored by Bennett. The British Columbia populist maverick then formed his own political group, the Reconstruction party. Without him, Bennett seemed to have lost the reformist zeal he had displayed during his radio talks. Although I was in the full bloom of youth, I didn't see rosy days ahead for the Conservative party.

But, while I was troubled by the danger signals on the federal front, there were worse troubles in the provincial field. The PEI election of 23 July 1935 will not soon be forgotten by Islanders. When the 1st Queens Tory incumbents, Walter Mackenzie and Thomas Wigmore, called at our house in Victoria, my mother asked them how things were going. Mackenzie replied, 'very well.' Her expression obviously prompted him to say: 'Don't you think so, Mrs Macquarrie?' Her reply was: 'Far from it.' But neither she nor any other Conservative could have realized how far from well things really were. On election night, the returns showed the Liberals the winners of all thirty seats. The premier led a legislature where there was no official opposition. It was a situation unprecedented in the British parliamentary tradition. There would be no Conservative government in Charlottetown until 1959.

The 30 to 0 Liberal triumph of 1935 was celebrated at a great victory picnic held at Premier Lea's farm in Victoria. Gleeful Grits, including all thirty MLAS, assembled on a beautiful July afternoon for a jubilant day of self-congratulation. I was there too, but came by a less jocose route. The Victoria Women's Institute had been asked to cater the picnic meal. My mother, the president and a charter member of the Victoria branch, was there and took on the task of making the tea on an iron range set outside in the field where the festivities were. At such Women's Institute events mere males were allowed to pour tea. When I was serving one chatty and vivacious Grit lady, she turned to the person next to her and inadvertently struck the big agate pitcher from which I was pouring. At least that is the way I recall it. Perhaps it was my lack of ease in the heart of enemy territory. But I felt remorse at spilling tea even on a Grit. As for the celebrating Grits they had a glorious day. To be in Prince Edward Island in summer is joy enough. To have won 100 per cent control of the provincial legislature must have made it truly heaven for Lea and his fellow Liberals.

A few years before the Liberal picnic I had developed a personal reason to appreciate Walter M. Lea. While at Prince of Wales College at age fourteen, I often went to sit in the visitors' gallery of the Prince Edward Island legislature. I recall that on my first visit as I was lined up waiting for the public to be allowed to enter, Mr Lea walked down the corridor en route to his seat. He stopped, welcomed me, and gave me a helpful run-down on the legislature's procedures. Considering I was only fourteen years old and not a Grit-leaning lad at that, I was most grateful to him for his courtesy and consideration.

Walter M. was a highly intelligent and confident person and was not hesitant to take people down a peg or two if that seemed appropriate. Once, when serving as deputy minister of agriculture before he became party leader, he was host to a prominent agricultural official from Ontario. Mr Lea gave him a good tour of various aspects of the agricultural scene in which the Island was – and still is – a leader in many fields. But nothing he was shown – herds of cattle, flocks of sheep or poultry, grain forage, or potato crops – seemed to impress the Ontario guest. They were either bigger or better in Ontario and often both. Mr Lea endured all this with the composure expected of a host and public servant.

Later, after dinner at Mr Lea's fine farm home, the guest eventually retired. Not long after, the household heard fearful sounds emanating from the guest room. When Mr Lea entered, his Ontario guest pointed to a small live lobster reposing under the blanket. 'What is that creature?' his terrified visitor asked. Lea said: 'Why, that's just a bed bug, although I'm sure that yours in Ontario would be bigger than that.'

Less than five months after the great victory, Walter Lea was dead and for the second time I attended the funeral of a Prince Edward Island premier. People came from far and wide and I had never seen so many people in the Victoria United Church. If I had to use but two adjectives about Walter M. Lea, I would choose honourable and intelligent. He was succeeded by his chief lieutenant, Thane Campbell, a Rhodes scholar, a lawyer, and an excellent speaker, whose son Alexander would later attain the premiership and retain it longer than any incumbent before or since.

Thane Campbell was the most scholarly premier of my era. At the last Prince of Wales convocation in which I was involved, he gave an appropriate and learned address. He said the classic rule for a speech was to begin with with an apothegm and end with an epigram. He also told an amusing story about two ladies who had a cottage on a quiet beach on the north shore of PEI. They complained to the local sheriff that they were a bit embarrassed by some young men who swam in the nude near their cottage. The lawman suggested that the lads do their swimming farther down the beach and avoid offending the ladies. When he later asked the women if everything was now all right, they said: 'Well, not exactly. We can still see them with the spy glass.' This little yarn was to indicate the difficulty politicians had in avoiding public scrutiny.

While no Liberal ever attained an election victory equal to that of Walter Lea, there was a long series of one-sided wins in provincial contests. Considering that my own career took place in an era not outstandingly Tory-tainted, I suppose I should be thankful that my youthful exposure to politics inured me to adversity and defeat.

For me the beautiful PEI summer of 1935 was not brightened

when, on 14 August, I heard that Bennett had finally dissolved Parliament and would have his rendezvous with fate and the electorate on 14 October. By then, Stevens was not only out of the cabinet but had established the Reconstruction party. All three party leaders came to Prince Edward Island during the campaign. The use of radio had increased markedly. I remember a nasty little talk by William Duff, a Liberal MP from Nova Scotia. One of his cracks was that Stevens hadn't served in the Great War because he had flat feet – but Bennett hadn't because he had cold feet. I presume Mr Duff was reacting to some Tory reflections on Liberal leader Mackenzie King's patriotism.

The embattled Conservative party had trouble finding candidates. The problem was particularly acute in the province of Quebec, as it had been before and would often be later. But Quebec was not the only place where candidate recruitment was a problem. When Bennett came to Charlottetown on 5 October, no candidate had been nominated for the Prince constituency. It didn't take a genius to figure out that, if the Liberal incumbent A.E. Maclean could hold the riding against the Tory sweep of 1930, he was unlikely to be beaten in 1935. But Bennett did not like constituencies going uncontested and he insisted that there be a candidate in Prince. He backed his insistence by signing a personal cheque in his suite in the Charlottetown Hotel. I was told that it was for $1000. Even at the 1935 value of the dollar, I cannot believe that that amount would cover even a token and belated election campaign. It was an indication of the loyalty and decency of Frank Arnett that he was willing to become the sacrificial lamb. He lost to Maclean by 4170 votes. In 1930, he had lagged by 1573.

On the other end of the Island, one of the finest public men we ever produced also did something far beyond the normal call of duty. Senator John MacLean resigned his seat in the Upper House and allowed Bennett to reward the long and illustrious career of John A. Macdonald by appointing that highly popular Tory to the Red Chamber. Not surprisingly in Kings County – where it used to be said that if you greeted every man you met with 'Good day, Mr Macdonald' you would be no more than 50 per cent wrong – another member of the clan was chosen to run in the new senator's place. Dr A.A. (Gus) Macdonald, affable, devoted, selfless, was the typical family physician in those days of meaningful doctor-patient relationships. My mother and her people, all of whom were from the Souris area, knew him and loved him well. But despite his enormous personal popularity, Dr Gus must have had misgivings about the prospects before him. He had, after all, seen his long-held provincial seat of 1st Kings go Grit in the PEI election of 23 July in that non-Tory year of 1935. Like Frank Arnett in Prince, the genial physician saw his opponent chalk up the biggest majority in the history of the constituency. Another doctor, T.V. Grant of Montague, was the winner. Dr Grant continued in the House of Commons for many years until he was appointed to the Senate in June 1949. Kings County, as well as having the best beaches in PEI, also seemed to have the best luck when it came to Senate appointments!

Considering everything in those 'Down with the Tories' years, the one-party 1935 meeting in Crapaud Hall (not Victoria to my great regret) was a fairly good affair. My father and I had walked the two miles to the meeting and were well pleased that, even without the confrontations of earlier joint rallies, there was still a goodly crowd to hear our Tory standard-bearers.

Both members detailed for their followers the efforts they had made for their constituents. Myers vividly recounted their presentation regarding car ferry rates to the minister of railways and canals, R.J. Manion. As Myers put it: 'He's an Irishman and as hot as the devil.' Manion did agree to lower the rates between PEI and New Brunswick. They recounted other achievements and the partisans attending the meeting, like myself, my father, and other loyal Tories from Victoria, cheered them for their accomplishments.

Nor was it all local issues the two men discussed. There was a good review of the Bennett government's achievements, especially in reference to the Empire Trade Agreements, assistance to agriculture, and assaults on unemployment. Bennett's reform platform was examined and exalted. There were plenty of attacks on the Grits. Laissez-faire, which Bennett had made almost a nasty expression in the 1930 election campaign and in his great radio speeches, was talked about. I hadn't heard of laissez-faire before 1930, but it was clear it was not a good thing. At Crapaud and on the hustings, the expression *ultra vires*, meaning outside the powers of a government, was much talked about. The nasty Grits were threatening *ultra vires* as a fate for Bennett's good and helpful legislation.

But in our hearts we knew that the Crapaud meeting was not like the Victoria gathering of 1930. The one-party affair was much duller theatre. The obese Chester McLure had declared that the Tories were not afraid of their opponents on the platform or anywhere else, but we felt that our boys were slightly leery of an open debate with the Grits. Although we didn't blame them, we regretted that prudence had been exalted over valour.

The Grits were bound to win in 1935 and only a myopic fool doubted it, but the doughty gladiator Bennett showed no despondency or despair when he spoke at the Forum in Charlottetown in October 1935. Along with his candidates in Queens, the well-dressed and impressive John Myers and Chester McLure, he marched confidently to the stage looking anything but a loser, although he was carrying on an exhaustive national campaign. He was introduced by the brilliant and stentorian Dr W.J.P. MacMillan, the provincial leader who had been walloped in July 1935 when, under my Victoria neighbour Walter M. Lea, the Grits had won every seat in the Island legislature. Bennett began by saying: 'There's no gratitude in politics, ladies and gentlemen; otherwise Dr MacMillan would be the perpetual premier of this province.'

It must be said that Bennett made the best of the occasion. He was neither apologetic nor mealy-mouthed. (Who could imagine him being either?) To the eternal credit of the people of Prince Edward Island, he had a fine crowd. In July, the provincial Tories had been annihilated, but in October they came out in great numbers to hear their national leader, the prime minister of Canada.

Just over a week after Bennett's Charlottetown speech Canadians went to the polls and inflicted on him and his party a humiliating defeat. The Liberals elected 171 members to the House of Commons, the Conservatives 39, of whom 25 were from Ontario. The *Charlottetown Patriot* made the sarcastic comment that when Parliament opened the Tories wouldn't need a special train for their Maritime contingent since only one Conservative, Alf Brooks of Royal, New Brunswick, had won.

In Queens, Myers and McLure had 7262 and 7767 votes compared to 10,326 and 10,303 for their Liberal opponents, James Larabee and Peter Sinclair. The two Reconstruction candidates received 1604 and 836 votes. I don't remember any congratulatory parties that night. The Tories' election rum was drunk for solace rather than celebration.

The results in the Victoria poll were as depressing as in the constituency at large. Because the Conservatives had been the governing party they had the naming of poll officials: deputy returning officer (DRO), poll clerk, and constable. This was a bit of patronage. In 1935 the poll was held in the store of Neil Penpraise who had the distinction of being the smallest man in the village, weighing in at one hundred and a half pounds, as he put it. Jim Knox and not Jabez Lea was the DRO. He was probably the most genial deputy returning officer of the many hundreds on duty that day. When the counting started at six o'clock, Jim pulled out a painful series of ballots marked for Sinclair and Larabee. After a while he said: 'Well certainly to Christ there must be one in there for Myers and McLure. I'm sure I put in one myself.' At that he plunged his arm to the very bottom and came up with the first ballot for the Reconstruction candidates, Ings and Hughes. This brought sustained bipartisan laughter from those standing in the poll. It was a bit of a fluke that he found a ballot for the H.H. Stevens party. One of the candidates won 5 votes in Victoria poll, the other 4. McLure and Myers won 55 and 57 as against 57 and 73 in 1930. The Liberals had jumped from 81 and 88 to 114 and 113. Bill MacLeod, a local Liberal, said to my father that evening: 'Well, I guess, Wilfred, you fellows will be walking the streets for the next four years.' Little did we know that closer to twenty-two years would pass before a Conservative government would take office in Ottawa. The wait for a provincial Tory victory would be even longer.

2

From Despair to Port Hope

The year 1935 was depressing on the international front as well. In grade 9 I had been fascinated by an inspirational piece of writing called 'The Hope of the World.' It prompted me to become an enthusiast for the League of Nations which was the subject of the story. Disappointed at the league's handling of Japanese aggression, I still hoped it would act on the Italian invasion of Abyssinia. For a while it looked as if sanctions would be imposed. In November I was thrilled that a Canadian at Geneva, Dr W.A. Riddell, was winning worldwide attention for his suggestion that to make sanctions effective they must include the essentials for the Italian military forces especially oil. But my euphoria was as short-lived as Dr Riddell's time in the spotlight. He had had the support of the Bennett government but his new political masters had no desire for strong measures. I was hurt and angry. My father, who was neither a historian nor scholar, seemed to have recognized Mussolini's rascality long before it became conventional wisdom. He also said that Mackenzie King was showing his usual mealy-mouthed attitude.

In the aftermath of the Conservative defeat on both the federal and provincial fronts, there weren't any political meetings to attend. Hard-core Tories would gather to commiserate, but there was no new organized party activity. With not a single elected

Tory in the province and an election four years away, there was no incentive for girding up the loins.

Certainly I would have had the time for political meetings. In May 1935 I had finished my two years at Prince of Wales College, had qualified as a first-class teacher, but was too young to be licensed. I was also too poor to go on to university. Chester McLure hoped that I would go into law. Instead I went into a year of unemployment. There were few opportunities for gainful activities. I picked potatoes a couple of times for fifty cents a day. Being quite unused to such labour I was probably overpaid. But my year off was a great opportunity for reading and I made frequent use of the Crapaud Library, which like others in PEI had been opened in 1934 through then Premier Macmillan's acquisition of a splendid $60,000 U.S. grant from the Carnegie Foundation. I also continued to build my stamp collection and took a correspondence course in short-story writing. Skating, swimming, and walking kept me reasonably fit and community activities must have provided some mental and spiritual development.

But I maintained my interest in politics and through the newspapers kept abreast of Bennett's visit to South Africa, Australia, and New Zealand. I read too of reports of his ill health. But it was three years after the débâcle of 1935 before the Conservatives faced up to the question of leadership. They called a national convention for July 1938.

They probably could not have tackled the leadership issue much earlier than 1938. Both Bennett's attitude and his health made for uncertainty. In any case it is not easy to get up off the mat in good condition after being knocked out as decisively as the Conservative party had been in 1935. An early meeting would have been a gathering of badly bruised people given to recriminations and hurt pride. As the old saying puts it, victory has a thousand fathers but defeat is an orphan. Bennett himself was the chief scapegoat. Harry Stevens was also a target for recriminatory blame. Indeed, he was regarded by some as a turncoat who had aided King. To change a mood of gloom to one of even limited optimism requires the healing grace of time.

I read all I could about the convention. Bennett apparently

would have yielded to a draft, but none came. Former leader Arthur Meighen was rumoured to be ready for a comeback. Stevens could have been coaxed but there were no coaxers. Herridge told the delegates their resolutions were a bunch of junk. He was not nearly as well received as his seven-year-old son, who made a brief speech of thanks for a gift he had been given. From what I read and what Chester McLure told me, I was expecting Dr Robert Manion to win. I was pleased at the success of the convention and caught a little of the optimism with which the 1800 delegates left the Ottawa Coliseum on 7 July with a new leader, a new name, and, perhaps, some new hope.

I would have loved to attend the 1938 convention. No one had asked me and this is not surprising. I was but nineteen and there were not many teenagers at Tory conventions in those days. Had there been an opportunity, I might even have managed to afford the trip to Ottawa with the reduced convention rates available for railway and hotel rooms. At that time, as a first-class male teacher in Prince Edward Island, I was actually earning over $600 a year in a one-room school in the picturesque and pleasant Island community of Bonshaw, eight miles from Victoria.

But, if I didn't get to the Ottawa Coliseum, I tried to keep abreast of developments both in Canadian politics and international affairs. I suppose teachers tend to stress to their students their own priorities as students. In Bonshaw and in every other school I gave strong emphasis to current events, my favourite part of the curriculum in my own days as a pupil. My beloved home province is an island, but we are not insular in so far as that word implies ignorance of, or disinterest in, the outside world. In my native village the world situation commanded much attention among the men who gathered at Wright Brothers' store. One might be inclined to use the expression 'Hot Stove League,' but my father often said of his good friend Miner MacNevin, the owner-proprietor of the store: 'Miner is a great man but very poor at operating a stove.' I remember too the many Sundays when Ab Howatt, an intelligent and well-read friend of my father, came up to talk over the world situation. It was later said that the New World was unaware of what was happening in the Old during the thirties.

From my own very clear recollections that was a somewhat superficial analysis.

At that time we didn't have television; the closest we got were U.S. newsreels which were shown as part of the cinematic offerings at local theatres. But the tragedies and iniquities reported in the newspapers and on the radio touched our hearts and souls. We were traumatized and sometimes downright frightened by the cruel Japanese invasion of China. The brutal Italian campaign against the underdog Abyssinians wounded us. I remember well going to our next-door neighbour, Mrs Jabez Lea, to listen to the frightening and frightfully vulgar outpourings of Adolf Hitler. We knew too of the awful sufferings of the Spanish people and others in their bloody civil war. I remember being deeply saddened by the assassination of the diminutive Austrian Chancellor Engelbert Dollfuss. Even more crude and frightening was Hitler's annihilation of Dollfuss's successor, Kurt von Schuschnigg, for he destroyed the man and his country too.

In Bonshaw I was lucky in my boarding-house and was extremely well looked after by Mr and Mrs Theophilus Beaton. Mr Beaton was a nephew of John Myers, and the general merchant and leading citizen of Bonshaw. When I heard on the radio on 13 March 1938 about the German seizure of Austria, I rushed breathless into the store. 'Herr Hitler has just entered Vienna,' I said, repeating the radio bulletin verbatim. 'Toff' Beaton replied at once: 'Yes, and if they don't look out the bugger will be in Charlottetown.'

Mackenzie King, after a visit with the German chancellor, had reported that there was little to fear from Hitler. But there were deep anxieties among other Canadians. I can still remember the tension in the air when the nazi soldiery entered the Rhineland. The tragic decline of the League of Nations was ominous. The threats against Czechoslovakia over the Sudetenland were felt in Victoria, Prince Edward Island, although Neville Chamberlain thought that it was a 'quarrel in a far-away country between people of whom we know nothing.' Putting it simply, while Canadians were still borne down by the economic depression in their own country, they were not unmindful or uncaring about the outside world.

Although I was interested in him and his cause and heard him speak over the air and at meetings, I never met Manion. I came close when, in 1940, I went to Moncton with my elder brother Scott to join the RCAF. In this venture he succeeded and I did not. On the way back, our CNR train included Manion's private car. I walked through the day coaches to the rear of the train having some idea I might meet the leader. But, when I reached the appropriate car and the porter reminded me that it was a private coach, I withdrew. I would like to think it was because of my solicitude for the privacy of a busy man, but it was more likely a case of my being chicken. So I failed to get into the RCAF and into the presence of my party's national leader. And besides, Moncton was never one of my favourite cities!

One of my father's Victoria friends, Harry Clark, was much more persistent. A few months earlier, he was on a train which included the private car of Finance Minister Charles Dunning, who had been given refuge in one of the Queens seats in 1935. With him was Premier Campbell. Not only did Harry get into the presence of these lofty figures, he successfully hit up the both of them for a donation to the Victoria Unions hockey team.

Although it is now half a century ago, I have a clear recollection of the election of 1940 and the cheap trick which triggered it. Mackenzie King had promised in the House of Commons that there would be no election until a session of Parliament had been held. But when the members had been called to Ottawa on 25 January they were told that Parliament had been dissolved. Manion, the leader of the opposition, first heard of the call to the hustings as the governor general was reading the speech from the throne. Of course, he and his party were unprepared for an election.

The embattled Manion and other prominent Conservatives decided that in a wartime situation, a non-partisan appeal would be helpful. Recalling Robert Borden's election campaign of 1917, he promised to form a broadly based national government. Indeed, during the election, Manion and his candidates ran not under the label National Conservatives but National Government. Unfortunately, the strategy got nowhere; Mackenzie King and M.J. Coldwell for the Co-operative Commonwealth Federation (CCF) announced that neither the Liberals nor the CCF would join such a government.

But I remember thinking for a while that the promise of a national government might bring political dividends. In Queens, a new candidate was required since John Myers, deciding that twenty-eight years in politics was enough, had withdrawn his candidacy. Chester McLure's new running mate was a prominent Charlottetown businessman, J.O. Hyndman. I attended the convention that chose him and recall his saying that he had not even considered a political career until Dr Manion came out four-square for national government. He easily defeated four prominent Tories. At the time skilled Liberal propagandists tended to debunk the national government notion as camouflage for the Conservative party, suggesting that only faithful Tories won nominations as Manion supporters. The Queens nomination disproved such allegations and there were others although, of course, most of the nominated candidates were Conservatives.

John Myers was not favourably impressed by the development. He said he had been at a great many Conservative meetings but had never seen J.O. Hyndman at any of them. After the convention, as many of us were rehashing events at the Morell Hotel, one old Tory expressed puzzlement and noted: 'If the new man is counting on his looks he won't get far.' But in fact he did do pretty well. Hyndman was 1205 votes behind the second-running Liberal, J.L. Douglas, but more significantly he was 232 votes ahead of his running mate and long-time Tory, Chester McLure, a skilled and assiduous campaigner. In those days, and often since, Conservatives drew such comfort as they could from coming close. Hyndman's political effort in 1940 was his last. The indefatigable McLure was to run again and win again.

At the time of the election I was principal of a two-room school in Albany, about ten miles from my home town of Victoria. The ill fortunes of Toryism must have helped erase my youthful appearance for I discovered my name on the list of voters prepared by the enumerator. Because I would not be twenty-one until the following September, I was not qualified to vote in the 26 March election. A few of the leading Tories of Albany suggested I ignore that detail and vote anyway. I had no great difficulty in resisting such a temptation. It would be highly improper to begin one's use of the franchise by voting fraudulently. Also, the Prince constituency in which Albany was located had not elected a Conservative since 1904. It was such a safe Grit seat that Mackenzie King himself had found refuge there in a 1919 by-election. In 1940 the Liberal candidate was Finance Minister J.L. Ralston, who had won the seat by acclamation in January 1940. As well as being a big-name candidate, Ralston was well regarded in Prince and indeed throughout the province. He was a sure winner.

But partisan fervour dies hard and the Albany Tories fought the good fight. For true devotees of politics there is always some fun in the political skirmishing on the poll level. The chief mogul of the Albany Liberals was Vern MacLeod, general merchant and splendid citizen. Good poll workers in Prince Edward Island never let a possible vote go to the other side by default. One lady, who might now be described as considerably retarded, appeared at the poll and asked for assistance in voting since she could not read the ballot. She was read the names of the candidates but giving their party designation was not allowed, and agents of rival candidates made sure it was not done. This unfortunate lady was apparently not acquainted with any of the candidates but insisted that she wanted to vote for Vern MacLeod. Being told that there was no such name on the ballot she explained her quandary. 'Vern MacLeod told me he would give me a bag of flour if I voted for him and I want to keep my word.' Needless to say, the genial MacLeod was not soon allowed to forget this revelation.

Although I had no illusions about Dr Manion's party winning a seat in the *terra inimica* of Prince, I was not so discouraged about Queens or the nation as a whole. Dr Manion's meeting in Charlottetown was well attended and he was warmly received. Dr MacMillan as usual took a prominent part in the speech-making and suggested, on the strength of the good Conservative showing in Charlottetown during the provincial election of 1939, that the party could carry Queens.

In full flight, he produced an unusual reason for not voting for Mackenzie King. Holding high a full-page Liberal advertisement showing King at the head of a group of marching Canadians, he twice declaimed the caption 'Marching forward with Mackenzie King.' 'I'll tell you where he would march. South of the border like he did in the last war. Where was he last Dominion day? Unveiling a monument to his rebel grandfather. There's traitor's blood in that man's veins. I'm a doctor and I know.'

What his professional brother Dr Manion thought of this use of medical 'knowledge' is unknown. Certainly he didn't look upset as MacMillan, the gold medallist of McGill's Medical School, gave his public diagnosis of the incumbent prime minister of Canada.

There was widespread use of radio in the 1940 campaign. I remember being very favourably impressed by M.J. Coldwell, who seemed to do all the speaking for the CCF in our area. He had a splendid, well-modulated voice with excellent diction and a good deal of common sense.

At least I heard spokesmen from all the parties. It was not that way in all partisan homes in Canada. Many years later Chief Justice Thane A. Campbell spoke at St Dunstan's University in Charlottetown. One of the bright young priests on the faculty told me he had no idea that Campbell, the former Liberal premier, was such a good speaker: 'In my home when he was premier, we weren't allowed to listen to Grit politicians.'

The election of 1940 was another disaster. The Liberals won 184 seats to 39 for National Government. The Tories then made it worse by their shabby treatment of Manion. He had been chosen partly on the illusory ground that, as a Roman Catholic married to a French Canadian, he might make some headway in Quebec and form a working arrangement with Union Nationale premier Maurice Duplessis. Manion was a decent, sensitive man who saw the need for reform. But even before the election he was being undermined by the right-wingers of the party so much beloved by the Tory tycoons of old Toronto. After it he was dropped with indecent haste.

Politics is not as gentle as a pink tea and we should not be too upset at its rough edges. But the treatment which my party gave to Robert Manion was despicable. My stern Presbyterian God had a good deal of vengeful righteousness. Perhaps for their ruthless stupidity in 1940, the Conservatives deserved another seventeen years in the political wilderness.

I left my election poster of Manion in uniform on the wall for a good while after the election. There was something a bit sad in its message: 'I'll fight for you again. Bob Manion.'

As was so often to be the case, I saw the 1940 election from the vantage point of the losers. My home was not one which rang with praises of Mackenzie King. My father should have forgiven him a little of his Grittism because King was a continuing Presbyterian, but I don't recall that aspect of the man's life being mentioned, at home.

At that time and thereafter, I read *Maclean's* magazine regularly, turning first to 'Backstage at Ottawa' by the Politician with a Note Book. A very perceptive article summing up the election on May 1940 closed with a splendid tribute to Prime Minister King:

Meanwhile Mr. King sits in Laurier House, or looks out over the Ottawa River from the window of his West Block office, monarch of all he surveys. He has come a long way from the cub reporter of the old *Toronto Globe*: a long way from the bitter, black years of 1917, when his star was in stygian eclipse. Not since Macdonald and Laurier has any political leader wielded such power; or campaigned with more success; or gauged Canadian sentiment with such uncanny skill. Lapointe, Ralston, Howe – all are potent figures. But King is the Chief; vanquisher of Meighen, Bennett, Manion; Nemesis of the Tory party.

It hasn't all been by chance.

It took me some years to work up enthusiasm for Mackenzie King. Shortly after the 1940 election, the full fury of Hitler's blitzkrieg fell upon Western Europe. We listened avidly to the sad news broadcasts and became devoted to the oratory of Winston Churchill. As a boy I used to urge my father to wear his naval service badge. Once in a while he humoured me, although he thought it a bit too large and ostentatious. I suppose in the old-fashioned language of the days, ours was a patriotic family. I was the only one of four brothers who didn't join the military forces. A half-brother was in the army in both the Great War and World War II. God knows I kept trying, but without success. I was thrilled one day to come home from the naval recruiting office in Charlottetown to report that I had made it as a sublieutenant in Royal Canadian Navy. My father was not so impressed. He thought that any navy which would enter me at such a rank was obviously not a great fighting force. But all his irony was in vain. When I went in to do the final attestation, someone took a more careful look at my documentation and discovered that I was only twenty and not the required twenty-one. I was shattered then but, years later in the fullness of time, I realized how fortunate I had been. I would have made a lousy member of any military group.

The furore in which I was caught up doubtless lowered the priority I gave to domestic politics. It also explained in great measure some of the things the Conservative party did. After peremptorily dumping Manion, the leaderless, luckless, and often clueless Tories had to do something in the face of the dominance of King and his enormous contingent of Grits in Ottawa. Going back to the pre-1927 era, a caucus and executive group decided to return to their third last leader, Senator Arthur Meighen.

I hadn't known much about Arthur Meighen. In my last years at school, I was impressed by a speech included in one of the English 'readers'. Older Conservatives on the Island recalled his great oratory, but I had read enough of Canadian history to know that Mackenzie King had outfoxed him in earlier elections. What made these moguls of the Tory party so sure he could come out of retirement and turn the tables on King now?

Canadian Conservatives probably had a yearning for leaders with fire in their eye. R.B. Bennett was much more flamboyant than the mugwump King. As the war raged, there were calls for vigorous national leadership. Who better to provide it than the peerless orator Arthur Meighen? This dedication to the maximum war effort soon expressed itself in a call for conscription, and no one was more identified with that policy than Meighen. Because of conscription, the Conservatives had no one in Quebec. Some at the heart of the party tended to act as if Quebec didn't count. And it was not long after the dumping of Manion that the party began to get embroiled once again in the conscription issue, which Manion had warned them against. There was considerable interest in the return of Meighen and I followed carefully the course of the by-election campaign in York South, the constituency which he hoped would send him back to the House of Commons. It was supposed to be a safe seat but on 9 February 1942 the CCF candidate defeated Meighen by over four thousand votes. Another gloomy night for Tories. I remember my brother Clifford saying: 'The old party is being brilliant these days. In one fell swoop we have lost a seat in the House and one in the Senate.'

It was not until a dozen years after this sad event that I met Arthur Meighen. During the early fifties I visited him several times in his office in Toronto. We talked mostly about Sir Robert Borden, whose career I was studying. Always Meighen was courteous and candid. My letters to him were answered promptly and helpfully. On one visit he took me to lunch at the Albany Club, whose affluent precincts I have rarely entered since.

I made full notes as soon as our discussions were concluded and I therefore have a clear recollection of his comments. Once I asked him about the oft-repeated rumour that Mackenzie King, the self-proclaimed faithful follower of Laurier, had wanted to join Borden's Union government. He answered with great certainty. 'Borden told me that he did and the word of Sir Robert Borden was good enough for me.' But he went on: 'Did you ever wonder why King, so defensive about himself, left those allegations unchallenged for so long? He had to wait until the two men who knew the truth had left the scene. Newton Rowell carried the message to Borden. After their deaths the great denial came out.'

He also gave me a magnificent one-liner on King's propensity to pose as a supernationalist. Meighen said that our status as an autonomous member of the Commonwealth had actually been attained by Borden, who was not interested in the filigrees and niceties of declarations and the like but in reality. After Borden, all that was left for King was to 'burst heroically through open doors.'

I shall always cherish my contacts with Arthur Meighen. Once when I was visiting him a telephone call came from his old colleague Sir Thomas White. Despite the most careful eavesdropping I couldn't discover what it was all about. When he hung up Meighen explained: 'Sir Thomas is still writing poetry and I wish he wouldn't.' Meighen sometimes was unclear on the events of preceding hours, but although he was eighty his magnificent and capacious memory was strong on the era with which I was concerned. I was fortunate too in later developing friendship with two of the Canadians who knew Meighen best, Grattan O'Leary and Eugene Forsey. Not in those early years, nor indeed now, would I claim the understanding of him that these two possessed. Yet even then, and certainly now, I sensed a tragic grandeur about this intellectual giant and fearless warrior, who in politics attained so much less than he deserved. On my last visit he gave me an autographed picture.

Long after my brother's gloomy comment on the by-election loss, I read a succinct and sophisticated analysis by one of Canada's leading historians, J.L. Granatstein.

The primary effect of Meighen's defeat was to destroy the hopes and plans of those who had arranged his selection as leader in November 1941 ... Meighen's defeat brought the Conservative party as close as it has yet been to extinction. The delegates at the Ottawa conference had had the choice of Meighen or chaos put before them; they chose one, but after York South they had both.[1]

I remember well the flat feeling of despondency which enveloped Island Conservatives after Meighen's defeat in February 1942. But I didn't at the time appreciate the importance of a major and positive response to that reverse which came within six months. During the days 5–7 September 1942 about 150 people gathered at Port Hope for an informal conference called a 'Round Table on Canadian Policy.' Similar meetings in late years were called Thinkers' Conferences. I attended several of the subsequent conclaves but my knowledge of the Port Hope gathering comes from reviews of the conference, press coverage, and interviews with participants, many of whom I later came to know well. In my considered view the Port Hope meeting was the most important and intellectually innovative of them all. The Port Hope Round Table was the inspiration of one of the finest and ablest Conservatives in my generation, J.M. Macdonnell. Macdonnell was deeply troubled about Canadians becoming disillusioned by both the old-line parties and being attracted to the novel group, the CCF. He feared a situation in which all leftist elements would go to the CCF and the reactionaries go to the Liberals. He thought such a dichotomy the prelude to class war. After careful consideration with the powers that be and the would-be powers, Macdonnell sold the idea of a meeting of Conservatives who would not detonate all their energies on leadership preferences or short-range tactics but rather concentrate on long-range policies.

The Tories were fortunate in having Macdonnell come to the fore. He was a first-class scholar with a splendid record at Queens, Oxford, where he was a Rhodes scholar, and Osgoode Hall. His military record was also impressive. He had attained the rank of major and brigade major in the Great War. The old expression, 'a gentleman and a scholar' fitted Jim Macdonnell well. He combined a sensitive idealism with a positive pragmatism. He had already raised money for the Tory cause when the acting leader, R.B. Hanson, had told him of the paucity of the purse. In organizing the Port Hope Conference he sought to elevate the party's policies and profile.

In July 1942 Macdonnell had written three articles for *Saturday Night*, which I often read even in those youthful days. In these he set the scene for the upcoming assembly of concerned Conservative Canadians. Macdonnell saw that a high-handed government with an enormous range of controls over its people might put in jeopardy the basic constitutional freedoms. He argued that a free and healthy party system was essential to the working of a parliamentary democracy. Urging thoughtful Canadians to become concerned about politics and indeed party politics, Macdonnell wrote in his first article on 11 July 1942:

The great secret of the British parliamentary system is that it has devised a plan whereby there is always before the public an alternative government in the form of a body loyal to the constitution, known to the public, always available to replace the existing government – I mean, of course, His Majesty's Loyal Opposition.

As he warmed to his theme in his second and third articles the eloquent Macdonnell struck a sense of urgency. Noting that the party system can only function efficiently if Parliament is supreme, he deplored the weakening of the position of Parliament by order-in-council government.

Macdonnell didn't confine himself to exposing the Liberal threat to the freedoms essential to a functioning democracy. He argued that the Conservative party was the only possible counterbalance to a Grit autocracy. The CCF had defeated Arthur Meighen in a supposedly safe Tory riding. The CCFers standing in the public opinion polls was impressive. They were once again talking about the big breakthrough. Macdonnell warned *Saturday Night* readers on 16 July that the way to freedom was not via the CCF.

Can we then look to the CCF? The answer is simple. The CCF would cure us with the hair of the dog that bit us. Instead of doing with a minimum of regimentation they would give us more than ever.

But Macdonnell was too wise and too sensitive to waste his readers' time in mere Grit-bashing or CCF-thumping. He outlined in crisp and measured prose some of the values he thought his party should embrace.

More and more the grave danger of the disappearance of various forms of freedom is coming to be realized. In these circumstances, the party that clings to what is good in the past may find its support vastly increased overnight. But only on one supreme and inescapable condition. It will not be enough to urge people to follow us merely as a refuge from untried experimenters. We shall have to satisfy people that we are dynamic as well as sound and sane. We shall have to convince them that we do not propose to put new wine in old bottles, that we do not propose to deal with new and formidable problems by a mere prescription of old remedies.

While Macdonnell feared the effects of a CCF government, he was not unaware of the CCF appeal to important elements in the Canadian electorate. He clearly saw that the Conservatives had to compete for some of the very votes at which the CCF was aiming. Putting it in simple terms, the Tories had to move to the left or run the risk of losing valuable and long-held ground to the CCF. The Port Hope Conference was a major landmark for the party of Macdonald and Cartier.

In his third and final article, on 25 July, Macdonnell wrote:

The National Policy of 1878 is often misconceived. We often forget that it was primarily designed to provide employment. What is the 1942 equivalent? Remember all that has happened in the interval, and particularly the changes brought by war. The 1942 equivalent I suggest is a broad measure of social security. The first element of this would, I suggest, be an assumption of responsibility of the State to see that every citizen is provided with employment at a wage which will enable him to live in decency.

In this same, and in my opinion the best, article, Macdonnell did a brilliant job in marrying a sensitive social conscience with a basic appreciation of the free enterprise values of our type of society.

We have during this war learned a new sense of equality and partnership. If that is so it should make us ready to agree that the state must hold itself responsible to see that its citizens have a national minimum – a kind of every citizen's charter – which ensures a decent livelihood for every citizen and opportunity for his children. And if we who believe in free enterprise make clear our willingness that the state should accept this obligation, then those on the Left, except the most fanatic, would surely consider the reasonableness of our position and would hesitate long before they throw away the blessing of freedom.

I have heard many speeches by Conservative politicians in my country and have read countless articles on Conservatives and Conservatism but I consider the foregoing paragraph to be the most sensible, sensitive, and significant statement of all.

As I see it, our party at its best has always been ready to call in the power of the state to redress grievous and grave inequalities within the citizen body. Sometimes today I hear Conservatives talk about the party as if it is, and always was, nothing more than a northern extension of the rigid rightist Republicanism typified by Ronald Reagan and his ilk. Even in our worst days the Canadian Conservative party was never in the mould of the Falwells, Kirkpatricks, and Reagans. Our tradition is quite different from Bible Belt Republicanism or the rigid anti-leftist rhetoric of some of the recent stars of U.S. Republicanism. It is not so far-fetched to state that, if the Tories in the forties had not gone to Port Hope, they might have become a spent force lingering on the political stage well behind the ebullient CCF.

Apart from his excellent articles, which gave a worthy intellectual foundation to the Port Hope Conference, Macdonnell handled the tactics and strategies with skill and sensitivity. Not being as vainglorious as some politicians he demurred from acting as chairman at Port Hope. A Bay Street businessman might not be an ideal symbol for a new-wave Toryism. With his usual good sense and sound judgment he secured the services of H.R. Milner, a competent and respected lawyer from Edmonton. Milner was an excellent chairman. Chosen as secretary was Rod Finlayson, a Winnipeg lawyer, who had been R.B. Bennett's private secretary and one of the authors of Bennett's stirring 'New Deal' radio speeches. Both of these articulate westerners did a splendid job in making the Port Hope Conference the resounding success that it became.

Macdonnell, concerned but unobtrusive, did not neglect his responsibilities. One of his tasks was to obtain the acquiescence of the party leader, Arthur Meighen, to the conference while at the same time indicating that neither the leader nor members of the national caucus were expected to attend. It was important that this be arranged since Meighen's desire for an early leadership convention might have scuppered the aims of the Port Hopefuls. In the end all was resolved sensibly and courteously. While Meighen would hardly say 'amen' to all the policy statements from Port Hope, he gave the conference his blessing and there was no anti-Meighenism at the gathering.

In these days of the short memory-span it is only the archaic person who wishes to recall what was on television the day before yesterday. Yet, as one who cares about the historic continuity of our great party, I feel today's Conservatives will cheat only their own intellectual selves if they disregard or downgrade the Port Hope Conference. Certainly one of the major historians of Canadian conservatism did not underestimate it. To J.R. Williams, 'The Port Hope Conference represented the opinion of the most advanced group of social thinkers within the party.[2]

About the Port Hope Conference there was much that was downright clever. It was a major achievement to bring together a group of the party faithful at a policy conference and keep their minds on anything but leadership. At Port Hope they really did talk about policy. As I ponder the attitudes of many of the Port Hopefuls, I do not leap to the conclusion that the gathering was a conclave of left-leaning Red Tories, to use a more recent label. If one were to generalize, one might say that the delegates were, in the main, a group of intelligent and concerned pragmatists. If the party was to go anywhere it had to tack to port. In the years that followed, Conservatives would have reason to be grateful for the collective wisdom of the worried men and women at Port Hope.

Then as now, the Conservatives were not the darlings of the press, but Port Hope did get good coverage. In part this stemmed from the shrewd preconference work of Macdonnell, Finlayson, and Milner.

Grant Dexter of the *Winnipeg Free Press* wrote on 16 September 1942: 'At most the conference was revolutionary. The ruins of the present Conservative party were dynamited, the ground cleared and the foundation laid for a new party. In the clean-up scarcely a vestige remained of the grand old party. At the lowest estimate the conference recorded the first definite signs of health, of lusty life, in the Conservative party since the disaster of 1935.'

The *Montreal Star* said of the Port Hope resolutions on 17 September:

The program it drafts would make Sir John A. Macdonald's bones rattle in their coffin, and out-Herridge Herridge by a long margin ... It does not make a move to the left. It takes a leap, and a long leap in that direction. Some of its policies are apparently intended to demonstrate that it could be far more extreme than anything the CCF has suggested up to date.

Some of the policies which shook the brier bush did recall Bennett's 'New Deal' radio talks. Others went beyond anything he had proclaimed. State intervention was called for where necessary. So were stiffer laws against monopolies. The delegates called for the establishment of a central farm bank and a price stabilization corporation. Collective bargaining and labour representation on all government boards and commissions was advocated. A social security program called for full employment for all able and willing to work.

The Port Hopefuls urged low-cost housing, slum clearance, federal aid to education, retirement insurance, and increased old age pensions at a lower age. Mothers' allowances and a form of medicare were advocated. The party of John A. and the National Policy called for the elimination of economic protectionism and urged the government to integrate the Canadian economy with that of the British Commonwealth and the United States. The women of the party were impressive at Port Hope and a women's association was formed. As well, the conference called for the adoption of equal pay for work of equal value.

The perceptive people at Port Hope were in the advance guard of their party. Some of their far-sighted proposals were not adopted for years to come. Often they were belatedly put into effect by

Liberal governments with great fanfare. For those of us who are inheritors of the Conservative tradition it is salutary to recall and acclaim the vision of the Port Hope pioneers.

The one area of the Port Hope Conference which troubles me is that vexed question of conscription. There were 10 or 11 delegates from Quebec (of 175 in total) and it is surprising that they accepted such a clarion call for all-out conscription. It is hard to believe that it was really necessary for the Conservatives to get onto conscription. R.B. Hanson saw it as an issue which would entangle the Liberals without any involvement by the Tories, who still suffered the wounds from their former encounter with the issue.

The Port Hope policy statement and the conference itself received a good press and the venture was widely acclaimed as a smashing success. It was also one of the bright spots in the dreary period of Conservatism from 1939 to 1945 which J.L. Granatstein described as the Politics of Survival.

Sometimes I let my fancy carry me into attaching special, almost superstitious, dimensions to the name Port Hope. Certainly our party was always at its best when it was seen to be left leaning. At those times there was reasoned, wholesome optimism about our future. Perhaps a new trek to a new Port Hope might be salutary in our party's present lot and condition.

At Port Hope, the Conservatives had been able to concentrate on policy and had brought forward some excellent and timely suggestions for a better Canada and a healthier Tory party. But after they came down from the philosophic mountaintop, the Port Hopefuls had to face that chronic problem of post-Macdonald Toryism – leadership. The thinkers of Port Hope were anxious to have a decision made on a permanent leader. They realized that, no matter how attractive their platform, a leader with a fresh mandate and a viable party organization was essential. In addition a convention was the only body which could adopt officially the Port Hope manifesto.

Meighen, as we have seen, was anxious to get out of an unwelcome and, for him, impossible role. Only days after the Port Hope Conference concluded, he took the initiative in calling a leadership convention. In a public statement announcing the convention call, Meighen reiterated his conviction that the party should continue to advocate national government and conscription. Apparently neither the defeat of the 1940 general election nor the disaster of his own by-election in York South had shaken his faith in these nostrums.

In Meighen's 23 September press statement announcing the convention, there was another brief but highly significant paragraph:

Therefore, it is my hope that the doors of the coming convention will be open to all citizens who, regardless of former party affiliations, are animated by these principles and resolved to give them effect.[3]

This ecumenical statement from a prince of Tory orthodoxy was revealing. Meighen not only was calling a convention but he wished to call the shots as to the choice of that convention.

In the late summer of 1941 the Victoria Conservative poll committee met in our home in Victoria. Chester McLure was there and told us of Meighen's grand design to recruit long-time Manitoba Premier John Bracken for the national leadership of the Conservative party. It was regarded as the ultimate in party strategy.

This appeal for open doors was a reaffirmation of fidelity to the goal of national government. Indeed it was much more. If John Bracken was to bring former non-Tories into the party ranks, it was extremely important that no rigid litmus test of historic party loyalty be applied to those Canadians desirous of attending the convention.

In making his party more amenable to accepting Bracken and convincing Bracken to doff his own Progressive party label and join the Tories, Meighen had much to do. He found the Port Hope policy statements extremely helpful in persuading the Manitoba premier. Meighen himself did not think much of the resolutions produced by Macdonnell and the other Port Hopefuls, but they were useful in convincing Bracken that he was being asked to lead a national party committed to progressive policies.

The prudent prairie premier was not rushing to accept Meighen's invitation. He had never been a Conservative; he was designated a Progressive. Some wag said his closest link with the party was his father's attendance at Sir John A. Macdonald's funeral. But he noted the eagerness of the national Conservatives to recruit him. They had designated Winnipeg as the locale of the convention and taken other measures to show their desire to accommodate him. They were also ready to show further signs of cordiality.

The Conservative party in convention at Winnipeg in December 1942 was clearly prepared to accept the Port Hope policy statements. Members of the policy committee presented the draft resolutions to Bracken at his home, and after many hours of discussion he also found them acceptable. Another hurdle had been dealt with. The courted leader thought the party's policies sufficiently progressive for him.

The nuptial rites were proceeding nicely in those wintry days when a serious hitch developed. Meighen and other Bracken backers had at one time hoped their man would win by acclamation. But Saskatchewan MP John Diefenbaker soon put the kibosh on that notion by declaring his candidacy. Howard Green and H.H. Stevens, who had rejoined the Conservative party in 1938, also announced their candidacy, as did Murdoch MacPherson, the former attorney general of Saskatchewan. Seeing no unanimous draft Bracken wanted something else. The outward and visible sign of an inward and spiritual grace was a change in the party name. At its first plenary session a letter from Bracken was read to the assembled delegates. In it he noted with satisfaction that the party through its adoption of Port Hope was becoming progressive. If it would just change its name by associating the words Progressive and Conservative, he would say 'I do.' No leadership convention before or since ever had such a request.

If Bracken and his backers thought this ploy was a winner they soon found how wrong was such an assumption. The *Winnipeg Free Press* of 10 December 1942 said Bracken's letter could be compared 'to the throwing of a stick of dynamite into a crowded Sunday school picnic.' Delegates resented the suggestion that the

Conservatives were joining the Progressives rather than the reverse. Instead of welcoming it as a gracious acceptance, angry Conservatives saw it as an ultimatum. The convention almost broke up in bedlam. Meighen later wrote Bennett that 'one would have thought there would be bloodshed before the prefix "Progressive" could be affixed to the name of the party.'[4]

Luckily, before the convention tore itself apart the wise counsel of J.M. Macdonnell prevailed; he suggested that the name-changing resolution be deferred until the leadership vote was taken.

Political scientist Ruth Bell, a careful student of Conservative conventions, is doubtless right in describing the 1942 gathering as the most dramatic one in Canadian history.[5] Certainly there was great tension before the deadline. After being rebuffed on the name issue Bracken's intentions on the nomination were shrouded in mystery. Ruth Bell's examination of his nomination form suggests that he didn't meet the deadline and someone else signed it for him. Meanwhile Sidney Smith, popular president of the University of Manitoba, had presented his own nomination form to Ruth's husband, Dick Bell, secretary of the convention, with instructions to withdraw it if Bracken entered. Because of the strong showing by MacPherson, Bracken required two ballots to win the leadership. The final figures were Bracken 538, MacPherson 255, and Diefenbaker 79.

At the time of the Winnipeg convention, I was living in Summerside where I was teaching at high school. I had rented a house and brought my parents up for the winter. We followed the convention doings carefully amid hopes that things would improve for the party. Because I had long followed election statistics as avidly as many people follow athletic contests, I had noted that Bracken seemed to be losing ground in Manitoba. It is folly to postulate what I would have done had I been a delegate, but I was enormously impressed by what I had read about Sidney Smith. Had he run he might have been my choice.

After the leadership vote, the Conservatives adopted the name Progressive Conservative which we have retained ever since. I don't think anyone at the Winnipeg meeting commented on the appropriateness of the designation.

In 1854 when John A. Macdonald, in effect, founded the party he wrote: 'Our aim should be to enlarge the bounds of the party so as to embrace every person desirous of being counted as a progressive Conservative.'[6] And that was a long time before Bracken! I was delighted with the name change and for years have found comfort in the 'progressive' part and I've always tried to underline its importance.

Professor Arthur Lower of United College, who would soon become one of my academic heroes, wrote about the convention in the February 1943 issue of *Canadian Forum*:

All the candidates made bad speeches, Mr. Bracken included. But out of him, as the disjointed, icy particles tear themselves from his lips, there stick two qualities that have redeemed many of his speeches in the past and have not deserted him now, character and sincerity. Without brilliance and without presence he dominates the platform.

The Conservative party's second Winnipeg convention may have ended as merry as a marriage bell but the euphoria was short-lived. Of the Bracken-Tory liaison, Lower, a Toryphobe, had written in *Canadian Forum*: 'A more incongruous match there has seldom been.' Poor Bracken's move to the national political stage was unfortunate for him to say the least. He would be destroyed and almost devoured by the party he had been persuaded to save.

One of his first problems concerned his getting into the House of Commons. Mackenzie King had offered to extend the usual courtesies but he had said the same thing about Meighen in York South; the Liberals there had aided and abetted the CCF in bringing Meighen down. The seats open for by-elections didn't appear all that safe and John Bracken wasn't really anxious to get into the hurly-burly of the House of Commons.

His opponents openly criticized him for cowardice; his own people privately deplored his reticence. In the end he didn't enter the lists until the 1945 general election. Instead he tried vainly to lead the parliamentary party from the gallery. He denied that he was afraid of the cockpit of the House of Commons but declared that, as a former provincial politician, he should give priority to getting to know the whole country and give the people of Canada a chance to know him.

Bracken was not idling his time away by any means. He was giving attention to party organization and bringing some able people to his side. He was also travelling far and wide across the Dominion and meeting thousands of Canadians. In the spring of 1943, he made a well-planned visit to Nova Scotia and Prince Edward Island. He touched not only the large centres but the small communities as well. In PEI he met many groups in various parts of the province and then held a wind-up meeting in Charlottetown. My father met him in the morning at the little village of Bradalbane and later in Charlottetown. He came back impressed by Bracken's folksy informality and the strength of his handshake. He was naturally pleased that the leader recognized him and called him by name at the Charlottetown gathering. By such small gifts are politicians judged. It was my father's opinion that Bracken was better in his informal off-the-cuff remarks at the small meeting at Bradalbane and much less effective in his formal address to the rally in Charlottetown. He was 100 per cent right.

Unlike my father, I didn't meet John Bracken during his first visit as leader to PEI. My teaching duties inhibited heavy involvement in politics and I was still chafing about my failure to enter the military and was seeking some alternative activity in the wider world. Among the many efforts to get overseas in some capacity was an appeal to the YMCA International Service. This wasn't successful but I did get an offer to join the staff of the YMCA in Winnipeg.

In the early fall of 1943, I moved to Winnipeg to take up duties with the YMCA and to enrol at United College. My four years in Winnipeg in 1943–7 were happy. I learned a great deal as a staff member of the YMCA. My time at United College was rich and rewarding. A liberal arts college with a gifted faculty it also brought me enduring friendship. I was class president of both third- and fourth-year classes. I served a period as prime minister of the student model parliament – one of my 'ministers' was Sterling Lyon, later premier of Manitoba. And best of all I met Isabel Stewart.

Our graduation banquet at the Fort Garry Hotel will always remain a bittersweet memory. As I was at a tailor shop picking up my borrowed tux, I had a telephone call from my boss at the YMCA, Charles Forsythe, telling me that word of my father's death had just come through. Mr Forsythe said they had debated whether to tell me or wait until after the graduation jollification. He said he thought I was of the stuff that could take it.

Actually, there was little choice. Telling only Isabel and my close friend Bob Mitchell I did my master of ceremonies duties and delivered the valedictory address as if I had no personal sorrow. It was a memorable evening, my first real date with Isabel.

When I moved to Winnipeg in 1943, I still recall my surprise that so little was ever said about the departure of the long-time premier. It was almost as if he had never been. No one seemed bereft by his departure or thrilled by his assumption of a new role on the national scene. No one seemed to hate John Bracken. On the other hand, no one seemed to love him. He was not capable of raising or lowering the political or emotional temperature by a single degree. John Diefenbaker always knew what to do with an audience but Bracken had no such gift. I had always wondered why Arthur Meighen, so eloquent himself and so critical of others' oratorical limitations, seemed unconcerned about Bracken's inability to make a good speech.

Even after the passage of so many years and the most careful scrutiny of documents, it is not easy to explain the rapid decline of Bracken and Brackenism. He was anything but a charismatic leader, but God knows Mackenzie King was not one either and he was the most successful and sustained party leader in our nation's history. When asked if his fellow Irishman George Bernard Shaw had many enemies, Oscar Wilde replied that he was not important enough to have enemies but that none of his friends liked him. John Bracken must often have felt betrayed as he looked for support and understanding from those who had beguiled him into the uneasy chair of leadership. Bracken had become a somewhat tragic figure before he had been leader for a year.

During his years as national leader Bracken made a great many speeches. Some of them are uninteresting or just plain dull. Few of them give much clear insight into the man or his mission. One exception is the speech he gave to the party's annual meeting in Ottawa on 3 March 1944. In it, he sought to give meaning to the Progressive part of the party's name:

The job of the Progressive Conservative Party is to make good on the word 'Progressive,' – that means to save all that is worth saving from the economy of the past, and supplement it by all that is worthwhile from the new knowledge of today. It means the building back into our economy of one essential to its success – the confidence it needs and must have, if it is to function properly; and it means providing for one major change in the attitude of the State towards its economy and its human resources – human welfare must be made the primary function of the State and not just one which is incidental or secondary or a by-product of some system.[7]

One of the most difficult issues for Bracken and his divided and dispirited caucus was the legislation on family allowances of 'baby bonuses.' The measure would provide $5 monthly for each child under five years old and larger amounts up to age sixteen. The annual cost was estimated at $250 million, no puny sum in 1944. Once again the Conservatives were torn apart by the legislation. Some rash and unworthy public utterances were made by Tories which grievously injured the party. On the whole, these insensitive outbursts came from the expected sources, but Bracken's own role in the episode is hard to understand. We can be sure that both the leader and the party were wounded in what appeared to be an early caucus hostility to the measure.

Bracken, the Progressive, had talked a great deal about social security measures and the state's responsibility for meeting the minimum needs of its citizens. He might have been expected to support the family allowance measure but in the early stages he had seemed to oppose it. He was critical of the cost and thought it had all the earmarks of a political bribe. A Toronto Tory, Herbert Bruce, described the family allowance legislation in the Commons on 31 July as 'a bribe of the most brazen character, made chiefly to one province and paid for by the taxes of the rest.'

If Bracken really did not know that the marriage of Toryism and Brackenism was on the rocks almost everybody else did. It seemed a long, long way from that heady night in the Winnipeg Auditorium in December 1942.

Bracken, with some fancy footwork, ended up by refusing to oppose family allowances in the House of Commons, but the party, thanks to the ringing utterances of some of the Ontario bigwigs, once again underscored its anti-Quebec image and lost thousands of votes there and elsewhere as a result of this perceived insensitive stance.

Bracken succumbed to the Ontario wing of the party on another issue, conscription. Mackenzie King thought that his mid-April election call would find the war ended before voting day. Once again he was right. But, despite the fact that the war in Europe had ended and thousands of troops were freed from duty, there were still Tory calls for conscription for the Pacific theatre of war. Among those calling for it was Bracken. At this stage, I gave up. His was, with all charity, a wholly idiotic stand. Perhaps, under terrific pressure from the Toronto group, Bracken was cracking under the strain. His statement that Quebec resented not having its youth conscripted is hard to explain otherwise.

In the 1945 election, the Progressive Conservatives won sixty-seven seats, the best showing since 1930. King's victory was a narrow one, but considering all the sins a long-standing government had to answer for, the fact that he won at all was remarkable. A far duller man than Winston Churchill, King survived while the dynamic British leader went down to defeat.

For me, the best news was the election of Chester McLure in Queens. He had stood in every election since 1930 and his victory was a tribute to his careful, earnest, and persistent campaigning rather than a reflection of Islanders' judgment on national issues.

The federal Conservative caucus had a western leader, but it was more heavily dominated by Ontario than ever before. It would only be a matter of time before it would have an Ontario leader as well. Bracken had worked hard in the House of Commons and brought sound organizational reforms to his caucus. He had also gained many seats, but he was seen as too dull, too dry, and not politically smart. Worst of all, he had lost an election. The premier of Ontario had actually won two. A Tory winner was a *rara avis* in those days. The party was as anxious to summon Premier George Drew of Ontario as he was to hear the call.

Oddly enough, I do not remember election night 1945 all that clearly. With whom did I sup sorrow or seek grains of comfort? These details my memory somehow does not provide. Needless to say, it was felt as another defeat, like the slaughterings of 1935 and 1940 and the shattering York South by-election of 1942. But to anyone who could recall our scraping through with thirty-nine seats in the preceding national election, sixty-seven seats in the House of Commons constituted a change in the desired direction. And unlike Manion in 1940 and Meighen in the 1942 by-election, our leader won in his own constituency.

But Bracken's days as leader were numbered. He had a divided and bickering caucus and was constantly under pressure from George Drew and his friend George McCullagh of the *Globe and Mail*. However, it was not enough for the long-suffering Bracken to have to deal with fractious and factious colleagues. He had to swallow some of his most deeply held opinions before yielding up the cup of anguish and frustration of the Tory leadership.

Bracken had been one of the great enthusiasts for the 1940 Rowell-Sirois Report on Dominion-provincial relations. All along he had seen a strong Dominion government as a necessity in a country where regions and provinces differed so widely in economic strength and resources. But Drew had become an opponent of centralization and a champion of provincial rights. During the Pontiac by-election of 1946, in which Bracken campaigned, he too adopted a provincialist stance. This opportunistic strategy, designed to please Drew and Quebec Premier Duplessis, did not pay off. The seat was won by the charismatic Social Credit candidate Réal Caouette. The Progressive Conservative trailed, winning 7487 votes compared to 11,412 for Caouette and 10,379 for the Liberal.

During the 1945 general election Mackenzie King had nastily

suggested that a vote for Bracken was a vote for the management of the Dominion by the Toronto heavies George Drew and George McCullagh. The disingenuous King was probably not far off the mark. Had Bracken attained the prime ministry he might have been able to stand up to the two Georges. But he never won the top job and never really was able to win arguments with the Ontario chieftain and his tycoon publisher friend. A John Diefenbaker or a Pierre Elliott Trudeau might not have been so polite and long-suffering as Bracken.

John Bracken was never in a position to become the unchallenged master of the federal party. He did not develop the diehard loyalist following that John Diefenbaker had for many years. Nor did he have the kind of regional or provincial support that sustained Robert Stanfield. Against the dynamic, aggressive, colourful Drew and his Toronto cohorts, Bracken was not a towering champion.

I remember being attracted to George Drew in the 1930s. While not living in affluence on my PEI teacher's salary, I nevertheless bought his book, *Canada's Fighting Airmen*. Although he was an artilleryman rather than an airman, I thought that the outspoken politician in far-off Ontario was a doughty fighter himself. I did not meet George Drew until after he became our national leader, though I had been well aware of his impressive personality and substantial record of achievement. Clearly here was a man who had lost no time in his climb to success. In December 1938 he was chosen leader of the Ontario Conservative party and soon thereafter was elected to the legislature. The election of 4 August 1943 brought him to premiership and began the long Tory reign in Ontario which lasted until the defeat of Premier Frank Miller in May 1985.

When in 1948 the Progressive Conservatives were once again seeking a national leader, it is not surprising that they looked in the direction of Queen's Park. The shrewd, practical, experienced Chester McLure was immediately enthusiastic about the prospect of the Ontario leader going federal. John Myers and most other prominent PEI Tories had a similar view. When Bracken resigned on 20 July 1948, Drew was the heir apparent – a shoo-in. Nor did anyone doubt that he had called the Ontario election for 7 June 1948, just three years after the previous one, to ease his transition to the federal scene.

In 1947 I had left Winnipeg and joined the department of economics and political science at the University of New Brunswick in beautiful and historic Fredericton. Chester McLure arranged for me to be accredited as a youth delegate to the convention called for 30 September 1948 in Ottawa. The magnitude of Drew's first ballot victory there surprised no one.

There is nothing like a hyped-up meeting of your own party to raise the morale of the faithful. It is not surprising, therefore, that the assembled Tories in Ottawa's Coliseum were ebullient when the gallant colonel was given command. After all, the wily survivor Mackenzie King had finally gone. There was no war, and so the spectre of conscription had vanished. It was really only a matter of time before we would enter the victory kingdom so legitimately established by the great Sir John A. Macdonald. This time we'll really wallop those Grits, we thought. Just issue the electoral writ.

It is not surprising that Progressive Conservatives were complimenting themselves on acquiring such a great vote-getter. While, fortunately for some of us, looks are not everything, they are a good part of it. George Drew was certainly a handsome man. He was six-foot two, and seemed tanned at all seasons. He had kept his athletic figure and his military bearing. Immaculately dressed, he was not likely to be ignored in any crowd. One journalist had labelled him Apollo Belvedere.

But he had more than good looks and good clothes. He had a fine resonant voice which came over very well on radio, still a major medium of communication in his day. In the 1940s less attention was paid to the leaders' wives than is now the case – the era of bachelors King and Bennett had been long. In the lovely and popular Fiorenza, however, Drew had a devoted helpmate. She was a gifted linguist and at one political gathering in a cosmopolitan area she had spoken English, French, Italian, and German. During the Drew era I often thought that Mrs Drew should have been brought further to the forefront.

But there was more to the new leader than externals. His record in public life was impressive. He was fifty-four. He had served in the municipal field and had been in provincial politics for ten years. He had sat on both the government and opposition sides. His victories were significant but he had known also the temporary effects of defeat. In 1943 he had gained a minority government. His good administration and shrewd tactics – plus some CCF blunders – enabled him to score an electoral triumph in 1945.

In the events in the Ontario legislature which triggered the 1945 election, Drew outwitted CCF leader Ted Joliffe and the renascent Liberal leader Mitchell Hepburn. The magnitude of his electoral victory deluged his major opponent, the CCF. As Bracken fumbled and failed, it was natural that federal Conservatives cast longing eyes at the triumphant, dynamic Ontario premier.

During his active public life George Drew's political enemies liked to depict him as an insensitive reactionary without much concern for Canadians and Ontarians not of the privileged classes. Sometimes his patrician manner helped make these allegations credible. But if one judges the man by his works and not his style, these charges do not hold up. His record as premier of Ontario is one of enlightened, progressive, and sometimes daring leadership.

While I believed then and still think that Drew's record and his status as a Tory actually in office were his biggest assets at the 1948 convention, his proven pugnacity was also a significant factor. In Prince Edward Island at this time we tended to prefer vigorous politicians. During my four years in Winnipeg (1943–7) I generally found the legislators dull and tepid, certainly in so far as the front-line parties were concerned. Perhaps this was in part a legacy of Bracken's tendency to discourage partisanship.

I could not see anyone else but Drew as the party's standard-bearer in 1948. Diefenbaker had been on the national scene for eight years and I had been attracted by many of his activities and populist utterances. He was coming through as a highly progressive politician with a good deal of colour and panache. I had not met him at that time. Donald Fleming, considered a young candidate at forty-three, had been in the House of Commons for three years. I had never seen him but was favourably impressed by his successful efforts to master French.

I had few reservations about Drew. The loss of seats in the 1948 Ontario election was just a bit disturbing. As a Maritimer who had lived in the West, I was naturally aware of anti-Ontario feelings in many areas outside that rich and important province. But we in the boondocks nevertheless recognized that Ontario is where the harvest of votes is reaped. Out of 262 seats in the House of Commons, Ontario had 85. Drew, therefore, was seen as having a substantial power base.

By 1948 there had been a good deal written and said about the Drew-Duplessis axis. Some months before the convention, the Ontario premier had publicly declared his desire 'to walk arm in arm with Mr. Duplessis.'

Drew was nominated by Ivan Sabourin, a Quebec Conservative with close ties to Premier Duplessis. What to do with Quebec remained the perennial Tory problem. Drew had decided on a close relationship with the Quebec premier. The power-hungry delegates at the 1948 Progressive Conservative convention were willing and eager to try again to find a way to the votes, if not the hearts, of a sizeable block of Quebec electors. The great majority of delegates at the 1948 convention were motivated by strategic and tactical considerations rather than those of ideology. Some old pros believed that we had failed by trying to appeal as a party of the left. The left was too crowded and now we must turn to the right.

But the delegates from the nation's far-flung constituencies did not vote for Drew because he was seen as the darling of Bay Street. Few of them had many contacts with the great financial centre and many might not have known or cared where Bay Street was. The Progressive Conservatives at the Ottawa Coliseum voted for Drew because they thought he was an able man and, more important, able to win.

Drew was the first contender ever to win a Conservative convention on the first ballot. The magnitude of his victory was a tribute to his presentation. After six years of Bracken's unexciting performances, Drew's public personality was a marked contrast.

At the convention, as he always did, George Drew came across as convinced and convincing in whatever he said.

On 25 May 1949 I attended the provincial convention of the Young Progressive Conservatives (YPC) of Prince Edward Island. The federal election campaign was by then under way and everyone attending the meeting in the Charlottetown Hotel was filled with optimism. Perhaps this was one of the first occasions when my contrariness (or independent judgment) brought me into trouble. In a chat with Colonel Ernie Strong, who had run a close second to the Liberal winner in the Prince constituency in 1945, I opined that the current Tory candidate, Brigadier J.H. Price, would not win in the upcoming election. A few minutes later, Colonel Strong introduced me to Price saying: 'The professor here was just telling me you won't win.' Extricating myself from this opener was not easy. I could only say that I would be delighted to be wrong and that if so it would not be the first time.

The program brochure for the YPC convention featured the handsome George Drew on the cover and carried the slogan, 'The Progressive Conservatives of Canada on the March!' This latter was an indication of a new confidence in the breasts of the faithful Tories young and old.

But there was no great comfort in the Prince Edward Island results of the federal election held on 27 June 1949. As I had predicted, the excellent Brigadier Price lost to a local Grit, J. Watson MacNaught, by 173 votes. The charming and gallant Lieutenant-Colonel John A. Macdonald lost in Kings to a new Liberal candidate, T.J. Kickham, by 597 votes. In the dual riding of Queens, Wing Commander J. Angus MacLean again failed to attain victory. The only Tory elected in PEI was the old maestro, Chester McLure, who topped the poll in Queens. On election night, while deploring the defeat of three of our excellent candidates, Islanders could draw some solace from the fact that on PEI the Tories had at least held their own, something that could not be said of the party as a whole.

I suppose it is never easy for a partisan to see his party lose. But in 1949 we were shaken by the grim fact that the great George Drew had not done nearly as well as the mediocre John Bracken.

On the morning after, the Progressive Conservatives had 41 seats in the 262-member House of Commons. In 1945, in a House of 245 members under Bracken, we had won 67 seats. O Fearful Fate! In the home province of our new leader PCs lost 23 seats. The prairie man Bracken had 48 Ontario colleagues in his caucus. Drew would have just half that number.

The 'morning after' quarterbacks in our own decimated party and in the ranks of the impartial observers were quick with their explanations of the Tory débâcle. The 1949 election focused more on the cult of personality than any preceding national contest. The public relations experts were more important and pervasive. Superficially it might have seemed that, in any such leader-to-leader confrontation, the handsome, experienced Drew should have had the advantage. Louis St Laurent was not an obvious charismatic figure, even in our own age where that adjective has been outrageously overworked. He came across as a well-mannered, well-heeled lawyer with a sedate, dry presentation. As someone said, he sounded like a mathematics professor speaking to a very dull class. He was twelve years older than Drew and, although there was not then the fad for juvenility which now prevails in Canadian politics, this should have helped the PC leader. But something went wrong on Madison Avenue, or 141 Laurier, the PC headquarters. The courtly, stately lawyer from Quebec, who was anything but a sansculotte, came through as a man of the people. George Drew was dubbed as the pompous, overbearing representative of Bay Street.

In those parts of the electorate where closeness to the corporate élite was not a political asset, Drew suffered. But there is no evidence that the Conservative party was benefiting from open hearts or open purses of Big Business in the 1949 election. As one party bigwig put it, we got the name but not the game.

I first saw Mr St Laurent during the York-Sunbury by-election campaign in 1947 when, as secretary of state for external affairs, he came to the University of New Brunswick to speak on behalf of the Liberal candidate, Dr Milton Gregg, the university president. As well as being interested in the Progressive Conservative party, I was interested in international relations and impressed by the kind of leadership St Laurent and Lester Pearson were giving on the world stage. I also thought he spoke a good deal of sense in his low-key speech which, appropriate to the locale, was essentially a lecture. I remember one other thing about his dealing with an audience. It was very warm in the meeting room. St Laurent, noting a group of students showing their discomfort, gestured to them to remove their coats, which they gladly did. This anecdote underlines the vast difference between the dress code of 1949 and 1991! But I marvelled at the time how St Laurent could convey his message without removing his own jacket. It was a sensitive bit of rapport.

When in 1948 the Liberal party had called a convention to select King's successor, we all knew it was a coronation rather than a contest. St Laurent was King's chosen successor. He was from Quebec and the alternating French-Anglo pattern was seen as vital by the Grits. He was also a big figure on the international scene and the successor to the great Ernest Lapointe. But Tories (and I am sure many Liberals too) wondered how the starchy lawyer would perform in the rough and tumble of election campaigning. For some time after he became leader there was still doubt. Not by any means did he strike sparks with the voters. Sometimes he showed a testy arrogance and an unattractive brittleness.

But a strange thing happened on the way to the election. The precise, sedate prime minister became 'Uncle Louis.' It is said that it all 'just happened,' that he talked to some children one day at the railway station, and thereafter became the darling of our young ones and, of course, of the old ones to whom the young ones belonged. Professor J. Murray Beck records a fascinating account of the St Laurent image, referring to a campaign meeting in Hawkesbury, Ontario: 'he acted the part of a father at the family table and "talked as a wise and kindly father would talk and the people stared at him spellbound." A member of parliament cried ... and when it was all over, he cried again and said, "Ah, he is the pappa of us all." '[8]

I am sure that no Canadians saw the PC leader as a benevolent

At a brilliant ceremony the Conservative party was recently united in marriage once more with a beauty of Quebec. Miss Isolation of 1949, offspring of Mr Maurice Duplessis. Mayor Houde, a distinguished wartime guest of the Canadian Government, was best man. The Union Nationale guarded the doors, which were sealed by Mr Duplessis's ancestral padlocks. The bride's face was hidden in a veil worn by her grandmother in 1911 and her mother in 1930. She was gowned in traditional blackmail and carried a simple bouqet of wild bigamy. Shotguns were carried by the proud parents, Mr Duplessis and Mr Drew. Mr Duplessis wore the medal presented to him by Colonel Peron of Argentina. Mr Drew wore a boyish smile. Mr Diefenbaker and Mr MacDonell wore sackcloth and ashes. The premises were tastefully decorated with Fleur de Lis from Mr Duplessis's private conservatory. The groom's gift to the bride was a veto over future Conservative party policy. After the exchange of nuptial vows the gathering followed the local tradition by burning a copy of the North Altantic Pact. In a happy little speech, Mr Duplessis stressed the glories of democracy and the need of campaign funds. Mr Drew pledged the happy married couple to a long lifetime of convertibility. The groom modestly remarked that he had not been so pleasantly married for quite some time. After the cutting of a large cake baked in St James Street, the bride and groom left for a honeymoon at Niagara Falls, which the groom will go over, as usual, in a barrel. (Cartoon by Arch Dale, *Winnipeg Free Press*, 2 June 1949)

father figure or a kindly Uncle George. A favourite appellation was 'Gorgeous George,' but those who tagged him with that were not doing it to assist him or his party.

Perhaps it was coincidence or accident of location, but I thought the 1949 election somewhat notorious for the mean-spirited nature of some of the appeals on the grassroots level. In the Liberals' underground campaign, the old were told that if they voted Tory they would lose their old age pensions. Other sectors of the electorate were warned that a Drew government would do away with family allowances. These subterranean appeals were, of course, aided by some of Drew's unfortunate remarks of 1945. This unworthy type of vote-gathering was used against Progressive Conservative candidates for a good many years.

But I have long since learned that even the most sound and rational explanations by those who fail to win are often treated merely as the excuses of poor losers. So it must be admitted that there were many positive reasons why the Liberals won such a great victory in 1949.

In their shrewd use of the nation's prosperity, the Liberals greatly enhanced their party's electoral appeal. I well remember the popular slogan of the campaign: 'You never had it so good.' There was, among Canadians, a feeling of well-being. The PCs preaching blue ruin were unable to excite or alarm a reasonably prosperous citizenry. For those who cared about foreign policy, we were making a good impression on the international scene. Mr St Laurent himself and his secretary of state for external affairs, Lester B. Pearson, were seen as enhancing our respect and influence abroad.

In 1949 the PCs were again almost shut out in Quebec. The famed Drew-Duplessis axis failed to get us votes in Quebec but probably cost us plenty in the other provinces. In 1945, the PCs had won one out of sixty-five seats in Quebec. In 1949, they managed to win two out of seventy-three.

3

Professor to Politician

Between 1949 and 1953 I intensified my political involvement and activities. During my two years at the University of New Brunswick (1947–9), I had attended political meetings and become identified as a committed Progressive Conservative.

Indeed my political orientation had preceded me. After my graduation from United College at the University of Manitoba, in the spring of 1947, I had written to a number of Maritime universities seeking some opportunity which would allow me to further my studies. The best response came from the economics and political science department of UNB. The chairman, Dr J.R. Petrie, wrote to offer me a teaching fellowship at the then princely sum of $2400 a year. Fredericton is a beautiful town which one of my United College professors, Dr Carleton Stanley, said made him think of Anthony Trollope's *Barchester Towers*. I taught a large class in economics and two smaller political science classes. I also had an opportunity to work towards a master's degree combining political science and history.

But the most impressive thing about UNB was the person who brought me there. Dick Petrie was a top-notch economist, a dynamic personality, and a man of strong opinions which he expressed freely and with great panache. When I arrived at UNB, I was early told that Petrie was on very good terms with 'the Beaver,' Lord Beaverbrook. The reason given was that he was the only faculty member whom the noble publisher and university chancellor could not drink under the table – doubtless another apocryphal yarn like many which float about at universities.

Petrie later told me why I had been offered the fellowship, rather than some other applicant. Apart from being satisfied with my academic record and references, he had more important criteria. 'I said to myself, "He is an Islander, of Scottish descent and a Highlander to boot. He's a Presbyterian and there's a damn good chance he's a Tory."' Petrie nominated me for membership in the St Andrew's Society, which I found to be a more lively group of Scots than one might expect to find in a city with such an English patina as Fredericton.

As with many colourful people, Petrie was an iconoclast. On occasion over a social glass he was wont to declare in reference to a left-wing faculty colleague: 'If we have another war my first patriotic act will be to get a Sten gun and shoot that old bugger.' If, as I presume was the case, this declared intention was passed on to the intended target, it doubtless did little for Dick's popularity in that quarter.

Petrie was a real dynamo, open and candid with his loyalties. He wore his Conservative fealty with prideful gusto. After the departure of UNB President Milton Gregg for the corridors of power in Ottawa, there were rumours that Dick Petrie might become the new president. This did not happen. His outspoken support for the PCs would have been a factor. After all, UNB was a provincial university and in New Brunswick the Liberals were solidly entrenched. Instead Dr Albert Trueman, president of the University of Manitoba, became UNB's new president. I thought then and think still that the university missed a good bet in not calling Petrie to the presidency.

It is likely that my open identification with an opposition party provincially and federally was less than helpful to my own career at UNB. When I left for PHD studies at McGill it was my understanding that after two years I was to return to UNB. This was the view of Petrie and others at McGill and UNB. In that less-bureaucratic era the agreement had not been documented or formalized. It was what we called, in those pre-feminist days, a gentlemen's agreement. In any case, it was not carried out and, instead of returning to Fredericton, I went to the Prairies once again. As with many of life's disappointments, the UNB fiasco proved a blessing and helped bring me into a meaningful and enormously satisfying political career. But there is more to be said about the years at UNB where I served on a university faculty for the first time in my life. However lowly my place on the academic totem pole, it was still a worthwhile learning experience.

Some aspects were less than exciting. For the first year I was assigned a room in a residence for single faculty members in the Alexander College campus of the university. This was an abandoned military establishment and if there were any amenities there I did not recognize them. The kitchen was definitely not *cordon bleu*, the atmosphere was something between primitive and shoddy, but the rent was reasonable. The depression of the environment was lightened by the people who shared the experience. Bob Gilmore, a Vermonter in the history department, and Ralph Hicklin of the English department were sparkling people to have around. Hicklin, who died tragically young, became one of our country's greatest experts on ballet. I knew of his great love and knowledge of the field in those far off days of 1947–9. A lovely New Brunswick lady, Mrs Nellie Taylor, was the college nurse and often invited us to her Alexander College apartment for some relaxation, good conversation, and, blessedly, good food.

Although Gilmore and I were closer friends, I admired Hicklin's turn of phrase. The wife of a faculty member he immediately dubbed 'Lady Macbeth.' One day I remarked that we had not seen him at lunch at the Lady Beaverbrook residence on the main campus where good food was served. Referring to a fellow faculty member whose wife was very much pregnant and who ate regularly at Lady Beaverbrook, Hicklin replied: 'Honest to God, I just couldn't face his profundity and her rotundity today, so I sent downtown for a restful hamburger!'

I had some involvement in the 1947 York-Sunbury by-election. The wife of General Ernie Sansom was a going concern, to use the vernacular. I recall addressing a meeting of the Women's PC association of which she was provincial president. In the preamble of my speech, I noted how important the women of the country and the party were. I pointed out that there were more of them than of us and in the reality of the situation they had more money. (Think of all the rich widows!) For some far-fetched reason this innocuous ad libbing of mine made the national news. I would have thought that everyone knew these facts and the well-known should not be news.

I tried to be helpful in the by-election despite my faculty status. I called in at Sansom headquarters more than once and talked with Mrs Leo Cain who was in charge – a charming lady. In 1949 I was asked to take on a major campaign role, not by Mrs Cain but by a big Tory connected with the *Fredericton Gleaner*. I doubt if it was an official invitation but in any case I was not able to stay in Fredericton for the 1949 general election. From 1947 I recall an amusing comment by one of the people on the UNB custodial staff who was an ardent CCF supporter. He said: 'I can't understand why this is called a by-election. Surely with Lieutenant-General Sansom running against Brigadier-General Gregg it can't be anything but a general election!'

My years at UNB ended with the Tories losers on all fronts. Milton Gregg's impressive by-election win of 1947 was followed by a big victory in the general election of 1949. In June 1948 the Liberal government of John B. McNair won forty-seven seats in the provincial legislature to five for the PCs. This lopsided victory prompted some smart-ass Grit to gloat to Milton Gregg that the Tories did not even have enough to be pallbearers. What this gloating Grit did not foresee was that one of the five, Hugh John Flemming, would in 1952 reverse the provincial humiliation of 1948 and make a major contribution to the Tory federal revival in the Atlantic region. What I didn't foresee was that in 1987 the provincial Conservatives would not elect even a single member.

In the late 1940s it was not all that easy to parade in the raiment of Toryism. I well remember a breakfast in the stately old Homestead Inn, to which I moved after the rigours of Alexander College. I was talking a Progressive Conservative line to some of the other residents when Professor McAndrew of the French department entered and said, with dripping sarcasm: 'That sounds like George

Drew.' Noting too much the sardonic tone and too little the actual words, I said in bristling response: 'It is well known that when there is no good argument, certain people resort to the smear technique.' Whereupon McAndrew retorted: 'I wasn't smearing you. I was merely likening your words to those of your great leader.' What else could I do but depart the dining-room without even finishing my lovely cup of tea? My judgment of his motives had been sound; my response to his tactics anything but!

My years at McGill did not offer many opportunities for political activity. Neither Montreal nor Quebec was fertile ground for Progressive Conservatives in the years 1949–51. My graduate studies, my teaching load, and my duties as dean of residence in Presbyterian College kept me busy enough in any case. Besides, I had married Isabel Stewart in December 1949 and she joined McGill's mathematics department in 1950. But we were able to get to Prince Edward Island for the summer and there I found opportunities for political activity. At annual meetings of provincial districts I was sometimes asked to address the assembled Tories. In those days these were gatherings of the faithful few. After being swept from the legislature in 1935 the provincial PCs had lost every subsequent election, and the fidelity of the truly stalwart was essential to keeping hope glimmering.

Interestingly enough it was a federal breakthrough which gave the greatest satisfaction to PEI Tories. In one of four federal by-election victories on 25 June 1951 the Queens constituency elected J. Angus MacLean with a majority of 453 votes. MacLean had lost in 1945 and 1949 and there was Tory jubilation in the little province on that June night. I recall literally dashing across the street to tell Mrs Wallace Stewart the moment the radio had conceded MacLean's victory. She was the widow of one of my father's friends on the Victoria poll committee. Afterwards my wife and I joined Frank and Florence Myers to go to Charlottetown for some celebration.

During the campaign I had made a radio address on behalf of MacLean and was gratified by the comments I heard thereafter. About a month before the election we attended a rally addressed by George Drew in Charlottetown. In a chat after the meeting he was lauding the PC candidate in Brandon, an area my wife knew well, and she made the comment that unfortunately that kind of person doesn't always get elected. I remember George Drew actually blushing at that remark which, although made in all innocence, might be misconstrued by someone who had often been elected himself.

The Brandon by-election was to have a profound effect on my own political career. With no return to UNB, I was in the academic job market and was engaged to fill the vacancy at Brandon College created by Walter Dinsdale's election to the House of Commons. Dinsdale was extremely helpful to me in my new duties and in a short time I regarded him as one of my closest friends.

Elected on the same day as Angus MacLean, Walter became a western stalwart of the Progressive Conservative party, winning election after election with massive majorities. At the time of his death in 1982 he was the Father of the House, although that designation of seniority of services is less used in the Canadian Commons than in the Mother of Parliaments.

Some parliamentary constituencies are dubbed 'safe seats.' There are some in Quebec which have been held by the Liberals for as long as the mind of man recalls. In Ontario there are a few rock-ribbed Tory seats. Then there are the swing ridings where the electors seem to have an uncanny knack of being on the side of whichever party wins nationally. Brandon was in neither category. It belonged to no party nor did it hitch rides on the national bandwagon. In 1935, when the West repudiated R.B. Bennett with much thoroughness, Brandon stood by the Tory member it had elected in 1930. In a by-election in 1938, a former Prince Edward Islander, J.E. Matthews, had won the seat for the Liberals. He retained it until his death in 1950. It would appear that when Brandon voters had a good member who served them well they gave him their sustained support.

It was an agreeable coincidence that I had participated in the Queens by-election and then moved to the constituency of Brandon, in which the PCs had scored another victory. A very few days after moving to Brandon I attended a Conservative strategy meeting at the spacious home of 'Cam' Donaldson, Brandon's representative in the Manitoba legislature. After the business of the meeting was dispensed with, Cam asked me if I ever took a drink. I replied with a definite affirmative, whereupon he invited me into the study. I do not recall its being lined with books but it was a genial place in which I would spend a good deal of time over the next four years.

The victorious by-election campaign was much on the mind and the tongues of the Brandon Progressive Conservatives, with whom I was to be closely involved during my stay in the City of the Wheat, as Manitoba's second metropolis was called. The Liberal party had nominated a prestige candidate, Dr J. Grant MacEwan, dean of agriculture at the University of Manitoba, author, historian, public speaker, and much else. In those heady Grit days the Liberal establishment doubtless thought that their man of eminence would have no trouble defeating the young professor from Brandon College. But the PCs had a candidate of unblemished record, immense energy, a decorated war veteran, and son of a popular Conservative politician. Walter Dinsdale sparked a lively organization which far outmatched the MacEwan Liberal campaign. Subtly they capitalized on MacEwan's outsider status. The PC slogan 'A Brandon Man for Brandon, Man.' hurt the man from Winnipeg, a place which many Brandonites find less than endearing. In portraying MacEwan as a parachutist the Brandon PCs naturally did not stress the fact that he too had been born in Brandon.

I was told that the Liberals outspent the Progressive Conservatives by a large margin. One of MacEwan's big campaign events was an open-air barbecue at which the Liberal candidate would speak and press the flesh. At such a gala affair a band was necessary. But it proved difficult to engage such a group of musicians. Eventually one was found. The Salvation Army Band provided splendid musical background. One of its members, Walter Dinsdale, cornetist, must have found the setting particularly interesting. Not always does a candidate have such a ringside seat at his opponent's major campaign pitch!

George Drew had come into the Queens by-election campaign, addressing a mass rally. The Brandon Progressive Conservatives did not feature their leader during the by-election. This was probably the old western suspicion of the east, and especially Toronto, at work. It might also have been a tacit recognition that the Brandon electors were candidate-centred in their political judgments. Believing that their Dinsdale could take on the Liberals' MacEwan, they wished to avoid any adverse fallout from heavy emphasis on the national leaders. In Walter Dinsdale they did indeed have a winner. A social worker, religious leader, university professor, he seemed to be a natural as a politician. He was an inveterate worker, a constant campaigner, a devoted constituency man. As I observed him in action for the first four years in his constituency and later as a parliamentary colleague, I never ceased to salute his performance. Putting it simply, he never missed a trick. Nor did he ever duck a responsibility. His own constituency was always in the forefront of his priorities, as it must be with any successful MP. But Walter served a broader arena. He worked diligently for the PC cause throughout Manitoba and the West. He was also a parliamentary champion of the youth, the churchy population, and a host of good causes which needed a spokesman and advocate. He was assiduous in his attention to all the people he represented.

Many good MPs are defeated because of adverse national trends or perceived deficiencies in their leaders, but some can ride out any political storm. Walter Dinsdale was one of those. Diligent concern for one's constituents is the basic ingredient for political longevity for any politician. Sometimes it is not enough, too strong a tide is running, but it is nonetheless the best bulwark of survival. Regardless of the opponent – and he had many of differing appeals and propensities – regardless of national leaders and national issues, Walter Dinsdale survived magnificently.

Not bereft of political ambitions at the time, I am grateful for the opportunity I had to observe Walter Dinsdale in political action. Although they were totally unlike in so many ways – age, physique, background, geography – he was in a sense for me a second Chester McLure, who in many ways was my role model.

Life in Brandon was full and interesting. Isabel and I, after spending a short time in a suburban motel, were lucky enough to find a lovely home with one of the finest men I have ever met. M.J. Tinline, retired superintendent of the Brandon Experimental Farm, rented us his home at a reasonable rate, retaining his own room and having meals with us when he was in residence. Not wishing to 'rust unburnished' after retirement, Mr Tinline became the superintendent of the International Peace Garden, a magnificent park area on the Canada-U.S. border between Dunseith, North Dakota, and Boissevain, Manitoba. When this noble international tribute to peace was established in the 1930s, the schoolchildren of Canada had been appealed to for assistance. As a wee lad in Victoria school I had, as a member of the Junior Red Cross, contributed my ten-cent piece. As I used to say to my landlord: 'I'm now checking up on my investment.'

I had no way of determining Mr Tinline's previous political allegiance. I naturally did not ask. He, as a long-time public servant, had known the virtue of discretion.

Mr Tinline stepped up his solicitation of private groups and gave many lectures with slides. Although qualified by age, Mr Tinline had never applied for old age security, arguing that he did not need the money. When Robert Winters, St Laurent's minister of public works, cut the Peace Garden grant, the devoted Mr Tinline applied for the old age pension. I recall his satisfaction as he told me: 'Here's $480 going to the Peace Garden that Mr Winters can't cut back.' All his old age pension cheques were turned over to the garden. A deeply religious man and a strong Sabbatarian, Mr Tinline did not hesitate to call Walter Dinsdale on Sunday, during his weekends home from Ottawa. The subject matter was his beloved Peace Garden.

Brandon, a city a little larger than Charlottetown, proved to be a pleasant place to live. Along with my college associations, some stimulating people on the faculty, and a pleasant group of students, I found many friends in the city. Brandon College had done wonders to survive in earlier days. I learned about professors who often had to wait for their cheques or be paid in kind. Although by no means plush in my time, things were a good deal better than marginal. Very much aware of the need for community support, Brandon College carried on a rich program of adult education. I found myself going out to many parts of western Manitoba to address local audiences. Generally speaking I found these sorties enjoyable, though not quite as pleasant as the fowl suppers which were gastronomic triumphs. I hear with sorrow that these delightful social events are rare in Manitoba these days.

I was delighted when the local radio station accepted my suggestion for a weekly commentary on international affairs. This was an initiative prompted by my recollections of a similar venture by Dick Petrie over CFNB in Fredericton. I think I was a bit less controversial than Petrie. Because of my position at the college and my known partisan affiliation, I tended to avoid comment on domestic politics. I often thought a fifteen-minute program was a bit long, but I enjoyed these Sunday afternoon talks and was moved by the friendly response of my listeners. In those impecunious days the $15 fee was welcome. Once in a while I 'made it' on some CBC current affairs program for which the fees were a little higher. As is usual with new arrivals, I had a busy speaking schedule in Brandon addressing a variety of service clubs and kindred organizations. I cherished the opportunities to speak to appropriate Scottish organizations on Burns Night and St Andrew's Day. The current affairs program of the Department of National Defence brought me to nearby military bases a good many times. Both the experiences and the extra income were welcome. Then, too, there was always a dram or two at the officers' mess.

While in Brandon I was active in both the provincial and federal PC organizations, serving for some time as president of the former and secretary of the latter group. For one interested in the political process it was a lively place to be in those years.

First came a provincial by-election. Cam Donaldson, although fond of party activity and an extremely effective party man, did not care for being an MLA. As he told the annual meeting of the provincial association: 'I should have had my head examined to go into it in the first place.' When Donaldson's resignation created a vacancy, the Brandon PCs chose Reg Lissaman, another businessman, as the candidate. Low-key, conservative in manner and method, Reg was a contrast to the ebullient, gregarious Cam Donaldson. He was the bane of those people who would now be called 'handlers.' When advised to make appearances in the Ukrainian area of town he demurred, pointing out that he did not normally go to events there. Urged to put in an appearance at the Baptist Church of which he was a member, Reg refused to appear as an active Baptist for mere partisan purposes. There would be no glad-handing, no baby-kissing, no cornucopia of promises in the Lissaman campaign. He was a good businessman, a man of principle, candid and direct, and so he presented himself to the Brandon electorate.

If Lissaman was a contrast to his predecessor Donaldson he was even more unlike Walter Dinsdale. I was fascinated during my Brandon years to have a federal member who did all the right things as a party candidate and a provincial member who followed none of the arts and techniques of public opinion management. But Reg Lissaman did win the by-election and succeeding contests and was an impressive member of the Manitoba legislature.

Then there was constituency reorganization as a result of a merging of the Brandon federal riding with the Souris constituency, represented since 1940 by J. Art Ross, also a Tory. In those days redistribution was carried on by the House of Commons rather than by commissioners as is now the case. It was not a great surprise that the Liberal-dominated House should find pressing need to reorganize two adjoining Tory seats! The situation was a bit delicate. Ross was the senior man. Dinsdale's political career was off to an auspicious start. The majority of the voters were in the Brandon rather than the Souris constituency. In the end all was settled amicably, and Walter Dinsdale became and remained the MP for the Brandon-Souris constituency which was created by the Redistribution Act of 1952.

The Brandon Conservatives were in the forefront of a move to make major changes in the provincial party. The premier, Donald Campbell, headed a coalition government of which Errick Willis, the Progressive Conservative leader, was a member. As a public personage, Premier Campbell was about as interesting as one of his predecessors, John Bracken. Putting it as mildly as possible, the Campbell government was faltering, if not moribund. There was little prospect, so Brandon Tories said, of their party going anywhere in such a lacklustre outfit.

But other Manitoba Tories had different views. A segment of the party viewed withdrawal from the coalition as a grave error. Manitobans had grown accustomed to the defusing of party hostilities over the years. In some constituencies members were repeatedly elected by acclamation. By presenting a united front the two old-line parties could keep out the leftists. (Former adherents of this school of thought in Manitoba might have been be tempted to say 'we told you so' during the Schreyer and Pawley regimes.) There was also the immediately practical consideration that, through coalition with the Campbell Liberal Progressives, the Progressive Conservatives would get some of their people into cabinet posts and gain all that goes with such advancement.

Withdrawing from the coalition had created ferment within the Manitoba party. Much more dissension was stirred up by the move to choose a new leader and, in effect, drop Errick Willis who had held the post since 1936.

These tensions were very marked at a stormy meeting of the provincial association in Winnipeg in 1953. I recall an anecdote of Mrs Dick Baker who, with her husband, was an active Brandon Tory. During one hectic session she had become separated from her husband. Because he had a heart condition she was a bit worried and mentioned this to one of the convention officers who was checking the credentials of voting delegates, of which Dick was one. He said: 'By God lady, if he has a weak heart he shouldn't even be at this meeting.'

When it was decided to call a leadership convention, three candidates emerged. The incumbent Errick Willis decided to seek a mandate as leader of the party, now in opposition to the government. J. Art Ross, whose federal riding of Souris was being absorbed in the new Brandon-Souris constituency, decided to run. He was viewed as having strong rural support and a broadly based popularity with the party's hard-core supporters. But the most interesting candidate and the clear front runner to the Brandon PCs was Duff Roblin, grandson of Sir Rodmond Roblin, premier of Manitoba from 1900 to 1915.

Duff Roblin, a prosperous car dealer, had been elected to the Manitoba legislature in 1949 as a non-coalition or Independent Conservative. He had made a highly favourable impression on party, press, and public. He was articulate, energetic, extremely well-informed, and clearly ambitious. It seemed to me that the Brandon PCs were almost unanimously in favour of Roblin becoming provincial leader.

In 1954, in an interesting exercise in party democracy, the three leadership contenders jointly addressed Progressive Conservative meetings across Manitoba. As president of the PC Association of Brandon, I presided over the meeting held in that city. And it was surely a meeting to remember. The hall was packed, the media were there in force, the interest was high, and the party faithful heard plenty of partisan rhetoric. I thought that all three candidates acquitted themselves well and any political party could be proud of them as standard-bearers. But by far the most impressive performer of the three was Roblin.

What I remember most clearly of that memorable gathering is not the oratory of the leadership hopefuls, but a few comments by the unostentatious local MLA, Reg Lissaman. After the speeches of Willis, Ross, and Roblin, he asked for the floor and, of course, was invited to speak. He walked to the front of the hall and flatly contradicted his leader, Errick Willis, on a major matter. Admitting that he was revealing a discussion in the PC legislative caucus, he stated bluntly that Willis was distorting the truth on a matter of serious import to the whole provincial party. To say that Lissaman's brief intervention was a bombshell would be an understatement. Followers do not do such things to their leaders in public. Party and caucus solidarity is not so readily discarded.

There were some Progressive Conservatives who thought Lissaman acted improperly in breaking the confidentiality of caucus meetings. But the vast majority supported him. They argued that unless it shook off its muted coalition past, the Manitoba Progressive Conservative party would get nowhere. They thought that a new and dynamic leader must be chosen. If in bringing this about the old leader was wounded, so be it. Some of these people were highly critical of Willis. I had heard them denigrate him since my first day in Brandon. Because a political party is not a communion of saints there is always a bit of spitefulness, and Errick Willis had been around a long time and made or acquired some enemies. But the prevailing theme was not spitefulness but the sadness of inevitability. Occasions arise where someone has to bell the cat. In this instance it was Reg Lissaman who performed the thankless task.

By the time the momentous Brandon meeting was held I felt that Roblin was headed for victory. The meeting itself seemed to buttress such a view. More precisely, perhaps, it made a Willis defeat wellnigh certain. As for Art Ross, everyone liked him but few planned to vote for him. The contest was between the new and the old guards, Roblin and Willis.

On the day following the Brandon meeting, the press had major coverage of the event. The *Winnipeg Tribune* described it as a Donnybrook. As the presiding officer, I took sharp exception to this description of what, in fact, was an orderly meeting. In a carefully worded statement, I gave the *Tribune* my version. To their credit and a bit to my surprise, they printed my counterpoint word for word.

It is now history, of course, but Duff Roblin did win the leadership and went on to become the best premier Manitoba has had in our time. He brought new life and vigour to the party and the legislature. Before he took over, the Manitoba Conservative caucus was essentially an Anglo-Saxon group from a southern corner of the province. Under Roblin the party broadened its base geographically and ethnically. The government which he formed in 1958 was progressive, efficient, and imaginative. I may be biased but I think his greatest accomplishments were in the field of education. Brandon College owes to him its continuing existence as Brandon University. Thanks to him it has developed and strengthened its role and function as a splendid institution of higher learning and community and cultural leadership. Instead of being an affiliate of the University of Manitoba, whose degrees its graduates earned, Brandon became a full-fledged university. This highly desirable change would never have happened without the sympathetic government of Duff Roblin. The province of Manitoba has reason to be thankful that in Duff Roblin it had the right man in the right place. I am always grateful that, as a member of the party structure, I was able to play a small role in having him assume the leadership of the provincial party in June 1954.

Errick Willis was gracious and magnanimous in the defeat which befell him at the convention and agreed to serve under Roblin. Because of his greatness of spirit the party avoided the wounds and scars which often follow a leadership struggle.

My contacts with Willis were always cordial. He used to refer to me as 'the other professor.' I presume this was a tribute to Walter Dinsdale. Perhaps, too, it was an indication that academics were not exactly thick on the ground in the Tory party. Later he became lieutenant governor of Manitoba. John Diefenbaker appointed many outstanding people to such posts, and Errick Willis was prominent on the list. He was an excellent lieutenant governor and clearly liked the job. He told me with relish of the time he went to Flin Flon to open the Trout Festival, one of the big events in the town. Planning to do a little hunting or fishing in the north, he left the official limousine and chauffeur in Winnipeg and drove himself in Mrs Willis's jaunty red sports car. As he pulled up to the front of the arena where the opening ceremonies were to take place, a commissionaire shouted at him: 'You can't park there. That spot is for the lieutenant governor and the old bugger is twenty minutes late already.'

In my youthful Winnipeg days I was a director of the Maritime Provinces' Association of that city. Years later, as a member of the House of Commons, I was invited to be the guest speaker at their annual meeting. One of the directors was Mrs Errick Willis, a woman of great beauty and charm. She said to me in reference to His Honour: 'This is one event to which he is invited because he is married to me and not vice versa.'

While I learned a great deal from, and thoroughly enjoyed, my participation in provincial politics, my big interest was still the federal scene. As secretary of the constituency association, I was at all the executive and general meetings and in on all the activities. George Drew came to town on occasion and, as with all visits of leaders, much time and attention had to be devoted to preparation. On one of these high level visitations the president of the Women's PC association, Mrs Roxy Cosgrove, was active in the planning committee. When we arrived at the Prince Edward Hotel for a noon event someone asked her about her husband. The gracious Mrs Cosgrove replied: 'Dear, dear, I'm afraid I left Jack at—.' Where exactly poor Jack was left I cannot now recall but it was at one of the places Drew had visited in his morning program. Mrs Cosgrove's devotion to the party was no light or transient thing.

On another occasion I thought that I myself was to be the victim of absentmindedness. I had accepted an invitation to go as guest speaker for the Progressive Conservative association in Carberry, a pleasant community between Brandon and Winnipeg. The affair was late getting under way and was long drawn out with a wide range of entertainment. Various people were called on to say a few words, and a bountiful lunch was served. The clock ticked on and still no mention of me. Just as I was becoming convinced that someone had been overcome by amnesia, the chairman recalled the meeting to order and began a generous introduction of the guest speaker. I had never before begun a public address at quarter to midnight.

Walter Dinsdale, a highly active and visible MP, had many prominent Tories visit the constituency. George Hees was one of them and, while I cannot recall much of the subject matter of his speech, I remember well his opening remarks. 'As the sultan said when he returned to the harem, "I know what I'm here for but I don't know where to begin."' I thought it quite a good opener, but I could not but hear one elderly lady's remark to her companion: 'That's pretty raw, don't you think?' Presumably they also belonged to the temperance wing of the party.

But the big political event of 1953 was the federal election of which Professor Murray Beck wrote, 'perhaps no two successive elections have had so much in common as those of 1949 and 1953.'[1] The leaders were the same, the issues and results largely so. It was a rematch for Uncle Louis and the Toronto colonel. The prime minister charmed the children at whistle-stops across 'this great country of ours,' as he invariably put it. Drew was as vigorous as ever, if perhaps a little restrained, in his fulminations against a government which he depicted as too long in office, too casual of peoples' rights, and too profligate with their money.

I attended many political meetings during and before the 1953 campaign and often heard and saw Drew in action. Other PCs were drawing national attention, especially John Diefenbaker who was a galvanic platform performer. George Hees, who had won the Toronto Broadview constituency in 1950, was becoming widely known and had travelled extensively even before he became national president in 1954. Donald Fleming, the scrappy, stocky MP for Toronto Eglinton, was developing an increasingly high profile. In the new party president, Léon Balcer of Trois-Rivières, the PCs had a handsome personable politician. A successful lawyer with a good wartime service record in the Royal Canadian Navy, Balcer had amiable connections with Premier Maurice Duplessis, whose provincial constituency was also Trois-Rivières. Like many other Progressive Conservatives, I had growing hopes that Balcer would become the party leader's Quebec lieutenant.

George Nowlan, a witty affable Gary Cooper type from Nova Scotia's Annapolis Valley, was becoming a strong regional representative. He too had served as national president, and had drawn media attention because of the number of times he had to contest the Digby-Annapolis-Kings seat. There had been deferred elections, by-elections, and general elections at which Nowlan was the star performer. Davie Fulton of Kamloops was a rising star from the West. Scholarly and articulate, he was also clearly ambitious. Howard Green, a veteran Vancouver MP, and G.R. Pearkes, VC, were established leaders in the British Columbia caucus. In Manitoba the winners of the by-elections of 1951 were gaining recognition. Dinsdale appeared more visible on the broader scene than Gordon Churchill and was active in the many Manitoba constituencies not represented by PCs in Ottawa.

In the Atlantic area, Angus MacLean seemed less interested in publicity than other new caucus members. Colonel J.A. Brooks, veteran New Brunswick member, was a solid if not showy performer. Douglas Harkness, winner of the George Cross, was gaining some recognition as a vigorous spokesman for his native Alberta.

The modalities of election machinery had for us a personal dimension in 1953. My wife Isabel was invited to teach mathematics at Acadia University in beautiful Wolfville, Nova Scotia. With our one-year-old daughter Heather and my seventy-six-year-old mother she rented an apartment there. Since the summer school ran from early July to mid-August she was not a resident in the constituency of Digby-Annapolis-Kings when the election writ was issued, but would still be at her university duties there on election day. Presenting her case succinctly to the revising officer, she succeeded in having her name added to the voters' list, although the Election Act was not clear that special provisions for teachers were intended to cover those engaged only for the summer session. Thus she was in a position to cast her first Tory vote for George Nowlan. For much of the summer I was working on the Robert Borden papers at the Public Archives in Ottawa but took some time off to be with my family in the lovely Annapolis Valley.

It was during that summer in Ottawa that I attended a joint political meeting somewhat reminiscent of those so long in vogue in PEI. In the Ottawa-Carleton constituency it was the custom for all candidates to hold an open debate on official nomination day. Because George Drew was the PC candidate, the meeting was of national significance and a large crowd filled the auditorium of Fisher Park High School. There was plenty of heavy partisan rhetoric from George Drew and George McIlraith, the well-entrenched Liberal MP for Ottawa West. McIlraith spoke on behalf of the Liberal candidate, John H. McDonald, who had also run against Drew in the 1949 general election. Candidate Eugene Forsey spoke well for the CCF. But I remember the speeches much less vividly than an incident triggered by McDonald. The PCs had made much of their promise to carve $500 million from the federal government's annual expenditures. At the end of his few remarks the brash McDonald went over to present George Drew with a long silver carving knife for the great pruning job. To say that Drew took this slightly juvenile stunt with poor grace would be an understatement. He literally kicked the knife away. Witnessing this revelation of temper I felt uncomfortable, embarrassed, and ill at ease. Later in the program Drew agreed to accept the knife and to have a picture taken with McDonald handing it over. This, he said, was the aim of the whole exercise anyway. But I still wished that I had not seen our national leader in such a bad moment.

In 1953, as the Liberal candidate at the Ottawa-Carleton meeting had implied, the Progressive Conservatives were giving top priority to reduction of government expenditure. One of their major advertisements, captioned 'Stop Squandermania,' castigated the Liberal government for monumental extravagance on many fronts. Declaring that 'a government that can't stop waste can't cut taxes,' the Conservatives promised: 'We can ... *we will*.'

Taxes were high at the time and no one enjoys paying taxes. PC election strategists believed that slashing government expenditures would have a powerful appeal to the Canadian electorate. The figure $500 million seemed huge at the time. Today a mere half billion would be a picayune sum indeed. The total federal government expenditure for the fiscal year 1989-90 was $142 billion. Canadians are aware, or should be aware, of the social impact of inflation. But the second government of Brian Mulroney encountered bitter public hostility to its programs of fiscal restraint.

I heard George Drew at more than one rally make points with his audience as he scarified the government for its outrageously casual attitude to the pillage of military bases. He told one meeting that he had known Camp Petawawa since he had trained there as a boy of fifteen, but during the election campaign Defence Minister Brooke Claxton had denied him the right to visit the scene of his early military service.

The charges of mismanagement or worse in the National Defence department gave the most spectacular dimension to the PCS' election campaign. I heard George Drew tell an audience about the disappearance of a whole military base at Farnham, Quebec. According to him everything was carted away unless it was absolutely unmoveable. There were stories of a railway spur being lifted and looted. In all these allegations the Tories were able to draw some credence from an investigative report by Colonel G.S. Currie. While it did not reveal all the things to which the PCS drew attention, the report of Currie, the National Defence investigator, found enough waste and incompetence to prompt many Canadians to believe there was something rotten in the state of Denmark.

In political warfare there is nothing much more effective than the skilful use of ridicule. In 1953 this was a major part of the PC campaign arsenal. By using the Currie Report on the administration of the Department of National Defence (DND), they were able to convince hosts of Canadians that crookedness had reached such an extreme that salary cheques were being issued to horses. From Bonavista to Vancouver Island, Canadians talked about the horses on the payroll. They found it hilarious when Tories talked about the strangely subsidized cavalry. 'What about horses on the payroll?' could sometimes throw a Grit campaign meeting off course.

In those days the reports of the auditor general did not then have the sexy political significance they later attained, but the auditor general, R.W. Sellar, was often quoted by Conservatives in the 1953 campaign. He had discovered that DND used eight different accounting systems. The very expression auditor general denotes impartiality and respectability, so it is not surprising that in their attacks on the St Laurent government's waste and extravagance, the major opposition party concentrated on the Defence department.

All in all the anti-waste campaign was great fun and well done, but it did not suffice. The big spenders continued to be the big vote-getters. Some Canadians might wish to see the St Laurent regime brought to an end. But, as Brooke Claxton put it, they were not prepared to let George do it.

As they charged Drew with inconsistency and deception in promising greater government largesse and lower taxes, the Liberals did a good deal of pointing with pride. Although there were problems and certain sectors of the population and regions of the country were having it hard, there was still a feeling of national well-being. While it was hardly as significant as family allowances, the St Laurent government's assistance to universities was popular with students, faculty, and parents. Although the man in the street might not have been excited, some opinion leaders were impressed by several nationalistic moves. A Canadian had been appointed governor general, the first after a long series of Britons. The Supreme Court of Canada, not the Judicial Committee of the British Privy Council, became our final court of appeal. Some important steps had been taken toward the long-talked-about repatriation of the constitution.

So perhaps there were horses on the payroll, taxes were high, some in the Grit hierarchy were showing the heady arrogance of too much power, but Uncle Louis won the day. Election day, 10 August, brought the national Liberal party its fifth consecutive victory. Little wonder that old Tories like my mother wondered if her party would ever win again. Little wonder either that Liberals were exultant about Uncle Louis's magic as a campaigner. Some, more ecstatic than reverent, declared that they would run him again even if they had to run him stuffed.

As we Conservatives surveyed the electoral battlefield on the morning of 11 August we had to scratch the ground pretty vigorously to find much comfort. Certainly we did better than in the 1949 election, which sent only forty-one PCs to the House of Commons. But while we had ten more than in 1949 we were only four seats stronger than at the time of dissolution. In the years 1949 to 1953 the PCs had done very well in by-elections, a situation far different from the Bracken years. Indeed in his party's by-election victories George Drew was certain that he could see a most significant and powerful trend towards the Tories. Out of twenty-nine by-elections we had won thirteen, five of five in 1951.

Perhaps because of Drew's strong provincialist stand, not a great vote-grabber in the have-not provinces, the PCs fared poorly in the Atlantic region. Newfoundland was even Grittier than ever. The Liberals won all the outport seats and captured the two in St John's as well. Was it all because of Joey Smallwood's campaigning for the Grits or was it a touch of anti-Drewism? In Nova Scotia we lost Colchester-Hants largely because Frank Stanfield chose not to re-offer. In New Brunswick, despite the 1952 provincial victory of Hugh John Flemming, the PCs did not do all that well. They recaptured the traditional Tory seat of Saint John-Albert. This brought the good looking, personable, and individualistic Tom Bell into the House of Commons.

In my own beloved province I found the results particularly depressing. Chester McLure, who had been our stalwart candidate in 1930, 1935, 1940, 1945, and 1949 went down to defeat in 1953. It was a shattering dénouement to a long and splendid career. Shortly after the election I telephoned him from Wolfville where I was visiting my wife, mother, and wee daughter. In resonant tones, Chester told me that the enemy was from within. He said his defeat came from the machinations of his running mate, J. Angus MacLean, who was re-elected.

In politics one sees much of the visceral and a good deal of the vindictive. Dual ridings, it seems to me, accentuate suspicions and exacerbate paranoia. When J. Angus MacLean was chosen as a Queens Conservative candidate in 1945, Chester McLure wrote me in exultant terms about his splendid young running mate. When in the election of 1945 McLure won and MacLean lost narrowly, I heard surreptitious charges that Chester was somehow collaborating with the leading Liberal candidate. I was dubious of these charges. My father simply said when the charges were raised: 'Bring me any Queens voter who was asked by Chester McLure to vote for him and the Liberal candidate Lester Douglas. After that I'll take these rumours seriously.' My mother, more direct and visceral, simply asked: 'How would it help Chester McLure to have one of the cursed Grits get in with him instead of MacLean?' In any case, base canards of hostility and competition between the two Tory candidates plagued the Progressive Conservative campaign in Queens.

It would have been such a splendid development had McLure won his last election, which 1953 would surely have been. I knew both McLure and MacLean and would not impugn the honour of either of them.

Once again in 1953 Quebec was the graveyard of PC hopes. The Tories lost votes in the Atlantic and western regions because Drew was perceived as being too much of a provincialist. In Quebec, where such a stance might be expected to win votes as in Ontario, the Tories won only four seats out of seventy-five, for a total gain of two seats. The Quebec premier, the other end of the much talked about Drew-Duplessis axis, was on holiday for much of the campaign. Drew had worked hard on his French and often spoke at length in that language during the campaign, but to no avail. Like Manion, his efforts to establish rapport with the francophone province proved unavailing.

Nor did the once-popular premier Drew score much better in the great and populous province of Ontario. His successor, Leslie Frost, had signed a tax agreement with the St Laurent government, and was rumoured to be less than enthusiastic about the federal party leader. Or perhaps Frost was giving credibility to the school of thought that big provinces like Quebec and Ontario express themselves most fully and effectively if they support one party provincially and another federally. Put simply, there was no Big Blue Machine at Drew's service in 1953. Out of eighty-five seats, the federal PCs won thirty-three, a gain of only eight, under the leadership of an erstwhile Ontario premier who had once scored great victories in the province.

In the West the Liberals lost ground, a foretaste of what would happen to them in subsequent contests. They dropped four seats in Manitoba and nine in Saskatchewan. Although in 1953 the notion that the CCF would be a serious contender for government had been abandoned, they did gain seats in the prairie provinces. The long-entrenched Liberal government did not heed Agriculture Minister Jimmy Gardiner's importunings about building the South Saskatchewan irrigation dam. They suffered for it in 1953 and would be further wounded for their insensitive intransigence in subsequent elections.

When the ballots were counted, some suspicions were confirmed. With the election so much a repeat of 1949 there was a low voter turnout. There were many more people in Canada in 1953 than there had been in 1949 but there were 200,000 fewer who voted. Perhaps there was some validity in the arguments against summer elections, or perhaps an election so much like the 1949 contest bored many voters. Surely it is one of the rights of citizens to be bored and disengaged if that seems to be the most sensible and sensitive response. The Liberals dropped 20 seats in the 1953 election, but with 170 seats in the House of Commons they were by no means on the ropes. For devout Tories it was not the best of all possible worlds.

We all knew that the PC campaign had not been a dud. Drew had been tireless throughout. Often at meetings during that long, hot summer he had taken off his coat and fought the Grits in his shirt sleeves. We had good people onside. Allister Grosart, who would later become the legendary advertising man, was working for Drew. Efforts had been made to emphasize the role of both youth and women.

I remember being depressed and frustrated at our defeat in 1953, and by the unfair Liberal tactics. Especially did I deplore the propaganda that George Drew was a narrow-minded, insensitive son of privilege from Bay Street, and that the well-established and well-heeled corporation lawyer from Quebec was the epitome of the people's friend.

My astute and intelligent wife listened sympathetically and politely. She then asked: 'But did you ever think that perhaps those other guys are, in fact, smarter than your people?'

A good question that!!

4

Learning to Run

If the Progressive Conservative party had had a leadership review mechanism in its constitution in 1953 many would have urged its invocation. The twice-repudiated Drew was apparently not going to lead his fellow Tories into the promised land. A growing number in the party were of the opinion that because of Drew's image the party could not win an election with him at its head. There were people in and out of the caucus who had a successor in mind: the dynamic Saskatchewan MP, John Diefenbaker. Many Canadians were ready to diagnose the PCs' problem. 'You have the wrong leader. You should have picked Diefenbaker.' I heard this repeatedly in academic circles and from the rank and file. One who believed this most strongly was Diefenbaker himself. Many of his contemporaries have told me of his feelings of being unappreciated, neglected, and held back.

But there was nothing in the constitution to allow the party to review its leadership. Nor is there any very effective mechanism now. The national Liberal party has none either. Today only the New Democratic Party (NDP) has a provision whereby the party votes on the question of leadership in the normal course of events at national general meetings. Perhaps it is easier for a party not likely to win national elections to have such a procedure. Many in the old-line parties would find it difficult to have a review of a leader who was prime minister.

Thus it was that the defeated Tories in 1953 could do little but mourn and murmur about their fate. Drew did not make it easy for them by resigning. He would not be daunted by the overt enemies across the aisle or by the covert dissidents in his own caucus. Interestingly enough, he eventually made a strong recovery from the dreary days following the 1953 election. With a great deal of help from a haughty Liberal government he was to reach an unprecedented position of power and prestige in his party.

The mid-fifties brought me increased involvement in the Progressive Conservative party. Thanks to Walter Dinsdale, I was elected third vice-president at the 1955 annual meeting in Ottawa. As I recall it, there were some murmurings within the PEI delegation about this honour coming my way so easily and quickly. Although not an onerous post, the third vice-presidency gave me a spot on the national executive and closer involvement with party matters.

Things were happening in Manitoba with Duff Roblin invigorating the provincial party. Walter Dinsdale thought I should seek the federal nomination in one of the constituencies bordering Brandon-Souris. Another serious proposition was that I move into the provincial political scene as part of the burgeoning Roblin team.

It would be inaccurate to suggest that I was being drafted. In fact, by 1955 I was eager to get into active politics as a candidate for public office. In those lean Tory years, nominations were not keenly sought after. But while not reluctant I had many things to consider. I liked Manitoba and was beginning to know it reasonably well, but I did miss the sea. There was also a strong emotional and sentimental attachment to the beautiful island of my birth and ancestry. When my long-time friend Chester McLure died in June 1955 this created a sort of vacancy in Queens. The successful and well-entrenched Angus MacLean would, of course, be renominated but a new running mate would have to be chosen. Chester had once predicted that I would become a member of the House of Commons. At the time I don't know that either of us thought of my fulfilling this prophecy as his successor in the Tory candidacy in Queens.

Chester McLure was a major figure on the Prince Edward Island political scene for a long time. He had befriended me over many years. I often wrote him for parliamentary publications which were promptly sent to me. On my first visit to Parliament Hill in 1950 he gave me a royal welcome. Many of the Progressive Conservative members were on the same corridor of the Centre Block, and most cases it was two members to an office. Chester led me down the hallway knocking on every door and introducing me as 'my friend and constituent, Professor Macquarrie.' Although I was then on the faculty of McGill University I had voted in Queens and in any case he was very much my MP. This was my first opportunity to meet some of the greats of the party like Pearkes, Donald Fleming, and Alf Brooks. George Drew was not in Ottawa that day. I had arranged for a special interview with John Diefenbaker which took place later in the day. He did not discuss internal party politics, concentrating on the villainy of the Grits. After each recital he would say, 'I tell you Mac, it's awful.'

Mr and Mrs McLure entertained Isabel and me in the parliamentary restaurant for lunch. The lamb chops were lovely and Mrs McLure made a comment to Isabel the cogency of which I would often recall in future years. 'You know, dear, if we weren't able to have meals here I don't think we could make expenses.'

So, as the year 1955 wore on, I found myself thinking more and more of getting into full political harness. There were possible opportunities on the provincial or federal scene in Manitoba, where I was now teaching. In my native Queens, the Progressive Conservatives would be finding a new standard-bearer for the next election. Nothing was certain by any means, but I had the feeling that it would be easier to gain a nomination in the West, but getting elected there might be harder.

At the same time as my pondering about the best and most appropriate avenue to entering politics, I was convinced that I was at a crossroads in my academic career. I greatly enjoyed my classroom hours and had not been neglectful of research. Some chapters from my PHD thesis had appeared in the *Canadian Journal of Economics and Political Science*, and I had been published by other university journals. But my thesis was not yet finished. There were too many intervals when I was so diverted by other things, often politics, that over several months I wrote not a word on my thesis. To broaden my opportunities in the academic world, it might be wise to take off enough time to finish the thesis and give myself a sort of academic refresher course.

So, after much reflection, I asked for and was given leave to absence from Brandon College for the academic year 1955–6. Since it was a leave without pay I was not surprised when the college was accommodating. It was at least clear that I would not be on the Brandon College faculty during the upcoming year, but would I be back in Manitoba in other activities more helpful to a political career? Should I instead re-establish myself in Prince Edward Island? Would something arise which would underscore and strengthen my academic interests? In seeking a leave of absence I was really revealing the uncertainty of this phase of my life. I felt that I was setting out for somewhere but didn't have a flight plan. This is not the most prudent way of travelling.

After marking examinations and clearing up other college and community responsibilities, Isabel and I set off in the later spring of 1955 with daughters Heather and Flora for the long drive to Prince Edward Island. I resigned from the Brandon School Board, to which I had been elected two years earlier.

Prince Edward Island, as everyone knows, is one of Canada's most beautiful areas and I was delighted to be home again in the summer of 1955. My mother and beloved Aunt Aggie were able to live with us in the old family home in Victoria. Proud parents as we were, we were pleased to have the children in the bosom of the eastern family. Flora they had never seen. She had been born in the summer of 1954. In this connection I recall a cute little incident which indicated a certain ambivalence in my political plans. Flora was born in Brandon in August while I was still in Winnipeg, serving on the summer school faculty. A fellow political science professor, Douglas Anglin, made the wry comment when I told him: 'I see since you aren't sure where you're going to enter politics you have arranged to have one daughter born in Prince Edward Island and the second in Manitoba!' He was right about my daughters' birthplaces but overestimated my political cunning.

Professor Anglin might also have thought I was hedging my bets in my newspaper writings. Early in my Brandon years I had accepted Lew Whitehead's suggestion that I contribute both columns and unsigned editorials for the *Daily Sun*. The extra income was welcome and practice helps one's facility of expression. Because there was no overlapping of readership of the *Sun* and the Charlottetown Guardian, I began to send my articles to the newspaper which proclaims proudly that it 'covers the Island like the dew.' The only difference was that while the *Sun* paid me $5 per column, the *Guardian* paid me nothing.

Without doubt the *Guardian* articles helped portray me as a political analyst and activist. The last time I saw John Myers, who died about a year after Chester McLure, he alluded to them. As I took leave of him, he said: 'You're a smart man, Heath, and we all admire your articles in the *Guardian*.' Being the witty iconoclast he was, he could not resist adding, 'but why in Hell do you have to wear that damn foolish cap?' He did not care for berets, of which I was becoming increasingly fond.

In 1955 there was a provincial election in Prince Edward Island and I was asked to speak in support of our candidates at several public meetings. All such invitations I accepted and enjoyed my participation to the full. Election day itself, 25 May, was not an unalloyed pleasure.

Although I had 'stood in the poll,' as the expression was, in Victoria for Mackenzie King's famous conscription plebiscite of 27 April 1942, my first exposure to this role in a provincial contest came in that 1955 election. I was drafted for poll duty because Walter Mackenzie, the Conservative candidate in First Queens, thought it might be anything but easy going in the small rural poll of South Granville, a pleasant community about fifteen miles from Victoria. He distrusted the Liberal deputy returning officer and asked me to be eternally vigilant against any kind of chicanery. For some time I found the atmosphere in the little house where the poll was held noticeably chilly. Later some voter came in and greeted me as 'professor.' Perhaps it was the traditional PEI regard for learning or perhaps my own amiability but in any case as the day wore on the social temperature rose to a comfortable if not genial level. Mindful of my stern terms of reference, I remained faithful to my assignment, not even making the usual breaks suggested by bodily needs and functions.

My devoted vigilance was probably not necessary since everything seemed to go well and fully in accordance with the Elections Act. After the votes were counted, the Conservative poll chairman in South Granville, Milton Weeks, invited me to his home for a pleasant and welcome meal. Before I ate I asked my hosts for an aspirin. My diligent sentry duty had brought on a rare headache. Within an hour the province-wide result was obvious and I reminded Milton that I had had the headache before the great Grit victory had been announced! Certainly the results were not such as to make any Progressive Conservative's health improve. The Liberals won twenty-seven seats, the PCs only three.

In the fall of 1955 I did some work at the Public Archives in Ottawa, digging further into the papers of that great prime minister, Robert Laird Borden. Ottawa is a lovely city but, used to the moderate weather of Prince Edward Island, I found its summer climate humid and debilitating and so was glad to have had the whole summer down by the sea. I continued writing for newspapers. I also did some corresponding with universities at which I might be interested in serving. I secured a John S. Ewart fellowship which would take me to the University of Toronto later in the year. Although some of my best friends had been denizens of that institution I was not counting the days until I settled in on its campus.

My wife, beloved partner and constant support, had gone the extra mile. She accepted an appointment on the faculty of prestigious Wellesley College, near Boston, and would take Flora and Heather with her. Luckily she would also be able to take a splendid Island lady, Mary Conkie, to help look after the children. No man of limited means could have a better opportunity to enter into a political career.

Taking my completed thesis chapters and archival notes with

me, I joined Isabel and for some months was a faculty spouse at Wellesley College. I was courteously received and even given a small office in which to do my research.

I enjoyed my visits to the Boston area. Although short of time and money we had some good experiences. The Boston Symphony is one of the greatest, as is the New England Conservatory of the Arts. In December 1955 we went to Ford Hall in Boston to hear Robert Frost, a special poet for both of us, read from his own poems. A week later, I heard Joseph Harsch of my favourite newspaper, *Christian Science Monitor*, lecture on the Soviet Union. At Christmas we attended service at First Congregational Church in Malden, where we were married in 1949. My mother and Aunt Agnes were wintering with my sister in Malden. We also visited my brother Bill and family in Wakefield from time to time.

The Wellesley environment gave me a good chance to recast one of my thesis chapters into a paper for presentation at the annual meeting of the Canadian Political Science Association to be held in Montreal in early June 1956. The paper, later published in the *Canadian Journal of Economics and Political Science*, was on the formation of Robert Borden's first cabinet in 1911. I enjoyed the discussion which followed my presentation. Among those participating was the unforgettable Eugene Forsey. As he always did, he enlivened the proceedings not only by his comments about Borden but by the manner in which he gave them. Forsey was an excellent mimic. So also, more surprisingly, was Arthur Meighen, from whom Forsey drew his Borden quotes, complete with Sir Robert's deep and measured tones.

The period from the late spring of 1955 to the autumn of 1956 was an eventful and decisive part of my life. It was also expensive. My salary at Brandon College had not been huge, but after the monthly cheques ceased I certainly noticed the difference. Without my wife's taking on a full-time position, I would not have been able to survive the phase of professorial suspended animation which the career change necessitated.

In order to do effective work at the Public Archives it was necessary to spend time in Ottawa. In earlier stints there I had stayed on a bed-and-breakfast basis with Mrs Caldwell in the Glebe.

That kind lady passed away and I then took up residence in the Bytown Inn on the corner of Albert and O'Connor. It was a charming little hotel with an excellent dining-room, of which there were few in the Ottawa of that day. But it was fortunate that the Public Archives had generous hours because my third-floor room at the Bytown was tiny. Passing through it was a hot water or steam pipe which seemed always at the very highest range of the thermometer. Sleep was difficult enough, and neither the temperature nor the space was conducive to sitting around there.

I always enjoyed working at the Public Archives and became acquainted with some splendid scholars in that Grand Central Station for researchers. Historian Donald Creighton was in almost permanent residence there as he worked on the biography of Sir John A. Macdonald, for which he would be so highly and justly lauded.

At the archives I made a friend with whom I am still on close terms. John Garner was a protégé of political scientist R. Mac-Gregor Dawson, for many years a prominent member of the faculty of the University of Toronto. That part of his background was not so rare, but John Garner was a Tory and from Saskatchewan at that. We had many good conversations and often walked to the Château Laurier for an affordable but excellent lunch in the basement cafeteria.

One day when Garner was not there I was anxious to complete a section of the Borden papers and therefore had little time for a lunch break. I asked the commissionaire at the archives whether he knew of a nearby place. He directed me to the Laurentian Terrace. I rarely handle a buffet line perfectly, usually missing some item. But at Laurentian Terrace this did not happen; yet the staff seemed enormously solicitous. I was wondering how the staff knew I was a greenhorn there. When I got back to the archives I told the commissionaire this. He said: 'Perhaps they knew you were a stranger there because it is a residence for female civil servants.' That I hadn't noticed this after all the times I had walked by the place must surely have indicated the strength of my intense devotion to my studies.

But in the nation's capital there were other powerful attractions. From the Public Archives to Parliament Hill is no great distance and I found it easy to move from the political battles of Borden and Laurier to the arena of confrontation between Drew and St Laurent. Walter Dinsdale, with his usual kindness, had provided me with a sessional pass to the gallery of the House of Commons and I made much use of it. I saw Angus MacLean from time to time and became acquainted with Tom Bell, who was the president of the Young Progressive Conservatives of Canada. He was a very astute young MP and had an appealing sense of humour. I visited Léon Balcer occasionally and found him a man of great charm and courtesy.

But the period of my most frequent presence in the gallery was in the weeks from 8 May to 6 June 1956, when the pipeline debate raged. I had long been convinced that C.D. Howe was a man of overweening arrogance. He had displayed his haughtiness before, especially in the preceding session in the debate over the Emergency Powers Act. He had become a favourite target of PC speakers across the country. His 'What's a million?' and 'If we want to do it who's going to stop us?' comments were quoted at many a Tory meeting.

Howe and his colleagues were impatient over the opposition's delaying the bill to authorize the construction of a pipeline from Alberta to Quebec. Their remedy was to impose closure, a limitation of debate. Closure had been invoked in the far-off days of the Borden government. In 1956 most Canadians had never heard the word before, but it sounded unwholesome and undemocratic. Although the motions were actually made by the Liberal House leader, Walter Harris, the whole pipeline imbroglio was associated with the dictatorial Howe.

From the gallery, day after day, I watched fascinated as the PCs and CCF fought against the government's steamroller tactics. Drew was powerful. M.J. Coldwell was vigorous and strong. But the stars were Davie Fulton and Stanley Knowles, CCF MP from Winnipeg North Centre, whom I had first met when I attended a CCF picnic at Kildonan Park in 1944. These two were brilliant in their knowledge of the vast and complicated rules and precedents of the House. Sharp in perception and quick on their feet, they proved themselves parliamentary giants. There were other members who were active and effective. Donald Fleming fought the Liberals with his usual vigour and tenacity. I don't know why I was absent from the gallery the day it happened, but he received national attention when he was expelled from the chamber for a day. Ellen Fairclough, PC member for Hamilton, had a Canadian ensign ready and draped it over the chair of her ousted colleague. As Fleming left the chamber, John Diefenbaker provided a neat historical touch by shouting, 'Farewell, John Hampden!'

When a prime minister is in the chamber he generally dominates it by his performance and presence. Certainly people like Macdonald, Laurier, Bennett, King, Diefenbaker, and Trudeau did. But, as I sat in the gallery during the pipeline debate, I was struck by the apparently minor role played by Louis St Laurent. I don't remember his being absent but I scarcely remember his saying anything . On the one occasion I heard him take part on an item (it was not the pipeline debate), he prompted a witty remark from G. Wilfrid Dufresne, the Progressive Conservative from Quebec West. Dufresne commented to his colleagues seated near him: 'Ah, he is making his maiden speech.' St Laurent seemed to be in the House but not of it. Incredibly he gave the appearance of one so detached as to be almost unaware of the ferment around him. Perhaps his adversaries were so obsessed with making C.D. Howe the villain that they had a blind spot for the prime minister. But there was, I believe, more to it than that. Perhaps he did not relish what was being done.

Another member whose stance puzzled me was John Diefenbaker. He was not in the forefront of the fight. I heard his speech and found it below his usual oratorical standard. I was later told that he did not believe the pipeline debate would be a good election issue. Did his half-hearted performance stem from that belief, or did he feel that the parliamentary fight would add too many laurels to Drew's brow? Whatever his motives, he did not put on the kind of performance which his immense talents would have made possible.

I was in the gallery on 31 May when the Scottish stalwart Colin Cameron, CCF member for Nanaimo, brought the House into a state of great tension as he read into the record a letter to the *Ottawa Journal* from Eugene Forsey. Cameron moved that Forsey's letter was an attack on Parliament and the Speaker, Ren Beaudoin, ruled the motion debatable. This had the effect of giving the opposition the floor for as long as they wished to debate.

On the subsequent day the Speaker reversed himself and the House went close to a condition of bedlam. I saw Drew, Coldwell, and others advance threateningly towards the Speaker. It was later said that the usually courtly Coldwell did not shake his fist at the Speaker. I had a good seat in the Members' Gallery and am satisfied that he did. It was a time of the most extreme tension. I sat there greatly exhilarated and a bit afraid. It would have been very bad indeed for our parliamentary system to break down in a mêlée of violence.

It was a stirring time. I was there when the opposition charged that members of the government had visited the home of Speaker Beaudoin and forced him to recant his ruling of 31 May. I heard George Drew move his motion of censure of the Speaker. This was an extreme and rare procedure. Today with the enhanced powers given to the Speaker it could not be done.

Drew sought to put his censure motion on Black Friday, 1 June, the day when the Speaker sought to put back the clock to the time before he had allowed Cameron's question of privilege. In the turmoil which followed this amazing stratagem the Speaker was able to forestall Drew by pointing out that such a motion required forty-eight hours notice. It must have been a strange feeling for a Speaker to hear, as he did on Monday, this motion: 'In view of the unprecedented action of the Speaker in improperly reversing his own decision without notice and without giving any opportunity for discussion, this House resolves that it no longer has any confidence in its presiding officer.' Naturally the Liberal majority defeated Drew's motion, but the Speaker's authority and effectiveness were ended nevertheless and the public career of a man of great charm and ability was over.

Sometimes the language was as extreme as the temperature was high. Davie Fulton described the government's tactics as 'the rape of our liberties.' Donald Fleming stormed that it was 'not any way to run a peanut stand let alone a Parliament.' As the government sought to use its majority to stifle debate the green chamber rang with cries of 'dictatorship,' 'guillotine,' and other such epithets. The emotion-charged atmosphere must have created much stress and strain for the members on the floor of the House. Even those of us in the crowded galleries felt a quickening of the pulse and elevation of the blood pressure.

The pipeline debate had destroyed a heretofore good Speaker. I hoped it would also destroy a heretofore bad government. Those tense hours in the Members' Gallery stirred anew my determination to find a seat on the floor of the House of Commons. To wrest a seat from those power-hungry Grits became my strongest goal, my deepest inspiration.

Although I put in many hours at the archives and broadened my knowledge of Sir Robert Borden, I did not finish my PHD thesis. This was unfortunate because all the other requirements for the degree – courses, written examinations, orals, and language tests – had been met long ago. But as 1956 progressed my chances of an early completion receded. I realized clearly that my priority was politics. My preference was to do it in the province of my birth and upbringing.

Persuading myself that becoming a candidate was a splendid idea had taken time but had not been difficult. persuading the Progressive Conservatives of the Queens constituency was a much tougher task. I knew it would require hard work, careful planning, and a good deal of luck. My Presbyterian father, with his penchant for predestination, would have chastised me for attributing so much to the element of luck. But I felt that to obtain the party's nomination in Queens would require a great deal of that ingredient and much else.

Over the years I have heard countless office-seekers claim that they had been urged to run. In some cases I am sure this was true. Many candidates are drafted or prevailed upon to run. An old American adage was that the office should seek the man and not vice versa. I was certainly not in that position in Queens. If I had sat mute and waited for something to happen, I would be lingering on the edge yet. Nor could I conceive any virtue in issuing a press release indicating that I intended to stand for nomination. It was necessary for me to find something in between. Testing the waters had to be done so delicately and gently as not to trouble or rile them. There is an element of salesmanship in politics, the product being the candidate himself or herself. I felt that I had no great aptitude for salesmanship; certainly I had no real experience. As a youngster I had sold Christmas cards and garden seeds for the Gold Medal Seed Company of Toronto, a big mail-order house. I generally managed to sell them all, perhaps with a little help from my parents with the slow sellers. My career as a newsboy for the *Halifax Herald* was a brief disaster. Peddling was not my art.

I knew that the job was one of enormous difficulty, perhaps the biggest challenge of my life. I believed I would make a credible candidate and an effective member. I was not yet thirty-seven years old and had the energy to take on the onerous duties that go with political and parliamentary life. I was also in a position to give it full time if I were to become an MP.

But one cannot hawk oneself like a huckster. For obvious reasons I was most sensitive about being perceived as a carpetbagger. I had left the Island for Winnipeg in 1943 and stayed there until 1947. With short vacations from the YMCA and a decidedly shorter purse, I had not been able to get home to the Island often. It was with immense regret that I had missed my father's funeral in 1947, but I was thankful that I had been able to get home at the time of his serious illness in 1945. My four years at UNB and McGill allowed long summers on the Island but these were often broken by teaching at summer school in Mount Allison or Acadia universities. The move to Brandon put me farther away than ever. So it was not surprising that many Islanders and many PCs did not know me.

Not only was my task difficult, it had to be done without undue delay. In the normal course of events the election would not come until 1957, a whole year away. But I felt I could not wait until 1957, nor could I expect the people in Manitoba to delay their plans and dull their strategies by deferring decisions until I was ready. An offer of special tasks that would subsidize me in the interim had come from Manitoba. The telegram from Duff Roblin revealed his sharp executive ability and persuasive personality. It closed with the request that I advise him what flight I would be on so that he could meet me at the Winnipeg airport.

I was certainly taking the Manitoba situation seriously. I was convinced that things were moving dynamically there and that Duff Roblin was a bright and rising star. But the idea of being an MP for Queens was a strong and growing lure. I advised some of my Ottawa-based friends about my interests and ambitions. George hees wrote the kind of letter at which he was a master: cheerful, positive, and friendly, just this side of effusive. He also underscored the importance of an early nomination. This is always sound advice especially for the party in opposition. I remember John Myers delivering a stern lecture to a Tory meeting at which other politicians had complained about the Grits surprising them with a snap election: 'It is not our business to be surprised. We know that the government has the power to call an election and it is our job to be ready for one no matter when they call one, whether it be spring, winter, summer or fall.'

In Queens the next election would be the first one in twenty-seven years without Chester McLure as a candidate. So adjustments would have to be made for the new era. Although I was helped by friends even at that early stage, I felt I had to make contacts myself. I accepted the idea of a blunt Island Tory, Wellington MacNeil, who used to say: 'It's a damn poor dog that isn't worth a whistle.' So I began a round of discussions with people I saw as potential candidates.

Colonel J. David Stewart, whom I had first seen at the funeral of his father, Premier J.D. Stewart, in 1933, was the mayor of Charlottetown. He was a handsome, articulate, prosperous businessman and very highly regarded. He would have won a nomination easily. In his capacity as president of the Canadian Federation of Mayors and Municipalities he had addressed the PC annual meeting in Ottawa in January 1956, and made a highly favourable impression. Recalling that Queens had the long-standing custom of choosing one candidate from the rural area and the other from Charlottetown, I knew that Stewart would be viewed as a natural for Chester's spot on the dual ticket. If Dave Stewart was interested in the Queens nomination I realized I had better take my political ambitions with me to Manitoba, pronto.

There were others. Walter Shaw had been deputy minister of agriculture for the province for many years. He was an extrovert and one of the most popular after-dinner speakers. He had resigned his job not long before the provincial election of 1955 in which he had run unsuccessfully in a district in which he did not reside. But he was a man of immense stature. I did not know whether he was interested in a switch to the federal field or hoping for a rerun in the provincial arena, perhaps in the role of party leader. As with Dave Stewart, I would not contest any nomination in which Walter Shaw was interested.

The incumbent leader, Reg Bell, one of three PC members in the PEI legislature, was another important person. The Tory loss in the recent provincial election made a change in the leadership a subject of widespread discussion. Reg Bell had served the party well. He was a great vote-getter in his own constituency, and had many friends who would have supported him at a Queens convention. Reg Bell had already spent many years in the political arena. Although nothing was put so explicitly, he was interested in a judgeship. Being a most excellent and successful lawyer, he did go on to a distinguished career in the Supreme Court of PEI.

One of the first people I consulted was Frank Myers, son of John H., who had been an MLA but had been defeated in the 1955 election. I asked him about his interest in the Queens constituency, and learned that he was not giving thought to running in any federal election. I told him of my own interest. He was impressed by the fact that I was being sought in Manitoba.

The reactions to my possible candidacy were not discouraging. Some of my close friends of earlier days were supportive. Typical was Cecil MacPhail, merchant of Bonshaw. When I taught in that community he had been a pupil, and remembered this in a positive way. Balm to my spirits and comfort to my ego was an unsolicited comment from John Colwill, prominent Conservative of Second Queens. In a general discussion of who would or should succeed Chester McLure on the ticket he said: 'You yourself would be the best man, Heath, if you should ever be interested.' Needless to say I did not hesitate to reveal my interest.

While sounding out the intentions of possible candidates, I had always to bear in mind that convention decisions are made by delegates and that without their good opinion I would fail. In too many parts of Canada at that time, there were constituencies where the internal party organization was moribund and nominations were decided upon by a very few big shots of the party or, in some cases, even by outsiders on the national or provincial level. But that sort of thing did not exist in PEI. PCs from every polling division could be expected to have their full slate of delegates at a convention. So as I went about making or renewing contact with especially influential PCs in Queens I knew that, in a sense, I was on display before the whole party. In the process of what came close to self-salesmanship there were restraints and inhibitions imposed by the circumstances or my own temperament. I could not possibly go door-knocking or glad-handing through the constituency. I had no special talent for that and I knew both myself and my fellow Islanders too well to consider such a course.

I did go to meetings of party executives. My position as third vice-president of the national party, innocuous post though it was, helped in this regard. I recall being at one meeting at which the Queens constituency president, Charles Phillips, was concerned about the upcoming annual meeting of the provincial association in Fourth Queens. That district had two Liberal MLAs as had been the case there for many years. It had been difficult to find a guest speaker. I offered to go and in short order it was arranged.

I remember that meeting very well. Fourth Queens, known as the Balfast District, was an area of strong Scottish tradition. A genial, thoughtful man, Frank Macdonald, chaired the meeting. It was a dreary, rainy night and the Belfast hall was far from filled. Claude Delaney of Albany in Prince County, one of the national directors, was there but left before the meeting was called to order. I met some good solid Tories that night and many of those Belfasters became my lifelong friends. I appreciated the opportunity of making contact with the PCs in Fourth Queens. Twenty-four miles from Charlottetown, it was about as far east of the capital as my home town, Victoria, was west.

There were other political activities. Frank Myers and his wife Florence were generous in their hospitality and there were political-social events at their home from time to time. I, as a friend and member of the Victoria poll committee, attended. In those days the farmers' market in Charlottetown was a social as well as a commercial centre. Friends helped me in arranging casual introductions to people like the popular meat vendor, Leith Brown, of Third Queens. All in all, the summer of 1956 was a fascinating time.

Directly or indirectly I was hearing that the people I regarded as heavyweights for the Queens nomination were not interested. Dave Stewart had an important and successful business which would not be fostered by his being in Ottawa for long periods. Walter Shaw had strong provincial interests. He did win the leadership and went on to do a splendid job as premier.

Years later during a federal campaign an Upper Canadian reporter described Shaw as one of the few people who could upstage John Diefenbaker on the platform. I well remember one of his great lines during the 1959 provincial election. He was excoriating the Liberal government for their unfilled promises in the 1955 election. As he went down the items on their platform he came to Rural Electrification and declaimed to his appreciative audience, 'My God to hear them tell it in 1955 they were going to electrify everything from the barnyard rooster to the distant hills.'

As the weeks passed in that beautiful Island summer of 1956, it began to appear that there were no potential candidates whose interest or intention would pre-empt my seeking the nomination. A general climate of receptivity was slowly developing and my optimism rose.

The catalytic event was an unexpected call which I received one evening in my Victoria home. Reagh Bagnall of Hunter River and Philip Matheson of nearby Oyster Bed Bridge came in for a serious talk about the situation. I was upstairs in the study doubtless typing something in connection with politics. If I had been competing for any sartorial awards I would have scored poorly. So informal was my attire that I had two quite noticeable patches on the knees of my trousers. I had met both these men some time earlier. It would hardly be possible for anyone interested in the PC party of PEI not to know Reagh and Phil. The former had been constituency and provincial president and a director of the national association. He had sound judgment and a deep dedication to the party. As Walter Mackenzie once said, Reagh Bagnall would drive his car to either end of the Island or telephone Ottawa a dozen times on party business and never dream of being reimbursed.

Philip had been in the provincial legislature but was defeated in 1955. He was a successful farmer, a great citizen, and a thoughtful person. As far as I know their mission was unofficial, but I sensed that they wished to test the seriousness of my interest and intent, and also to see at close range the person who might well become their party's federal candidate. I felt too that, if they were satisfied, they would be stalwart supporters and key advisers. Their position in the party was such that, if they thought the new guy was okay, that would be sufficient for a host of Queens PCs.

The discussion was excellent and candid. I told them frankly of my concerns. One was that the convention be held in the fall. On general principles it is good to give a new candidate sufficient time. In my case I would need to do a great deal of work to make myself known to the electorate of the constituency. On another matter, while it usually adds zest to a convention if there is a contest, I thought the upcoming one might prove an exception. Angus MacLean as the incumbent, and one who was doing an excellent job, would, if there were a vote, lead the poll. Considering that I was the one coming from behind, it was well not to convey the impression that Macquarrie had less than the full support of the party. Therefore an uncontested convention was the better course. My two callers could not, of course, give any guarantee but they understood my reasoning.

Somehow, without anything specific being said in the aftermath of the Bagnall-Matheson visit, I sensed my candidacy had moved from the realm of probability to that of likelihood. Before long the executive met and a convention was called for 16 September. In PEI they did not go in for open conventions and the selling of memberships at the door. To vote at any convention a delegate required a credential slip signed by his or her poll chairman. Each poll was entitled to five delegates.

It is the custom at party conventions for the movers and seconders of candidates' nominations to make brief speeches. These are important parts of the proceedings and sometimes the speeches of the mover and seconder can be very helpful. Needless to say I gave careful thought to this aspect. I thought the best possible person to move my nomination would be Mayor Stewart. He would have been a favourite son had he offered. Besides he was the very popular mayor of the urban centre where at least half the Queens voters lived. Since I was not a Charlottetown man I thought his public support extremely valuable. Everyone I mentioned this to thought it a great idea but could not be sure he would do it. A very direct man, Dave Stewart never hesitated to say no if he thought a negative the most appropriate answer. With a little trepidation I called upon the mayor and, as I expected, he did not beat around the bush. Happily his answer was yes. He told me to provide him with a résumé and I knew that I had one important job in the best of hands. In PEI we have long recognized the importance of maintaining a balance of recognition of Protestants and Roman Catholics. In the last mayoralty election Dave Stewart had defeated Alban Farmer, a well-established and respected lawyer who was also a prominent Roman Catholic layman. I was enormously grateful that he too accepted my invitation to second the nomination.

But that left the rural-urban balance to be considered. I asked close friend and backer Wilfred McAleer from West Queens if he would be interested in speaking in support. His reply was: 'Thanks but you had better get one of the old Scotsmen from the East.' I had developed a huge regard for Frank Macdonald and he agreed to my request to say a word or two in support. I thought it important to have someone from my own backyard involved and so I asked Frank Myers to close the paean of praise for my candidacy.

Needless to say I regarded 16 September as a red-letter day. I gave strict attention to my grooming and, while I did not prepare a script for my remarks and realized how important it was to refer to things said or done at that meeting, I nevertheless gave careful thought to what in a sense would be my maiden speech. Isabel and I took some of our Victoria neighbours with us and were at the Clover Club of the Charlottetown Canadian Legion in good time. The meeting was well attended and well conducted, with Charles Phillips in the chair and Bennett Carr, another who had encouraged me, as secretary. The people who spoke on my behalf were all splendid. Frank Myers noted that PEI had grown used to an outward brain drain but, with my seeking the nomination, we were getting one of our own proven assets back. Everything was going as merry as a marriage bell but, because it was a democratic convention, other nominations could be put forward. Had that happened it would have had an effect on my remarks. If there were a contest, I would have to make my pitch before the balloting and, if successful, speak to my fellow PCs after the vote. If I lost, my only task would be to show myself a good loser.

But there was no contest. I received the acclamation I had desired, and I was enormously cheered and deeply gratified. I found that evening an emotional experience. Many people I didn't know well or at all gave me their good wishes and assurances of support. One diminutive man strode up to me and said: 'I'm George Rogers in that big building just across the street. If there's anything I can do for you in any way, by God I want you to walk right in there and say so.' It was all heart-warming. I drove back to my modest Victoria home a thankful and happy man, sure now that I was to be an Island, not a Manitoba, politician.

Nor was my ebullience daunted next day by a comment I heard on Great George Street in Charlottetown. Angus MacLean and I were proceeding to the provincial PC office located above the Liquor Commission outlet. A poor chap down on his luck was standing in front of the commission apparently hoping for a handout. Seeing Angus and doubtless having read the convention story on the front page of the *Guardian*, he called out: 'Congratulations Angus. You'll be all right but the other bugger will get nowhere.' He didn't realize that I was the 'other bugger.'

That man-in-the-street comment was more than the basis for a delightful anecdote; it was reflected in the views of many astute observers. Dave Stewart had told one of my early backers: 'He'll get the nomination but I hope you're not counting on his getting elected.' While my delicate, careful negotiations and those of some of my friends may have had influence on bringing about an uncontested nomination, political history and statistics were highly significant determinants. On the face of it the nomination must not have looked all that attractive to possible contenders.

The figures for Queens in the 1953 election were: Neil A. Matheson (Lib) 10,351, J.A. MacLean (PC) 10,086, Cecil A. Miller (Lib) 9,991, and W.C.S. McLure (PC) 9,946. A Liberal had led the poll with a margin of 265 votes ahead of Angus MacLean. Chester McLure, who had won the seat in 1945 and in 1949 with the highest total, was at the bottom in 1953. The figures were not of themselves so commanding, but many observers seemed to detect a trend and that was a voter preference to split Queens representation between the two parties. The Conservatives had not carried both seats since 1930. The best the Tories could do in the elections of 1945, 1949, and 1953 was to elect one of their candidates. Was this a fluke, a matter of candidate popularity, or was it a definite preference? Although I knew that a split had been the result in three successive general elections, I could not believe it was a conscious pattern. It was well that I was not fazed by the figures and thought a total Tory victory not at all impossible. But well into the election campaign itself and certainly before it, I was told by many well-wishers and even some of my own poll chairman: 'I'm afraid it will be Matheson and MacLean again.' Naturally I did not go about quoting these prophets of doom.

Nor were the portents on the provincial scene all that propitious. After losing three seats in 1955, their worst showing since 1939, the provincial PCs did not look like sure winners next time. Thus it was that a certain lack of rosiness in the political outlook helped me win a nomination which, in a period of brighter prospects, I would have had enormous difficulty in attaining. As Shakespeare didn't say, 'there is a tide in the affairs of men which taken at its ebb leads on to fortune.' The Tory tide was soon to rise but of course we did not know that in the summer of 1956.

In the late summer of 1956 the new Tory candidate in Queens could feel that the universe was unfolding as it should. But not so for the national leader of the party. Like many other Progressive Conservatives in Canada I was shocked to hear that George Drew would not be leading the party in the next election. After a thorough diagnosis by his medical advisers and the most careful consideration on his own part, the gallant colonel decided to step down forthwith so as to allow the party to proceed quickly to select a new leader. There was a certain poignancy about it all. Drew had given strong, steady, and skilful leadership in the pipeline debate. The voters were finally becoming fed up with the unseemly and unceasing arrogance of the incumbent Liberals.

I was riled by the haughtiness of the Liberals during the great pipeline debate and, apart from my personal reaction, I thought it had made a profound impact upon many Canadians. Television was becoming a major medium in public affairs, and there were plenty of cameras on the Hill. I remember one night after the House rose a Liberal MP from Ontario was accosted by a hostile crowd outside the Centre Block. Possibly under the strain or the osmotic effect of the lofty leaders of his party, he gave the questioner a very snotty putdown. One of the citizens immediately commented: 'You've put closure on the House so now you would like to do it to the public!' That exchange was not ignored by the media people with microphones and cameras.

Some of the print reporters in the press gallery were not enthusiastic about the electronic invasion. But television did bring Ottawa to many thousands of Canadians. Interviews with the chief protagonists stirred new interest in the activities and utterances of the tribunes of the people. Television didn't (and doesn't) encourage in-depth contemplation of great issues but it helped establish or harden attitudes. That new word 'closure' took on evil overtones. It was the kind of thing those arrogant Grits were doing. John Diefenbaker, after he became the leader, correctly read the public reaction and said that under him no PC government would ever invoke closure. C.D. Howe, whose allegedly phenomenal gifts had made him something of a household god during the war and its aftermath, was becoming a *bête noire*.

Twice worsted in a national contest, George Drew, it seemed to many, might well triumph in his third try. But there would be no third try. Drew's resignation was effective on 20 September 1956, and a meeting of the national executive was called to arrange for a convention. Veteran Ontario MP Earl Rowe was selected interim leader on the promise, as he jokingly put it, that he would not run for the real thing. As a member of the national executive I attended the Ottawa meeting. Even that early in the game it was clear that John Diefenbaker would be the favourite. Donald Fleming and Davie Fulton were soon recognized as contenders. The convention was called for 12 to 14 December in Ottawa.

Back in Prince Edward Island there was much to do. Poll chairmen are the vital cogs in a party organization. Their committee members are key people also. Together they constitute representatives of the party and the candidate at the grassroots level. Not surprisingly in Queens, as in other constituencies, there were many well-organized poll committees. It is always necessary to keep each poll in an efficient and harmonious condition, and some were anything but. With an election likely in less than a year, an organization returning was important to us. Angus MacLean, who would have to return to Ottawa for the parliamentary session on 26 November, was naturally interested. I had the same concerns plus a strong desire to become better acquainted with those people who would bear such a heavy responsibility for my failure or success come the impending federal election. These poll workers' meetings sometimes combined several committees. Others were smaller gatherings of people from just one polling division. I have the warmest memories of these strategy sessions. Once in a while I ran across a crank or a smart-ass. But overwhelmingly these evenings were amicable and indeed uplifting. I used to bring along a sheaf of voting statistics for the poll and the district. Usually there were some grains of comfort from history.

It was a pleasant series of social contacts with a group of key people for whom I developed a growing regard and affection.

Sometimes, it being hospitable PEI, there was a bountiful lunch. In the Fredericton poll in 1st Queens we also had a drop of 'the crater.' I believe it was Elmer Wigmore, son of our popular former MLA of 1931–5, Tom Wigmore, who brought along a bottle. Although by that time no stranger to booze, it was my first time imbibing from the common bottle. Not only did I find the beverage excellent, I thought the sociability something quite precious in human relations. Our chairman, George Buchanan, showed good humour and good sense when, in closing the meeting, he said perhaps we had better have the bottle passed around one more time. That one was sufficient to finish it.

There were many calls on party people in their homes. Some of my friends drew me into social events which would allow me to meet numbers of people. I was invited to Bennett Carr's prenuptial stag party, which was a genial and interesting affair but a bit challenging too. I was not very familiar with stag parties as a social form but was not surprised when the telling of humorous stories became the item of 'business.' Clearly it was not the time for jokes suitable to a Sunday school class. Nor was it the occasion for anything so off-colour as to be crude. I believe I was fortunate enough to strike a happy and amusing medium.

It was after the nomination and the public awareness of my candidacy that I really became a topic of conversation. 'Who's this Macquarrie?' or 'Do you know this new man Macquarrie?' were oft-repeated questions. In many, many cases they brought negative replies, a matter of great concern to any candidate. Sometimes these inquiries were readily and positively met. Wellington MacNeill used to ask even some fellow Tories if they knew anything or had ever heard about 'this Macquarrie.' When he questioned my life-long neighbours, the MacLeods in Victoria, he received a fulsome and indeed flattering account. Later, when someone told the converted MacNeill of not knowing Macquarrie, he gave typical reply: 'Well you should know him; he's an Islander and his father before him. He's a very smart young man.'

One exchange on the matter of my identity had a charming and sentimental quality. Dr N.R. Bovyer, who had practised medicine in nearby Crapaud for more than fifty years, had retired in Charlottetown. Someone, knowing that the doctor had come from the same area as the new candidate, raised the usual question. He replied: 'I was the first man that ever saw him.' I visited him during the fall and on election day he was out to vote. I was told that he was quite emotional and kissed the ballot paper before returning it. It was the dear old gentleman's last vote.

In my efforts to increase my impact on the electorate I was inadvertently helped by a prominent Liberal. Premier Alex Matheson, in a radio talk on 'Provincial Affairs,' made reference to Professor Macquarrie and opined that the PCs really had me in mind for the provincial leadership. Such a thing had never crossed my mind or any other Tory's, but it certainly didn't do my public profile any harm.

On the day after the Queens convention Bennett Carr received a ribbing telephone call from his friend E.D. Reid, a successful Charlottetown businessman. Reid, a very fine chap and one of my opponents in a later election, kidded Bennett about the fallacy of trying to elect a professor, especially one who wore a beret. In some quarters the professor bit helped; in others it was no asset, since to many it suggested an impractical, visionary babe in the hardwoods of politics. I don't know about the beret.

After my nomination was reported to national headquarters in Ottawa I received a candidate's kit with helpful hints, speaking points, and the like. Some of these were useful, others not of great value in Prince Edward Island. What might be conventional wisdom in a riding like Montreal West or Vancouver East might be a 'no-no' in constituencies like Athabasca or Queens.

The national leadership campaign brought Diefenbaker, Fleming, and Fulton to the Island. Naturally I was at the meetings they addressed. Because I was a newly minted candidate, I for once kept my thoughts to myself in so far as leadership preferences were concerned. There was little doubt that Diefenbaker was the odds-on favourite of Island Tories. He had gained a larger vote in the 1948 convention than in that of 1942. And Islanders had not failed to hear that old refrain of the Drew years: 'You should have picked Diefenbaker.'

Although I was having a grand time and enjoying those eventful, productive days in the later summer and autumn of 1956, I knew it was a crucial period and nothing could be taken for granted. Perhaps it was my inner anxiety that led to what might be described as a minor incident with John Diefenbaker. He addressed a meeting in Charlottetown and in the course of his speech lauded his caucus colleague Angus MacLean. He made slight reference to me or the PC candidate for Kings, John Macdonald. After the meeting closed he asked if his address had been all right. I replied that it was splendid but also pointed out the minor billing given to the candidacies of Macdonald and myself. While I subscribed to any praise of MacLean, Diefenbaker would never win the prime ministership if only those already in the caucus were elected; people like Macdonald and myself would also have to join the ranks. I had no doubt that he did not like my answer. I suppose he expected me to praise his speech extravagantly, without the analysis. Perhaps I should have done so, telling the truth but not the whole truth as I saw it. But he had asked my opinion, and I had never learned the art of dissembling. I might have saved myself a bit of trouble along the way had I become more skilful in the use of soft soap and unctuous flattery. In the dining-room of the Queen Hotel the next morning Mrs Chester McLure said she was 'heartbroken' over Diefenbaker's speech. Of course, while she regarded it as a slight to me, she would be irate at the exaltation of Angus MacLean, who was very much in her bad books following Chester's defeat in 1953. After all, she had refused to accept Angus's hand of sympathy at Chester's funeral.

Dalton Camp, with his usual perspicacity, had told me that my big problem, or perhaps he said priority, was identification. In this connection I did some television talks and was grateful for the opportunity to present myself to people I had never met or who did not attend Progressive Conservative political meetings. I don't recall anyone so unimpressed as the farmer of Matlock, Saskatchewan, who, when he viewed Liberal MP Walter Tucker defending the St Laurent government's wheat policy, reached for his shotgun and emptied both barrels into the television set. (During the months when I was a House of Commons colleague of Tucker, I used to note how some of my sharp but slightly nasty

PC colleagues would wait carefully for Tucker to rise with a question or a speech. By snapping down their desk covers they made sounds somewhat like a gunshot.)

In general, while I suppose I heard the generous comments rather than the grousing ones, I believe that these television appearances were helpful. In Prince Edward Island television itself was in its early phase, and perhaps I benefited from the novelty of both the man and the medium. But as Victor Hugo once said: 'The perfect smile belongs to God alone.' I had no chance to let even successful events go to my head. One evening, after doing a five- or ten-minute talk on CFCY-TV, I drove to a PC meeting in a rural area and called in at the home of our poll chairman before the meeting. He greeted me by saying how well I looked on television an hour ago. His wife chimed in, saying quite innocently: 'I understand they use an awful lot of make-up on TV!'

Being a nominated candidate of the PC party in Queens gave me a new status and new responsibilities. It was sad that one of my first public appearances in this new role was as an honourary pallbearer at the funeral of John H. Myers. At the graveside his daughter – and my former landlady – Lulu thanked me for the tribute to her father which had appeared in the *Guardian*. This farewell to one of the greats of the party was also an assemblage of leading contemporary Tories.

In the course of our calls together I used to tell Angus MacLean that he had me at a disadvantage. In many parts of the constituency he seemed to have cousins or other relatives. The MacLean clan was much larger than the Macquarrie, who were far from numerous in the Highlands. His mother was a MacLeod and that too was a big clan. I had few relatives and on my mother's side most of them were in the eastern constituency of Kings. My best 'in' was through my earlier teaching contacts.

On 17 September after a busy day in Charlottetown I drove to Victoria, not by the Trans-Canada Highway, but by the longer but more scenic route, highway 19. This beautiful thoroughfare passed through Canoe Cove, where in 1936–7 I had my first teaching assignment. My landlady of that year was Katie Belle (Mrs Dan) MacLean who gave me the best of board for fifty cents a day. I told her I had just succeeded Chester McLure and that she was the first elector upon whom I had made a call. It was a pleasant reunion but I had no reason to believe that I could count on her x come election day. There was nothing in my recollection to make me regard her or her late husband, a fine chap who was one of the school trustees in my day, as anything but devout Grits. But one mustn't take anything for granted either negatively or positively.

As I resumed my journey to Victoria an incident occurred which I found most difficult to handle. I encountered a sizeable flock of hens on the road and, in spite of all due care and concern, I feared I had killed or named one of them. Should I report the tragedy? If so, to which farmer? With what I hope was not unworthy cowardice I drove on. Chickens were not supposed to run loose on a public highway and it would not have been smart for the new Tory candidate to hawk himself about among Grit farmers trying to explain the inadvertent slaughter of some far-ranging poultry.

Far worse than wandering hens were the dogs of Queens. While I am a longtime cat fancier, I was never very fond of canines. Some years before entering political life I had been bitten by a dog as I walked on a sidewalk in Victoria. Resenting this unprovoked attack, I reported the incident and the RCMP destroyed the dog. When some years later the late dog's mistress found my name on the ballot I am convinced she made sure no x was placed behind it. Luckily during all my canvasses, while often barked at, I remained unbitten. Dog owners normally play down the nastiness of their critters with such soothing assurances as, 'Oh, he barks but never bites,' or 'Just ignore him, he'll relax.' But Billie Carragher in Kellys Cross issued no such soothing syrup. When asked if his loudly barking pair would bite, he replied: 'Christ yes, they'd ate you!'

The Progressive Conservative Party's fifth leadership convention later that year was an impressive event with a large attendance and a full agenda. Much time was spent in policy seminars, with my old friend Dick Petrie taking a prominent part in the economics discussions. As usual, a large number of delegates were less than firmly convinced of the importance of talks about policy. To such people the leadership selection is the one and only job. Supporters of the candidates canvassed delegates and those whose names could be on the ballot pressed the flesh. I remember one group of delegates outside the Coliseum being greeted by Donald Fleming. As he was leaving he was asked if he was putting up a strong campaign. His prompt, clipped reply was: 'Yes, and a winning one.' After Fleming was out of earshot, Senator John Haig of Winnipeg said that he should not have said that. According to the old senator, it is poor strategy for a candidate to be seen as cocky or overconfident.

Although I found it an interesting meeting, it lacked the hoopla which marked later conventions. There were fewer gimmicks and demonstrations. Perhaps my low profile kept me less involved than some delegates. I voted for Donald Fleming but did not go about trying to persuade others. Nor did I wear a Fleming button.

Although not a Diefenbaker supporter – I did not vote for him at any convention he contested – I was nevertheless convinced that he was the obvious winner. The widespread belief that it was a sure thing for the prairie populist certainly diminished some of the excitement. The result was convincing and predictable: Diefenbaker 774, Fleming 393, and Fulton 117.

I think I would have voted for Donald Fleming in any case, but certain developments during the convention reinforced my inclination. Although I did not hear it from Balcer himself, I was told that there were certain anxieties among the Quebec delegates. Diefenbaker seemed to neglect some of the formulae which might indicate a sensitivity towards the francophone sector of the PC party. I'm sure Léon Balcer would have been happy to be given even an informal designation as the Quebec lieutenant. But this did not happen until years afterward when it was too late. Diefenbaker even stated his preference for seat-mate. It was not to be a Quebec MP, but George Drew, who of course did not plan to run for the House of Commons again. Indeed there apparently was not a place for a Quebecer on Diefenbaker's convention presentation. His mover was New Brunswick Premier Hugh John Flemming; his seconder General George Pearkes of British Columbia.

In the highly charged atmosphere of political gatherings, things become overblown and distorted. There were reports that Balcer was hostile and some Quebec Tories were contemplating a walk-out to demonstrate against Diefenbaker. The 1956 convention was not the only one to reveal Anglo-French tension, and the problem was not as serious in fact as rumour suggested. But I was of the opinion that Fleming might be more alert to the importance of developing new PC strength in the province of Quebec. And despite the fact that Diefenbaker made by far the best speech of the contenders, I stayed with Fleming who had made such a fine effort to learn French.

Conventions are social events. It was great to see Dick Petrie again and to renew contacts with other PCs on the national scene. Most agreeable of all was the opportunity to get to know better so many people in the PEI delegation. But when I drove to Welles-ley for the Christmas season I carried some misgivings with me. The party had been shut out of Quebec for so long that I was fearful that our choice of Diefenbaker might have assured continued failure in that important province.

While I was troubled about Quebec the focus of my thoughts and attention was the constituency of Queens. But I had to discharge one obligation of another kind first. I had been granted a John S. Ewart fellowship to the University of Toronto. The months I spent in Toronto in early 1957 were somewhat tentative. The office I was assigned in the political economy building was said to be the former cloakroom of the great Harold Innis, the legendary Canadian economist whose voluminous writings I always had trouble comprehending. Whether my cubicle was a former closet or not I never knew, but it did not seem to matter. The eminents in the building, like Vincent Bladen, seemed totally unaware of my presence or my interests. Of course they had no responsibility towards me. Somehow that neither troubled nor interested me.

But I was pleased to become acquainted with Professor Alex Brady, an expert on the Commonwealth. I remember attending a public forum on the Suez Crisis, featuring radio personality J.B. (Hamish) McGeachy; Peter Stursberg of the parliamentary press gallery, a specialist in international affairs; and my senior colleague of McGill days, Professor Burton Kierstead. McGeachy, an Englishman become a Canadian resident, strongly supported the actions of Britain and France. Kierstead disagreed. As he saw it, the future of both the Commonwealth and the United Nations was at stake. Stursberg was of a similar opinion, and I too found myself to be totally in accord with Kierstead's point of view. This put me against what Progressive Conservatives were saying in the House of Commons.

When not at my own academic pursuits I made contact with Islanders in Toronto and enjoyed attending the Islanders Club of that city, of which I soon became a member. I also spent a great deal of time on my portable typewriter in my digs on Huron Street, writing to Island Conservatives. Angus MacLean came from Ottawa to visit me and we had a useful talk about the federal political situation in PEI.

During those three months in Toronto I lived something of a monastic existence. In my office I pursued my academic work; my room on Huron Street was my political centre. I had the occasional meal at Hart House where I found the cuisine a cut below the fare at the Lady Beaverbrook Residence at UNB. Never having liked bars or pubs, I spent no time in that environment. I don't think I ever had a bottle in my room and of course not in the office. At that time Toronto, unlike Montreal, had few good restaurants so little time was spent in gracious living of that kind.

Despite the spartan nature of my life and the handicap of having my family in Massachusetts and my constituency in Prince Edward Island, the Toronto period seemed to pass quickly enough. Although never a great husbandman of money, I actually saved some of my funding from the fellowship. Clearly this was one of my best exercises in frugality; with an election pending I would need every penny.

I was already back in Prince Edward Island when Parliament was dissolved on 12 April 1957. The election was set for 10 June, a good date for Prince Edward Island. It would be all over before the great influx of tourists arrived and April and May would provide pretty fair travelling conditions for covering the rural areas.

Of course there is no time in the year which pleases everyone. Some might complain that the campaign would take place in planting time or the opening of the lobster season. And, of course, only the very rash try long-range weather predictions. Spring is often backward in PEI. It is the only season in which the climate of Ottawa is preferable. But the weather was no deterrent to our 1957 campaign, which I was to find the most absorbing and interesting two months of my life up to that time.

Once an election is called, political candidates and their organizations are very much the slaves of the calendar. One of the first documents put up on the wall is the election timetable. It is basically a diagrammatic countdown – the end of enumeration, so many days before polling day, official declaration day, and the like. Enumeration, or the compiling of the voters' list, is enormously important in urban areas. It also has to be done in short order in the first few days after the election call. In Charlottetown, as in other urban polls, enumerators from the two parties that came first and second in the previous election go from door to door to compile the roll of voters poll by poll. Our seasoned election experts in Queens considered this enumeration process very important because it gave a party representative the first opportunity to make a good impression on the electorate, as well as a chance to sample the public attitude. Since the enumerators go in pairs there would be no chance for proselytizing, but an observant eye and a still tongue can nevertheless learn a good deal. So a meeting of all the Charlottetown area poll chairmen was one of the first events. If the poll chairman can do the enumerating himself or herself that is generally considered a good thing. If the poll chairman chooses not to do so then his or her advice usually determines who the enumerator will be. As with all positions under the Elections Act, enumerators are not going to make a fortune, but it is a little item of patronage and there is usually no problem in attracting people to take on the chore. I found that many people like it, and in my opinion it is generally done extremely well.

Although the chief electoral officer always alerts the public to the importance of getting their names on the list, and political parties also use the media to inform the voters, there are always people missed. The preliminary lists are displayed in public places, but many voters do not trouble to look at them. If close to the election day committed voters find they have not been listed, they may take it out on the party they normally support. So for the first few days the candidates and their people are very much concerned with the enumeration process. Workers at the party headquarters are instructed to give top priority to anyone who drops by or telephones regarding names which should be put on the list. In the United Kingdom and other countries there are permanent lists upgraded through the year. Thus they avoid the flurry of activity at election time and election campaigns need not be so long. This matter has been studied in Canada for years and the merits of our system seem sufficiently convincing to assure its retention. The Canadian election process is noted for its fairness and efficiency and through the years we have been blessed with chief electoral officers of the highest probity.

In the interests of getting every legitimate voter onto the list, a revising officer is appointed for each urban constituency. In Queens it was normally a county court judge. I well remember my first encounter with this part of the election machinery. A prominent and enormously colourful Charlottetown attorney, Lester O'Donnell, who was assisting the Revising officer, called me in off Richmond Street to go upstairs with him and look at the list. He pointed to a name and said: 'Look at that. Old Joe—. Dead two years. Jesus Christ, dead two years!' So errors creep in even in the most highly organized processes.

Another of a candidate's early responsibilities is to appoint an official agent. This person handles the expenses and is responsible for a great many forms and documents required under the Elections Act. The candidate himself does not receive or disburse election funds. A very important and difficult task is that of financial chairman. Elections are costly and in 1957 increased use of television was making the expenditure greater than ever. The national party helped, but sizeable amounts were necessary beyond its contribution. Fund-raising is a task at which I am useless and I was never much involved or even interested in the process.

People whose integrity and ability I trusted implicitly took this job on for me, and they justified my trust.

A successful campaign requires careful budgeting and a good deal of specialization. Someone has to look after newspaper advertising and political parties pay a very high rate. Radio and television also require someone to be in charge, and good contacts with the appropriate people in the media can be enormously helpful.

We also had someone to take responsibility for the mailings, always a costly but important means of contact. The message had to be carefully considered, not too long, not so elaborate as to be considered extravagant, but not so modest as to be considered cheap. In that year we had no sophisticated office equipment and volunteers devoted many hours to addressing envelopes by hand. You don't do much for your cause by getting a voter's name wrong. Worse still is for a letter to be addressed to a citizen who had died since the enumeration. The campaign office was always alerted to the importance of avoiding slips of this kind.

Someone took responsibility for institutional visits. Calls at chronic care and senior citizens' residences had to be scheduled. Visits to the university and establishments with a number of employees were set up. I was never very fond of the calls on industries, feeling perhaps that a visiting politician might be viewed as a damn nuisance. I had a different view about calls at the nursing homes. I remember the wise and sensitive words of the gracious mother superior at the Sacred Heart Home when she escorted us to the floor of some patients who were becoming infirm of mind and body. She said: 'We must remember that these were all smart ladies at one time.' So long as he was there, Angus and I made our last call at the room of a gentle retired priest, Father Duffy. He always played a selection or two on the organ. I was keenly appreciative of the courtesy displayed by the people in charge of the various nursing homes and came away with a deep feeling of gratitude for people who in ministering to the elderly are performing such a noble service to society. My mother spent her last years in the Livingstone MacArthur nursing home and I know what splendid care they gave her.

One aspect of an election campaign for which the candidate always has a plenitude of advisers is the door-to-door canvass. There is almost complete unanimity that however much he or she is doing the candidate must and should do more. As with most things it is not all that simple. Given a small constituency and little else to do, I suppose a candidate could make a personal call on every voter. But I usually took with a grain of salt the boasts of those who claimed they had shaken every hand in their electoral district.

If it is impossible or impractical to canvass every voter, what is the best strategy? I was often told not to waste time calling on the hard-shell Grits. Some said it was not necessary to call on the stalwart Tories. Better to concentrate on the 'doubtfuls.' In small rural communities this pattern could be risky. Voters who have been supportive may resent candidates passing their lanes and calling on someone who may never have cast a vote for the party. Some who have been supporters may resent being catalogued with the undecided. And, who knows, some of the allegedly rock-ribbed Grits might not be as inflexible as their party bigwigs thought. Angus MacLean often told me of a small poll which had been normally in the Grit column but in the 1951 by-election gave him a narrow win. The Liberal poll chairman later told MacLean that his committee held the usual post-mortem and went over the voters' list with a fine-tooth comb. As the chairman put it: 'They gave you all the Conservative votes, and after much sorting out gave you *all* the doubtful ones, but they still couldn't account for two of your votes. I don't think any of them ever suspected that it was Annie and I who cast those two ballots!'

Despite these reservations and dubieties I did a great deal of canvassing in the 1957 campaign, and this is a skill requiring some common sense. To enter into argument or, even worse, to denigrate one's opponents or their party would be totally unhelpful. Angus MacLean and I were, happily, by temperament and judgment, given to the soft sell. We never mentioned our opponents' names or went about denouncing the Liberal party. We avoided trying to pin people down as to whether or not they would vote for us. All of them knew that we weren't going around selling Easter seals.

Tiring though it was, the cross-county traversing was fun. But not always. About two days after my triumphant nomination in Queens and two blocks after I drove away from an important social function in the Charlottetown Hotel, my car stopped moving. It is embarrassing for a grown man to be out of gas. Especially so for a man heading down the highway of political achievement. So I thought. Before many minutes passed two Charlottetown policemen drove by and noted my embarrassed immobility. The manner in which these gallant young men handled the situation prompted me to believe there was much validity in that old expression about police forces, 'Charlottetown's finest.' They certainly mitigated my chagrin about my own stupidity. These incidents helped me be more attentive to the fuel gauge, but it required a few more dry fiascos to rid me of my casual attitude towards the gas fact.

If I had my problems keeping fuel in the gas tank, I also had certain anxieties about destinations. In my seven years as a teacher in PEI I did not have a car or even a bicycle, nor did my father. Therefore I did not have an intimate knowledge of every highway and byway on the Island. I was not possessed of the innate sense of direction of my sailor father. I was more like my mother, who often got lost in the subway system of Boston, a city in which she spent many years. I recall here more than once going in the wrong direction and having to pay to get back into the subway system to continue a journey on a connecting line. Often was I bewildered when looking for some prominent Conservative I was told: 'Just go along the Markham Road until you get to Big Joe's place and turn right. You can't miss it.' But I could and did! When your political opponents and others have accused you of being something of an outsider, you don't relish appearing as someone who doesn't know where the hell he is going on the roads of Queens County.

But I wasn't the only politician with a slightly less than precise sense of direction. Angus MacLean, distinguished and decorated

RCAF officer, told me of an event which took place before I became his running mate. One of our faithful Tory poll chairmen had advised him of the importance of going to the funeral of a great old guy who had long supported the Conservative cause. Angus duly went to one of the leading Roman Catholic funeral homes and dutifully viewed the remains. Instead of good old Joe, he viewed an old lady in the coffin. Clearly he had gone to the 'other' Catholic funeral home. A short while later he heard that his attendance at the funeral had been much appreciated, especially since no Liberal candidate had shown up at the funeral of a faithful member of that party.

Possibly I was a bit hesitant about some aspects of keeping before the public. I was always ill at ease lest I should appear to be trying to gain political mileage out of people's bereavement. Generally speaking, I followed the practice of attending only those funerals to which I would have gone before becoming a political candidate. A letter to the bereaved seemed to me to be in better taste.

Some politicians are accused of becoming great churchgoers after the writ is issued. We had some of those in PEI but none surpassed a Tory candidate in a rural Queens provincial riding. He not only attended a goodly number of church services but managed to get himself into the choir in almost every case.

In some constituencies the nominating convention is a major event in the period between the call of an election and voting day. I always thought that the candidate should be in the field before the writ was issued. In 1957 I was thankful that I had been nominated early and I felt I had made good use of the time thus made available to me. I have heard George Hees on this subject many times; early nominations are good strategy.

In 1957 the election period was roughly two months. That would seem to be a long time, perhaps too long. But it is amazing how the days dwindle down to a precious few. The big election day calendar on the wall is soon filled. Visibility and participation are of the essence for the candidate. His or her days are long and the activities structured. In Queens we gave early attention to a series of public meetings set up in various parts of the constituency. Early in the campaign one special meeting had to be coordinated and the hall booked. This was the wind-up rally. It was our preference to hold it, if possible, on the Saturday before the Monday election. With the then forty-eight hour blackout of political broadcasts on television and radio, the pre-election Saturday was the last chance for candidates to make an appeal to a substantial sector of the electorate. After that they can do little but wait and pray. The wind-up must be an event which will help people to feel positive, happy, and kindly disposed towards the candidate and his cause. Above all else they must enjoy themselves. In 1957 we were able to feature Don Messer and his Islanders, including Charlie Chamberlain, Marg Osborne, and the other popular members of that grand musical group.

While we had far fewer meetings than those in which Chester McLure and John Myers participated during the 1930s, we nevertheless had to give thought to the timing and location of public appearances. I always insisted on a meeting in Victoria. Belfast Hall in Angus MacLean's home turf was another obvious location. We always had a meeting in Afton Hall in the southeast part of Queens. The important fishing and Tory centre North Rustico was another regular. In the western area, New London or Bradalbane were frequent sites.

I was always keen on making these gatherings more than old-fashioned political meetings, and so we sought to make them entertaining. Local entertainers were brought in. I remember my cousin, Marion Macquarrie, and my one-time pupil and long-time neighbour, Donald MacLeod, coming to York and singing. Our poll chairman Leith Brown remarked: 'Those MacLeods were strong Liberals. Think of that.' PEI has produced lots of good fiddlers and a good fiddler often lures a step dancer. So we liked to have some oldtimer or his young grandchildren perform. After a pleasant variety show interspersed with candidates' brief speeches, a fine lunch was served. Politicians are prone to consider their speeches shorter than does their audience, but Angus MacLean and I tried to avoid long-winded perorations. Commander John Kenny, who was our campaign manager, always reported meetings to the campaign committee the next morning. He timed our speeches to the second and told our committee about them.

These public meetings were one of my favourite parts of campaigning. It has been said that if anyone ever addresses a public gathering and six people applaud him he is never the same again. Perhaps! But apart from their effect upon the vote they were interesting from a sociological point of view. PEI is not a very large place, 2184 square miles, Queens County is but a part of it. Yet there was a different ambience as we moved from place to place. Meetings in Belfast were subtly different from gatherings in Rustico or York.

Charlottetown, Parkdale, Sherwood – the urban areas – were not given to political meetings. In one election Angus MacLean and I hired a hall in Parkdale and went there with a group of performers including some pipers. In fact we had such a well-structured program that the performers outnumbered the audience. It was always difficult to get out a crowd for political meetings in the urban areas. But if the Tories in 5th and 6th Queens were averse to coming out to political rallies they did their bit on election day. In all my eight campaigns I was gratified by the strength of my support in Charlottetown and environs.

But these meetings, as with all other aspects of a campaign, do not just happen. A good organization is essential and a poor one can be a ruination. In 1957, as subsequently, we had excellent people. One of the most encouraging and rewarding aspects of public life is the dedication of so many citizens to their party's cause and candidates. I shall be forever grateful to the hundreds of Progressive Conservatives who did so much for me in Queens constituency in the elections of 1957, 1958, 1962, 1963, and 1965, and in Hillsborough constituency in 1968, 1972, and 1974.

The whole of Prince Edward Island is dear to me. Those of us who come from small islands are blessed. As Lord Tweedsmuir put it, we can carry such homelands more easily in our hearts. But of all places on Abegweit the most precious to me is my birthplace, the beautiful village of Victoria. Here there was no problem of identification, no 'Who's this Macquarrie?' comment.

I would be judged politically by those who knew me from the beginning. The manifestation of attitudes towards my candidacy in my home community was enormously important to me. I suppose it is a combination of sentimentality and vanity which prompts a candidate to set a special store in carrying his own poll. Once again the statistics were not all that comforting. No one could remember the Victoria poll ever showing a preference for the Conservative candidate. Even in 1930, John Myers did not carry it, although it was his home poll too. The village of Victoria always seemed to be evenly split, but the Hampton part of the polling division was another thing. I remember Whit Howatt producing a voters' list and pointing to the numbers of Fergusons on it. 'There are a lot of them and they're all Grits.' So I was touched and grateful to hear of a breakthrough there. Captain Dan Ferguson, a man of great candour and integrity, told Walter Shaw that while he was a strong Liberal he was voting for Heath Macquarrie because his father Wilfred had been one of the finest men he knew. Miner MacNevin, the owner-manager of Wright Bros. store in Victoria, had been the confidant of nearly everyone in the village after serving the community for over half a century. While he kept a low profile in party affairs because of his business, Miner was an ardent Liberal. I never went in for asking people to vote for me outright. Still less could I take such an approach to my friends and neighbours. So I was all the more delighted when in the early days of the campaign Miner readily disclosed his support. As his daughter Hean, my sister-in-law, remarked, he had never taken such an active interest in all his years as a Liberal.

As the campaign progressed I had reasons for appreciating the results of all the years of community and family ties. One Sunday night the Reverend M.K. Charman made some pretty definite comments about the election. He urged the congregation to support good candidates regardless of party label or their own party preference. After the service Mrs L.D. MacLeod called in at our house and, without saying much, gave me the kind of embrace that loving mothers give. It was a potent message from a very powerful lady. She was a prominent community worker and, as I see it now, one of the early feminists. She was a woman of great strength of character and bigness of heart. She had been much moved by the preacher's words and had lost no time in showing it. A few days later I told my close friend Lloyd MacPhail about the clergyman's remarks from the pulpit. With his usual wit he asked: 'You mean to tell me that when he told them to vote for the best man you automatically thought he was meaning you?'

5

In with Dief

When the 22nd Parliament was dissolved on 12 April 1957, I was not taken by surprise. It was four years since the last election. The Liberals thought the pipeline issue was fading from public memory. Finance Minister Walter Harris was still presiding over substantial budget surpluses, and out of this affluence a few goodies were still to be bestowed upon the electors. While I had no intention of saying so for the next sixty days, I really expected that the St Laurent government would be returned. But I could see it suffering a reduction in its majority. As part of that process I was determined to exert a maximum effort to capture a PC seat in Queens.

The election call found me ready to give the campaign my full attention. I was finished with the work at the University of Toronto. There were no teaching duties and my wife was looking after the bairns in Wellesley, Massachusetts. I was also comfortably located at the Queen Hotel in Charlottetown at which I had spent a good deal of time before the election campaign began. It was a homey place with first-class cuisine. Among other residents were Mrs Chester McLure and her daughter Lena. My predecessor's widow had not lost her political instincts. In those days television sets were far less common than they are today. It is likely that the only receiver in the Queen Hotel was the one in the lobby. Mrs McLure once told me that, if I ever passed through the lobby when Bishop Fulton J. Sheen was on, I should sit down and watch him. 'Many of the people are strong RCs, dear, and they will appreciate it.' It was no hardship because I had great respect for Sheen's homilies. He was so much more profound and credible than some of the awful peddlers of salvation who fill the airwaves from the fundamentalist networks in our time.

Apart from the enumeration process, an early priority was the scheduling of public meetings in the constituency. In a way, my personal campaign had opened some months earlier. Shortly after my nomination I had decided to have a public function in Victoria and to have my good friend Walter Dinsdale come down to PEI to do the honours on my pre-election début as a candidate. We had a splendid social evening in Victoria Hall, to which a wide range of community leaders and political incumbents were invited. We made sure it was a non-partisan affair and Walter Dinsdale made a highly favourable impression. Remembering that Walter was also the seat-mate of Angus MacLean, we had organized another event the following night in the eastern area of Queens. The Belfast Hall was well filled and the two DFC members of Parliament were very much at home. On the intervening Sunday I accompanied Walter to the Salvation Army Citadel in Charlottetown. It was a pleasant and impressive service, but a new experience for me. It was the first time that I was asked to sit in the pulpit area when I was taking no part in the service. Another feature new to me was that the Army didn't excuse the guys in front from contributing to the collection. I'm not great at having the right change at hand, and would be quite inept in commercial transactions without the aid of credit cards. So, when I saw the tambourines approaching, I surreptitiously rifled my pockets. Luckily enough, I happened to have what I thought was the optimum denomination, a $2 bill. Less might have looked a bit tight; more might have seemed a bit showy in 1956. To have none at all would have been the worst possible situation in which to find oneself.

But, with the election call, our meetings had to be advertised as party functions, and their scheduling became an important part of our overall campaign organization. It is very hurtful to a campaign to have a meeting appear ill organized. It was therefore of great importance to engage a program organizer familiar with the area, its people, and its entertainment possibilities. We wished to have local performers and hoped their friends and relatives would come to support them. They invariably did. We had two appealing young men, Ken Campbell and Eddy Doiron, who, with their guitars, were always well received. Forbes Kennedy, a player on the Toronto Maple Leafs hockey team, made a big hit with the athletic group. Later my young son Iain was to admire Forbie most because he could take the cap off a beer bottle with his teeth.

A highly popular American politician of that era, Hubert Humphrey, used to talk about the politics of joy, and there is much in the life of an active partisan which is heart-warming and sentimental. I recall one of my later elections when my gracious and beautiful colleague, Jean Wadds, came down as guest speaker for the Victoria meeting. My house wasn't all that warm at that time of year but we went up to it nevertheless for some liquid refreshments after the close of festivities in the village hall. In the group were Jack Doyle, our oldest poll chairman, and Ken and Eddy who sang for us. I found it an evening of charm and warmth despite a somewhat low reading on my thermometer. There are some moments of unforgettable delight.

As I have already indicated, the vision and the interests of a candidate for the House of Commons are very much confined within the borders of his constituency. So was it for me in the 1957 election. I read the *Globe and Mail* and other expressions of the national press. I heard the national news whenever possible. But my concern was for that part of the globe between Victoria on the west and Wood Islands on the east – of Queens constituency, that is.

I don't recall Queens voters' having any negative feelings about John Diefenbaker, but in 1957 he was not the big issue. If, in his first election as national leader, he had political coat-tails, we didn't seem to see them in PEI. I don't remember in my speeches spending much time lionizing Diefenbaker, and certainly not in denigrating St Laurent. The odd crack at C.D. Howe and perhaps the insensitive Walter Harris might be in order. But certainly I didn't feel that I was running against Mr St Laurent; still less did I pick an oratorical row with the Liberal party. Unless I picked up some votes from the electors who had voted Liberal, I would be a loser and therefore a loner.

A few years ago an experienced and able journalist, Pat Best, asked me who helped me most in winning the 1957 election. Possibly he expected me to name John Diefenbaker. In any case he seemed somewhat surprised at my nominees, Liberal Walter Gordon and Tory Robert Stanfield.

I never tire of relating the great morale boost which Stanfield's 30 October 1956 accession to the Nova Scotia premiership brought me. I have repeated many times my comment to Isabel: 'I think now we can win the federal election too.' Nova Scotia's switch to the Conservative column was not lost on Island voters. Certainly the long-trailing PEI Tories received an enormous spiritual lift. Earlier in the year, Premier Hugh John Flemming of New Brunswick had won re-election. His victory was on 18 June. In the *Guardian* the next day there was a paid advertisement by the PC party of PEI warmly congratulating our New Brunswick brethren. As I recall it, Walter Hyndman had come up with the idea at a Tory executive meeting in Charlottetown the night before. Obviously he fast-talked someone in the *Guardian* to get the ad out in such record time. Putting it in simplistic terms, Island PCs were hitching a ride on the bandwagon of our neighbouring provinces. It did not hurt us in our drive to build up electoral momentum.

I didn't know Walter Gordon in 1956, and I'm not sure that I had even heard of him. But this stalwart Grit never went unmentioned in my campaign speeches. He was the chairman of the Royal Commission on Canada's Economic Prospects. That illustrious body came out with many recommendations for improving our national well-being, but I spoke of only one of them. This was the suggestion that the unemployed of the Atlantic region be assisted to move to other parts of Canada where jobs might be available. Gordon's report thoughtfully observed:

If it should turn out that there is not the necessary combination of resources in sufficient quantities to permit a substantial rise in living standards in the Atlantic region, generous assistance should be given to those people who might wish to move to other parts of Canada where there may be greater opportunities. But even if assistance is provided for those people who might be willing to move elsewhere, many people undoubtedly would prefer to remain where they are, despite the handicaps referred to ... People who so choose should at the same time be prepared to accept a different kind of life, or certainly life at a different tempo and lower levels of income.[1]

Anyone who knew the Maritimes would have realized that we had suffered for years from the outward migration of our people, especially those in their youthful and productive years. On television, on the radio, and at public meetings I scorned this proposal with all the righteous indignation I could muster. As I put it, no decent government should suggest that we move the Maritimers into more prosperous areas. The thing to do was to adopt national policies which would move the Maritimes into prosperity. I bridled at the suggestion that the people of the area where Confederation began should be shipped to Upper Canada on second-class, one-way tickets. I spoke from deep conviction but I also sensed that my tirades were striking a responsive chord. It would be impossible to quantify such a thing, but I'm sure that Walter Gordon brought many PC votes into the ballot boxes of Queens. Other Tory candidates in our region also drew political benefits from the distinguished Toronto businessman.

We had another gift from the gods in PEI. As a result of a statistical error or miscalculation on Ottawa's part, the Island had been overpaid on an equalization grant. Our wee province was put in the nasty position of 'owing' the federal government something like $1.5 million. In the post-Bennett era, provincial Grits had exalted the virtues of having the same team in power in PEI and Ottawa. Our little province did not have the luxury of disagreeing like Ontario, the Prussia of Canada, as Arthur Lower once described it. Nor could we be like Quebec, the pampered darling of Confederation. But after two decades of faithful alignment we were faced with a whopping bill. What price for staying on the same political team as the Ottawa biggies? We PCs urged Island voters to try another tack. Send those insensitive feds a message that we were capable of asserting our independence and our individuality. When, after special pleas from the Liberal provincial government, the St Laurent administration decreed that the 'liability' could be discharged in instalments and not necessarily in a lump sum, we Tories were unimpressed. I told my audiences that it reminded me of the kind-hearted farmer who was told that he must cut off the tail of his injured dog. He couldn't bring himself to do it in one fell swoop but, instead, cut off a bit each day.

In Queens the PCs benefited from the perceived niggardliness of the St Laurent government to the senior citizens. Despite their budgetary surplus they increased the old age pensioner's monthly cheque from $40 to $46. The Progressive Conservatives denounced this paltry increase and the Grits were dubbed the 'Six Buck Boys.' It didn't help them. Older voters and their kinsfolk are a powerful segment of the electorate, and the $6 increase has to go down as a major Liberal blunder.

Although I did not dwell on the issue, there were some Queens voters who resented the St Laurent government's handling of the Suez crisis. They felt that Canada should have supported the British-French invasion of Egypt. A few took exception to the prime minister's crack about the days of the European 'supermen' being over. But in the final analysis the Suez affair didn't have much effect on the ballot boxes of Queens.

The pipeline debate had not been forgotten, as the Grits had hoped. Diefenbaker, although he had not been a star in the parliamentary battle, made good use of the issue in the campaign. He waxed righteously indignant against governmental arrogance, and helped convince his audiences that it was a good idea to turn the haughty incumbents out. After all there were people voting in the 1957 election who had never lived under anything but a Liberal government. Many Queens voters, and not just devout Tories, told us it was time for a change. John Diefenbaker was coming on strong as a dynamic campaigner, and he was seen in the Maritimes as elsewhere as a new and interesting political figure. Mr St Laurent, then in his seventy-sixth year, sometimes appeared remote, tired, and bored by the whole thing. He was not good on television. Diefenbaker was. In the Maritimes we had two bright premiers who, with their organizations, gave full support to the federal cause. On the campaign front things were clicking well in PEI.

Progressive Conservatives in the Atlantic area attained an unprecedented measure of regional solidarity. On 11 May candidates and campaign managers from the four provinces met at the Brunswick Hotel in Moncton to map a regional strategy. I was impressed to meet so many PC candidates who, like myself, were making their political debuts. I was pleased to find them able, eager, and possessed of wholesome confidence for their futures. The conference was well organized. George Nowlan was a key figure and, with his ability and affability, set the tone. Dalton Camp, a native New Brunswicker and a major player in the national campaign, took an active role. From this campaign emerged the Atlantic Resolutions which were a regional platform for the Progressive Conservative party. The policy commitments were positive and possible, a far cry from the pessimism of the Walter Gordon approach. Many of the resolutions dealt with the kind of major corrective measures which had long been recognized as needed but too long denied. I am sure that every one of us at Moncton thought that we were in a position to do something really useful for our part of Canada. The two premiers were behind the resolutions and John Diefenbaker, to his eternal credit, adopted them as the holy writ for future Conservative government for action.

As I became more experienced in political campaigns, I realized that the leader's visit is a mixed blessing for the local candidate. In the first place, it requires a great deal of preparation, and many purely constituency functions are put off. For instance, it would be poor planning to have local meetings during the week the top brass was visiting. I recall that in 1957 Alan Scales, then an undergraduate and a PC, was assigned responsibility for the Diefenbaker visit. There were a great many things to arrange, from the composition of the agenda and the platform group to the sturdiness of the podium. Who was to receive him at the airport? Would there be a cavalcade from the terminal? Would he make any special visits to local VIPs? When was there to be a press availability session? In PEI there was always some concern about getting the leader into all three – later four – constituencies. Because of these local priorities, we often overworked the national leader, although it was the smallest province and might have been considered the easiest to cover. During his call on former premier W.J.P. MacMillan, Dief asked how things were going provincially. The old doctor replied: 'Not bad, considering we have a damn fool for a leader.' This was not the easiest conversational gambit to handle.

In 1957 Diefenbaker, like Drew in 1949, opened his campaign in the Maritimes and we had him in Queens early in the campaign. His Island-wide rally was held in the Rollaway Club in Charlottetown, which is not the greatest assembly hall in the country, but the meeting was a cracking success. He amused the audience, he interested it, he inspired it. There was much applause and the vibrations were good. Dalton Camp, the gifted wordsmith, wrote of the Rollaway meeting in his *Gentlemen, Players and Politicians*, likening it to theatre or a minstrel show with MacLean and Macquarrie as the end men:

Angus, sitting on the platform with his short legs crossed at the ankles, a fixed, dour smile on his square, dark face, motionless, his white socks gleaming. Heath looks inscrutable, his mouth turned down at the corners but smiling. White hair grows around the sides of a pink bald head, seeming like a halo under the spotlight, and grows long at the back. Macquarrie looks more like a Father of Confederation than Cartier.[2]

Dalton notes that at this meeting Dief shows that he has been reminded that Angus is not the only candidate in Queens, so he laid it on for both of us, 'spreading it thick.' He told the audience of Macquarrie that, along with his other values, 'we in the West toughened him up for a while.' It was all a veritable love feast. After the meeting Diefenbaker told us he had difficulty assessing the mood of a slightly sloshed heckler. Somewhat deaf, even in those early years, Diefenbaker thought the man was shouting

'Good-bye, John.' After sorting out the Island accent, he realized his friend was really saying 'Good boy, John.' After saying good night to the leader and his wife, some of us withdrew to my room for a nightcap and a highly upbeat appraisal of the day's event. Thus the prospect for victory in Queens was strengthened yet again.

As the national campaign wore on things got worse for the Liberals. Walter Harris wished to bring the $6 pension increase up to $10 but St Laurent said no. C.D. Howe was reported in big trouble with the western farmers. St Laurent's mass meetings were often a mess while Diefenbaker's popular appeal with the crowds was soaring. At Mr St Laurent's wind-up rally in Maple Leaf Gardens in Toronto the Friday before the election, an incident occurred which should have given us a hint of the depth of the Liberals' troubles. Just as the prime minister was getting into his speech a teenager walked up to the lectern carrying a St Laurent poster. He tore it up in front of the astonished prime minister. The chairman, doubtless fearing an assault on Mr St Laurent, grabbed the youth, who fell backwards down the steps, crashing his head onto the cement floor. Needless to say this took the shine off the big rally and, fairly or otherwise, added one final contribution to the label of unfeeling arrogance that was adhering to the Liberal party.

The day 10 June 1957 will long live in my memory. I took an early opportunity to get to the polling station in Victoria Hall where Isabel was one of our agents. Then I set out to visit the other polls in the constituency – I always enjoyed these activities. In truth there is little a candidate can do on election day except make ceremonial calls to the pollings stations. Once in a while one would detect a bit of tension in the air if there had been any incident or argument. Usually everything was orderly and restrained. About the only appropriate question a candidate can ask at the poll is about the voter turnout, and that is not a very profound inquiry. I called on rural polls in Western Queens and then headed for the Charlottetown district. Angus MacLean was following a similar pattern in the eastern part of the constituency. In Charlottetown I found a mighty row in progress between Bennett Carr and a Liberal activist, Mrs Gracie Roper. Bennett, in poll A, advised Mrs Roper that, since she was an agent for poll B, she was totally in error in intruding on the conduct of the voting in A. I declined to be drawn into this altercation. In the first place there would seem to be no chance of helping either myself or the situation, and besides I was anxious to get back to the Victoria poll to participate in the counting of the votes, and to share the moment with my loved ones. My mother was with us and my sister Mary had come up from Boston. As she put it, she wanted to be on hand to share the celebration, or, if it should go the other way, to help pick up the pieces.

Needless to say I was tense and eager as the vote tally proceeded in the Victoria poll. The 1953 results had underlined its status as a Liberal stronghold. McLure and MacLean had 53 and 59 votes to 104 and 101 for Matheson and Miller. When we finished the count on 10 June 1957 it was, to my great joy, a different story. I led the poll with 91, Angus had 77, Miller 82, and Matheson 74. A short while later our friend Howard Wood, a Liberal agent, told Isabel: 'With that kind of a vote in this poll Heath will win the constituency.' By that time I was out the door, down the hall steps, and heading up Victoria's main street to tell my mother and sister the good news. I guess that, like young David in his trip from Bethlehem to Jerusalem, I danced rather than walked the distance between the hall and my home. The emotions of my mother, unmitigated Tory, need not be delineated. That the first Conservative ever to win the Victoria poll was her son must have been a veritable cup of joy. But there was a disquieting moment for all of us. I had just relayed the news from the Victoria poll to mother, sister, and a few others when returns came in over the radio. The totals from a few Queens polls put me not at the top but at the bottom so far as the mainline parties were concerned. To say that we were all shaken and deflated would be inadequate. But, thank God, our sojourn in the Valley of Humiliation was of the briefest duration; the next and larger batch of returns put MacLean at the head of the Queens poll and Macquarrie second.

From then on the PC lead widened and, almost before I knew what was happening, I was the MP-elect for my home constituency,

the stomping ground of Chester McLure and John Myers. All of a
sudden we were in a joyous state of bedlam. The doorbell started
to ring; close friends and neighbours popped in without ringing
the bell. The telephone became active. One of our guests had let
little Flora out on to the veranda and thereby to the street. The
child had to be located. Congratulatory messages had to be received; arrangements had to be made to meet the media at several
locations. Murdock Stewart, our pollchairman for Crapaud, Victoria Tories, and people from the nearby polls dropped in. I remember giving Murdock Stewart a celebratory drink but I doubt
that I was able to 'light' long enough to get one for myself.

My dear mother, after many years of seeing her party trounced
by the Grits, was a little uneasy when I accepted the views of the
media who 'declared' me elected. Even when there was but one
more Queens poll to hear from, she counselled caution. 'You
know, dear, you can't trust some of them.' I presume she meant
Grits in general. In my overweening confidence I assured her that
the Green Road poll couldn't turn the thing around. She was right
about the Green Road results. Angus and I had 20 and 22 votes
respectively to 58 and 55 for Matheson and Miller, but, with a
plurality of nearly 1000 votes, I was not submerged by that one
poll.

The Maritimes were doing so well for the PCs from the very
beginning that the thought of a Conservative government was
assuming the shape of reality. So it was not just my victory but a
major political upset that we were experiencing. In 1930 John
Myers and Mrs Myers received at home election night. I would
be able and pleased to do that too, but 1957 was a different world.
We had to react to the widened role of the electronic media.

For the extremely important television coverage we had to go
to the transmitting facilities at Bonshaw, which was on the Trans-
Canada Highway, eight miles east of Victoria. After that we jour-
neyed another sixteen miles to Charlottetown. Not only was it
the geographic centre of Queens but also the place where the
other media outlets were located. We went to Charlottetown to
meet our own people and also the press, who were agog about
the political upsurge of the Tories in PEI and nationally.

It was, doubtless, a good harbinger of public life, but in many ways I had little control over my movements or my schedule on that far-off night when the people of Queens ushered me into my parliamentary career. After the big television interlude in Bonshaw, Isabel and I went on to the various public relations stops and ended up at the Community Centre on Stewart Street in Charlottetown. Here Angus and I with our wives Gwen and Isabel were with our jubilant supporters. Many of them, like Reagh Bagnall, Frank Myers, and Philip Matheson, could remember when the Tories last won nationally with the two Queens seats but many in the hall were too young for such memories. I hope we weren't boastful or blinded by our success but it was a great night – indeed an unforgettable experience. I'm sure I shook a thousand hands on that glorious evening. It was a long evening what with the many media interviews and many speeches. But I did not feel weary!

As the hours passed and the electoral returns from across the province and the country accumulated, we realized that it was, in political terms, a night of nights. PEI for the first time had gone solidly Conservative in a federal election. Orville Phillips, a dentist and RCAF veteran, had carried Prince constituency, a feat no Tory had accomplished since 1904. I had heard good things of my taciturn colleague during the election campaign, but I didn't think that he would crack that Grit bastion, Prince County. I knew the Eastern colleague John A. Macdonald better and was less surprised when he won. In the spirit of the Atlantic Resolutions the PCS of PEI stressed the 'Island Team' and I believe it helped all of us. When the election campaign began, the only 'sure' PC winner was Angus MacLean. To have four of us make it before 8:30 p.m. was not a bad Tory contribution from Canada's smallest province.

With the media looked after, we went to the home of Dr J.A. (Joe) McMillan for the finale of the glorious evening. Before 1957 I never knew Dr Joe McMillan. During my campaign, both before and after the issue of the writ, there was much anxiety about my identification. The Liberal slogan 'Who's this Macquarrie?' was getting under the skin of some of our PC chieftains. Good people

·that they were, they didn't wish to settle for one seat in Queens
if better activity and shrewder planning might give them two. So.
while the new candidate wasn't doing all that badly – in fact quite
well, some said – they felt they must make assurance doubly sure.
Their solution was to have someone really 'in' with the Queens,
and perhaps the Island, community become a patron of the new
candidate. It would be a great coup if that leading doctor and
prominent member of the community, Joe McMillan, could be
inveigled into supporting the number two PC candidate. After all,
Charlie McQuaid, our somewhat unofficial but engaged campaign
chairman, was Joe's brother-in-law. Joe was clever, articulate, and
respected, especially by his fellow Catholics. But while his background was Conservative no one regarded him as a card-carrying
Tory.

So it was that I was to be presented to Queens voters on the
media by a person deemed to have closer identification with the
community than I had. Once again I had a important exercise in
what might be called self-salesmanship. More was required than
in the case of Dave Stewart, since Dr Joe would be addressing the
total constituency, not just a party gathering.

Before presenting myself to my new would-be patron, I heard
the matter discussed by many leading Tories in Queens. Everyone
thought it was a great idea but some cautioned me against disappointment if the very busy doctor decided not be become involved. But as the talk went on I sensed a discreetly growing
confidence that the idea was becoming more feasible. Friends of
Dr McMillan were sounding him out, and the project was being
advanced. In many parts of Canada there is a tendency to see
Roman Catholic voters as being more kindly disposed to the Liberal party than to the Tories. How much these historic items
affected voting patterns during my career it would be hard to say.
But I recall Phil Matheson's view about getting Dr Joe McMillan
on side. 'The Catholic people of the Island are very proud of him
and they have every right to be.'·

Thus it was after much thought and discussion that I found
myself one afternoon face to face with Joe McMillan. I was not
surprised to find him a very impressive person. He was busi-

nesslike and direct. There was a little small talk. He asked me some sharp and searching questions. I supposed many of them were to elicit information. Others were to give him a chance to 'diagnose' me. Although less taxing than my oral PHD exams at McGill, it was, I knew, an enormously significant meeting for me. I realized that here was a man of influence and rare ability. He was clearly a very confident person, purposeful and intellectually sure-footed. The object of the exercise was to give him a chance to size up the new candidate. But I found myself appraising him. It did not require the full interview to convince me that whoever inspired the idea of bringing him into the campaign certainly knew what he was about. This man would be a tower of strength and a powerful advocate.

When it became clear that he would be supportive I was immensely grateful, and drew sustenance from a feeling of reassurance that everything would be well. Shortly after the interview, the party acquired time on television and radio and Dr McMillan presented me to the constituency via the airwaves in a brilliant and eloquent performance.

With dramatic flair Dr McMillan began his speech with: 'Tonight I break a lifetime of political silence' ... he then went on to give a highly favourable – yet convincing – appreciation of candidate Heath Macquarrie. So great was the impact of this radio-TV talk that George DeBlois approached Charlie McQuaid a few days later asking that he be allowed to make a personal contribution to my campaign by underwriting the printing of the speech in a pamphlet form and its distribution to the electors. This is the sort of gesture which comes more easily in a small constituency where people know each other better and perhaps care a bit more too. At John Myers's funeral, Mr DeBlois had promised his help and he had found a worthwhile way of making it available.

Later Dr McMillan, who had become quite a television star, appeared in panels with Angus and me, and also once with the four PC candidates on the Island. He spoke at public meetings and was powerfully and effectively supportive of our cause in 1957 and subsequently. He was always able to come up with some way to liven proceedings. I remember his advising me always to quote something from the latest edition of a newspaper. 'You can't let them think that you are not right up to the moment on these things.' I don't suppose Dr McMillan's role in 1957 was unique in the election of that year but it was unusual. Often a candidate is aided by an incumbent in another jurisdiction. Our MLAS were helpful to us in federal campaigns and we sought to return the favour in provincial contests. A former office-holder often is asked to use his influence in a campaign. But Dr McMillan was not in any of those categories.

So it was not surprising that Isabel and I ended up at Dr Joe's late on the night of 10 June 1957. So jubilant was our celebration at his and earlier ports of call that when we arrived in Victoria at dawn the birds were singing sweetly. So were we. And Joe McMillan's contribution to that night of victory went far beyond the excellent champagne with which we toasted the national PC victory in that evening more than thirty years ago.

Although Dr Joe remained a good friend to the end of his days, he was not involved in my last four elections. Knowing him was a great dividend in my political career. Happily, too, I was able to sustain the connection through his family. His son Tom moved my nomination for Hillsborough in 1968, the election in which he cast his first vote. His speech was excellent, truly of Dr Joe calibre. Ten years later, with my unconcealed support, he became my successor in Hillsborough. He won election to the House of Commons in 1978, 1980, and 1984, and served as minister of the environment.

But we did not stay on cloud nine for long. Although the congratulations and good wishes continued to come in by mail, telephone, and in person in the days following 10 June, so also did the demands and responsibilities of my new position.

The St Laurent government did not turn over the seals of office until 21 June, but many of my constituents did not wait that long to bring their problems and aspirations to my attention. In Prince Edward Island there are few labour-intensive industries. This always resulted in an outward flow of people seeking employment in metropolitan centres where business and industrial establishments had large numbers of employees. My mother and father had worked in Boston. Many of their siblings had found jobs and settled there. My sister and two brothers had followed a similar pattern in their generation. For those remaining Islanders who were not self-employed, the government was a very important potential employer. Combine this economic fact of life with a community where intense partisan interest prevails and you have little difficulty understanding that patronage is a subject of more than academic interest.

When in June 1957 I became a Progressive Conservative MP supporting a government in office, I found myself with a host of constituents who had been in a patronage desert for twenty-two years. Loyal and active Tories blocked from government appointments since 1935 were ready for their turn. I heard many lurid stories about the ruthless efficiency with which the Grits had wielded the axe and turned out the Tories in 1935. One of my people told me that his father had been a lighthouse-keeper but 'on the very day after the 1935 federal election the Grit poll chairman called and relieved my father of the key.' That was fast work. The son was now willing to take over the lighthouse and wished his party to act with the same dispatch as the Liberals in 1935. Others wanted jobs as potato inspectors, fishery inspectors, crewmen on Department of Transport vessels, and many other 'government jobs.' Some even thought that the road crews on the highways should be immediately replaced, even though the Liberals were still in office provincially. But two sources of jobs transcended all others in importance. These were the Prince Edward Island National Park, which stretched across the north side of Queens County, and the car ferry service from PEI to New Brunswick. Jobs on the car ferry were considered plums, and the National Park work patterns fitted in well with unemployment insurance procedures for the seasonally unemployed. Prince Edward Island fishermen could only fish for a limited time each year. The Department of Fisheries allowed only a part of the year for them to derive a living from their real calling. If you can fish lobsters for only two months, some other source of income must be found, and the unemployment insurance benefits are essential.

According to many of my stalwart party activists, the National Park had been an exercise in Liberal patronage. After the passage of thirty-four years, I still recall vividly the great pressure to do something about that nest of Grits who still had jobs in the National Park. More than once I was called to PC meetings in the 3rd Queens area and told that something must be done. At one such indignation meeting, I recall the Queens constituency president Charlie Phillips, after many names had been mentioned, rising from his place to offer advice. Charlie was a good man and not known as profane but he said simply: 'Mr Chairman I say that every damn one of them should go.' Naturally Covehead Hall, the meeting's locale, rang with applause. I knew this view, although instantly popular, was unrealistic and extreme. But at that phase I recalled my father's dictum: 'Those who got their jobs because of their politics should walk the plank when their party is out.'

Patronage occupied me during all my waking hours and sometimes beyond. During the 1984 election campaign the PC leader Brian Mulroney promised 'jobs, jobs, jobs.' In a somewhat different way this slogan would have described my basic preoccupation for two or three years after my election in 1957. When I went to PC headquarters on Great George Street in Charlottetown there were lineups. When I arrived home in the evening there were people there. One night the girl who was helping with the children was doing her hair and wished to get from the upstairs bathroom to the porch for some reason. She discovered the Bonshaw poll committee in the living-room and the Bradalbane committee in the dining-room. With great ingenuity she decided to go out the front door and come in the back door and thus reach her destination. But as she slipped out she found the French River committee on the veranda.

While I could and did respond to pressure from Queens Tories, I couldn't grant full and immediate satisfaction of all the demands. I had no magic wand of patronage and no amount of incantations of open sesame could get all the Grit appointees out of the National Park and Tories in their place. Some of my political advisers suggested I walk into the park and simply tell the superintendent whom to hire and to fire. Perhaps some of my Liberal predecessors had and used that kind of clout. For me at least, it was not quite that simple in 1957. I was inexperienced in the relationship of the elected politician to the professional bureaucrat. In practically every other department I was soon able to work out a sane and harmonious relationship. But the poor superintendent and I didn't get on all that well. Indeed there were times when I was at odds with the minister and his office in Ottawa. Between militant constituents and stubborn officials, my lot, like the policeman's, was not a happy one. In fairness to the superintendent he could hardly by expected to welcome a wholesale change of park personnel once the summer program was underway. On the other hand, things did get better and the park developed well when a new and more astute and diplomatic superintendent took over a year or so later.

It was an enormous task to assuage the yearning for government jobs. As for the car ferry service, a crown corporation, the CNR, was involved in the hiring process. From Queens alone there were enough job applicants to man ships far larger than those plying the waters between Borden and Cape Tormentine. I once told the CNR chief executive in Charlottetown that I could man the Queen Mary! But things had happened in the years since the Bennett government. Many of the crew members had tenure. Unions were becoming important. In short, there was no great source of jobs here, but as new positions opened up our people did very well.

The situation on the car ferries demonstrated how patronage had changed in a couple of decades. The civil service had earmarked more and more government positions. The spoils system was not what it had been in earlier years. Putting it simply, a change in government didn't automatically bring a potential harvest of appointments for the party faithful. Lighthouse-keepers and all sorts of people drawing Government of Canada cheques were not vulnerable to the winds of political change. The springs of patronage had been drying up in the twenty-two years between the Bennett and the Diefenbaker eras. I found it extremely difficult to explain this development to many of those most interested in firing Grits.

My heavy involvement in patronage matters was underscored

by the fact that the other Queens MP, Angus MacLean, was called to Ottawa to join the Diefenbaker government as minister of fisheries. I had to man the constituency fort alone and deal with all the job-seekers, not because Angus dropped the problems on me, but as a minister in a new government he was compelled to be in Ottawa most of the time.

There was one appointment which drew more attention and more applicants than any other. In a mood of overconfidence the St Laurent government had left ten Senate vacancies unfilled when they dissolved Parliament. One of these was from PEI. The last Conservative senator from PEI was John A. Macdonald, appointed in July 1935. A large number of Island PCs wanted the Senate seat. The 'Senate vacancy' file in my study was soon bulging. I had many letters, visits, and phone calls from would-be senators and their backers. There were some splendid people among them; many had rendered notable service to country, community, and party. Frank Arnett, our PC candidate in the 1930 and 1935 elections, called to see me. He felt a commitment had been made by Bennett and the party long ago. He would have made a first-class senator. H.F. McPhee seemed to be the first choice. After his untimely death there developed a consensus, although less strong, that Pat Morris should get the appointment. When he too passed on, it went to J.J. MacDonald, a stalwart PC, war veteran, and community leader for Third Queens. I was quite supportive of J.J., but as in all things I felt very sorry for all the other good people who had to be passed by.

When he was appointed to the Senate in 1957, J.J. became a cherished addition to the Island's parliamentary team at Ottawa. He was straightforward, unpretentious, and realistic. I shall long remember the first day I visited him in his Senate office on the east side of the Centre Block. I asked: 'Well J.J., how do you like the Senate?' His laconic reply spoke volumes: 'By God, how could you help but like it?' I have yet to hear a better appreciation of senatorial appointment.

It is easy to remember my first few months as an MP as one long, frustrating struggle over patronage allocation. Certainly it was a tough time but, I reiterate, not a surprising one. My anguish came from the fact that, even at my best, I could do so little to assuage the anxieties of my friends and supporters.

The summer of 1957 was filled with dawn-to-dark dealings with my constituents, but other aspects of the job assumed their priority. The PC national caucus was called to Ottawa for pre-session meetings. It was a veritable love feast and Prime Minister Diefenbaker was lionized. I remember one discordant note and that concerned a statement by Howard Green, public works minister, in which he knocked the patronage system. His widely quoted utterances had been anything but popular with my party supporters. At the caucus meeting I found that my Tory constituents were by no means unique.

It was during that caucus visit to Ottawa that Prime Minister Diefenbaker told me that I was to go to the upcoming United Nations General Assembly. 'Mac, I want you to go down there on the political committee and make a name for yourself.' To be the Canadian representative on the prestigious political committee struck me as a very high rating for a freshman MP. It turned out in fact that I was a parliamentary observer. In that role one is able to get an overview of the UN and of the total Canadian delegation. I found it a delightful and eventful experience. Along with everything else it was my first visit to New York.

I enjoyed the UN so much that I could have stayed in New York until the General Assembly wound up in December. But our PM was leading a minority government and I was recalled to Ottawa when the session got underway. Two senior Tory MPs, Harry White and Frank Leonard, were left at the UN. Although I gave high priority to the UN session, I regarded my role as MP as even more important, correspondence from Queens was answered promptly. I did broadcasts from UN radio to Charlottetown and Ottawa. I also wrote articles for the *Guardian* on UN matters.

Those months in the latter half of 1957 were jubilant times for me as a political animal. Not only was my party back in office, but we were doing well. The new prime minister was a hero. The party was filled with ambitious hopes of accomplishing great things. They were heady days. Howard Green, as well as being minister of public works, was a very effective House leader. Most of us were delighted when Sidney Smith joined the cabinet as secretary of state for external affairs on 13 September 1957. The opening of Parliament on 14 October was a special event with the Tories sitting in the high seats. The speech from the throne, outlining the government's legislative program, was a brilliant forecast of useful and helpful legislation. For the party and for the country, all the omens were good. For us Tories in 1957 it was most assuredly the best political period since 1930.

In his remarks during the throne speech debate, Mr St Laurent declared that the election had brought about not so much a change of government as a change of faces. As documents go, speeches from the throne are often innocuous and prolix. That written by the government in 1957 was more solid than most. Its content demonstrated that 10 June had brought more than a change of faces on the treasury benches. In tackling long-neglected inequities the new administration showed a strong sense of purpose. It was clear that promises and commitments made by the Progressive Conservatives were to be taken seriously. The Queen read the government's words, which announced:

In the legislative program to be laid before you, it is fitting that mention should first be made of measures to improve the lot of the senior members of our society. Accordingly you will be asked to increase old age security pensions and to shorten the period of residence required to qualify for them. Changes will be proposed in the terms of assistance offered to provincial governments to enable them to increase the payments to be made under the Old Age Assistance Act, the Blind Persons Act and the Disabled Persons Act to a corresponding level.

You will also be asked to increase the scale of war veterans allowances and to enlarge the groups to whom they are paid. Changes will also be proposed in several sections of the Pension Act.

In order to assure to the farmers of Canada a fair share of the national income, you will be asked to enact a measure to provide greater stability in the prices of their products. Every possible effort is now being made, and will continue to be made to seek new markets for agricultural products as well as to regain those that have been lost.

Due to inability to market their grain, prairie farmers have for some time been faced with a serious shortage of funds to meet their immediate needs. In order to permit them to receive an advance payment for the grain they can expect to deliver this year you will be asked to authorize a system of cash advances for grain stored on farms.

My government will strive to secure additional markets for the products of our fisheries and to promote the development of international rules to safeguard the living resources of the sea.

My ministers believe that a national development policy carried out in co-operation with the provinces, and in the territories, is needed to enable all regions of Canada to share in the benefits to be realized in developing the resources of this great nation. It is their intention to propose to you from time to time programs and projects to implement this policy.

As an immediate start upon a program of more extensive development in the Atlantic provinces, you will be asked to authorize, in joint action with the provincial governments, the creation of facilities for the production and transmission of cheaper electric power in those provinces. You will also be asked to provide assistance in financing the Beechwood project which has been under construction in New Brunswick.

My ministers will advance this national development policy further by initiating new discussions with the government of Saskatchewan in order to make possible the early commencement of construction of the dam on the South Saskatchewan river.

My ministers are pressing for a favourable settlement of international problems in connection with the Columbia river to clear the way for a joint program with the province of British Columbia to develop the immense power in the waters of this river.

My ministers will place before you a measure to ensure that those working in industries under federal jurisdiction will receive annual vacations with pay.

You will be asked to approve bills relating to certain railway branch lines, amendments to the Canadian and British Insurance Companies Act, and, in so far as the other business before you permits, to several other statutes.

I shall always regard those exciting far-off days in 1957 as the most satisfying time of my twenty-two years in the House of Commons. After the new cabinet had been sworn in, the irrepressible George Nowlan said: 'Show us where the cabinet room is.' Not a single minister of the new cabinet had ever served in government. The only privy councillor in the caucus, the Honourable Earl Rowe, was not included in Diefenbaker's cabinet. Yet with very few exceptions those greenhorns did a good job. They were a far more sure-footed group than some that followed them in later years.

Under our system, the spotlight's glare is so concentrated on the prime minister that his cabinet colleagues are not readily visible. Party leaders are not given to sharing the limelight and, certainly, John Diefenbaker loved a centre stage reserved for himself. But through caucus, the House of Commons sittings, and party events, the other ministers made some impact. The one I liked and admired most was Sidney Smith. While for some time he was a little ill at ease both in his parliamentary and departmental roles he had an innate affability which endeared him to me. I was shocked and saddened when on 17 March 1959 the prime minister literally ran from his Commons desk behind a messenger, who had come in with a whispered message. He quickly returned to tell us that Sidney Smith had suffered a fatal stroke. Only hours before Dr Smith had told me how happy he was with the way things were developing in the department and how much he looked forward to working with Norman Robertson, the new under-secretary. I rejoice that I was at the 12th and 13th General Assemblies of the United Nations when Sidney Smith was minister. Along with his charm and warmth his treatment of the delegation was impressive. At our morning meetings he gave us clear, candid, and wonderfully insightful accounts of his discussions with other diplomats.

Another man very easy to like was George Nowlan. Shrewd politician and skilled parliamentarian, he could have handled a much bigger assignment than that Diefenbaker gave him. He was minister of national revenue until August 1962, in the last days of Diefenbaker's political empire, he made Nowlan minister of finance.

I never really got to know G.R. Pearkes. Of course I wasn't used to the company of generals. Perhaps his English accent was a bit off-putting. It may well be that had I known him better I would not have considered him stuffy.

Ellen Fairclough, the first woman to sit in a federal cabinet, was another minister I did not know well. She struck me as a very bouncy type of person but I don't have many other recollections or impressions. Michael Starr of Oshawa was said to be the first minister with an ethnic background not French or British. In 1991 it is hard to believe that the fact should make headlines. I remember Mike Starr as a pleasant, unpretentious man. He was widely popular too, but apparently not a great favourite with the hot-tempered Liberal front-bencher Lionel Chevrier, who during one testy exchange threatened to go across and smash Starr in the jaw. At this stage the aggressive Don MacInnis of Cape Breton, who never feared a fight, shouted out: 'Yeah, but who's going to carry you back?'

Léon Balcer was also under rewarded and downgraded in the cabinet assignments. Doubtless this stemmed from Diefenbaker's grudge over Balcer's alleged hostility to him at the leadership convention of December 1956. He was named solicitor general. Today, with greater emphasis on internal security and more public discussion of capital punishment, the solicitor general is a sensitive and more important portfolio than it was in 1957. Certainly it was not a great plum for Balcer, who was Diefenbaker's highest profile francophone minister.

As I look back upon their performance, I am filled with admiration for the way in which the early Diefenbaker government handled things. In little over three months Parliament passed a spate of legislation of immense benefit to the people of Canada. I used to say on political platforms that the new government gave priority to the little man and the poorer provinces. Having always believed that a government should help most those citizens who most need help, I was especially pleased with the increase in old age security and other pensions. By a quirk of fate the Tories received credit for the $6 boost the niggardly Grits had granted, as well as for the $9 increase put into effect by the Diefenbaker government. The $6 had not been added to the monthly cheques until the Grits were out of office.

Although not precisely forecast in the speech from the throne, the other measure over which I was especially delighted was the Atlantic Provinces Adjustment Grant. This provided $25 million to the four Atlantic provinces. In the 1990s the sum may not seem large but in the mid-1950s it was no mere bagatelle. On the platform, in the media, and everywhere, I unashamedly boasted of the new government's attitude to the Atlantic region. I compared Diefenbaker's largesse with the penurious St Laurent attitude which had our little province 'overcharged' by $1.3 million. I also found numerous occasions to contrast the new approach with the Walter Gordon formula. For Prince Edward Island, the Atlantic Provinces Adjustment Grant meant an additional $2.5 million for the province to spend as it wished – with no strings attached. Considering that for the fiscal year ending 31 March 1957 the total PEI budget was $12,495,533, it is not strange that a government-supporting MP from the Island would exalt the Diefenbaker government. In later years John Diefenbaker and I were to fall out of favour one with the other, but I never hesitated to praise him for his treatment of the four seaside provinces. His sensitivity to our region was appreciated by the voters of Atlantic Canada. Except for Joey Smallwood's domain, Newfoundland, Progressive Conservative candidates did well in my region during the Diefenbaker heyday.

We weren't idle during the 23rd Parliament. The legislation was coming thick and fast, the committees were busy, and there were extended sittings. Often we spent Saturdays at our House of Commons desks. I made my first speech on 13 November. This was in the throne speech debate, which allows great latitude in subject matter. In this general debate certain traditions are followed. The opening sentence is given over in praise of the mover and the seconder of the motion. One also congratulates the Speaker on his appointment. This was a pleasure, since the handsome, poised, and impartial Roland Michener was already off to a good start. I showed my historic bent, if not my pedantry, when I recalled Sir Robert Borden's comment that a Speaker must be impartial, firm, courteous, and above all patient. I expressed the view that Speaker Michener had demonstrated all those virtues.

The throne speech debate offers an unparalleled opportunity for members to reveal a bit of their mental and spiritual make-up. Regrettably the press gallery never had the sense or took the time to listen to or read throne speech debates after the party leaders had spoken. Few reporters in the press gallery wrote of anything beyond the often theatrical exchanges during question period. This was the case before the televising of the House of Commons. The television cameras didn't create the art of hamming it up. They only accentuated it.

I had a great time making my maiden speech although I was unlucky enough to have the adjournment bell come in the middle of it, necessitating a return bout at the next sitting. The rules of the House forbid the reading of speeches. The ban is a gentle one since most speeches are in fact read. In my academic career I thought students deserved something better than the reading of a lecture so I had grown accustomed to the *ad lib*. If the auspices are good this makes for a better speech, but it is draining on the intellectual, emotional, and neural strength of the person speaking.

Over three decades have passed since that first speech in the Commons on 13 November 1967. I still like one of my opening paragraphs:

A maiden speech, as one member of this house observed years ago, is always a valuable exercise. To the new member it gives a rare opportunity to experience a deep feeling of humility, an attitude good for the soul as well as for the mind. To the other members of the house it affords an opportunity to show indulgence, one of the greatest virtues of men and especially, it is said, leaders of men.

Having once again posited my humility (a declaration some of my friends sometimes question), I went on to a subject on which I felt no modesty or humility. In the throne speech debate the tiro MP must laud his constituency. This was for me an easy assignment. Along with all its other virtues I unashamedly congratulated PEI for being the only 100 per cent province; I noted that it had, for the first time in its history, elected a full slate of PC candidates on 10 June. I recalled that 'twas not ever thus, that provincial Tories had been blanked out in 1935, and that neither they nor their federal colleagues had done too well since.

I obviously felt I owed my House of Commons colleagues reasons why PEI had repudiated the once popular Liberal party. My first item was the miscalculation which put little PEI $1.3 million in debt to the Dominion government. I explained the mathematical blunder as a result of a grave Ottawa miscalculation of PEI's population rise. 'It was because many of the young people of our province found it necessary to go to other parts of Canada and so, piling Pelion upon Ossa, we not only lost a great many of our people at the productive and energetic period of their lives, but we had to pay for it on top of that.'

I quoted with approval a comment from Premier Stanfield of Nova Scotia and urged that in making Canada work we must consider more than economics. I said that we voted Conservative because we expected a better deal from Ottawa. No Island politician should make a speech without mentioning PEI potatoes, which command a premium price on all agricultural commodity markets. As I lauded our spuds, the venerable Reverend Dan McIvor contradicted me by saying Irish potatoes were best. While highly respectful of the benevolent cleric who had vanquished Mansion in Fort William in 1940, I refused to budge on potato superiorities. When I ended my speech the dear old chap came over to tender warm and generous congratulations.

In concluding my speech the next day I referred approvingly to the proposal to construct a causeway between PEI and the mainland. I noted how important was transportation to PEI politics through the years.

I noted that I had hoped the old age pension would have risen to $60 but that I had accepted the explanation that the increase was 37.5 per cent over 1949 as against a 23 per cent increase in the cost of living. Perhaps this part of my speech was by way of self-preservation since the Queens election advertising had cited a $60 figure. Possibly it was an attempt to 'cover my ass,' to use an expression now much in vogue in the bureaucratic world.

There were some personal motives in my praising the government for increasing the allowable absence for recipients of the old age pension outside Canada. My father and mother liked to go to Boston to be with my sister and brother for the Christmas season. In order not to lose old age pension cheques they had to be back in late March – not a great time for weather in PEI. Many times my volatile sister used to say: 'Ma, you can get along without that old age pension cheque.' Highly practical in her response, my mother would say: 'Yes, but I can get along better with it.' She was but one of multitudes of Canadians who after years of service to this country had been harried by foolish regulations.

I concluded my speech with a discussion on foreign affairs and an expression of pleasure at the amount of space given in the speech from the throne to international matters.

Later in the session I spoke on a motion of human rights, talking about our own country's inadequacies in the field. I also dealt with the value of the Bill of Rights as against common law. My final speech in the short 23rd Parliament was on the Atlantic Provinces Power Development Act in which I quoted PEI Premier Alex Matheson as saying the St Laurent government had not given the Maritimes half a deal.

Before any of these speeches I received my first answer to an order paper question. This was on the construction of a PEI–New Brunswick causeway.

As I look over the yellowing Hansard containing my parliamentary utterances in my first year on the Hill I wonder how much I have changed since those halcyon days. It is likely that my arteries have changed more than my objectives. I see the muted degree of partisanship. My devotion to my party was there then as it still is, but the expression was restrained in comparison with the remarks of many of my colleagues. I didn't find it necessary to get into expressions of adulation for my party leader. Until rereading my maiden speech I had forgotten that in that early effort I had singled out Robert Stanfield.

My concern about and love for PEI was there as it always is, and my gratitude for my provincial homeland, an interest in the history of my country and my party, and an emphasis on world affairs remain today. Perhaps in 1957 I was more the academic than I am in 1991. It would be traditional to denigrate the brash freshman who made his initial foray into House of Commons debates in 1957. But while some values have been reinforced and new causes taken up, I find that my long years on the Hill have been evolutionary rather than marked by drastic alteration or traumatic conversions. My interest in the Caribbean was in its early stages. My deep and abiding concern for the victimized Palestinians was yet to be stirred. But whether or not the child is father of the man the emotional and intellectual ingredients of the mellowed senator of the 1990s were basically in place in the maiden speech of the neophyte of 1957.

While I had met a good many Progressive Conservative MPs before my entry into the House of Commons, most of the Liberals were but names in Hansard. I had long admired Lester B. (Mike) Pearson, but I didn't meet him until we were colleagues in the House. Similarly with Jack Pickersgill, Paul Martin, Jimmy Gardiner, and the other bigwigs of the Grit establishment. I was quite shattered by the appearance of Mr St Laurent. He seemed a broken and bewildered man. I frequently saw him walking the halls alone. In the parliamentary dining-room he was often at a table by himself or with his son Jean-Paul, the member from Témiscouata. Once or twice I had a little conversation with the former prime minister, and his grace and courtesy were still appealing. But the manner in which many prominent Grits had dropped their once-courted leader was sad and shocking. It doesn't pay to lose in politics. Mr St Laurent would have been saved a great indignity had he retired before the 1957 election as he had sometimes thought of doing. But, of course, the Liberals were not going to give up the great vote-getter of the 1949 and 1953 contests. It was all sad, sad, sad.

After the surprising defeat on 10 June 1957, Mr St Laurent did tender his resignation and on 15 January 1958 the Liberals chose Mike Pearson as his successor. I watched the television coverage of the Liberal convention and heard Pearson's boastful promise to lead the great Grit party to victory soon. No doubt he was carried away by the euphoria and hype which is a part of political conventions. Within days his promise of a quick victory led Pearson into a deep vale of humiliation. On the very day he took over as leader of the opposition Pearson moved an amendment which, if carried, would have been regarded as want of confidence in the government, necessitating an election. But despite his bravado at the convention he really didn't want an election and, just in case the NDP and Social Credit might be tempted to vote the Tories out, the Liberals tried to put forward an amendment which the smaller parties would under no circumstances support. With this in mind, under Jack Pickersgill's auspices, the Liberals produced a dilly of an amendment. It roundly condemned the government for its economic and other policies and called for its resignation and replacement by a Liberal ministry without the formality or bother of an election.

It was an unhappy début for poor Pearson. Diefenbaker's response was devastating. He scorned the timidity of the new Liberal chief who wanted office but not an election. He compared Pearson's strident statement at the convention with his tepidity in the House. 'On Thursday there was shrieking defiance; on the following Monday there is shrinking indecision.' In the face of Diefenbaker's blistering attack and his exposés from a hidden economic report of the St Laurent government predicting recession, Pearson was an almost tragic figure. It may be inelegant so to phrase it, but Diefenbaker wiped the floor with Mike Pearson that day. As Jack Pickersgill, no enthusiast for Diefenbaker, put it: 'I doubt if a more effective destructive speech was ever made in Parliament.'[3] The next day, the eloquent Colin Campbell wondered whether Diefenbaker really believed in the humane slaughter of animals. He thought that the prime minister had used quite an arsenal against one forlorn sitting duck already crippled by a self-inflicted wound.

I'll certainly never forget the explosive day when Diefenbaker nuked Pearson, but in that stirring period another drama was before us when the 23rd Parliament went into history. Early in the day on Saturday, 1 February, Howard Green asked the pages to leave the government lobby, told members to guard the doors and then he let us in on the big news. The PM was to fly to Quebec where the governor general was in residence and obtain a dissolution. We were enjoined to secrecy and told to be on hand when Diefenbaker returned. Thus, skilfully and appropriately, Howard made all of us a part of the drama. I'm sure every one of us heeded his instructions and appreciated his shrewd exercise in teamwork.

It was a bit tedious to then have to deal with the supply items of citizenship and immigration before the House in committee of the whole but in late afternoon things livened up. Diefenbaker generally had a good sense of drama and he certainly had it then. As six o'clock, the adjournment hour, approached, he entered the chamber which had been fluttering with rumours all day. After the report of the committee of the whole had been received and the Speaker resumed the chair, Diefenbaker rose and said: 'Mr. Speaker, today I made an historic trip by air to the citadel of Quebec City ...' then followed criticism of Liberal obstruction and the need for dissolution. There were a number of points of order and it was clear that some opposition members expected that other party leaders would have a chance to respond to Diefenbaker. In this they were disappointed. After announcing that he had obtained a dissolution and that the election date was set for 31 March, the prime minister concluded by saying: 'As the proclamation points out, this parliament is now dissolved.'

The sitting of Saturday, 1 February 1958, was a triumphant one for us Tories but there was a tiny cloud in the picture for those who chose to see it. The ever-courteous Speaker Roland Michener was of course unable to hear the protests of the opposition members who argued that since the order in council had already been signed before he rose, Diefenbaker himself had no right to speak. Michener, declaring his view that 'this House of Commons has no further existence,' said it only remained for him to leave the chair. But he did ask to say one word on his own behalf: 'I do so with regret because of the co-operation I have received from all members of the house on all sides.' On this comment from a very fine Speaker, the 23rd Parliament went into history. One of the briefest, it was probably one of the best in our nation's existence.

Nearly thirty years later Jack Pickersgill had some caustic comments about Diefenbaker's coup of 1 February 1958, later dubbed by Liberals 'Black Saturday.'

There was not the slightest excuse, nor the least vestige of constitutional justification, for the dissolution of a Parliament which had been elected only seven months before and in which the government had just won a crucial vote to keep it in office. Yet the governor general apparently raised no question when Diefenbaker asked for a dissolution.'[4]

As the former Liberal minister saw it, Diefenbaker's action was the closest approach to a claim of absolute power for the prime minister ever made in self-governing Canada. But the state of the public mind was such that 'this virtual coup d'état was not publicly challenged.' Pickersgill confesses that he thought of doing something but admits that in the wake of the confidence motion fiasco he was not riding high as a strategist.

Pickersgill was right about the state of the public mind. John Diefenbaker's stock was so high and the Liberals in such low waters that no one was troubled about constitutional improprieties or House of Commons procedures. The Progressive Conservatives were holding an annual meeting at the Château Laurier on the weekend of 1 February and a more jubilant assemblage could not be imagined. Everyone was in high spirits and before the night was over, some of us were into other spirits too.

Although all the omens were good, overconfidence in politics must be avoided at all times, and so we in Queens lost no time in getting our campaign under way. Despite the season we ran an active and well-organized campaign starting with a heavily attended nominating convention on 20 February. there followed meetings throughout the constituency often starring members of the new cabinet. We also had a good advertising campaign and frequent television and radio appearances with Dr Joe McMillan a feature performer. Diefenbaker spoke in Summerside in Prince constituency, as well as in Charlottetown, and was lionized. The Atlantic candidates had another get-together, this time in Halifax because the media opportunities were better there. Everything seemed in order but we weren't taking any chances. One day as we were having lunch in Milton's Old Spain restaurant in Charlottetown a constituent asked us how we thought things were going. Both Angus and I replied with caution, indicating that we hoped everything would be OK. Whereupon our hearty constituent said: 'You damn fools, if you don't know you're going to sweep things this time you're the only two people in Queens County that don't know it.'

He had it right. On election day our victories were huge in Prince Edward Island terms. A few more votes and our Liberal opponents would have lost their deposits, an unheard of thing in PEI for candidates of the old-line parties.

The Liberal candidates were J.O.C. Campbell, a prominent Charlottetown lawyer, and E.D. Reid, successful businessman and potato dealer. On television Campbell used to challenge us to point to one new job in PEI created by the Diefenbaker government. It's never smart to respond to the other fellow's taunts or challenges so we didn't. I could have referred to some recently hired Tories on the National Park and the car ferries but somehow I didn't think that was what Campbell meant!

The vote totals were MacLean 13,969, Macquarrie 13,480, Campbell 7540, Reid 7787. 'Twas a famous victory. Although I worked hard in 1958 I could have won without lifting a finger or even being in the constituency. In 1957 I had had to fight for my success and survival every inch of the way. In 1958 I was borne into office. The Diefenbaker coat-tails were like a flying carpet in that winter campaign of 1958. The same political momentum which brought me such a stunning victory in Queens carried a massive contingent of PCs to Parliament Hill. In a House of Commons of 265 members 208 were Progressive Conservatives. It was the most sweeping victory in the history of our country. Nova Scotia, Alberta, and Manitoba joined PEI in the 100 per cent Tory club. The Liberals didn't win a seat west of Ontario and in that great province they only elected 14 of their candidates. The CCF dropped from 25 to 8 seats, losing their leader M.J. Coldwell and the veteran Stanley Knowles in the slaughter. The Social Credit party, which won 19 seats in 1957, was swept out altogether in 1958. Quebec elected 50 PCs to 25 for the Grits. In the distribution of parliamentary seats, the Progressive Conservatives were the only national party on the scene. It was a broadly based mandate such as no government had ever received before. We were amazed by its magnitude. Even the voter turnout, 79.6 per cent, was an unprecedented high. Diefenbaker had asked for a working majority. This the Canadian voters had given him. But they gave it in such a generous manner as to produce a sweep. When a bandwagon gets rolling it sometimes gets overcrowded.

Although the immensity of the victory had not been foreseen, there had been general expectation that the PCs would win. Nineteen of the Liberals elected in 1957 decided not to take to the hustings in 1958. The 1958 election was, perhaps more than any earlier one, a combat between the leaders. In this it brought our electoral confrontations more in line with the battles fought every four years in the United States. Parties and candidates were of some importance but the election was highly presidential in style and substance. Those of us who fought the battle in the constituencies found national headquarters had a much heavier impact than ever before. Allister Grosart was very much the chief architect of the contest and American values and clichés were not too difficult to detect.

In a gladiatorial encounter of this kind, the Liberals were outclassed. Diefenbaker had long been a magnificent campaigner. He was at his best in the 1958 election. He stormed and barnstormed across the country with obvious relish, slashing the Grits with hyperbolic delight. The famous 'hidden report' provided ample grist for his histrionic mill. He told the Canadian voters that the Liberals had been warned of the economic problems but, instead of doing anything about them, they covered up, they hid, they ignored. It was great theatre. As the first winning Tory leader since R.B. Bennett in 1930, he was almost a novelty. People whose lives had been lived under Liberalism were excited and exalted.

They were ready and eager to touch the hem of his garment and, of course, to vote Tory – even though the party's campaign literature was short on the name of the party but long on that of its leader.

The unfortunate Grits and their hapless leader were undermatched from the beginning. Leaster Pearson was a man of wit, charm, and warmth. But he was sadly deficient when placed before a large audience which, of course, is the very kind of audience a political party wants during an election campaign. Bill Foster, the young son of my friend and fellow Tory Gerald Foster, graphically described his first sight of Pearson on television: 'He sounds just like Foster Hewitt when the Leafs are losing.' Pearson tried to defend his style, or lack of it, by staking out a higher road than his opponent. Not for him were 'quivering clichés or evangelistic exhortations, oracular fervour, or circus parades.' And in one of his best lines, he warned the Canadian people not to 'confuse motion with progress, agitating with action, or platitudes with performance.' When I heard him I thought it was all very apt but all apt to be ignored.

As I noted earlier I did not agree with those who thought Bennett's 1930 campaign was evangelical. I could not disagree with those who so dubbed Diefenbaker's performance of 1958. He excited and stirred great gatherings of Canadians as he told them of his vision. The vision was largely of the North but had broader parameters. A few years later, Martin Luther King proclaimed: 'I have a dream.' The Bible declares that young men shall see visions and old men dream dreams. The terminology is interesting. The young Southern Baptist and the older Canadian Baptist evoked the ethereal, and for a while it took on a glowing substance.

The Diefenbaker vision added a degree of nobility and vigour to Canadian nationalism. It was heady stuff in the 1958 Canadian election. The Liberals, naturally, sought to belittle all that 'vision' stuff but, as Lucy Maud Montgomery might have put it, they should have saved their breath to cool their porridge. Canadians weren't reading any footnotes or listening to any 'buts.' They were prepared to follow Diefenbaker and were enthused about the northern dimension of Canada. When any Tory speakers did take the trouble to discuss their Grit detractors they invoked history to their cause. Had not the ancestors of those same Grits mocked John A. Macdonald's opening of the great North-West which brought us truly *a mari usque ad mare*? Had they not jeered that there was nothing in the West but Indians and buffalos? Had they not described the northern acquisition as nothing more than an ingathering of igloos? In the euphoria of 1958 the Liberals were seen as a bunch of sour naysayers.

I don't remember the word 'charismatic' being used in 1958. Nor did I use it in the political science courses I gave at university or hear it applied to politics in my student days. But, as something of a Presbyterian activist, I had heard the word in a religious connotation. To many Canadians it seems that the word was hewn from the rock when Pierre Elliott Trudeau dropped onto our national stage. But if we think of charisma as the capacity to inspire followers with devotion and enthusiasm – a dictionary definition – John Diefenbaker had it in abundance in 1958. I doubt if he was divinely inspired as were the apostles on the day of Pentecost long, long ago but he was a consummate actor and could get through to the audience, which in this case was the Canadian electorate. He certainly stirred and aroused the Canadian voters who, while given to excesses and excitement over such things as the Grey Cup and the Stanley Cup, rarely let their nationalism show. In 1958 it showed and glowed under the fervent Diefenbaker inspiration. It was a splendid election and exciting theatre.

In the 24th Parliament, which convened on 5 May 1958, the Progressive Conservative caucus had to change the room for its weekly meetings. The largest of them all, the Railway Committee Room, became the scene of our Wednesday morning conclaves. It was a long time before I became acquainted with all our new members. Some of our Quebec MPs I never did get to know well. In the chamber there were more of our members sitting on the Speaker's left than there were Liberals and NDPs. It is customary on Thursday for the opposition house leader to ask the government house leader to outline the business for the coming week. One day a smart BC Tory, John Drysdale, sitting in the front row of the rump, rose with serious mien and directed the traditional inquiry to Government House Leader Gordon Churchill. All of us in the chamber seemed to enjoy the ploy.

It was difficult for any Tory to be anything but jubilant in 1958. John Diefenbaker was the man of the hour, the darling of the press, and the object of something like adulation from his party. It seemed that the world was his oyster; everything was going his way. One journalist declared he was the luckiest politician ever. Who else, he asked, could elect 208 members and one of them not be Charlotte Whitton? The feisty and brittle Ottawa mayor had run in Ottawa West but lost to veteran Liberal George McIlraith.

Few of us thought about it at the time and fewer still mentioned it, but in the magnitude of the victory lay the seeds of destruction. Too much was expected of a government so strongly outnumbering its opponents. Political leaders, by their very nature, have a high quotient of vanity. In 1958 we had a host of MPs anxious to be noted by their leader. One western member introducing Diefenbaker in his constituency declared that even John A. Macdonald paled into insignificance compared with John Dicfcnbaker. The rank and file were prepared, nay eager, to be adulatory. The victorious leader did not discourage them.

It was not surprising that, after their electoral triumph of March 1958, the PCs should be forgiven for extreme confidence in their invincibility. Strong feelings of self-esteem often lead to hubris. A comfortable majority would have been better than the sweep of 208 seats. But party technicians cannot fine-tune the electorate's expression of will.

The party enjoyed a honeymoon until the 1950s ended. The Gallup Poll held favourable, party unity was strong, the prime minister's image was a positive one. The Diefenbaker government continued and extended many of the policies which had made it popular during the 23rd Parliament.

The appointment of Major General Georges Vanier as governor general in September 1959 was a most popular move. A distinguished soldier and diplomat, Vanier was the first francophone to occupy the post and it would be difficult to think of anyone who could have filled the office with such grace and distinction.

He became a father figure and in himself an embodiment of the bilingual basis of our country. The strikingly beautiful Madame Vanier was unforgettably impressive. In their dignified style, their gracious charm, and true appreciation of their role, the Vaniers were, I believe, the most distinguished denizens our historic Rideau Hall ever had. Every day of their occupancy of our nation's highest office, I rejoiced at the rightness of the appointment and felt gratitude that the first citizens of the land brought inspiration to so many Canadians in all walks of life. In some more recent successors, I have not found such compelling reasons for pride.

Nineteen fifty-eight was a big year for the Progressive Conservative party. It was also an eventful one for the Macquarries. An American political observer noted that the Kennedys liked to have their wives pregnant during election campaigns. We didn't plan it that way but Isabel was noticeably in the family way that year. Indeed some of my supporters were suggesting that it might be prudent to have her vote at the advance poll. This was not necessary and Iain Heath did not join the family until 18 April. He was thus born into a country that was overwhelmingly Tory.

Before the election I had heard from a former Brandon colleague, Cecil Evans, about a conference of parliamentarians sponsored by the Society of Friends. This gathering scheduled for August was to be held in Clarens, Switzerland. Needless to say, I was most anxious to go, although the necessary family accommodations were not easily orchestrated. Fortunately, we were able to make highly suitable arrangements for all those left behind.

Neither Isabel nor I had ever been to Europe and the prospect of the Quaker conference filled us with anticipation. In those days one was advised to make one's first trip to Europe by boat. We went from Montreal to Southampton on the Italian liner the ss *Homeric* and found every day totally pleasant. Good weather, good music, good food, and good shipboard company made the whole voyage a most happy episode. Our first trip in a British train from Southampton to London had all the satisfaction of a novel experience.

Considering the paucity of my contacts and the primitive nature of my communications at the time (MPs had no long-distance telephone rights), our itinerary was remarkably full and interesting. As an executive officer of the Canadian Branch of the Commonwealth Parliamentary Association I knew the general secretary, Sir Howard D'Egville, who had founded the CPA in 1911. He and his people gave us every courtesy. We toured Westminster, met some British parliamentarians, and received half-fare passes on British Railways. George Drew, now our high commissioner in London, received us warmly and his deputy, George Ignatieff, helped make arrangements for our later visits to the continent.

Watson Jamer, agent general for the Atlantic provinces, was kindness itself. He had secured reservations at the Kensington Palace Hotel, a lovely hotel but too rich for our budget. After two nights we moved to the top storey of Prince's Lodge.

Later we went by the Flying Scotsman overnight to Edinburgh and were charmed by that Athens of the North. We attended morning service at St Giles Cathedral where that grim zealot, John Knox, had thundered against the devil so long ago. His 1958 successor was much less sulphuric, which was just as well. I never liked the Hell and Damnation type of sermon. St Giles was an impressive and prosperous-looking congregation but there were many empty pews on that summer morning.

On our arrival at the railway station in Edinburgh, Isabel had sprained a tendon in her leg and required attention at an infirmary. For the rest of our British trip she received medical care at each of our stopovers. We developed a warm appreciation of their medical service. Had a fee been levied for these services our budget would have been still further assaulted. I couldn't but compare it with our experience in New York the preceding fall. At our hotel she had paid two successive doctors $10 in an unsuccessful attempt to have a cinder removed from her eye. The comparison reinforced my view that state medicine was not such a bad thing!

Our trip by rail to Inverness was a moving experience. Inverness itself is a little gem of a city and the Station Hotel there a charming hostelry. Nearby Culloden evokes exquisite and painful memories for those of us of Highland ranks. A number of Macquarrie supporters of the Bonnie Prince had been taken to the New World in 1747 as prisoners of war. It is often said that Scotland has much history, mostly tinged with sadness. It has a rugged and striking beauty and the trip from Inverness, the capital of the Highlands, down to Oban is one of majestic glory. Oban is a bustling and friendly fishing centre and an important entrepôt for the Hebrides. After staying overnight we went over to Tobermory, on the beautiful island of Mull, the homeland of some of the Macquarries.

My visit became something of a pilgrimage when I set out from Mull to the nearby island of Ulva, the ancient seat of the small Macquarrie clan, which had been visited by Dr Samuel Johnson and James Boswell in 1774. From the Mull mainland I signalled the boatman for the little island and he promptly rowed over. His first question: 'Is her ladyship expecting you?' was slightly off-putting, for while I had written the owner of Ulva, Lady Congleton, I had had no reply from her concerning our visit. I assured the Ulva boatman that Lady Congleton would, I was sure, receive us. But neither my credentials nor my appearance was altogether impressive. After hours in heavy rain we looked anything but spick and span, to say nothing of appearing important. A frantic search in all my sodden pockets failed to find a House of Commons card. When the dubious old oarsman brought us to the entrance of Ulva House the best I could do was send in a message on a serviette which I had inadvertently pocketed at breakfast time in the Tobermory Inn. At this stage Isabel asked the traditional wife's question: 'Are you sure you know what you're doing?' But the granddaughter of the Canadian Lord Strathcona was not easily shaken from her hospitable instincts and we were well received in the ancestral heart and home of the Macquarrie clan, albeit we were the only Macquarries on the island.

The visit to Old Scotia completed, we travelled to Paris, Brussels, Bonn, and Bern. Even in 1958, a mere thirteen years after the carnage and destruction of World War II, the prosperity of the area was apparent. Paris was beautiful, exciting, and expensive as I expected it would be. At the Brussels World Fair we were well treated by Glen Bannerman, our commissioner. In the Belgian capital, a senior member of our embassy took us under his wing. At Bonn, the city of Beethoven, we were entertained at dinner by Escott Reid, our interesting and dynamic ambassador to West Germany. In Bern, the quaint and quiet capital of Switzerland, we were house guests of the Canadian ambassador, Edmond Turcotte. At all of these stops in Europe, we enhanced our awareness and appreciation of the cultural inspiration to so many Canadians.

The week-long conference of international parliamentarians at Clarens was stimulating and interesting. The Quakers, with their commitment to world peace, clearly showed their expertise and contacts on the international scene. Theme Speakers were of a high calibre, including Philip Noel Baker, Bruno Kreisky (the Austrian chancellor), and Herr Holstein, one of the intellectual fathers of the European Community. There were four congressmen from the United States, two members of Ireland's Dail Eireann, two from Britain's House of Commons, and representatives of the national parliaments of France, West Germany, Austria, Italy, and Norway. Paul Martin and I were the two members from the Canadian House of Commons.

I have been at many conferences of parliamentarians in the decades since. They were held in many locations under widely varying auspices. Yet somehow I think of the 1958 gathering as the most pleasant and effective of them all. While we had some recreational events such as a trip across the lake to Evian and visits to Geneva and other historic Swiss centres, it was a low-key, low-budget affair. A few of us went for a daily pre-breakfast swim. Paul Martin, Isabel, the socialist lady from Austria, and Charles Haughey of Ireland were among the early morning dippers.

Paul Martin was a good fellow delegate. He guided Isabel and me around the Palais des Nations in Geneva where he had served on the Canadian delegation to the League of Nations in the late 1930s. He also took us to Reformation Park where great statues of the major Protestant reformers look down from the noble platform. Paul recalled that he had also introduced Mackenzie King to what he jokingly called 'these awful people.'

Paul Martin used the Canadian Mission facilities at Geneva more than I did. He once came back in the limousine and gave me an official envelope which he said he had opened by mistake. It was a wire from Sidney Smith asking me to be a delegate to the 13th General Assembly. He congratulated me on this, but a day or so later I was the bearer of news which took him aback. This was to the effect that the House of Commons had supported the Diefenbaker government's resolution providing simultaneous electronic translation of House of Commons debates. Martin seemed to feel that this move might well consolidate Tory strength in the province of Quebec. While the move didn't bring immediate political dividends to the Progressive Conservative cause in Quebec it was a splendid development. I am proud that my party took the initiative. Prior to that, while MPs had the right to use either English or French, they in effect didn't have the right to be heard and understood.

The exciting European safari over, we returned to Canada, family, constituency, and Parliament. My stint at the United Nations kept me in New York all fall of 1958. Because of family responsibilities, Isabel was rarely with me. I found it a very busy period, filling as I did the Canadian chair on the fourth committee. I kept up a heavy correspondence with my House of Commons office and with the constituency. I also made frequent radio broadcasts from UN radio not only to CFCY in Charlottetown but also to CFRA in Ottawa.

Things went well in 1958 and also in 1959. By 1960 it was apparent to many Tories that our days of easy popularity were over. The glowing vision of early 1958 was fading. The energetic and purposeful thrusts of the early days were not so apparent. There were many outside the party, and some within, who feared that the prairie crusader was not, in fact, a good administrator. It was said that the country was suffering from Diefenbaker's difficulty in arriving at decisions. One critical journalist opined that the prime minister preferred to keep some major decisions dangling because as long as the matter was unresolved many people were dependent upon him.

Then too there were problems on the economic front. The small, aggressive, and well-organized parliamentary opposition made capital in the House of Commons about unemployment, inflation, and the weak Canadian dollar.

Four Liberal front-benchers – Pearson, Paul Martin, Jack Pickersgill, and Lionel Chevrier – used question period to good effect. They were known as the Four Horsemen of the Apocalypse and were adept and persistent in casting gloom and anxiety on the government's sins of omission and commission.

6

Out with Dief

Sometimes I am guilty of understatement. Once, in the House of Commons, I declared that I was probably not John Diefenbaker's favourite member of the Progressive Conservative caucus. A chuckling Flora MacDonald later told me that my assessment was not faulty. On another occasion I was confessing that if the then-reigning Liberal prime minister, Pierre Trudeau, offered me a Senate seat I would accept with alacrity and that in fact I would have been delighted to go there under a PC ministry but that I was never called. The gentlemanly Harold Danforth of Essex-Kent said: 'I'm sure the Chief wanted you to go somewhere, but I don't think it was to the Senate!'

On my part I had never voted for John Diefenbaker at any national convention. Possibly there are people and personalities whose chemistry is antithetical. Yet I was an early admirer of the prairie MP from the time he entered the House of Commons in 1940. As I saw it, he championed many good causes and put forth his eloquence on behalf of worthy humanitarian crusades. Perhaps he was a wild-eyed populist, as Valerie Knowles described him, but I thought he was a valuable addition to the Conservative party. He gave us new dimensions and broadened our appeal. That such a bright star should shine in the Stygian darkness of the Grit fiefdom of Saskatchewan made him all the more a Tory gem. I followed Diefenbaker's career, read his speeches, and often quoted him.

But, when I became acquainted with him, my enthusiasm for the man diminished rather than enlarged. I found him vain, suspicious to the point of paranoia, and extremely difficult to converse with no matter the subject. If manners indeed make the man, as William Wykeham, the bishop of Winchester, put it long ago, I early found myself put off by both the manners and the manner of the man Diefenbaker. Those extravagant qualities and gestures which made him such a hit with partisan audiences seemed to put his credibility in doubt in a direct or face-to-face situation. In short, I often found myself questioning his intellectual integrity and his sincerity. If some of his emotions and sentimental commitments were phoney might not many others be equally dubious?

So I was not totally surprised when the lustre began to fade for the electorate by the time we had reached the 1960s. The man with the vision was seen by an increasing number of Canadians as a man of indecision. Too often he was moved not by pragmatism, but by his prejudices. In 1958 the province of Quebec joined the rest of Canada in giving massive support to Diefenbaker. In part, the success was attributed to Premier Duplessis allowing or ordering his Union Nationale fieldworkers to get out and work for the prairie potentate and the PCs. But even had Duplessis sat out the federal election as was his custom, Quebec would have gone Progressive Conservative. Not having one of their own as national Liberal leader in 1958, they could do the previously unthinkable, and vote Tory. Had St Laurent not been replaced by Lester Pearson, the federal Liberals would not have been trounced in 1958 despite Diefenbaker's appeal or Duplessis's collaboration.

The Tory sweep of fifty of Quebec's sixty-five seats in 1958 was a magnificent breakthrough. Its magnitude made all the more painful the plummet to fourteen seats in 1962. There were many reasons for this drop and not all the responsibility may be charged to Diefenbaker. He did not speak French or even read it very well.

But in those days a leader's ability to communicate well in French seemed to be much less important than it is now.

The tragically early death of Paul Sauvé, the dynamic successor to Duplessis, had profound repercussions on the federal Progressive Conservative party. I had hoped that this admirable young man, son of one of R.B. Bennett's ministers, would one day become the national leader of our party. In his hundred days as premier of Quebec, Sauvé had offered new dimensions to the barnacled Union Nationale. There had been an opening towards the federal institutions of government. Had Sauvé been in office longer the national government and party might have found an earlier appreciation of some of the powerful and sometimes turbulent forces motivating Quebec's social and political developments.

It is surely an important priority of a political leader to maximize the potential contribution of the members of his caucus. Many of our fifty Quebec colleagues in the 24th Parliament confessed that they never felt useful or much wanted. For part of that time we didn't have simultaneous translation in the House and certainly not at our caucus meetings. Diefenbaker was responsible for correcting the first shocking deficiency by having facilities installed in the Commons. Few anglophone MPS spoke French, and communication between members from Quebec and other provinces was inhibited. Sometimes, too, there were reflections of the attitudes of a party long dominated by English-speaking Canadians, some of them not noted for their broadness of outlook or interest in the aspirations of francophones. I recall a special caucus to discuss a private member's bill to provide bilingual cheques for the federal government. While I was not a constant participant in caucus discussions, especially in those days of my callow youth, I did express my astonishment at the hostility to two languages on Dominion government cheques, considering that our paper currency had been bilingual for a long time. I said that the people of my constituency would accept them in Chinese so long as they were negotiable. This incident occurred in the 23rd Parliament where we were in a minority. Fortunately our caucus eventually realized the sensitivity of the situation and voted for the bill. But it did reveal some rather niggardly views.

In spite of the Commons translation and bilingual cheques, I cannot remember Diefenbaker ever showing much awareness of the urgent need for the party to reach out to Quebec. Much of his failure stemmed from his passionate fondness for nursing grudges. Léon Balcer, a member of the House since 1949 and a popular man with the national party which he had served as national president and youth president, could have been enormously helpful to Diefenbaker. But Balcer was essentially outside the pale even when he was in the cabinet. Diefenbaker never forgot or forgave Balcer for his hostility and plotting at the time of the 1956 convention. He could have been a useful Quebec lieutenant, but Diefenbaker didn't want a Quebec lieutenant. As was often the case, Diefenbaker, despite his massive vanity, was motivated by impulses of insecurity even when he had 208 seats in a House of Commons of 265 members. To him plots and plotters abounded. As the years went by, in fact, the number of true believers decreased until the Diefenbaker enthusiasts lost their majority status. From the Prairies, where support had been modest in the 1957 election, came most of the real stalwarts. Much of Quebec, the cities, the youth, and the academics became cynical. As early as 1960 it was clear that the glorious days were over. After 1958 there were no more electoral crusades. The best we could do was stage a series of holding operations.

In the election of 31 March 1958 the PCS won 54 per cent of the popular vote compared to 33 per cent for the Liberals and 10 per cent for the CCF. This lead decreased in the Gallup polls until the polls of 28 September 1960 showed Liberal popularity at 43 per cent and the PCS at 38 per cent. It was in those years that John Diefenbaker gave frequent expression to his contempt for polls: 'Polls are for dogs!'

But while pollsters in the 1960s were much less important in the electoral process than they are in the 1990s, it is always better for a party to stand high in these samplings of voters' opinion than to trail. Many concerned Conservatives found the negative readings disquieting. The cancellation of the Avro Arrow contract was the most traumatic single event in the years between the 1958 and 1962 elections. I recall frequent and highly emotional discussions at our weekly and sometimes special caucus meetings. More than once the prime minister described the Arrow as a beautiful and magnificent aircraft, but one that by the time it would be in production it would be obsolete. Such problems in the field of sophisticated technology are not unknown today. Through all the agonizing weeks, there was no doubt about the gravity of the decisions which had to be taken. There was no lack of awareness of the serious impact of the unemployment which cancellation would create. Nor was the political leadership insensitive to the pride many Canadians felt in producing a plane of such sophisticated capacity. There was much discussion about the loss of skilled technicians and engineers in a highly competitive and increasingly important phase of industry. In retrospect, the importance of the latter was under appreciated, since the bulk of the Arrow's designers and creators were lost to the United States where they could continue working in their field.

But while it was by no means a wanton blunder, the Arrow cancellation was poorly handled. The abrupt closing of the plant and layoff of 11,800 Avro employees in one day were viewed as brutal acts. The government tended to blame Avro management for the shoddy treatment of the workforce. But the Canadian electorate stored its resentment not against Avro and its belligerent president, Crawford Gordon, but against John Diefenbaker and especially his candidates in the affected regions. John Pallett, whose constituency had a heavy concentration of Arrow workers, saw his whole life pattern shattered by the Avro Arrow closure. He was but one of many Ontario Tories whose political future was blighted by the traumatic event.

The Arrow fiasco accentuated a problem which seemed always to bedevil the Diefenbaker government – unemployment. Surprisingly, in the light of R.B. Bennett's experience, John Diefenbaker did overcommit himself on his guarantees to protect Canadians from the pains and pangs of unemployment. His opponents lost no time in resurrecting his promises and renewing the oft-used chant of the real Depression era: 'Tory times are hard times.' At political meetings across the land, the Four Horsemen of the Apocalypse and their kind paraded the jobless figures and shamelessly blamed Diefenbaker and his government for the problem. The figures remained stubbornly high despite a host of governmental make-work programs. Unemployment insurance benefits were extended, technical schools were built at a rapid rate, but still the jobless statistics were bad.

Year	1957	1958	1959	1960	1961	1962	1963
Percentage unemployed	4.6	7.0	6.0	7.0	7.1	5.9	5.5

In later years I saw other governments unsuccessful in their efforts to bring about full employment. For years under Pierre Elliott Trudeau the figures were bad. But no one seemed to receive the opprobrium that fell upon the Diefenbaker government. Was it that we later grew accustomed to unemployment? Or were the Grits of the late 1950s and early 1960s better, sharper critics than the Tories in opposition?

While our constitution provides that five years is the life of a Parliament, in practice elections are generally held at four-year intervals. Since the last contest had been on 31 March 1958 it was generally assumed that 1962 would be an election year. Certainly there was much talk about it. John Diefenbaker took an almost childish delight in teasing the press and the country about dissolution. There was much talk in caucus.

Diefenbaker's indecisiveness had become well-known by 1962, but it must have been difficult for him to find a good time to go to the country. Public opinion polls were not encouraging. On 20 January 1962 Gallup found 42 per cent supporting the Liberals to 38 per cent for the PCs. In March and May the Liberals widened the margin.

The PCs were faced with serious economic problems. The unemployment figures were stubbornly high. There was anxiety about the rising cost of living. The pegging of the dollar at 92.5 cents U.S. came during the campaign and added to our political lexicon the word 'Diefenbuck.' The Liberals had thousands of these printed and circulated them enthusiastically. A weak Canadian dollar seemed a terrible thing in 1962. Today some of us would have to rack our memories to recall the Canadian dollar standing as high as 92.5 cents. Economics used to be called a dismal science and Diefenbaker was never very successful in discussing the subject. He and Finance Minister Donald Fleming were made to appear bewildered and incompetent on the currency question.

The government was also seen to be incompetent in its dealings with James Coyne, governor of the Bank of Canada. His was hardly the sort of public office designed to make him a popular figure, and Coyne's personality was not endearing, but the government found it difficult to silence or sack this difficult person.

Economic issues predominated in the 1962 campaign. There was none of the drama of the pipeline, or the vision of 1958. The state of the nation's economic health makes for a gutsy issue but not necessarily an exciting one. Diefenbaker liked to have someone to oppose. A cast of unseemly and ill-intentioned 'theys' were an essential backdrop to a Diefenbaker crusade. Some of this flavour was found in his attacks on the bureaucrats, eggheads, and other 'Pearsonalities' supposed to be leading the evil Grit attack on the Man of the People. In a fascinating way he also effectively denounced these new figures as 'the same old bunch.' There were suggestions our winner of the Nobel Peace Prize was soft on communism. Canadian voters whose ancestry traced to Eastern Europe were led to believe that the PCs were prepared to stand up to the Soviet overlords in their homeland. Some PCs contended that the Russian leadership was pro-Pearson. There was considerable interest in Diefenbaker's tale that his strong speech at the UN on behalf of the Ukrainians had prompted Nikita Khrushchev to pound his shoe. A good story, but the boisterous Soviet leader had done his thumping act three days after the speech of the Canadian prime minister, when Britain's Harold Macmillan was at the podium.

But while the beleaguered and sometimes disbelieved prime minister was not the man who stormed the country in 1957 and 1958, he was still a tough and competent campaigner. There were nasty and violent scenes at some of his meetings, especially at Vancouver and Chelmsford, Ontario. The old fighter stood his ground and became something of an object of sympathy. The stance of an underdog with his back against the wall was one he made the best of. The Gallup figures over the period of the 1962 campaign are highly interesting. On 9 May it was 45 per cent for the Liberals to 38 per cent for us. On 9 June, 44 Percent to 36 per cent. On 16 June, two days before polling day, it was 38 per cent to 36 per cent. Election day percentages were 37.5 for each party. Diefenbaker's campaigning must be given a major share of the credit for stemming the Liberal advance.

It must also be remembered that Pearson was a poor campaigner and despite all the slick u.s.-style techniques, the Liberals failed to set the political heather ablaze. True they increased their House of Commons seats from 48 to 100, but they had expected to do much better. One spoiler for them was the province of Quebec. The pcs dropped from 51 to 14 seats but the Liberals won only 35. The surprising beneficiary from the Tory crash was the Ralliement des Créditistes de Québec, which captured 26 seats. Their leader, Réal Caouette, a folksy spellbinder, captivated many Quebec voters, especially those in rural areas. He lured voters to his movement who might otherwise have gone Liberal and given Mike Pearson a majority. I didn't meet Caouette until we became House of Commons colleagues. I thought him one of the most interesting and colourful members of that assemblage of practising politicians. He was witty, sharp, and a fascinating debater. I later found myself breaking with my party and supporting his motion not to adopt the Union Jack as our second flag, but to ask the next Commonwealth leaders' meeting to adopt a flag to be used as a Commonwealth symbol by all members of the association. Perhaps Caouette might not have done so well had either of the old-line parties been led by a Québécois, but I think he would have made a major impact in any case.

I did not enjoy the 1962 election much. I had seen John Diefenbaker at countless caucus meetings and had become aware of his endless capacity for spite and bitterness. I had grown accustomed to a government with the biggest parliamentary majority in history acting as if it was in a minority position. Long before I met L.B. Pearson I had admired his statesmanship and the kudos he had won for Canada on the wide screen of international affairs. The promulgation of the notion that he was soft on communism was a despicable strategy. The most ardent Diefenbakerites in our party were not the Conservatives I most admired. But I kept my reservations and anxieties on a private plane. It was later to be alleged that internal party division had weakened the Tories in the 1962 campaign. Not so. We did not all exult in the orgies of hero-worship which marked many of the MPs at meetings of the caucus and of the House of Commons. But every Tory incumbent did his or her best.

Until the disruptive and kamikaze Liberal caucus of John Turner's leadership, it was conventional wisdom to regard the PC party as being the most obsessively self-destructive of all time. A more careful look at the bitterly spiteful leadership years of John Diefenbaker might present a picture of a Tory party amazingly homogeneous and patient under provocative, blustery, and often paranoic leadership.

In religion a Calvinist and politics a pragmatist, I worked very hard in the 1962 campaign. I did have a good many requests to speak in other constituencies and felt duty-bound to accept most of them. This is a touchy area for any person running for the House of Commons. Because you are interested in your party's future as well as your own, you cannot simply say: 'Please leave me in my own bailiwick.' On the other hand, it is most dangerous to be seen by your own constituents as cocksure or uncaring. Thus, I avoided being in another province when a major political event was being staged in Queens or in a neighbouring PEI riding. Never wishing to be too far from home, my 1962 canvassing and guest speaking was pretty well confined to Atlantic Canada.

I 'ran scared' in every one of my eight elections and certainly in 1962. But down deep I hoped to win and could not bring myself to believe that a government with such powerful parliamentary backing would be ousted. On 18 June things turned out very well for me. I received 11,590 votes in Queens as compared with 13,480 in 1958. My running mate, Angus MacLean, had 12,117 as against 13,969 four years earlier. I never did grow to appreciate MacLean always leading me at the polls but, since I always won comfortably in the dual riding of Queens, as I did later in the single-member constituency of Hillsborough, I didn't spend much time on the statistics. He had, after all, earned a high place with the electorate before I entered the lists.

The outside experts of the fourth estate tended to explain the Tory sweep of PEI as a result of the Diefenbaker government's pre-election promise to build the causeway which would link PEI to the mainland. I couldn't be anything but publicly in favour of the permanent link after the Conservative provincial government of PEI proclaimed itself the 'Party of the Causeway.' But I never took it all that seriously. I knew too that, while it had its enthusiastic Island supporters, there were others of a different opinion. As old Mr Leard of Cavendish put it, 'It's the foolishest thing I ever heard of.'

It is a rare election campaign that doesn't produce abundant promises. Just a few days before dissolution, Léon Balcer, minister of transport, told the House that a new car ferry would be built for the Wood Islands–Caribou, Nova Scotia, route which served eastern PEI. When that happy warrior George Hees came to the Island, his first question to me was: 'What do you want me to promise them at the meeting?'

I doubt whether Island voters were lulled or gulled by the dangling of future goodies. But there was a widespread sense of gratitude for what the Diefenbaker government had done for the little province. As Premier Shaw often put it, 'John Diefenbaker is the greatest friend the Island ever had.' In the other Maritime provinces a similar feeling helped hold the area against any strong Liberal advances. Premier Stanfield was highly supportive.

But even in Atlantic Canada things were much tighter than in 1958. The Liberals gained three seats in New Brunswick and recaptured two traditional Grit seats in Nova Scotia. In Newfoundland the Liberals won six seats, leaving Jim McGrath of St John's East as the only Tory. Even in Prince Edward Island there were ominous signs. While Margaret Macdonald and Orville Phillips retained Kings and Prince ridings, the vote for each was less than the total vote of their opponents.

In the Prairies, as in the Maritimes, the electorate proved itself capable of political gratitude. The energetic minister of agriculture, Alvin Hamilton, was given credit for finding vast markets for unsold wheat, prices were good, and even the weather co-operated to give the PCs a smashing electoral triumph. Out of forty-eight seats the Conservatives won forty-two. The Liberals, Social Credit, and the NDP divided the other six seats equally. Tommy Douglas, the recently chosen leader of the NDP, was trimmed in Regina. Pierre Elliott Trudeau is generally credited with alienating the prairie voters, but the Liberals had lost the West long before he became *El Caudillo*.

On 18 June 1962 the Maritimes and the Prairies brought the only good news the PCs received. No fewer than 92 caucus colleagues went down to defeat, but with 116 members we still outnumbered the Liberals by 17. I walked with sadness down the corridors of the Parliament Buildings as I noted on the office doors the names of many close friends who had been casualties of the electoral battlefield. It was not a knockout but the party certainly hit the mat in 1962.

One good thing about the election was that for the first time we were given a decent respite from parliamentary sittings. John Diefenbaker had always seemed to be obsessively devoted to keeping the House of Commons in session. He clearly did not believe the old maxim that, for the government, the worst day when the House is not sitting is better than the best day when it is. But he was in no hurry to have his minority government meet Parliament in 1962. In fact the 25th Parliament did not convene until 27 September. Since there is no place like PEI in the summertime, I was delighted.

The electoral damage of 1962 left Diefenbaker dazed and badly shaken. In 1957 he hadn't thought he was going to win. In 1962, surrounded by a host of courtesans hailing his invincibility, he was not prepared for the reality of election night. I had seen Mr St Laurent in a post-election trauma in 1957 and have known of other politicians absolutely shattered in the wake of an electoral setback. With Diefenbaker's excessive vanity and capacity for histrionics it must have been a most unsettling period for those around him. He spent a good deal of time behind the walls of 24 Sussex Drive. It was not a great time to be a Progressive Conservative and even less stimulating to be a part of the governing process.

Diefenbaker's last gasp as prime minister was the saddest part of his career. He still displayed all the idiosyncrasies of the past but seemed neither physically nor emotionally up to the job of leading a party or a nation. Later, when the burdens and responsibilities of the prime ministry were removed from his uncertain grasp, he experienced a sort of rejuvenation.

The gravity of the economic situation forced the government to take drastic steps in the days following the 1962 election. An austerity program was proclaimed, including increased tariffs, cuts in government spending, tight money, and heavy borrowing abroad to buttress the exchange rate. Naturally the prime minister was denounced for concealing the country's grim economic situation until after the election. Nor did all Canadians share my satisfaction about the three-month delay in calling Parliament. Some in the press and other parties thought it quite improper to take such fundamental economic measures with the House of Commons *in absentia*. The *Canadian Annual Review for 1962* was quite exercised about the situation, referring to

a nation apparently hovering on the brink of financial collapse, a government rejected by two-thirds of the electorate refusing to meet Parliament, a defeated ministry borrowing millions of dollars and levying new taxes by unusual means, a Prime Minister presuming to speak for the nation in London before his dubious mandate had been confirmed, and the life of the administration hanging by a thread held by the whimsical Réal Caouette.[1]

But there was worse to come. The government had been clobbered in June. Before year's end it was seen to be falling apart. Some weeks prior to dissolution in 1962, Robert MacLellan, MP for Inverness-Richmond, and I went to British Columbia for meetings with students at the University of British Columbia and the University of Victoria. We found a number of them upset about the lack of clarity in the government's attitude to providing nuclear potential to those Canadian forces assigned under the North American Air Defence Agreement (NORAD) of 1957. But the issue was by no means a major talking-point in the 1962 campaign.

Things were to change dramatically in a very few months. At the party's annual meeting in December 1962, the subject was on the agenda for panel discussion. I remember Howard Green cautioning us not to have himself and Douglas Harkness, minister of national defence, on the same panel. Howard Green had become a strong champion of disarmament and had made a good impression as well as some progress at the UN and other international forums. He was passionately against nuclear warheads for Canadian military forces. He was also against nuclear testing. Douglas Harkness, who dealt with the Americans closely on the matter, believed Canada was defaulting on agreements made by the Diefenbaker government. These divergent views made for a profound cabinet split which could not long endure. After weeks of vacillation Diefenbaker finally came down on Green's side and saw to it that his views prevailed in the resolutions passed at our less-than-jubilant annual meeting at the Château Laurier. The most recent Gallup poll had shown 54 per cent support for nuclearization. Diefenbaker always pretended to scorn public opinion polls but his chief opponent did not. Lester Pearson, who had been against nuclear arms all along, announced on 11 January 1963 that he thought Canada should nuclearize its forces for 'those defensive tactical weapons, which cannot effectively be used without them but which we have agreed to use.'[2] The prime minister's public statements were masterly in their imprecision.

In a farewell statement U.S. General Norstad, supreme commander of the North Atlantic Treaty Organization (NATO), contradicted Diefenbaker's interpretation of Canada's commitment on the nuclear issue. The American State Department also issued a sharply contradictory statement. It was a nasty bit of intrusion on the part of our big neighbour. It seemed clear at the time that we had made commitments regarding nuclear arms, but the actions and attitudes of the American administration were quite inexcusable. The U.S. ambassador, the military leaders, and the State Department went far beyond the bounds of proper diplomatic relations with a friendly country.

There were times when it seemed that Diefenbaker would take a strongly anti-U.S. stance. Considering his distaste for John F. Kennedy it might not have been too difficult for him to mount such a confrontation. He liked to have enemies to attack and who bigger than the glamorous and aggressive U.S. president?

I remember caucus meetings in which members implored the PM not to go on an anti-U.S. kick. In the end such a course was not chosen, but there was little pro-American expression at PC gatherings, and our big ally got few favourable mentions in the 1963 election campaign.

If they had not known it before, Progressive Conservatives attending the annual meeting realized that the nuclear arms issue was rending the party. On 3 February 1963 the nation was galvanized by the resignation of Douglas Harkness. Over the years I have noted that many resigning ministers cite personal or family reasons for their departure. Not Harkness, who candidly referred to 'irreconcilable differences' between himself and the prime minister.

The Commons sitting on Monday, the day after Harkness's departure from the cabinet, was one of almost unbearable tension. Pearson moved a motion of non-confidence based on the government's indecision and confusion on both national and international matters. If the two smaller groups supported the Liberal motion, the government was doomed and another election imminent. Robert Thompson, the Social Credit leader, began his speech before the six o'clock adjournment. Although critical of the Tory government, he was careful not to say how he and his group would vote on the resolution. In the two hours before the evening sitting, the situation could have been salvaged. Thompson had set out conditions for his support. Those who claimed to know him well declared that a simple phone call from Diefenbaker could have stroked him into supporting the PCS rather than the Grits. But no such call was made, no other interventions were efficacious, and Tuesday night the vote on the motion would bring the government down.

Tuesday, 5 February was like the last day before an execution. There was little to do but wait. Two of my colleagues, Denny Hanbridge and Orville Phillips, had pleasant news which must have eased their pain about the party's loss of a confidence vote. Hanbridge was appointed lieutenant governor of Saskatchewan and Phillips senator from Prince Edward Island. I was having lunch in the parliamentary dining-room with my Island colleague when one of the waitresses came to advise him he was wanted on the telephone. Both of us thought it would be in reference to the Senate appointment. When Orville returned to the table he told me it was Diefenbaker on the line. He then sat down and poured himself a second cup of tea. I was amazed at his calm. Diefenbaker told him to make sure that he didn't go into the chamber to vote that night because by that time he would be a senator. Hanbridge was similarly cautioned.

That afternoon Nathan Phillips of Toronto was seen in the official gallery of the House. This prompted a foolish rumour to the effect that Diefenbaker was so rattled that he appointed the wrong Phillips and that he had intended to give the Toronto mayor an Ontario senatorship. This preposterous rumour was widely touted by some Liberals in Prince Edward Island. Over two decades later, it was brought up in the Senate. Having been with my Island colleague at the time he received the good news, I was able to declare the falsity of such a report.

As if the parliamentary drama were not enough, we were having hectic days within the Progressive Conservative caucus. Across the country there were strong expressions of hostility over Diefenbaker's handling of the nuclear issue. Stalwart old-line Tories were furious. Along with Gordon Churchill, I attended an Ontario PC student federation weekend meeting at Caledon and was astounded at the bitter criticism by many of our most active students. Diefenbaker and Green were their special targets. I fear I did not convince these critics when I stoutly defended Howard

Green. The disaffection had reached the cabinet room itself. A number of ministers thought the departure of Diefenbaker would avert defeat in the non-confidence vote and give the party and a new prime minister a chance to regain the support of the country. It was reported that Social Credit members would have liked to see the popular George Nowlan as prime minister. Some dissident cabinet ministers thought that Diefenbaker would be just the man to become chief justice of Canada! Diefenbaker told Donald Fleming that he would become prime minister before the day was out. We bobbed in a sea of rumours under a cloud of uncertainty.

It was never clear just how many ministers were a party to the contemplated *coup*. George Hees, Léon Balcer, and Mac McCutcheon were prominently mentioned. Perhaps there was never much chance of ousting Diefenbaker, as the 'nest of traitors' had done to Sir Mackenzie Bowell in 1896. It was thought that if enough ministers stood up against Diefenbaker, ready to resign if he didn't, that he could be prevailed upon to quit. But he wasn't the resigning type. Not for him a quiet, gracious withdrawal like Bracken's. The troubled cabinet dissidents didn't plan a very effective revolution. Little was done to elicit support among backbenchers. Perhaps they gave too much importance to the element of surprise which might have been vitiated by consultation with a broader cross-section of caucus members.

In the accounts of this particular crisis, it is generally claimed that Diefenbaker snuffed out the rebellion by having the caucus called for a time earlier than the cabinet meeting of Wednesday, 6 February. Instead of the PM meeting a strong group of dissenting ministers in the cabinet room, those same ministers would be forced to face a caucus predominantly against them and for 'the Chief.' Credit for advancing the hour of the caucus meeting is given to the loyalist fellow Saskatchewanian, Alvin Hamilton.

That PC meeting in the big Railway Committee Room will be long remembered as an emotional orgy. Ministers who had already written their formal resignations apparently decided not to tender them. We went into the meeting expecting that George Hees and others would announce their departures. Instead the meeting became an emotional extravaganza almost reaching the soap operatic proportions of a love-in. I have read many times that the eloquent speech of Senator Grattan O'Leary was the most decisive intervention. I take second place to no one in my affection for Grattan O'Leary and admiration of his eloquence. Of course he made a great speech; he always did. But, in my opinion, the most powerful message was that of the gentle, able, and undemonstrative Alf Brooks, who had been on Parliament Hill since 1935. He didn't have a full panoply of oratorical techniques, but he was enormously convincing. An excellent speech was made by another unpolished rhetorician but a highly respected person, Angus MacLean. Perhaps it is revealing that I chose to say nothing.

After the hyperbolic close of the meeting, when Diefenbaker and Hees left the caucus almost arm-in-arm, I was one of those who accepted an invitation from George to go to his office for a drink. After the emotional draining of that meeting, it was a capital suggestion. I recall Jim McGrath's accolade: 'Today, George, you're ten feet high.' It was a grand salute but, despite his recantation at caucus and his promise to 'knock Hell out of the Grits,' George resigned within days and sat out the 1963 election. Pierre Sévigny resigned the same day. Other important ministers chose not to run. It was not an auspicious beginning for the election campaign, which, following the government's defeat on the confidence vote, was set for 8 April 1963.

I probably enjoyed election campaigns and the political process as much as any member of Parliament; otherwise I would hardly have devoted so much of my life to electioneering. But I could have done without the 1963 campaign. It began on 6 February, less than eight months after the 1962 election. It is important in any campaign to get back to one's constituency and show vigour, enthusiasm, and above all optimism. If these attitudes can be displayed with realism and conviction, all to the good. Some of my people were a bit bewildered by what was going on within the national party. Because my children were attending school in Ottawa I would not be able to have them and Isabel on the Island with me. My house in Victoria was closed for the winter. In those penurious days MPs had very limited telephone and travel privileges.

But, as often happened, when I got to the Island and interacted with people in the constituency association, my spirits were restored and my morale boosted. As the campaign progressed I began to enjoy it greatly. This, in part, was the result of some of the preposterous antics of the Liberals. The 1963 campaign brought forth the 'truth squad,' captained by the redoubtable Judy La-Marsh, Liberal MP for Niagara Falls. She and her two cohorts were to follow Diefenbaker about the country and puncture the inaccuracies of his statements. To say that the scheme did not work would be a major understatement. At Moncton, early in the campaign, Diefenbaker made mincemeat of the squad as it literally sat in the spotlight. It lived on only in the derision heaped upon it, not only by the prime minister but by every PC speaker on the hustings.

Another Liberal gimmick was the release of homing pigeons, who were bright enough to fly and flee the role assigned them. A third smart-ass scheme, the use of nasty colouring books, failed to amuse, arouse, or interest either the children or the adults of the land. At every meeting I addressed in Queens or elsewhere, I found a highly appreciative audience as I made much of the Grits' slick tricks. It was as effective as lambasting Walter Gordon in 1957 and much more fun.

Things looked so bad for the Tories in 1963 that we had nowhere to go but up. And up we did go – but not enough. Diefenbaker, once again, showed amazing resilience and his usual capacity to attract sympathy. As Jack Pickersgill put it, Diefenbaker was trying to weep his way back into office. The U.S. magazine *Newsweek* carried a cover picture of Diefenbaker which would have upset Count Dracula or Mephisto. Both the picture and the lead article were crude and vicious. Diefenbaker used them to the hilt. It was those nasty Americans, in cahoots with the horrid Grits, who had inspired it all. He criticized the U.S. press, as well as nearly all the Canadian press since few newspapers supported him.

The party was not flush with funds and the battling prime minister did not have a chartered plane for his cross-country tours. But of this he made a virtue, claiming that like Harry Truman in

1948 he was with the people, not soaring above them. He drew large crowds at whistle-stops. It was not long before we realized that the 1963 contest was to be a closer affair than expected and certainly livelier than 1962.

If anyone expected a clear and rational discussion of nuclear weaponry, which the election was supposedly about, they were disappointed. Some rational souls might feel that, if the Bomarc-B missile was functional only with a nuclear warhead, the non-acceptance of such warheads was not a good contribution to North American defence. Campaign meetings in 1963 didn't feature this kind of discussion. Nor can I recall any sustained arguments about whether or not the CF-101B Voodoo interceptors were of much value without nuclear weapons, which experts declared essential to their full effectiveness. But then I suppose no experienced politician should expect a careful discussion of issues during an election campaign. A political campaign may be many things; an academic seminar it never is.

Lubor Zink of the *Toronto Telegram* on 20 March noted sadly that Diefenbaker's 'fury of emotionalism ... had struck a responsive chord in a politically illiterate public. Many of Diefenbaker's vintage campaign speeches read poorly and were difficult to report, but they were performances. It may be that the public was a bit confused as well as mesmerized by the old maestro's histrionics. Certainly not all his audience was perfectly clear about what he had in mind when, in the catalogue of his evil enemies, he listed 'an invisible incognito.'

For all his fervent campaigning, Diefenbaker was not able to diminish the Liberal lead as effectively as he had in 1962. The Gallup poll of 23 February showed the Liberals with 44 per cent to the PCS 33 per cent. Samplings on 23 March and 6 April both showed 41 per cent to 32 per cent. The election-day results gave the Liberals 42 per cent of the vote as against 33 per cent for the Conservatives.

Lester Pearson, despite his clutch of election specialists, was no more successful in endearing himself to the voters than in 1962. Since their leader could not win in a personality contest, the Liberals emphasized program and policies. Premier Lesage of

Quebec was more cooperative this time around. The promise to set up a Royal Commission on Bilingualism and Biculturalism was considered especially important in Quebec. A distinctive Canadian flag was promised. To 'get the country moving again' a whole series of actions was promised, in 'sixty days of decision' which would bring Canadians an abundance of blessings.

On the day of the election we had a fierce winter storm in Prince Edward Island. I had to break off my afternoon visits to polling stations to get to the Charlottetown Hotel, next door to CFCY studios, before the highways became too treacherous. In Queens constituency things went well. I received 11,608 votes and Angus MacLean 11,666. Our Liberal opponents Ira Lewis and Alex Gillis had 9257 and 9144. The usual minuscule vote went to the NDP. But the news from Kings and Prince was bad. Senator Phillips' successor, Lorne Monkley, was behind veteran Liberal Watson MacNaught 8387 to 8967. Margaret Macdonald lost to a bright young man, John Mullally, by 4304 votes to 4705.

The defeat of Margaret Macdonald was distressing to me. Her husband John A. was my office mate and one of my closest friends. I well remember arriving at Toronto's Malton Airport in early January 1961 en route to address a PC youth meeting in Calgary. I heard my name on the PA system. It was a call from our secretary, Bonnie Howatt, telling of John A.'s death. I immediately cancelled my flight west and returned at once to Ottawa and prepared to go to his funeral in Cardigan.

Before many months the question of a by-election candidate arose. I was highly instrumental in his widow Margaret's being nominated, although she was by no means eager for the role. I did all I could to assist her. Happily she was elected on 29 May 1961, becoming the first woman member of the House of Commons from Atlantic Canada. That night I had a call from Allister Grosart the national PC director. John Diefenbaker came on the phone to express his thanks, saying 'I'll never forget you, Mac.' Margaret won in the 1962 election. With her loss in 1963 she had run in three elections in three years. Politics is not an easy life. For her harder than for most participants.

Over in Newfoundland, my good friend Jim McGrath went down

to defeat. We also lost Shelburne-Yarmouth-Clare and the two seats in Halifax, the other dual riding. Atlantic Canada, despite John Diefenbaker's largesse, elected 20 Liberals to 13 Progressive Conservatives. My friend Donnie MacInnis defeated NDP Vic McInnis to regain Cape Breton South, the seat once held by Clairie Gillis, the first CCF member from Atlantic Canada.

The Liberals' good showing in the Atlantic region was ominous. When the returns from the Eastern Standard Time zone started coming in, our gloom in the suite at the Charlottetown Hotel deepened. In Quebec the PCs won 8 seats, the Liberals 47. Surprisingly, Caouette's group held on to 20 of their 26 seats despite a fierce Liberal campaign against them. Conservative strength in Ontario fell to 27, little better than R.B. Bennett had done in 1935. The Liberals swept Metropolitan Toronto and most other urban areas to capture 52 seats. On the Prairies the Liberals won a grand total of 3 seats to 41 for the PCs. British Columbia elected 6 Liberals, 4 PCs, and 9 NDPs.

During the campaign there was the usual talk of an NDP breakthrough. It didn't happen. They dropped to 17 seats. Apart from Caouette's group, 2 Social Credit were elected in Alberta and a like number in BC. The two smaller parties had brought down the government, thereby triggering an election in which the NDP lost 2 seats, the Social Credit 6. I don't know what second thoughts their leaders had on election night.

Many of our good PC supporters and party officials could not make it to the Charlottetown Hotel election night. Many who did stayed all night because the weather and road conditions prevented them from reaching their homes. Fortunately we had ample refreshments in the suite, including good Puerto Rico Ron Bacardi. So we made it through the long wintry evening until BC results were in. The Liberal total had risen from 100 to 129 seats. Our side had dropped from 116 to 95. After less than six years the Progressive Conservatives were once again to be out of office. Not gracious in yielding power, Diefenbaker had not conceded victory or hailed Pearson as the winner. He referred to Mackenzie King's staying on after the 1925 election. Once again the Pearson

Liberals had failed to reach a majority. They were 4 seats short of the magic number 133.

As I drove my colleague Angus and my wife Isabel to the airport Tuesday morning through great walls of snow, there was little hilarity in the air. Angus MacLean likened our trip to Napoleon's retreat from Moscow. I was a little surprised at his gloom. He was normally a calmer person than I. The next day I flew to Moncton and caught the Ocean Limited to the nation's capital. On board I met some of the defeated Tory incumbents on the way to Ottawa to pick up the pieces. There were recriminations aplenty, with Diefenbaker blamed for their losses.

In Ottawa there was some lingering thought that Diefenbaker might hold on to the government and meet Parliament before resigning. This dream was shattered when it was reported in the press that a handful of Social Credit members from Quebec had indicated their intention to support the Liberals in the event of a parliamentary challenge.

On 22 April in that bleak year of 1963, I was just outside the main entrance of the Centre Block when a formally dressed Lester Pearson came out heading purposefully for the East Block, which housed the Privy Council office. Although I was careful to be unobtrusive he broke from the little procession and came over to thank me for a personal note I had sent him when we were both registered at the Charlottetown Hotel during his campaign visit to PEI. Over the previous four years I had found him genial and courteous. In my note I had wished him well in all his endeavours except the partisan one which had brought him to PEI. His gesture on the day he assumed the prime ministry was typical and an indication of the decent and unostentatious man he was.

An event of an entirely different emotional range was a visit to Howard Green in his East Block office. I found him at his desk, his personal items neatly packed, the surface of his desk bare. Like the candid man he was, he blamed himself for his defeat after twenty-eight years representing a Vancouver riding. 'Heath, I allowed my organization to get too old as I gave attention to other things.' Long before I had met Howard Green I had heard that he was a most astute constituency-minded politician, whose Vancouver-Quadra organization was always strong and efficient. But being a senior minister and secretary of state for external affairs had taken its toll. Whether he wished to say it or not, national trends had been playing in his constituency as well. One positive note for him was that Paul Martin would be his successor as foreign minister. 'Paul's a good internationalist.'

After the 1962 election John Diefenbaker had been criticized for the long delay in calling Parliament. Lester Pearson was most anxious to get the legislative mill going. Diefenbaker had resigned on 22 April. The new prime minister met Parliament on 16 May. Doubtless it would have been helpful to Pearson and his cabinet ministers to have had a period of assessment of their new responsibilities. But he had foolishly made an enemy of the clock by his grandiose promises of 'sixty days of decision.' Diefenbaker had been denounced for not producing a budget. On the fifty-third day of the countdown, Walter Gordon brought in his. It was immediately apparent that it was a premature birth.

I don't remember any budget getting anything but a lambasting from the opposition parties, but the deluge of scorn which fell upon Walter Gordon's first budget was unprecedented. For its preparation he had brought in a small brain trust from the Toronto world of finance, which he knew so well. Confidentiality is of the essence in the budget-making process. And so, before anyone had read the document, Gordon was embarrassingly on the defensive for bringing in 'outsiders' and breaching the sacred confidentiality. In content as well as in its conception the Gordon budget was a wretched fiasco. Major portions had to be withdrawn and it was a tattered wreck which finally passed the Commons. It was a poor start for one of the touted geniuses of the new administration.

The day-to-day life of a member of the House of Commons is normally a good deal easier when he is in opposition rather than sitting as a government supporter. If he is keen on question period, he is much more likely to be recognized by the Speaker if he is an opposition member. If he is bursting with oratorical fervour, he will not have too much trouble getting on the speaking list. At House of Commons committees he has a far better chance to interrogate ministers or other witnesses, since government supporters are expected to make it easy for ministers piloting legislation through the House or committees. For an opposition MP the pressure is less and the opportunities for parliamentary participation greater. He might even find some chance to exercise a bit of independence.

Those on the quarterdeck of political parties naturally prefer any independence by individual members to come in very small doses. During our six years as a government caucus, I heard many exhortations against pairing. From 1957 to 1963 our whip would declaim: 'Pairing helps only the opposition. Don't pair.' After the 1963 election the revealed truth was that pairing was in fact a diabolical device designed to help governments. Therefore, 'Don't pair.'

In the face of such unrealistic strictures, the individual MP must work out something on his own. It would be difficult for a secretary of state for external affairs to do his or her job well if it is a parliamentary risk to leave the country. I often accommodated my friend Paul Martin by telling him that, while I 'couldn't pair,' I would not in his absence vote to jeopardize the government. Once, when he asked me to cover him during a visit to Poland and a couple of other East European countries, I replied in a note suggesting that the safest thing would be to take me with him! I saw him pass my note to Jack Pickersgill. Within two hours I had a phone call from Pickersgill asking whether I would like to go to the Soviet Union on the inaugural flight of the Air Canada–Aeroflot service. I went. I never thought I was adept at angling things for my own advantage but I did quite well that time.

But constituent relations mark the greatest difference for the MP on the right or the left of the Speaker in the House of Commons. While he or she may have a far better entrée with a minister (and much depends on the the minister), the government-supporting MP has also more problems. Much more is expected. My bulging file of Senate applicants in 1957 was a case in point. Patronage, although often seen as a helpful lubricant, can also bring a good deal of trouble. Angus Maclean used to say that when you obtain a government job for someone you often create one ingrate and nine soreheads.

Opposition MPs may not sit in caucus once a week with a prime minister and ministers, but, on the other hand, they are not held responsible for the administrative errors or omissions that gall the electors – poor postal service, inflation, unemployment, high interest rates, recidivism, and a host of other things. Despite all of these realities I didn't find my first years in opposition all that agreeable. The House of Commons in session was very much a bear pit. Scandals and allegations of scandals tainted the air.

Prime Minister Pearson showed great courage in Winnipeg by going before the annual meeting of the Dominion Command of the Canadian Legion with his distinctive flag proposal. But the House of Commons flag debate did not enhance the institution or bring lustre to the country. While there were some excellent and eloquent speeches, the whole process was marked by obstruction and petty politicking. Thirty-three sitting days and almost 300 speeches were made in the six-month controversy. The prime minister's suggested design featured three red maple leafs from the coat of arms and blue borders symbolizing the oceans. ('The wholesome Sea is at her gates. Her gates both East and West.') This was immediately dubbed 'Pearson's Pennant' by Diefenbaker. A House committee favoured a one–maple leaf design. This bore a considerable likeness to the logo of the NDP whose MPs joined the Liberals in voting for it. Diefenbaker declared that the one–maple leaf flag would never fly.

Eventually it did, but at the cost of much bitterness and discord. Léon Balcer, Diefenbaker's seat-mate (they sat together but did not converse), rose to ask George McIlraith, government house leader, to impose closure. Some Progressive Conservative party meetings went on record for a cessation of the debate. I thought the most shocking thing of all was John Diefenbaker's performance at a national executive meeting of the party in 1965. Although some kinds of ballots, like those on leadership, were anathema to him at the time, he put forward an amazing questionnaire. In it, he asked the executive members whether he should attend the ceremonial proclamation of the new flag. The bill had passed both Houses and received royal assent. But so toxic was the atmosphere in our party that few seemed to notice the outrageousness of an officer of the House of Commons, the leader of Her Majesty's Loyal Opposition, asking such a question of a party dedicated to parliamentary institutions. How preposterous even to consider boycotting such a state occasion. In the end he attended and wept as the Red Ensign came down.

Frank Walker, editor of *Charlottetown Guardian*, once told me that for many distinctive flag enthusiasts the concern was not over what would be on the flag: 'What they are really interested in is to take something off, that is, the Union Jack.' Once, a bit unkindly, I fear, I had said of one of my Tory colleagues: 'The only flag he would like is a Union Jack with a Union Jack in the corner.'

At one caucus meeting the maple leaf was taking quite a buffeting with prairie members saying that maple trees were not native to their part of Canada. One of our Quebec members rose to say that there was a lion on the Red Ensign. 'Perhaps lions roam Saskatchewan but they are not native to Quebec.' But, blessedly, the anger and anguish of the flag debate soon dissipated. Many Canadians, in PEI and elsewhere, who swore they would never accept the new flag now display it with pride and affection.

The closeness of the election results in 1963, and the scandals, fumblings, and bunglings of the Pearson government had a profound effect upon the Progressive Conservative party. Had we won the 1963 election the internecine quarrelling over the leadership would have been quieted for a while. Had the Liberals won big in 1963 or captivated the electorate or soared in public opinion polls after the election, the pressure for a change of command in our party would have been vastly strengthened. John Diefenbaker would not have stepped aside gracefully or graciously; he would have had to be dragged out screaming and blaming. But there would have been far more Tories ready to do some of the pulling.

We Conservatives were in a strange position in the early sixties. The poor performance of our own government got us out of office in 1963. The poor performance of the Pearson government rendered us incapable of taking the measure which would have rejuvenated us. Canadians had turned against John Diefenbaker but they weren't turning to Lester Pearson. Many of the party, although exasperated by Diefenbaker, wondered whether even he couldn't do a better job of administering the country than Pearson. We were caught in a bind which for several years made for acute discomfort and discouragement within the party.

Not long before the 1963 election, the annual meeting of the PCS had passed a motion of confidence in the leader. But what delegates said in the meeting-room was often quite different from what they said in their own rooms or in the bars of the Château Laurier. One newsman described the annual meeting as a hotel full of hypocrites. Not surprisingly, considering the 1963 election results, there was even more rumbling at the annual meeting of February 1964. Recalling the unreality of the unanimous vote of confidence in 1963, some PCS were advocating a vote by ballot on the leadership issue. This evoked a highly emotional response from Diefenbaker. At his most histrionic he said: 'I want to know where I stand' and, ominously, 'I want to know where you stand too.' In our national elections we had long ago given up open voting. But the secret ballot seemed not good enough for party decisions.

So once again confidence in the leader had to be proclaimed in a stand-up vote. As one of the thirty or so who voted in the negative, I learned how the ant must feel when stepped on by a large boot. We dissidents were a tiny, scattered group in the crowded drawing room of the Château Laurier that day.

Annual meetings and conventions are often occasions for people to have a good time. There was not much of that sort of thing in the Tory gatherings of the 1960s. The stresses and strains were painful and enervating, and the ache and the agony would continue for a long time. In those difficult years some bowed out of the protracted fray, but I still marvel that so many in the party, the elected members and the rank and file, continued on course.

The rebels (we would graduate to 'termites' later) had been

mightily overwhelmed in the great stand-up vote of confidence in February 1964. But disaffection with Diefenbaker continued.

The flag debate had been particularly hard on our eight Quebec MPS and on 15 January 1965 they had jointly asked the party president, Dalton Camp, to convene a meeting of the national executive to consider calling a national leadership convention. On Saturday, 6 February, the members of the national executive, along with Mrs John Diefenbaker, spent most of the day in PC headquarters at 161 Laurier Avenue West in Ottawa. And what a day it was! Léon Balcer, not a spellbinder at best, didn't make a very impressive opening statement. With his usual courtesy he spoke, not in his first language but in English, to accommodate the great majority of his listeners. Diefenbaker was his dogmatic worst – not for him the way of conciliation. Erik Nielsen, the leader's chief hit man, strongly criticized the officers of the party and argued that the national executive lacked the authority to do what the Quebec MPS had requested. Nielsen was never a great favourite of mine and I thought some of his accusatory attacks in the House on Pearson and his ministers had been unnecessarily excessive. He was always well briefed and forthrightly tough in his advocacies; however, I found nothing commendable in his interventions that day.

The vote on the item which might have led to the calling of the convention was close. It was a long way from the pro-establishment stampede of the 1964 meeting.

In the abortive revolt of 1963, Diefenbaker's people had had a caucus meeting called prior to the fateful cabinet meeting. In 1965 the strategy was repeated. The caucus met the day before the national executive. After four hours a standing vote of confidence was taken. The majority stood. Indeed it was difficult for those of us who didn't stand to get even a rough count. The chairman, Mike Starr, probably showed kindly diplomacy in not calling upon the nays to stand. There was a long-standing tradition against votes in caucus. Consensus rather than majorities were to be sought. But, in those days of grim infighting, many conventions were cast aside. Perhaps the caucus vote had an influence on some members of the national executive. Some of us who belonged to both groups changed neither our votes nor our views. Speaking of groups, we were given membership in two others that day: the party leader described the pro-convention types as 'termites' and 'chiselers.'

Robert Stanfield, the only premier to attend the 1965 national executive meeting, must have brought great comfort to the Diefenbaker people. He and others from his province gave unwavering support to the arguments of Diefenbaker, Nielsen, Churchill, and their ilk. Discussing the meeting on the following Monday, the irrepressible Heber Smith declaimed: 'With Stanfield and his Nova Scotians there, Dief didn't need even one Horner.'

The stormy meeting of the national executive had revealed once again the intensity of the disagreement over John Diefenbaker's continuing leadership. Although the Diefenbaker establishment had gained a reprieve, the bitter meeting, although an *in camera* affair, demonstrated to the party as a whole the wide measure of disaffection and anxiety. It was not just a handful of malcontents who thought that the party should review its relations with the leadership and vice versa.

The most regrettable fallout from that fateful February meeting was the loss to us of Léon Balcer. At the 1963 annual meeting it seemed that there had been a reconciliation between Diefenbaker and his most senior Quebec MP. At a carefully staged ceremony Balcer seemed to have been anointed Quebec lieutenant. After the 1963 election Diefenbaker debunked the notion. In his exasperation Balcer, in calling for the national executive meeting, had declared that the Quebec MPs were ill at ease and uncomfortable within their own party. The action, or rather inaction, of the national executive had done nothing to allay their discomfort.

The situation was especially painful for Balcer. He had been an MP since 1949, an amazing political longevity for a Quebec Conservative. He was a man of modesty and forbearance, but he was at a crisis point. I remember well being one of a considerable group calling on him in his Ottawa apartment importuning him to stay with the party whatever happened. I had flown up from

Charlottetown at my own expense. Doug Harkness, Heward Graff-tey, and a good many of the other 'dissidents' were there. We had a good, candid discussion, but in the end we lost Balcer. Once when I begged Léon to be patient a bit longer he told me why I might be talking about quite a long time. 'When he [Dief] likened himself to Sir John A. Macdonald, Sir Wilfrid Laurier, and Mack-enzie King I could hold on. But when he began his references to how old Gladstone was when he was prime minister, I had to give thought to getting out.' He eventually sat as an Independent in the House and did not run in 1965. He moved to provincial politics and unfortunately, as I saw it, ran not for the *Union Nationale* but for the Liberals. He lost and left politics for good. Clearly the PC party was in a bad way if it had to lose a stalwart with such a record of service as Léon Balcer had. Some years later I nominated him for the Order of Canada. I had the same lack of success which crowned my earlier efforts with the nomination of Howard Green. Looking over the roster of the Order it would seem that Liberal ex-ministers do much better than their Pro-gressive Conservative counterparts.

Another Quebec MP, Rémi Paul, also quit the field, saying that he couldn't win or even save his deposit running under Diefen-baker. Théogene Ricard declared that he would stay with the old man. When I asked Paul Martineau, MP for Pontiac-Témisca-mingue, whether he too was staying with the old man he gave me a fine and sensitive reply: 'No, Heath, I'm staying with you and others like you.' Paul Martineau, briefly a minister in 1963, was a highly articulate and intelligent man. I vividly recall his taking on Diefenbaker after one of his caucus tirades.

For most people it is painful to the nerves and to the soul to be forever in an adversarial position. A sort of uneasy lull followed the unfortunate national executive meeting. I often thought of the words of the poem, 'They stood aloof, the scars remaining.' The Liberal decision to go for a 1965 election brought termites and Diefenbakerites into a pattern of coordinated if not congenial action.

Lester Pearson had won the Nobel Peace Prize for his efforts in conciliation and mediation in 1956. Inadvertently and unwillingly he had become a peacemaker again. To bring the Capulets and the Montagues of Torydom into an alliance in 1965 was a weirdly wonderful achievement. It was not a holy alliance and it would not last beyond the closing of the polls, but it was great theatre. One day the public read that George Hees was giving up the presidency of the Montreal and Canadian Stock Exchange and returning to the fold. Sévigny was also 'willing' if he could find a seat. A fascinating newspaper photograph showed John Diefenbaker and Douglas Harkness shaking hands at the Calgary airport. A host of 1963 dissidents rallied to the cause. Eddie Goodman, who had become one of the hostile 'them' in Diefenbaker's eyes, was asked to become national campaign chairman and gamely accepted. In the fall of 1965 so many Conservatives had their best foot forward that the biggest peril was inadvertent tripping. John Diefenbaker explained his call for unity as a response to 'the serious condition of affairs of this nation.' The *Globe and Mail* of 4 October wondered whether the ecumenical move was based on 'high purpose or simple ambition.'

When I pleaded with Léon Balcer to stay with us, I dwelt on the basic truth that the party was more lasting and more important than any leader. Diefenbaker's unity kick did have some effect. In 1957 and even more in 1958, the Progressive Conservatives were a Diefenbaker party. The leader was stressed, the party label obscured. But, as I look over my own Queens constituency advertising from the 1965 election, I note a distinct downplaying of Diefenbaker. Gallup poll figures for the campaign indicate that John Diefenbaker, in sharp contrast to earlier elections, was not running ahead of the party in popularity.

It would be naïve to suggest that the united front of Torydom was based on charitable motivations. Eddie Goodman reports that James Johnston, one of the Diefenbaker inner circle, dubbed the election slogan 'Let's give the old bugger another chance.'[3] Although they may not have used such language I heard many PCs voice the same sentiments. And, once the election had been thrust upon us, there was little else that pragmatic Tories could do so why not do it with good grace.

Perhaps many Progressive Conservatives allowed themselves to be more gullible than ordinarily. One older member of the party told me that the wrong people were suggesting that Diefenbaker resign. 'He won't listen to his enemies but if his friends advised him to go he might be more receptive.' To this well-intentioned advice from a man I respected I could only say: 'And how long do you think such a person would remain in the 'friend' category the moment he proffered such advice?' During the 1965 campaign 'insiders' and 'peacemakers' spread the illusion that after this election the old man would step aside. I had no trouble in recognizing the total unreality of such a scenario. There was about as much prospect of his stepping aside voluntarily as of my becoming the Prince of Wales.

There was a good deal of hard realism behind the staging of our solidarity chorus in 1965. Astute politicians with their own axe to grind would, naturally, have made a careful analysis of the political situation then prevailing in Canada. The period after the 1962 election made it apparent that the incumbent leader of the Progressive Conservative party could not easily be cajoled or jostled out of the top seat. *Ipso facto*, the Conservative leadership would not be easily attained, but with the uncertain pace of the Liberals it was worth striving for. In short, anyone nursing ambitions of becoming the national leader of the Progressive Conservatives could not afford to stand aloof in 1965. Barons ambitious to wear the crown dared not offend the old king or his cronies. Some, who in 1962 had described the then prime minister as a 'raging maniac,' in 1965 advised the Canadian people to re-elect him as prime minister of the country.

There were many big names participating in the 1965 election, but if we had had the modern software of computers and word processors at that time I am sure that an index would have shown that the most frequently mentioned name was not that of any 'biggie' in either of the historic national parties. Until I heard his name mentioned in the House of Commons I had not known of the existence of Lucien Rivard, whom the u.s. authorities sought to extradite on a narcotics charge. Apparently he had been an active Liberal – a case of poor judgment but not of total depravity. But I later learned things which indicated that highly placed Grits

were feathering him. There were serious allegations that prominent, government-connected people had offered bribes for his
release. At the time I thought that Mr Rivard was probably not a
wholesome character and that some of the Quebec Grits were
being a bit casual. I didn't realize that this undistinguished person
was to become a *cause célèbre* in a Canadian election.

When Rivard escaped from prison in Quebec in early March
1965 the Pearson government was embarrassed beyond measure.
It was said that not until Rivard was finally captured in July did
Pearson begin to think realistically of calling an election. At countless meetings across the country Diefenbaker would say: 'It's a
lovely warm night, just like the one when Rivard asked to flood
the rink.' I haven't studied the meteorological records, but the
autumn of 1965 must have been one of the warmest on record
because the Chief certainly used that line to great advantage. Later
on, when Rivard was recaptured and Pearson felt it safe to call
an election, the old maestro still had good lines. As Pearson, like
all PMS, went across the land promising goodies including sports
centres, Diefenbaker had a choice comment about the hockey
arenas. 'I wonder who will flood them now that Rivard's back in
jail?' One has to be careful when making comparisons, but I cannot recall a dirtier campaign to that time. People in the highest
offices of the land were accused of having ties with those engaged
in vice and corruption. Regrettably there were dirtier ones since.

It is agreeable to have people laugh with you but not such fun
when they laugh at you. One of the potent weapons against the
Pearson government was simple derision. Some of the great car-
toons of the time featured Pearson himself as a small, bewildered,
and tattered man dithering in circumstances beyond his control.
He was constantly pictured as a man of misadventure and mis-
fortune. Personally I never doubted his integrity but it was sometimes difficult to respect his judgment.

In my twenty-two years in the House of Commons I missed only
one of the press gallery dinners. Since the members of the press
can invite only one guest each, back-benchers are honoured to
receive bids to these high-spirit extravaganzas. Despite the often
bibulous atmosphere of which I was generally a part, I have the

most vivid recollections of Mike Pearson's performance at one of them. This was the year when the skits and songs were featuring the Mafia connections of prominent Liberals seen as pals of Lucien Rivard. When called upon to speak Pearson produced a black glove and put it on his right hand.

Looking back over the intervening twenty-five years or so, I still recall Pearson governments as tainted and vulnerable. Erik Nielsen and other PC accusers were extreme in their taunts and charges, but there were unwholesome and unworthy actions on the part of those charged with the responsibility of governing the country. The inquiry into the Rivard affair by Chief Justice Dorion of Quebec revealed many disquieting things. Guy Favreau, Pearson's minister of justice and trusted lieutenant, departed that post and in effect terminated what once had seemed a brilliant expanding career in public life. Other Quebec Liberals came under a cloud of suspicion. Pearson himself appeared unaware of the grave significance of some of the malfeasance around him. He claimed lack of knowledge of events which it later transpired had been reported to him at the highest level. This allowed John Diefenbaker to charge him with 'selective amnesia,' not a sterling quality for a prime minister!

The ostensible reason for the 1965 election was the Liberals' desire for a parliamentary majority. Surely more important was Pearson's desire to rise above the morass of his administration and attain from the people of Canada a mark of confidence which his efforts and his basic integrity deserved. In many ways, and certainly for the Conservative party, it would have been better had he received the endorsement he so dearly sought.

We had fought elections over autocratic government, over visions, over economic incompetence, and over nuclear weapons, but it was hard at the time, and still is hard, to define an issue which pervaded the 1965 election. I suppose a campaign is always an exercise in choosing the good guys over the bad guys but, if it is only that, an election is something less than satisfactory. Professor Murray Beck's election guide is prescient. His chapter on the 1965 gladiatorial contest is entitled 'It isn't much to come out of an election.'[4]

But those of us who wore our party's colours had to don our arms and wage the political fight. Once again I was busy every waking hour and accepted a good many calls to speak in various parts of the country, especially in Atlantic Canada. After our party had been shut out of Newfoundland in the 1963 election, I had been given some sort of unofficial caucus responsibility for that province and had made some enjoyable visits there before and during the election.

In the final days of the campaign, speaking in Angus MacLean's home area of Belfast, even I had dropped my usual gentility and put on the mantle of criticism. I said, again as the *Guardian* of 5 November reminds me: 'This is the first election in the history of Canadian politics where the government has asked the people not for a mandate on certain policies or issues but only for more power.'

When the last speech was made and the final round of partisan applause given, there was not much to celebrate in the 8 November 1965 election. Despite all Diefenbaker's oratorical magic and the party's exercise of unity, we gained only two seats and lost marginally in the popular vote. The Liberals had increased their standing by the same wee margin so things were much as they had been before the unnecessary election.

Prince Edward Island by itself provided the Tory increase. Kings and Prince returned to the PC party. In the former, Melvin McQuaid, an able provincial minister, had won over his highly personable cousin, John Mullally, by 140 votes. In Prince, a most attractive and able newcomer, the Reverend David MacDonald, who had just joined the party, defeated cabinet minister J. Watson MacNaught by 767 votes. David was one of the truly bright lights added to our parliamentary caucus in the 1965 contest.

Atlantic Canada, often cited as an area adept at picking the winning side, did not do so in 1965. The PCs won 18 seats, the Liberals 15. Seven of theirs were in Joey Smallwood's Newfoundland. The Liberals also lost a seat in Ontario and two of their precious few in the Prairies. With their nine gains in Quebec the governing party had a net national gain of two seats. Once again public opinion polls indicated that Pearson had lost ground during the campaign. Electioneering was obviously not his forte.

The scandals, so luridly described across the land and the networks, hurt the Liberals. Diefenbaker's campaigning once again attracted many voters. In some areas the Liberals were hurt by the flag issue. Diefenbaker lambasted them for creeping republicanism.

The morning-after psephologists had plenty of material from which to explain what had happened. There was, of course, the initial difficulty of deciding who had won. Was the strong showing of the PCs the major achievement? Or was the remarkable thing the survival of a government with such an image? On election night I had said to my PC friends at the Charlottetown Hotel: 'I believe the big news is not that the Liberals failed to get a majority but that a government so tarnished should win at all.'

In Queens we did very well in what was for me my fifth and final campaign in the old dual riding. The 1965 results were MacLean 12,588, Macquarrie 12,305, MacGuigan 9626, Jones 9143.

In 1957 most Liberals and a good many Conservatives thought only one PC would be elected in Queens. It took what I thought an interminable time for the slogan, 'We'll get Macquarrie this time,' to die down. In 1965 the Liberals put up a bright young Island native, Mark MacGuigan, a relative of the cardinal and a member of a leading Grit family. He had more university degrees than I had and was younger and better looking. He was also a Catholic and I wondered whether somehow in the dual riding this might hurt me. Perhaps his candidacy did maim me a bit; after being only 58 votes behind Angus MacLean in 1963, I had 285 votes fewer than he in 1965. MacGuigan was 483 ahead of his Protestant running mate 'Bus' Jones. Once again psephology was difficult even on the constituency level. Perhaps I lost some votes for not being sufficiently devoted to John Diefenbaker, but I did not hear anyone so declare. With a margin of 2677 over the leading Liberal, I had little interest in quibbling over the details of the vote.

On the Island all the national issues were in play along with others of a purely local nature. In an effort to capitalize on the pro-causeway sentiment, Liberal candidate Watson MacNaught had staged a ceremonial 'opening' at the site of the New Brunswick terminal. Whether or not he chose Cape Tormentine rather than Borden to indicate that it was the mainland joining PEI rather than vice versa I never knew. But what everyone knew after the sod-turning festivities was that Premier Walter Shaw had not been invited. This discourteous omission was used to the hilt by the Tories in all three Island constituencies. Even without Mac-Naught's booboo I believe David MacDonald would have won Prince. Very likely Mel McQuaid would have carried Kings also and Angus and I had not been seen as in jeopardy. In the Maritimes by this time, there were a number of incumbents who were becoming strongly entrenched.

The most important and helpful issue in the 1965 election was the PCs clear-cut promise to pay $100 per month in old age security pension. In 1965 that amount had considerable purchasing power. I had always been well received at senior citizens' residences, but in the fall of 1965 the welcome was beyond anything previously experienced. Recipients of the OAS and their kinsfolk could remember well the 'six buck boys' and the nasty means-test red tape of the Liberal days. In all my years of politics I never found a more effective promise insofar as winning votes was concerned.

A sadly disappointed Pearson was despondent after the failure to win a majority. His minister of finance, Walter Gordon, taking responsibility for advising an election, tendered his resignation. After a holiday in the Caribbean, a somewhat restored prime minister returned to his office, and six weeks after the election announced a major reconstruction of the cabinet. Among the new ministers were Jean Marchand, Robert Winters, Joe Greene, and John Turner. Two heavily and perhaps unfairly criticized Quebec ministers, René Tremblay and Maurice Lamontagne, had resigned before the shuffle. The second Pearson government had a generally calmer time than his first. He presided with grace and charm over our centennial celebration and on 14 December 1967 he announced his resignation. He left the prime ministry on 20 April

1968. I saw him occasionally after he left office. Once in a Senate committee room he met with a group of people interested in foreign affairs and gave us some informal off-the-record recollections of his diplomatic years. He had an engaging sense of humour and was a splendid raconteur.

Pearson would have served his country as an elder statesman in the mould of Sir Robert Borden. Tragically he died before he could fully grace this role. In 1988 I was honoured to be asked by Stewart McInnes, minister of public works, to serve on a committee to present recommendations to the government on a statue of Pearson for Parliament Hill.

The 1965 election was the fifth John Diefenbaker had contested as leader. (For Pearson it was the fourth.) After the stalemate of this latest encounter it became the conventional wisdom that a change of leader was essential. A strong dissenter from this view was John Diefenbaker. But as week followed week the pressure for change strengthened among active PCs who had done their best for the leader and the party in the 1965 election. Yet there was no mechanism in the party's constitution for dealing with the situation. Does a leader once chosen have some semi-divine right to continue, or should the party which placed him in the leadership in the first place have some rights to determine who shall be at its head? John Diefenbaker and a substantial segment of the party apparently believed that a leader once chose remained there at *his* pleasure. Others thought that if political parties are a handmaiden of democracy they should themselves be structured democratically.

Addressing the annual meeting of the YPCs, I had urged that John Diefenbaker ameliorate the tension by calling for a ballot on his leadership. I also expressed the view that he would win such a vote. But in the aftermath of the 1965 election, Diefenbaker and his people were adamant against such a notion. I was soundly denounced for such apostasy and in one or two confrontations was in danger of being physically attacked. Not being a pugilistic type I didn't relish the prospect of being a bruised and battered balloter.

Most people like to be admired and praise is sweet to the human ear. Many politicians enjoy adulation and John Diefenbaker could accept a great deal of it. In politics there are always fawning types who are eager to feed the vanity of the top man. I can recall countless standing ovations and special tributes to the various anniversaries in Diefenbaker's life. Lowell Murray once said: 'That man has more feast days than the blessed Virgin Mother herself!' In these rituals everyone was expected to stand and cheer, and of course all did. To have a vote of confidence handled in the same way was deemed a clever stratagem. Overwhelming them with numbers became a favourite technique. It had worked so well at the 1963 annual meeting that it was expected to outfox the discontented for a long long time.

Dalton Camp, who had been elected national president at the annual meeting of February 1964 with the support of the Diefenbaker people, was giving much thought to the basic question of leader-party relations. We were among the speakers at a weekend Conservative Youth Conference at McMaster University in Hamilton. On three successive mornings I lectured on the party's history. That the young people were of stern stuff was shown in their excellent attendance. The most important discussion I had was one with Dalton Camp after the day's agenda was completed in which he outlined his thinking about the leadership situation. He was considering standing for a second two-year term as national president on a commitment to call a national leadership convention. Needless to say, I was all for this as were Pat Nowlan and others in on the discussion. Dalton obviously had quietly canvassed the opinion of party people and before long launched his re-election campaign in front of a couple of Tory audiences.

Although in the 1965 election Conservatives had donned the mantle of ecumenical equability, goodwill and forgiveness were not much in evidence after the campaign. One of Diefenbaker's moves to consolidate his own group in control brought about the firing of Flora MacDonald from her post at national headquarters. A tremendously active, able, and popular figure, Flora's dismissal brought a shocked reaction from PCs all across the country. If Dalton Camp needed anything to strengthen his resolve, Flora's sacking provided it. None of us was surprised when he became the target of a fierce barrage of criticism from the Diefenbaker forces. The battle lines were drawn; the field of conflict would be the annual meeting of November 1966. A bloody confrontation it would prove to be.

While he was still prime minister, John Diefenbaker had suggested that Arthur Maloney run for national president. Maloney had told me about their meeting in the PM's private railway car in Toronto at which Maloney agreed but stipulated a condition. He wished to be given a senatorship. The Liberals had established something of a tradition of presidents being appointed to the Upper House.

To obtain Maloney as their candidate was a major coup for the Diefenbaker group. He was one of a politically active family. Among criminal lawyers in Canada he ranked at the top. With a ready wit and an infectious Irish charm he had legions of friends. He had been elected to the House in 1957. Our offices were not far apart and I knew him well and fondly. Had all things been equal I would have been in the forefront of his active supporters in 1966. But in those days there was, for many PCs, one transcendent question – leadership. Believing that it was imperative that the party express itself on the leadership, I had to support the Camp candidacy even if it meant voting and working against an old and dear friend.

Strangely enough, while my relations with Art Maloney had been warm and cordial from the first, it was a long time before much geniality developed in the contacts between Camp and myself. He had left UNB before I arrived there and I heard about him only through Tories like Dick Petrie who tended to scorn him as an acolyte of Premier John McNair and the Grit party. Some years later during my summers at the archives in Ottawa, I met him at Bracken House when he and Bill Rowe seemed to be handling the PC national headquarters very well. After I became an MP and Dalton was the party's national director, I inadvertently did something which embarrassed him and put a chill on our relationship. In a report at a high-level party meeting he had made a shrewd appraisal of some of the factors causing our great drop in electoral strength. He said that the party in making a god of their leader had made sheep of themselves. Speaking to an Ottawa Women's PC group, I used this line, properly attributing it to Dalton and agreeing with it wholeheartedly. I hadn't expected that a back-bencher speaking to a local PC group would hit the press. I soon found how wrong I was. Not only did my comments receive media coverage but they made the popular Max Ferguson show, one of my favourite CBC radio programs. As usual Ferguson's skit was delightfully clever, but Camp resented my giving currency to a comment made *in camera*. It is always difficult to set the record straight. As a member of the House of Commons I was on the list for the printed party minutes containing Camp's speech. Apparently I also received a copy as a member of the national executive. One of the two was marked confidential, and the other was not. Unfortunately I had used the latter. I doubt whether my justification of good faith would have carried, so I lived with my minor infamy.

Not inadvertently I then passed through a period when I considered Dalton too soft on Diefenbaker. I was certainly not in his corner when he appeared as the anointed successor to Egan Chambers at the annual meeting of 1964. Nor was I enthusiastic about his non-voting at the controversial national executive meeting in 1965. But I did appreciate his summoning of the national executive on that occasion in response to the call from Balcer and his Quebec colleagues. He was a very active and effective national president in the 'unity' campaign of 1965. By that time Camp had been proven a brilliant strategist in provincial campaigns in many parts of the country. Powerful provincial politicians had reason to praise his political prowess.

So it was that when Dalton Camp discussed with me and a few others his strategy on the leadership issue, I knew a good deal about him and had given much thought to his virtues and verities. I was totally supportive of his course of action. Knowing as he did John Diefenbaker's capacity for venom, Camp was revealing himself as a man of great courage. In staking his re-election on the convention issue he could very well become the fall guy. To me, the other termites, and party people sadly convinced of the need for drastic change, Camp became something of a champion.

In the weeks leading up to the annual meeting I devoted long hours to the Camp cause. Even in my own elections I did not enjoy the one-on-one canvass of people's support. But we knew we had a struggle on our hands, so there was no course but all-out campaigning. There was much strategizing; I recall many conversations in my office or on the telephone. I was often in touch with David MacDonald, Gordon Fairweather, Jean Wadds, Jed Baldwin, Gordon Aiken, and other parliamentarians. Lowell Murray and Flora MacDonald with their contacts all across the country were powerful workers in the Camp camp. There was a thick aura of tension and suspicion and people were judged by the company they kept. My lovely third floor office in the West Block was deemed one of the centres of conspiracy. One day I noticed MPs Gordon Fairweather and Alf Hales in serious conversation on the parliamentary lawn. With a little memo book in hand I opened my window and shouted: 'Aha, Hales, I've got your number now.'

At one party meeting John Diefenbaker, at his denunciatory best, spoke of 'termites being moved by personal ambition.' Later Jim MacDonnell, the father of the Port Hope Conference, long-time MP and past president of the national party, rose with a comment: 'I may be a termite but since I am also an octogenarian it is doubtful that I am motivated by personal ambition.'

The explosive confrontation of the Campites and Diefenbakerites at the annual meeting of November 1966 still glows and pains in my memory. My niece Hazel was visiting us from Boston and registered as an observer at the meeting. She was quite unprepared for the intensity of the battle and remarked: 'I was never noted for impressive breasts but they seem to draw an inordinate amount of attention here. Not until the tenth person had peered and growled at me did I realize it was the Camp button that was turning them off.' I recall many times greeting fellow delegates in elevators only to have the cordiality end when someone would say in horrified tones, 'Oh, I see you're one of them!' A Maritime MP knocked a Camp student to the floor. The venerable Senator Grattan O'Leary, who moved Camp's nomination, was spat upon. Years after, Walter Baker told caucus that he had literally saved Heath Macquarrie's life, in providing his Château Laurier room as a haven for me when a prairie colleague was ready to tear me limb from limb. It was a terrible three days. Many old friendships were shattered; many loyalties torn asunder. For years after, Dalton Camp was depicted as a Machiavellian monster, a scheming regicide. Seeing him at close range through those fateful, fevered months, I can testify to his dignified composure and his cool competence throughout. There was no venom, no viciousness in his attitude. Some of his lieutenants and followers often displayed more intensity of feeling than he did.

From the beginning Camp had sought to make his crusade much more than a pursuit of personal re-election to the presidency with a commitment to a leadership convention. He sought to stimulate Conservatives to look deeply into the role of a party in a democratic society. He was interested in policies as well as structures. In his many speeches across the country there was no sniping at the national leader. Indeed he didn't mention John Diefenbaker's name. In broadening the range of his appeal Camp sought to attract more people than those who regarded Diefenbaker's departure as the *summum bonum* of the party's existence. Some wag said he was trying to encourage people to vote for Camp and for a convention and still be able to feel loyal, faithful, and respectable. On Camp's effort to lead the fight yet keep above the fray, Peter Newman made the eloquent comment: 'he transformed himself into the embodiment of an irrefutable cause: the reform of the Conservative party.'[5]

Obviously he had some success in this approach. Some less philosophical types supported him because the party's constitution provided that presidents be elected by ballot – a victory for Camp would *ipso facto* be a vote for a convention in the only way that the inadequate procedural rules could provide. So it was that there were delegates who voted not out of enthusiasm for Dalton Camp but in a desire for a leadership convention.

I don't enjoy reliving those emotional days, but there is one part of the record of that fateful annual meeting which I can set straight. It has been recorded that the Camp forces rushed into the Château drawing room and pre-empted all the good seats long before the meeting began. On the contrary, I remember that Jean

Wadds and I discovered a host of Maloney supporters occupying many rows of seats well in advance of the meeting. She immediately urged the YPC leader to get his young people down to the hall. I phoned Isabel and Hazel urging that they find seats at once. Our people did respond well. A look at newspaper photographs will show many Maloney placards in the front rows; Camp signs are also evident. Considering the zeal in both camps, it would be surprising if such were not the case.

I have spent a lifetime attending public meetings and listening to parliamentary speeches. I have never found it necessary to heckle or interrupt anyone's remarks. I was profoundly distressed at that opening meeting to hear John Diefenbaker being booed and heckled. His remark, 'Is this a Conservative meeting?' was really a well-deserved rebuke. Nor is it sufficient justification to recall that the preceding remarks of Dalton Camp were nastily and consistently interrupted. Sitting in the row behind me was a Maloney supporter whose loudness was matched only by his unpleasantness. Into the folklore about the 1966 meeting has gone the allegation that the Camp people sent around a note to spur their people to harass the leader during his speech. There was indeed a note and I wrote it. The message was that things were going our way and for God's sake don't spoil it by heckling Diefenbaker. Jean Wadds and Doug Harkness knew of my effort. I'm sure that Fairweather, David MacDonald, and other Campites would have the same recollection.

The only culpability, if that is the word, which I would accept over the incident was the refusal of many of us to stand in ovation at John Diefenbaker's entrance. We had often seen the standing ovation technique used to melt the opposition. I am still convinced that, had everyone in that hall stood, such an action would have been seen as a ringing endorsation of Diefenbaker and Maloney. The Camp candidacy and the Camp objective might well have been swept aside in a gesture of respect not intended as a judgment on the crucial issue facing the meeting. I take no pride in my part in this particular episode but it had been conditioned by bitter experience.

O tempora! O mores!

The 1966 annual meeting remained divisive and nasty to the end. Dalton Camp won the presidency by a mere 62 votes, defeating Maloney 564 to 502. A subsequent motion to call a convention passed 548 to 209. By that time, as the vote shows, many anti-Camp delegates were no longer in the hall. They were, instead, thronging around John Diefenbaker in a nearby room. The cheers for the old chieftain were highly audible to those in the ballroom as they took the steps that would lead to the selection of a new leader. Diefenbaker was to have spoken at a closing banquet; both the feast and the speech were abruptly wiped off the agenda. Once again it was not a glorious time to be a practising Tory.

In the aftermath of the bitter warfare at the Château Laurier there was a sort of replay on Parliament Hill. As I entered the opposition lobby I noted a table with official-looking documentation. While there were no flowers or candles it seemed to have something of a shrine-like aura. It was the famous declaration of loyalty. 'We, the undersigned Members of Parliament of the Progressive Conservative Party, request that the Right Honourable J.G. Diefenbaker continue as Leader of our Party.' Before the document was removed from the lobby it had been signed by seventy-one MPS.

The Diefenbaker forces had returned to the old strategy of interposing the caucus, where he was strong, against party bodies in which he was not so popular. But this was the first time caucus had been invoked *after* the party had registered an opinion. It was also interesting that, instead of the traditional stand-up ovation it was in writing. It was almost as if, after fighting the ballot at party gatherings, the Diefenbaker forces were producing one massive ballot of their own. The numbers showed that in the caucus the leader had a large majority of support. In his memoirs Diefenbaker listed also those who did *not* sign, describing it as 'revealing.'[6] The list read:

Gordon H. Aiken	H. Ray Ballard
Martial Asselin	Richard A. Bell
Gerald W. Baldwin	Thomas M. Bell

Siegfried Enns	Marcel Lambert
Gordon Fairweather	David MacDonald
J. Michael Forrestall	Heath Macquarrie
E. Davie Fulton	J. Patrick Nowlan
Lee Grills	L.R. Sherman
Heward Grafftey	Heber E. Smith
Alfred D. Hales	Georges-J. Valade
Douglas Harkness	Jean Wadds
W. Marvin Howe	Eldon M. Woolliams

There were few surprises in this list although I had not expected that the numbers would reach twenty-four. Ten months after the signature the seventy-one loyalists were divided and supporting candidates other than Diefenbaker in the 1967 convention. Some ran against him. It was all really very sad.

Of John Diefenbaker it cannot be said that he went quietly. When the leadership convention was convoked in September 1967 he became a candidate and stayed on until the third ballot in which he won but 12 per cent of the votes cast. Had he made his intentions clear earlier he doubtless would have made a better showing. One of his actions at the Toronto convention was ironically amusing. He had walked out of the annual meeting ten months earlier. At the Convention he walked in with pipers piping and interrupted the proceedings with a vengeance, which he doubtless enjoyed.

John Diefenbaker remained on the party and national scene for another decade. For his successor, Robert Stanfield, who had done so much for him, he was a thorn in the flesh. After his own resignation the usually mild and correct Stanfield publicly rebuked Diefenbaker for his harassing of Joe Clark.

From the departure of his old adversary, Lester Pearson must have drawn some relief, although he himself resigned the leadership of his party a few months later, in December 1967. There was a short period of civility when Stanfield sat across from him in the House of Commons, and Pearson invited Stanfield to lunch at 24 Sussex Drive. As they strolled the grounds, Stanfield, an avid gardener, noted a particular shrub and asked his host: 'After it's through blooming do you transplant or cut back?' Pearson, no great horticulturist, replied: 'At that stage I phone the National Capital Commission.'

There can be no doubt that Dalton Camp was the catalyst of a fundamental change in the Progressive Conservative party. Apart from his skill as a strategist under the heaviest fire, he was one of the most profound thinkers our ranks have produced. Yet, for a long while after his epochal victory, he became something of a pariah in our party. Many who were delighted to have the leadership question open were eager to dissociate themselves from the deed. There were times when a casual observer might be pardoned for believing that Dalton Camp must have marked all those ballots himself. Would-be successors to John Diefenbaker naturally wanted to get the votes of as many of his admirers as possible, so carrying the badge of Camp was no help.

Throughout the bleak years of semi-exclusion, Camp went his imperturbable way. In his writing and his speeches he added lustre to Progressive Conservatism. I used to say that while he looked like Dean Rusk he spoke like Adlai Stevenson. Not all who are gifted in oral expression are equally blessed in the written medium. Camp is an expert communicator in both.

7

Noblest Roman of Them All

Although, as I have noted, he had an indirect but significant influence on my victory in 1957, I was not an early fan of Robert Stanfield. I heard his speech at the 1956 leadership convention in Ottawa, but I can't remember whether or not I met him. In the late summer of 1957 I went to Shaw's Hotel on the north shore of the Island to greet him and his wife Mary. Carrying on a conversation with him was somewhat laborious and challenging but, as my wife reminded me, he did try to chat with her. In 1960 he and I were on the Air Canada flight which marked the inauguration of service from Halifax to Britain. It is difficult to recall anything he said or did. Our own premier, Walter Shaw, was the star of the show insofar as the Atlantic premiers were concerned. Although I didn't warm to the too forward Joey Smallwood, I at least remember him.

As the years passed and I learned more about Stanfield's political and administrative skills and accomplishments in Nova Scotia, I developed a great respect for him. But I certainly could not see any reason, other than sheer loyalty, for the intense admiration which so many of my Nova Scotia colleagues had for him.

But when, after much travail, the way was opened for a national leadership convention in 1966, he already had impressive credentials. After a long period trying to resurrect the Nova Scotia provincial party in his role as president, he agreed to accept the leadership in 1948. It must have been a tremendous act of faith to take over a party which held not a single seat in the legislature.

In his very interesting book on Robert Stanfield, Geoffrey Stevens suggests that he was 'the most forgettable member of an unforgettable family.'[1] Of the Stanfields, Stevens writes that in their own quite different way they were to Nova Scotia what the Kennedys would later become to Massachusetts.

After Robert Stanfield became our leader I was guest speaker at a British Columbia political meeting. I spent little time on the issues of the day but talked mostly about the quality and qualities of our new leader. After the meeting a gentleman told me he was greatly surprised at many items in Stanfield's background: 'I can't understand why you people don't make more of him.' Certainly in all the years of Stanfield-Trudeau confrontation it was Trudeau who came across as the man of intellect. But Robert Stanfield was a brilliant scholar.

Although the national annual meeting of 1966 had gone successfully insofar as I was concerned, it had been an emotionally draining experience. The 'morning after' was fraught with tension and I welcomed the healing pause which the Christmas recess brought. As always it was uplifting and pleasant to get back to Prince Edward Island and see friends, especially at the New Year's Day levées in Charlottetown.

But the respite was brief. The PC national executive decided early in 1967 that the leadership convention would be held in Toronto in September. It was clear that the air would be filled with candidates' calls for the national party's attention and support. By mid-February three candidates, John Maclean of Brockville, Davie Fulton, and George Hees had announced their entry into the race. Amid these declarations of willingness came a statement of quite a different kind. The premier of Nova Scotia stated on 24 January that he had neither the intention nor the desire to enter the federal sweepstakes, but he didn't make an unequivocal statement that such a move was completely ruled out.

I was one of those Progressive Conservatives who spent the first half of centennial year dedicated to a cause but without a candidate. There were a number of reasons why Stanfield didn't enter the lists when the other would-be leaders did. In the first place he was not a man to jump either to conclusions or decisions. He would mull it over carefully.

He had also decided to hold an election in Nova Scotia and he could hardly conduct that campaign if he were seen as having one eye on Ottawa. Nor would he have time during a campaign to give thought to the national scene. So we Stanfieldites knew we had to wait until the 30 May election was over and a decent interval after that. It would be unbecoming for him to accept the reconfirmation of his Nova Scotia electorate by saying: 'Thanks awfully. Now I'm buzzing off to Ottawa.' Many, many times I discussed the Nova Scotia election with my wife and caucus colleagues in the pro-Stanfield group. It would be a real help if he could win with an increased majority. But having won thirty-nine out of forty-three seats in 1963 it was a bit unrealistic to expect him to achieve an increase. But he did and I remember my rejoicing on the night of 30 May to see the PC seat total reach forty. Never mind that the legislature had been increased to forty-six seats. He had still won more than ever! George Drew and John Bracken had lost popularity with their provincial electorates just before moving to the federal scene. Not so Stanfield.

The big victory in Nova Scotia made Stanfield's candidacy more attractive to a growing number of Conservatives. My West Block neighbour and close friend, Mike Forrestall, was active every day in contacting people to stimulate their interest and advocacy. During early summer it was a sort of chicken-egg situation. Many in the party might admire him but would be reluctant to make a commitment without knowing whether he might run. On the other hand, Stanfield could hardly be expected to make a move without some indication of the type of support he would get. I remember Forrestall and myself joining a number of caucus people in a visit to Grattan O'Leary in his Senate office. We besought him to use his influence and eloquence to prevail upon our somewhat reluctant gladiator. O'Leary had enormous admiration for Stanfield and, great party man that he was, agreed to go to Halifax. As it eventuated he met with Stanfield in Toronto where, as the premier put it: 'he gave me quite a going over.'

In the pro-Stanfield forces could be found the great majority of the 'Camp followers' (one of our gentlest cognomens): Douglas Harkness, Jean Wadds, David MacDonald, Gordon Fairweather, Jed Baldwin, and nearly all the MPs who did not sign the loyalty oath of November 1966. But not all those who backed Camp for the presidency in 1966 supported Stanfield for the leadership in 1967. In fact one of the most distinguished of the twenty-four, Davie Fulton, was himself a candidate.

In the non-parliamentary group there was also a range of choice. One of the best people in the Camp camp was Lowell Murray, Fulton's campaign manager. Other prominent Fultonites were Brian Mulroney and Michael Vineburg. Maritime Progressive Conservatives were strongly behind Stanfield. All ten MPs from Nova Scotia were Stanfieldites. I would have been delighted had there been a unanimous declaration from PEI's MPs but we did get 50 per cent, with David MacDonald and me for Stanfield from the beginning. Throughout the spring and summer I was made aware of the great respect in which Robert Stanfield was held and how many people, Tories and others, wished him to bring his wisdom, decency, and outlook to the national scene. Across Atlantic Canada he was very much the favourite son.

I remember that long summer of 1967 as a time of immense excitement, a good deal of optimism, but also of a debilitating degree of tension and uncertainty. Every day there was a new rumour, another well-based report. Stanfield will never run; Stanfield has already decided to run. Roblin is out; Roblin will certainly run. Dief is just waiting for the best time to enter. The Chief is behind Hamilton, Fleming, or Starr, or perhaps even Roblin. The rumour mills rolled erratically and noisily, but they rolled without ceasing. This uncertainty was in part a result of the fact that some of the principals had not made up their minds. In part too it was motivated by wishful thinking. At times the rumour mongering was a part of someone's strategy for his own victory and someone else's defeat.

Throughout it all there was the speculation about what John Diefenbaker would do. When he took to the airwaves in January 1967 to call for a convention, he thundered that he was not about to render a swansong. Generally I think that most of us greatly overestimated his power to make kings or destroy pretenders.

Political conventions are not without their pain, even for those who do not seek the crown. I well remember a telephone call from Donald Fleming whom I had supported in 1956. He told me why he had decided to seek a return, and of his confidence that he was responding to a 'genuine draft.' Although he had some excellent people behind him like R.A. 'Dick' Bell, I had some reservations about a number of others who had done the drafting and said to Fleming that if Diefenbaker ran many of these would leave Fleming high and dry. I didn't enjoy saying these things. Nor was I in any way heartened when after the vote in September Fleming reacted to his having been let down. In any case I had to tell my friend and former colleague that I was totally committed to Stanfield whose candidacy I still expected.

I didn't know Stanfield all that well and it would be presumptuous for even a close friend to try to read his mind. But even when the most negative reports were coming out of Halifax I was able to keep the embers of hope alive. It seemed to me that this man had a deep and genuine interest in the national party. More profound still was his concern for the country. I recalled that he was invariably present at meetings of the federal PC party. Not every Tory premier showed up at such gatherings.

Although he didn't make waves or headlines, he made a good many speeches outside Nova Scotia. Often he indicated a serious national viewpoint on important issues facing the Dominion. Stanfield's speech at the meeting of premiers in Charlottetown, 14 to 15 August 1961, was an example of his sure feel for the national scene. This meeting was called to discuss general financial matters and one important specific item – the establishment of a cultural centre at Charlottetown to commemorate the initial meeting of the Fathers of Confederation held in that city in 1864. Dr Frank MacKinnon, political scientist and principal of Prince of Wales College, had convinced the leaders of all ten provinces and the Dominion that it would be a splendid idea if all of them would support the erection of a fitting memorial in the cradle of Confederation. His dream was realized, and the Confederation Centre is today a splendid theatre for the performing arts and nucleus of cultural riches benefiting all who visit it.

Stanfield's performance at this meeting was in keeping with such an historic theme. He spoke in French in honour of the new Quebec premier, Jean Lesage. He reminded his counterparts of the historic role of the Maritimes in the confederation process. 'After all, we fathered this country. We have some responsibility for the way it behaves as it grows up.'

Certainly these were splendid words but I always set more store by his address in Montreal in April 1964 when he told the Canadian Club some of his thoughts about the kind of Canada he envisaged. In that speech he again talked about foreign ownership, trade, and general economic issues. But doubtless the most important part of his address dealt with relations between anglophone and francophone Canadians. He supported a bilingual public service, at a time when some Tories were denouncing Pearson's moves in this direction: 'English-speaking Canadians should welcome the French language and culture in Canada as a continuing fact.' He also came out in favour of a distinctive Canadian flag and a national anthem. That Montreal speech was not the think piece of a politician bound by the borders of his own province. It was, I thought, the first glimpse of Robert Stanfield, Canadian statesman, and I for one liked what I saw. I always recalled this contribution to national issues when told that Stanfield had no ambitions beyond Nova Scotia. The Montreal speech became my lifeline to optimism in the uncertain days before Stanfield announced his candidacy.

While Stanfield himself is a direct and straightforward man, there was a good deal of toing and froing in connection with his decision to go federal. There was much speculation at the time that his plans were likely to be affected by Duff Roblin's intentions. I believe that Stanfield would have stood aside had his fellow premier from Manitoba entered the lists. He was in Charlottetown in August the day Roblin announced his candidacy and he revealed enough to convince me that, had Roblin moved earlier, he would have had no competition from Stanfield. Since, as it turned out, the two premiers led the pack all the way, Roblin's hesitancy may well have cost him the crown. In light of what happened in the Canadian political scene in subsequent years he may not be filled with regrets.

Then there was the Dalton Camp question. Our hero of the 1966 annual meeting was probably the most brilliant political operative in Canada, having handled election campaigns in a number of provinces including Nova Scotia, Manitoba, New Brunswick, Prince Edward Island, and, of course, federal contests. Both Stanfield and Roblin had strong reasons for recalling Camp's support and skills. His struggles to open up the party leadership would have been amply justified if either Roblin or Stanfield came forward as a candidate.

Until one of the premiers moved, Camp was in a most difficult situation. There were those in the party in 1967, especially in his strongly supportive group, the so-called Eglinton Mafia, who thought he himself should run. I remember attending a meeting in the Centre Block of the Parliament Buildings with many of my pro-Camp colleagues. Two of Dalton's close friends and confidants, Chad Bark and Don Guthric, had come down from Toronto to sound us out on Dalton's candidacy. There was a good discussion of the question. Every one of us expressed unbounded regard for Dalton and appreciation of his work and worth. But most declared with regret that they could not recommend that he be a candidate. Not surprisingly, they thought that he would become a target for those who had been worsted in the 1966 meeting. In the kind of emotional upheaval his candidacy would cause, they saw not only anguish for him but the grim likelihood of defeat as well. I said I appreciated their views but, in the final analysis I doubted that our party was so blessed with brains that we could unequivocally turn down a man of Camp's special calibre and qualities. Only Gordon Fairweather supported my view. At the time the prospect of Stanfield's candidacy was not bright. He, of course, was the first choice of both of us.

A lesser man than Dalton Camp might have gone into a state of dudgeon over the reaction to whatever leadership ambition he nurtured, since the parliamentarians were not the only ones to express reluctance to support him. But he responded to the call to serve another's cause yet again. Adding a bitter ingredient to his cup was the fact that this time he was expected to work for others but do it all *sub rosa*. At Stanfield's press conference in the Red Chamber of Province House in Halifax, an ebullient crowd of prominent Tories were in jubilant attendance. Two of the most jubilant, Camp and Finlay MacDonald, had been requested to absent themselves. Both men did so without demur. Officially Robert Stanfield's campaign manager was Maurice Flemming, president of the Nova Scotia PCs, who had defeated Camp's friend Finlay MacDonald at the party's annual meeting. The man in charge operating from a figurative underground bunker was Dalton Camp. One wouldn't use the word Byzantine about the city of Halifax in the Year of Our Lord 1967, but there were some interesting strands to follow or unravel.

I recall being somewhat surprised to hear at one stage that everything was set for Stanfield to declare his candidacy except for Ike Smith's opposition to the idea of Stanfield's leaving Nova Scotia. Knowing the enormously high regard each man held for the other I required a little explanation. My Nova Scotia informants told me that as a prerequisite to going federal, Stanfield wished to feel that the province was in the capable hands of Ike Smith. For a number of reasons, among them the fact that the provincial election had been so recent and the possibility of problems on the industrial and economic front, Smith was not eager to don the mantle of leadership. Eventually, after much discussion and negotiation, the issue was resolved and Smith, a man loyal to his party and his friends, adjusted to Stanfield's departure.

So it was that when Robert Stanfield entered the leadership race he had Nova Scotia solidly behind him and was almost as strong in the rest of Atlantic Canada. He had substantial support in the parliamentary caucus. He was backed by Dalton Camp and a cadre of extremely bright people. His entry won widespread favourable comment in the press. It was an auspicious launch with most things in place. In the end, of course, it would be the man himself who would carry the day. Most appropriately there was at hand the slogan used in the 30 May provincial election: 'The Man with the Winning Way.'

Whatever else the centennial leadership convention did for us, it didn't do much for my summer. Everyone knows the Island is the best place to be at that time of year. But the exigencies of the convention strategy required me to leave the blessed isle far more than I liked. Even when I was there the telephone was incessantly active. Then in August came the Montmorency Thinkers Conference. Without doubt Montmorency Falls is a beautiful and historic spot but it is not PEI.

Within minutes of arriving at the Maison Montmorency, Mike Forrestall told me of the greeting given earlier to a group of arriving delegates by one of the Dominican brothers. 'Ah, you have come here to build upon the ruins of the future.' In coming months there were times when some PCs wondered whether this charming man's expression might not be prophetic. Certainly there was trouble enough in some quarters about the 'deux nations' concept of federalism, which became associated with the Montmorency Conference and one of its illustrious guests, Marcel Faribault. That prominent businessman and constitutional expert had appeared at the Fredericton Thinkers Conference in 1964 and nothing he said at Montmorency surprised me. I thought him a brilliant, if brittle, man whose candidacy for our party would be a great boost for us. He also had good contacts with the popular Union Nationale premier of Quebec, Daniel Johnson. Faribault believed that a constitutional document should recognize that Canada is composed of two founding peoples with historic rights, 'deux nations,' who have been joined by people from many lands. When 'deux nations' was translated into 'two nations' rather than 'two founding peoples,' hackles were raised. (Actually 'two founding peoples' was an atrocious expression. It totally ignores the fact that we had people here ages before Jacques Cartier or John Cabot left their home ports.) Before the year was out the argument over two nations would become sharp and nasty. At Montmorency the majority of participants had no great anxiety about the expression.

Another controversy developed later over Dalton Camp's closing speech in which he suggested that the vast funds voted to national defence should be diverted to foreign aid instead. There were Tories who agreed with him, but more was to be heard from those who regarded such views as akin to the kind of poppycock emitted by the peaceniks of the NDP.

On the whole I recall the Montmorency conclave as an uplifting affair which would help the Progressive Conservatives get back into the mainstream of contemporary Canadian thought. It is always difficult for delegates to a leadership convention to keep their mind on policy. By having a policy gathering before the convention, this problem was circumvented. While the Montmorency people worked out a consensus on important matters, they did not and could not bind the party to them. In addition to the 'deux nations' theory, the Montmorency gathering favoured constitutional rights for the French language in the legislatures and courts, repatriation of the constitution, entrenching the Bill of Rights, and other progressive items which Canadians now take for granted.

By a clever decision, all leadership candidates were invited to attend but not to participate. In that way delegates were given a kind of sneak preview of the roster. The most unostentatious of them all was Stanfield. He had no cadre of supporters or big-time operators about him. Rather he went his own solitary deliberate way. A good many people called me aside and suggested that his supporters at least take him under their wing and present him to the people they knew well. Having already offered my services I knew that Stanfield was doing it his way, and that even the most well-intentioned intrusion was neither necessary nor appreciated.

Returning from Montmorency I felt that it had been a worthwhile exercise. Participation had been excellent. Not all the people attending were Conservatives, but it was good for a cross-section of our party to meet with some leading Canadians who were not motivated by partisan considerations – certainly not of the Tory kind. Montmorency helped our party look like a modern, moderate, progressive aggregation of people. Despite his almost painfully low-key performance, I thought Stanfield had made a good impression.

The sixth leadership convention of the Conservative party was the first to be held in Toronto. It had more delegates than any previous gathering, and it certainly had the most intensive media coverage and the most elaborate hoopla. Over 2200 delegates cast ballots, and there were hosts of non-voting delegates and observers in attendance. In fact, an important section of the Progressive Conservative party was on display for the week. The television age was upon us and it was a wide-open convention in more ways than one. The demonstrations, the parades, the hijinks of supporters of competing candidates – Robert Stanfield, Duff Roblin, George Hees, Alvin Hamilton, Donald Fleming, Davie Fulton – may even have rivalled the soap operas for countless television watchers. The calmest candidate won some attention for eating bananas during the long intervals between votes. When asked why, Stanfield quipped that you could eat a banana quietly.

It was all very exciting, noisy, and at times a bit dangerous. Stanfield, who always refused to take himself too seriously, told one interviewer he knew that many delegates had come for the excitement. Therefore he did not plan to win on the first ballot!

The Progressive Conservatives came to Toronto without knowing whether or not the incumbent leader would be a candidate. Diefenbaker was housed in the best suite in the Royal York Hotel where he held court. Donald Fleming, Alvin Hamilton, and Duff Roblin paid calls and had conversations with the old Chief. But when Dief's former comrade in arms, Howard Green, sought to pay his respects he was rebuffed. Much hurt by this, Green told me that it must have been because he was an open supporter of Roblin. It was a mean and petty attitude for Diefenbaker to take towards such a man as Howard Green.

Apart from personal contacts with delegates, the candidates had two occasions to present themselves and their views to the assembled PCs. On Tuesday, 5 September, each hopeful was asked to put forward his views on policy. It was a major test for all the candidates. Stanfield won new friends and votes with a tightly structured speech, well reasoned, low-key, but not weak. In some ways it was different from, and a good deal better than, the usual frenzied appeals by people seeking delegate support. George Hees gave one of his trade and commerce booster speeches. Duff Roblin, having been told by one of his advisers that it was a question and answer session, had no set speech like the other contenders. But he prepared himself while others spoke and did well when his turn came. Before the Tuesday night session there was some chit-chat about which candidates would appear most proficient in French – Roblin, Fulton, or Fleming. Not much was expected of Hees, Starr, or Hamilton. With his usual delightful candour Wallace McCutcheon had earlier told a reporter that he spoke no French and if anyone had questions they had best be put in English. The candidate most at home in French was none of the front runners but John MacLean.

The Tuesday speech helped Stanfield a great deal. Despite the uncertainties and rumours it became clear that, between Tuesday night and Saturday, Stanfield's stock was on the rise. The *Toronto Telegram* had an active polling team at the convention and the paper prominently featured the results favouring Stanfield. Uncommitted delegates must have been impressed that the Nova Scotian with the winning way seemed to be victory-bound again.

In convention organization the Stanfield group was also the leader. Nothing was left to chance. The hospitality suites were superbly run. The demonstrations were excellent. The pretty girls, the pipers, the bands seemed always to be in the right spot. Someone quipped that Stanfield may have been the quietest candidate but he had the noisiest demonstrators. The big party on Friday night featuring Don Messer and his Islanders was a grand success.

John Diefenbaker's last-minute entry, ostensibly motivated by a desire to save the party and the country from the iniquitous 'deux nations' theory, was a divisive but not a discombobulating gesture. Its effect was minimized when the convention decided to table rather than debate the Montmorency conference report. Then and now, the Diefenbaker strategy is hard to fathom. Did he really think he could win even with all the anti feelings that 'deux nations' could foster? It is hard to believe that such an experienced politician could so overestimate his strength. He must have known that many of his erstwhile supporters had gone public in favour of other candidates. Some of them would recant but many would not. In the end he let himself in for a humiliating defeat. If he was seriously fearful of 'deux nations' he could have taken a stand against it long before the last minute for nominations. I remember a comment by the CBC's gravel-voiced Norman Depoe who said that John Diefenbaker didn't know what 'nation' meant in French but he did know he didn't want two of them in Canada.

Good speeches were made by the leadership hopefuls. Naturally I was most interested in Stanfield's and was well satisfied with his performance. He came across as calm, cool, and contemporary. My wife was sitting with my Brandon College successor, Professor Norma Walmsley, who had not been an enthusiast for Stanfield up until then. After the speech she said: 'Even if he can't win the election we must have him as leader. I would prefer to lose with Stanfield than win with Roblin.' A perceptive and prophetic comment. One of Stanfield's sentences was widely praised: 'There is a time for discussion and a time for decision; and I accept the responsibility of knowing when one must end and the other must begin.' Some of his former Nova Scotia colleagues later told me that he lived by that.

The pattern of the balloting was revealing. In the first place it was clear that the party wanted a new face. Not only did the delegates reject the old Chief, they were less than enthusiastic about those who had been with him. On the first ballot the candidates who were not caucus members led the field with Stanfield getting 519 votes and Roblin 343. Fulton won 343, Hees 395, Diefenbaker 271, McCutcheon 137, Hamilton 136, Fleming 126, Starr 45, John Maclean 10, and Mrs Sawka 2. I had thought that Stanfield would have had at least a hundred more votes than he received. But I was not surprised that he led the field and that Roblin was second.

Certainly Roblin was an appealing candidate. He was articulate, ambitious, intelligent, and informed. He had administered Manitoba with efficiency. It appeared that he had made a most favourable impression on Progressive Conservatives in Quebec and he was considered the favourite candidate of Premier Daniel Johnson. Surely Roblin's credentials were most impressive even apart from his ability, unique among the candidates, to play the bagpipes!

As we went from ballot to ballot in Maple Leaf Gardens, it was clear that many delegates were similarly drawn to Stanfield and Roblin. In the main the supporters of the caucus and former caucus candidates didn't shift to others in that group but to one of the premiers. But the MP candidates were no slouches. George Hees was a sterling success as minister of trade and commerce and a long-time politico who must have made countless friends in the party. Alvin Hamilton was an innovative idea man and a top-notch minister of agriculture. Donald Fleming had come second in 1956 and was a most able parliamentarian. I found Fleming's campaign somewhat sad. He seemed so confident, brisk, and ever so sincere, but he alone seemed to believe he was going anywhere.

Davie Fulton, a star in the pipeline debate and a most brilliant man, had leadership capacity. Perhaps he was hurt by his failure in BC politics when he didn't win a legislature seat. Geoffrey Stevens's comment is acerbic and painful: 'The front benches in the House of Commons were lined with tired loyalists, men of slender talents who had been sucked dry by years of submission to the Diefenbaker ego.'[2] I think this might apply to some caucus seniors but not to the contenders in 1967.

During the convention there were many explanations why Stanfield was chosen over Roblin. Certainly the role of Camp was significant. There were able people in Roblin's campaign group but they were not as competent and skilled as the Stanfield-Camp people. Some said that Roblin and his people underestimated Camp and overestimated Diefenbaker. Some of the Campites among the delegates thought that Stanfield had shown himself more daring in entering the fray without too great sensitivity about Diefenbaker's wishes or intentions.

Political conventions are usually exciting events. They can also be wearing and wearying. Although the Stanfield people were confident, they were never in the position of the Bennett, Manion, Bracken, Drew, or Diefenbaker forces in earlier leadership contests. With so many candidates and Roblin's steady strength, there was no time for relaxing and certainly no temptation for complacency. It was too hot and too noisy. I remember Saturday as a great day but an inordinately long one. The modernity of our arrangements didn't make things better. There were long delays in counting the ballots. Grattan O'Leary was not satisfied by the explanation that the adding machine had broken down. 'God Almighty, surely there's more than one adding machine in a city like Toronto,' was his exasperated comment.

But eventually the great throng of Progressive Conservatives accomplished what it had come to Toronto to do. The party had a new leader. The old leader, who had left the Maple Leaf Gardens just as he had departed the annual meeting in 1966, returned and was on the platform for the final rites. He made an appropriate speech. Stanfield, who had always seemed to rise to the occasion during the convention, once again did a splendid job. He was brief, modest, humble and conciliatory. He was gracious and generous in his references to John Diefenbaker. He revealed his appreciation of the importance of the healing balm of unity for the party. Before concluding his remarks, he declared his determination to get along with 'that fellow Camp.' Had he not paid that measure of respect to Camp, my satisfaction in the convention outcome would have been significantly and seriously diminished.

But there still lingers in my mind an indication that at this momentous occasion I allowed my dedication to overwhelm my common sense. Because I had been one of the early ones to try to persuade Stanfield to enter the fray, I felt it was incumbent upon me to do all I could to support him. I therefore decided to take a sort of post-Lenten vow of abstinence from alcohol until the voting was over. The results of the final ballot didn't come until almost 10:30 p.m. Although I got to the Royal York as fast as I could and to the reception room even faster, I ran afoul of Ontario's archaic liquor laws. After 11:00 p.m. on Saturday, good citizens of that great province were not allowed to drink in public. I took a long lingering look at the bottles behind the bar, but a look was all I got. I thought that George Drew's liquor reforms had fallen short. Our room at the Royal York was comfortable and there was plenty of ice, but I hadn't had time to buy a bottle of West Indian rum or even champagne. Not wishing to hawk my aridity about among my friends, I retreated to said hotel room where we retired weary, happy, and vindicated – but most fearfully dry! I had been much less provident than Winston Churchill who, recounting his first retreat to an air raid shelter in World War II, recalled taking down 'a bottle of brandy and other medicinal comforts.' But once dry was enough. At no subsequent convention was I caught in a rumless state.

The weeks which followed the centennial convention were euphoric. Newspaper editorials were enthusiastic. The *Vancouver Sun* described Stanfield on 11 September as believable in the role of a future prime minister. Of the outgoing leader the *Sun* noted prophetically: 'His presence in the House of Commons, as a continuing symbol and reminder of internecine differences if not as a focus of internal disaffection could not fail to be embarrassing to a new leader.' The *Ottawa Citizen* on 12 September believed that under Stanfield 'the back-biting and personal antagonisms should be gone.' As the *Toronto Star* saw it on the 11th, 'There is nothing bland about Mr. Stanfield. In real terms he is tougher than his predecessor. He has a reassuring knack of puncturing nonsense.' The *Hamilton Spectator* of the same day saw Stanfield as 'an engaging combination of diffidence, wit, integrity and competence [who] testifies by his very person that we are entering a new era of federal public service.' The *Evening Globe* of St John of that day noted that 'behind the cool exterior is a man of vigour and action.' The *Windsor Star* saw the new leader as steady and solid with a rough-hewn countenance reflecting 'strength of character and of conviction, a dedication of principles and a determination of purpose.' The *Globe and Mail* saw Stanfield as 'a low-key business-like man not given to pyrotechnics ... Calm reason will accompany him into the House.'

It was good to see a truly good man gain such a good press. Many Conservatives thought that the Toronto convention had restored our hopes. With a wise, moderate man like Stanfield at the helm, the wounds could be healed and success be ours at an early date.

8

The Best Prime Minister We Almost Had

Canadians enjoyed Expo '67 and celebrated the centennial of Confederation with gusto and excitement in all parts of the Dominion. The Progressive Conservatives did their part by putting on the best and liveliest political convention in our nation's history. But, as the warm glow of the centenary faded, so did the Progressive Conservatives' rosy prospects. With the success of 1967's celebrations behind him, Prime Minister Lester Pearson decided to resign the irksome burdens of office. His long career in diplomacy had been a glittering success crowned by the Nobel Peace Prize. He had made a magnificent comeback after the defeat of 1958. In five years, the Liberals had moved from having only forty-eight seats to a minority government. But Pearson's tenure in the highest elected office in the land had been ill-starred.

By 1967 he must have been yearning for release from all the blunders, accidents, scandals, and fiascos which marked his prime ministry. The record shows that much was accomplished under the Pearson government, but it was overshadowed by the day-to-day falterings of many of those about him. When, on 7 December, he walked over to the National Press Building to announce his resignation, few on Parliament Hill were surprised.

There was much interest in the Liberal leadership convention called for Ottawa in April 1968. Theirs was also a large, colourful affair. There were also a large number of candidates. Cabinet ministers included Robert Winters, John Turner, Allan J. Mac-Eachen, Joe Greene, Paul Hellyer, and the veteran parliamentarian Paul Martin. Eric Kierans, a former minister in the government of Premier Jean Lesage, was also a contender. But the big entry was that of Pierre Elliott Trudeau, the minister of justice, who announced on 16 February. From that time he became the man to beat, and his campaign for delegate votes drew far more attention than any of his rivals. He had become a highly exciting public figure. Dashing, unconventional, supposedly enormously attractive to beautiful women, rich, brilliant. He was an expert at judo, drove fast cars, was a great swimmer and diver, a clothes horse, and much, much else.

I had been in the House of Commons across from him since 1965 and seen him perform as parliamentary secretary to the prime minister and later minister of justice. I had seen him at social receptions in Ottawa. I hadn't realized that he was so unique and unusual, but we Tories were soon to find out. I remember when Grattan O'Leary came into caucus reporting on the crowd cheering Trudeau on Parliament Hill. 'We are up against a real star this time. I haven't seen such crowd appeal since Rudolph Valentino.' During Trudeau's campaign for the Liberal leadership and the subsequent election campaign, Canadians read and heard the word 'charismatic' which had not been familiar to them before. Another word, even more ominous for PCs, came into being: 'Trudeaumania.' Canadians of all ages, especially the urbanites, were mightily attracted to this dashing new politician.

After Trudeau's victory I made some phone calls to friends and constituents. One eastern colleague was profoundly depressed. He asked rhetorically: 'They have a swinger and we have a square – which one do you think will win?' Another call to a vice-president of the PEI Progressive Conservative party brought a muted response. I was soon to discover why. He was giving thought to running for the Liberals, which he did.

There was little time between the Liberal convention and the election call. On 23 April 1968 the new prime minister dissolved Parliament with the election date set for 25 June. The governing party was using the glamour and publicity of their convention as a boost for the electoral contest. Being able to time elections is one of the great advantages of office.

The 1968 election was a very important one for me. The Redistribution Act of 1966 had had a profound effect upon Prince Edward Island. No longer would constituency boundaries be based on county lines, to which Island voters had grown accustomed over many years. There would no longer be a member for Kings, one for Prince, and two for Queens. Henceforth there would be four single-member ridings: Cardigan, Egmont, Hillsborough, and Malpeque. In the House of Commons, both Angus MacLean and I had fought against the recommendations of the Redistribution Commission. Since the historic system had worked well and since all PEI constituencies were – and would remain because of constitutional protection – considerably less populous than the national average, why make a disruptive change. No matter how it was sliced, Prince Edward Island would have four seats in the House of Commons, no more, no less. But, not surprisingly, our efforts were unavailing. The new constituency of Hillsborough was totally within Queens and comprised the Charlottetown area and a rural section. Malpeque had the eastern part of Prince and most of the remainder of Queens. It did not take a genius to conclude that, for the incumbent Queens members, Hillsborough would be the preferred riding. But neither Angus MacLean nor I lived in the new Hillsborough constituency. My home, Victoria, was in Malpeque. His was in Cardigan to which an eastern part of Queens had been assigned.

On the face of it, it might seem that I should run in Malpeque where I lived and that Hillsborough might go to Angus MacLean who was the senior man. Had I taken that view, things would have been simpler. But I assumed that, since neither of us was resident of Hillsborough and both had represented its people in the old Queens constituency, I should not automatically take a self-denying stance. It would be most unhelpful to have both MacLean and Macquarrie contest the Hillsborough nomination convention. Two men who had run in Queens for five successive and successful elections as running mates could hardly appear as competitors before their own party. So it was decided that the executives of Malpeque and Hillsborough would meet in joint session and make a decision. The two incumbent members would accept the verdict and run in the constituency indicated by the joint executive.

At that meeting we were asked to say a few words. When my turn came, I began by saying I would accept the meeting's verdict and run in either Malpeque or Hillsborough. I expressed the view that MacLean might be a better candidate than I for Malpeque, stressing that he was a farmer and that Malpeque was a major agricultural area. I also noted that the RCAF base would be in Malpeque and that Angus was a distinguished RCAF veteran. As for Hillsborough, I thought that as an academic I might have good contacts with the important University of Prince Edward Island community.

Angus MacLean and I then left the meeting and walked around Charlottetown a bit and ended up at the Charlottetown Hotel. We were, in effect, doing something akin to watching the chimney of the Sistine Chapel at Vatican conclaves. After what seemed a long time, one of the executive members, Emmett Austin, came to get us and we went back and heard the verdict, that MacLean should run in Malpeque and I in Hillsborough. It brought great satisfaction to me but not to my colleague. He was greatly surprised and was not prepared to accept the decision of the joint executive.

There followed a period of anxiety and tension. To say that the joint executive decision was not unanimously acclaimed would be an extreme understatement. There was much grumbling and mumbling among those who thought Angus MacLean had been ill-treated. Appeals were made to the national leader, Robert Stanfield, to intervene. Not surprisingly, he did not elect to do so. Efforts were made to overturn the decision. A meeting of the poll chairmen of 5 and 6 Queens provincial districts was held and a petition drawn up to the effect that MacLean and not Macquarrie be the Hillsborough candidate. Since this was a formidable group of the poll chairmen of the Hillsborough constituency, their united protest would have been highly significant.

Naturally, I wasn't at this meeting, but apparently the mood was somewhat altered by a late appeal from one of the poll chairmen who rushed to the meeting after arriving at the Charlottetown airport. Alan Scales, an able young lawyer and businessman, presented a strong case. As I understand it, he dealt with what their efforts for MacLean might do to Macquarrie. He put the case so strongly that a substantial number said that, on reflection, they did not wish to sign the protest document. This successful and skilful intervention made things somewhat easier for me. In succeeding weeks, I was able to re-establish cordial relationships with nearly all the party people who had been hostile to the joint executive's decision.

Redistribution often brings difficulties and discord for candidates and for parties. We were somewhat unique in that we had the dividing up of a dual riding with two long-time incumbents. For a while after the joint executive meeting, there was speculation as to whether Angus MacLean would contest Malpeque. I always thought he would, but I was uncertain about repercussions in Hillsborough.

I faced my strongest opponent in 1968. Jack MacAndrew was program director at the Confederation Centre of the Arts, which put him in close contact with many Charlottetown people, especially the young and artistically inclined. He was a highly proficient communicator. He also turned out to be a very hard worker with an inventive mind. Every day of the campaign, I realized that there was a strong alert opponent just across the way. The fact that he was a good friend of mine didn't make it any easier.

Developments on the national scene prompted the most careful attention at the constituency level. The Stanfield campaign at the leadership convention had been a model of efficiency. The same could not be said about the election campaign. Only a myopic optimist could have believed that things were going well. The bang-up opening staged in Winnipeg should have been a smashing success. But, despite the star-studded cast featuring Premiers John Robarts of Ontario, G.I. Smith of Nova Scotia, and Walter Weir of Manitoba, along with Duff Roblin, Alvin Hamilton, and Marcel Faribault, it failed. Some of these men, especially Faribault, spoke well, and there was a large audience. But there were so many speeches that the rally had gone off national television before the leader, Bob Stanfield, began to speak. There were similar blunders in other places. The big Toronto rally bombed. The Tories had a propeller-driven aircraft, a DC-7 dubbed 'The Flying Banana,' while the jet-age prime minister naturally zoomed across the country in a stretch DC-9 which flew at twice the speed of Stanfield's vintage plane.

Nationally the PCs were outflown, outclassed, and outman-oeuvred. Often Stanfield was put on the defensive for the 'deux nations' policy, which lent itself to misinterpretation and mis-understanding. He was often questioned about what appeared to be his policy in support of a guaranteed annual income. But even if the Progressive Conservative campaign had been sure-footed and well directed, the party would not have won in 1968. The Trudeau phenomenon was the prevailing political fact of life. The new hero was the darling of the masses and the classes. He appealed to the broad-minded, to the latitudinarians, and the lib-ertarians. He also won support from some of the bigoted. To the anti-French elements he was seen as the person who would put Quebec in its place, whereas the former premier of Nova Scotia was viewed as a patsy to Quebec. At one and the same time, Trudeau was welcomed as the greatest swinger and the toughest strong man ever to come down the pike.

Nor were Prince Edward Island and the Hillsborough consti-tuency immune from Trudeaumania. In his cross-country search for delegates before the Liberal convention, Trudeau had received a hero's welcome in Prince Edward Island. Our popular and able premier, Alex Campbell, led 200 people to greet him at the air-port. Campbell was the first premier to 'go for Trudeau.' Later in the day, 300 people jammed the Charlottetown Hotel to hail the conquering Grit hero.

When two months later he again came to Charlottetown during the election campaign, Trudeau was greeted by a massive crowd at Confederation Square. Charlottetown is a small city but it is still a city, and from my room in a nearby hotel I kept close tabs on the expression of Trudeaumania in the heart of Hillsborough constituency. The report confirmed my view that, if Trudeau's appeal were effective electorally in Prince Edward Island, it would be most felt in Hillsborough. But I was not despondent and we continued our campaign strategy as originally established. I never spent much time in talking about the personalities on the other side, and this exciting visit didn't frighten or deflect us. But we didn't slacken our effects either.

When Stanfield came to the Island, he was over an hour late but he certainly didn't do our cause any harm. There was a good crowd at the airport and our local people had organized a motorcade from the airport to the Charlottetown Hotel. After the Stanfield party had checked in and gone upstairs, I was asked to invite Stanfield's son Max to meet the young people who formed a large part of the group in the crowded lobby. When I phoned the suite, Stanfield himself answered and called Max to the phone. This was so like him. Introducing Stanfield at the meeting that night, I welcomed son Max too, advising the ladies not to be overcome by Trudeaumania but to kiss Max first. He later told me, 'and I though you were my friend!' Stanfield's children were most supportive in his campaign as was his lovely vivacious wife Mary.

Stanfield did very well in Prince Edward Island, carrying all four seats. My majority in Hillsborough was 1956. In Atlantic Canada the PCs won 25 out of 32 seats. Newfoundland had gone solidly Liberal in 1965. In 1968 only one of its constituencies elected a Liberal and that was Don Jamieson in Burin-Burgeo. The Newfoundland result brought me special satisfaction since it meant the return of my friend Jim McGrath to the Ottawa scene. Of Nova Scotia's 11 seats all but 1 went PC, the exception being Cape Breton-Highlands, held by that master politician, Allan J. Mac-Eachen. In New Brunswick the split was 5 to 5 with the Acadians remaining with the Liberals. That situation would continue until Richard Hatfield ushered in a new political alignment in the province. Except for Newfoundland the PC victors were, in the main, incumbents. This must, of course, be considered an important factor in the overall regional result. But many old-timers were wiped out in other parts of Canada in the face of the forces of Trudeaumania. Much credit must be given to the strength of Robert Stanfield in that part of Canada where people knew him best. Indeed it is not too much to say that there was a regional form of Stanfieldmania going for the Tories.

The PCs fared ill in the rest of the Dominion. As against 25 Atlantic MPs, the combined PC total for the two giant central provinces was 21, this out of a total 162 seats. It was a real shellacking. Defeated in the central provinces were such luminaries as Marcel Faribault, Jean Wadds, Dalton Camp, Dick Bell, Wallace McCutcheon, and many other able Tories. Nor did we do well in the West. The three prairie provinces elected 25 Progressive Conservatives, 15 of them from Alberta, the Tory bastion of the West. The party was wiped out in British Columbia whose voters had a heavy case of Trudeaumania. In the process the western voters defeated such top-ranking House of Commons material as Duff Roblin, Davie Fulton, and Alvin Hamilton. Seeing so many of his 'enemies' go down to defeat, John Diefenbaker commented from Prince Albert with a detectable element of gloating: 'The Conservative Party has suffered a calamitous disaster.'

In Hillsborough I had the immense satisfaction of having a united and able group of workers whose efforts led on to a splendid victory against a first-class Liberal candidate. But later in the evening, with our own thank yous made on the media and our constituency celebration over, the outside world came into focus. As we watched the national returns on television in room 411 of the Charlottetown Hotel, we saw reason for increasing gloom as we left our region and time zone. I would go back to a much smaller caucus in Ottawa than I had left. The high hopes of the 1967 convention were pretty well shattered. Even if it was not unexpected – after all we could all read Gallup polls – it was flattening.

Our party had dropped 25 seats, to 72; the NDP had gained 1, to 22. The Liberals, with 155 seats, now had a comfortable majority. But there were some compensations. At least it was not a minority government situation with the possibility of another election in a year or two. Having gone through six in eleven years I wasn't hankering after another, at least not until my campaign debts were paid off. Also there would be no recall of Parliament until September. This meant a full summer for me in PEI which is the place to be.

As I tried to find some grains of comfort on the morning after, I turned my thoughts to 1958 when the once-proud Liberal party suffered a much more severe drubbing than the Stanfield Tories a decade later. Naturally I didn't see it clearly then, but Robert Stanfield with his limitless patience and strength of purpose was just the man for the long haul. The next federal election for him would be a vastly different affair from the 1968 encounter. Some political observers have compared the 1968 election aftermath to Stanfield's position twenty years earlier in Nova Scotia. Then he headed a party with no seats and faced a long and wearing road ahead. But in many respects things were tougher in 1968. True, he had a sizeable caucus group in the House of Commons. But numbers aren't everything. Since I have been quoting a number of sages and savants in these pages, modesty fails to deter me from recalling a comment I made to Geoffrey Stevens over fifteen years ago:

His problems were immense ... The caucus was not his caucus, really. He put his own Nova Scotians in a separate category and even they didn't always stay in that category. He had, say, a dozen to twenty supporters in caucus, plus the Nova Scotians – less than thirty altogether. It was not a tremendous cheering section for a man who needs a bit of cheering. If he were a normal man prone to getting discouraged, he would have needed more support than that. God, I was impressed by him as those years went by. He endured much. I would put him up against Job in terms of patience.[1]

In Nova Scotia in 1948 Stanfield had nowhere to go but up. Not so in 1968. Under his leadership the caucus had shrunk to seventy-two from the ninety-seven in Diefenbaker's last fling. After Stanfield's selection as national leader in September 1967, the Gallup Poll stood at 43 per cent for the PCs to 34 per cent for the Liberals. Readings in March 1968 were PCs 34 per cent to 42 per cent for the Liberals. In the election of 1968 the PCs won 31.4

per cent of the popular vote. As well as patience, Stanfield required vast reserves of hope.

The techniques and method so successful in Nova Scotia were followed on the national scene. He had traversed Nova Scotia and he decided to do the same in the vast Dominion. He went everywhere, logging an enormous and wearying number of miles. A few years of this and he felt able to tell a nationwide audience that he now knew Canada pretty well; he still wondered whether Canadians knew him well. But his biggest problems were not in Bonavista or in Prince Rupert but in the very heart of the parliamentary party.

One of Pierre Trudeau's great aims was to attain equality for the French-speaking Canadians in the government service. From the beginning, Stanfield thought the PCs must support such a goal. He believed it would be wrong and politically dangerous for the party to be against the measure. This was in line with views he had expressed earlier. But unfortunately for him there was a hard-line group in caucus ardently opposed to the Official Languages Bill. This was primarily a prairie group plus Robert Coates, veteran Nova Scotia member. The group was aided and abetted by John Diefenbaker. I shall long remember the day he came into caucus and urged opposition to the bill. Stanfield's face was a model of immobility as he heard the call to defy the party leader's policy. After his exhortation, the man from Prince Albert departed the meeting.

Worse was to follow. On second reading, the bill might have gone through 'on division,' that is, without a recorded vote. But enough members of the Antis rose to their feet and thus forced a recorded vote. Those who voted against the measure were Messrs Cadieu (Meadow Lake), Coates, Diefenbaker, Dinsdale, Downey, Gundlock, Horner, Korchinski, McIntosh, Moore, Muir (Lisgar), Ritchie, Schumacher, Simpson, Skoreyko, Southam, and Stewart (Marquette). Needless to say, Robert Stanfield didn't like these goings on and the next Wednesday's caucus heard an angry and aroused leader. He was particularly irate at the five standees who had prompted a recorded vote and exposed the party's split for all to see. He said their stupidity was exceeded only by their malice. This tough approach buoyed the spirits of the MPs in Stanfield's corner. Whether it did much to assuage or placate the dissidents was more difficult to judge. Some of these blamed Stanfield for the heavy losses in the election. Others didn't understand the man and would not try. As for John Diefenbaker, he had never been noted for enthusiasm for any Conservative Party leader other than himself.

Robert Stanfield did not lack realism and we may be sure that he knew that his seventy-two-member caucus was far from being a Hallelujah Chorus. In fact he may have been given too much to the reconciliation process. I think the closest I came to serious criticism of Stanfield was when I once told him in Charlottetown that I thought he sometimes didn't know his friends from his enemies. If one looks at the caucus structure under him it is clear that he had many ardent Diefenbakerites in committee chairmanships which made them frequent party spokesmen in the House of Commons. There was certain ambivalence about the situation. Stanfield was denounced by some sore Tories who viewed him as a creation of Dalton Camp. Others who had worked hard to get him into the leadership felt somewhat let down, as they saw what they considered the continuing prominence of so many old-guard types in the new regime. But, of course, the party and its leader needed the old and new elements if a viable political structure was to be built. The role of the reconciler is not easy, but Stanfield did achieve great successes in his efforts at bringing about some harmony.

Our new leader had other troubles after the 1968 defeat. One of the most serious was certainly not of his choosing. In the fall of 1970 terrorist groups in Quebec carried out activities of such violence as to bring on a major reaction from the government and people of Canada. The kidnapping of a British diplomat, James Cross, and later the Quebec minister of labour, Pierre Laporte, shook us all. Before it was over Mr Laporte had been murdered, the army had been sent into Quebec, and the War Measures Act proclaimed. Hundreds of suspects were rounded up and jailed;

only sixty-two were charged and of these only eighteen were convicted. The War Measures Act had never before been invoked in time of peace.

The country's representatives in Parliament were traumatized by the violent events in a country which always prided itself on its preference for evolutionary rather than revolutionary change and ballots rather than bullets. It was a frightening time. Many of us had scarcely heard of the FLQ, the Front de Libération du Québec. Terrorism was something we read about in remote and less orderly countries. To find our own media filled with stories of kidnappings, threats of violence, the wild talk of revolutionary cells was for all of us a new and upsetting experience. There were many of the dramatic ingredients of television thrillers with the terrorists' communiqués read over radio stations.

The country and its institutions were shocked and mesmerized for a few days. Rumours circulated that the government of Quebec was nearly paralysed and that an interim alternative group was governing the province. Ottawa's response when it came was Draconian. NDP leader Tommy Douglas likened it to using a sledgehammer to crack a peanut. But the prime minister was not apologetic. When asked about the use of troops he had one of his sharp smart answers. 'Well, there's lots of bleeding hearts around that just don't like to see people with helmets and guns. All I can say is: "Go on and bleed!" When asked how far he would go, Trudeau's reply was 'Just watch me.' As well as the members of the Department of National Defence, a host of policemen were hauling Canadians to jail. There was a massive assault on the rights of Canadian people. Those cherished liberties and institutions of freedom seemed to recede before the eyes of Canadian citizens. It is now easy to accept that Tommy Douglas was right. But in 1970 even many of the great supporters of human rights were strangely silent. I recall novelist Morley Callaghan as being one strong voice against the extreme measures. He spoke bravely and powerfully on a national television program but his was a minority voice. Nor can I exculpate the politicians.

The Progressive Conservatives were naturally much concerned. One didn't need a PHD in history to recall that the Liberal Party of Canada had a strong authoritarian cast. C.D. Howe and his orders in council and postwar controls were not forgotten. The War Measures Act was indeed a heavy measure. But the dramatic intensity of events was carrying the public along and the electronic media gave the image of the prime minister as a strong decisive leader. In this climate of opinion to talk about such things as a Bill of Rights or freedom of the individual was deemed naïve by many and almost traitorous by the toughies in the law-and-order group.

The night after the War Measures Act had been proclaimed, party leaders addressed the nation. The steely-eyed prime minister came on as a no-nonsense strong man. Tommy Douglas was solicitous of civil liberties. Stanfield, who followed Trudeau on the program, sought a reasoned, balanced approach. He could accept for the time being the imposition of the War Measures Act if the government would bring in a new bill strong enough for the situation but with a less drastic assault on the civil liberties of Canadians. It was not a great performance but it was a tough assignment. When national security is an issue, there is always the thought that the government may have much more information than the opposition. Certainly we all felt that that was a possibility. Then there was the ethnic equation. In the Conservative party there always seemed to be an element easily moved to anti-Quebec sentiments. The FLQ was a separatist and terrorist organization, and it was not an enormous leap to create the impression that all the terrorists in Quebec were separatists and most separatists were terrorists. I recall some government apologists coming close to using the two words as if they were interchangeable. Many Conservatives thought Stanfield's television talk was weak and wishy-washy. To some it was but an extension of his softness on Quebec.

All in all it was a terrible time. The speeches of the leaders had come fairly late in the evening but that didn't stop the telephone calls of protest through the night. One of my Charlottetown friends, Dr J.C. Sinott, called me in great anxiety. He was a splendid party man but wanted to know: 'What in the name of God Stanfield was up to.' His was not the only critical call I received. Indeed the party as whole and certainly the leader's office had a clear signal of disquiet from the rank and file. In this, of course, they were reflecting Canadian public opinion as a whole. In this troubled time I had one call which came as a balm to my shattered faith. Art Wright, a former constituency president and close friend, telephoned to say that the government was wrongfully overreacting and that the time to be a civil libertarian was when civil rights were being assaulted. Art wanted me to vote against the act.

But while one night was over, the agony of 1970 was still upon us. I had emotionally and intellectually prepared myself to vote against the War Measures Act in the House of Commons. It is not the custom to take votes in caucus but my impression was that a substantial, if not overwhelming, majority were ready to vote against it. But with the deepening crisis, and the increasing assaults on our leaders, we felt overwhelmed by a sea of tumultuous and frightening events. I was no recent victim of insomnia, but on the night before the vote I slept not a wink. I was not troubled by the thought of being in a minority as I now read the party's changing attitude. I had been in such situations before. Nor was I unprepared to be criticized and misunderstood. That too was not unfamiliar to me. But what was the right thing to do? It seemed a very personal matter. I always felt there was something grandiose if not self-righteous about people who too readily display their conscience. But on the War Measures Act I felt that all I had learned and believed in over the years was somehow being tried and tested. My agonized uncertainty did not end until the vote was called. In the roll call I stood with all members of my party and supported the War Measures Act knowing in my head and heart that it was an improper and highly ignoble thing to do. In my thirty-four years on Parliament Hill, I have doubtless done many foolish things and said many more. But the only occasion on which I still consider I was fundamentally wrong was on this vote. The only worthy excuse I could advance was that I had avoided a rift in the caucus. Stanfield was sufficiently under attack without adding to his problems the charge of having a fractured caucus.

The trauma on the Hill began to wind down for us. I recall our outspoken whip, Bob McKinley, advising us about the Liberals' new legislation, the Public Order (Temporary Measures) Act. As he put it, this was 'to help us out of the mess we had got ourselves into.' I regarded the new bill as something of a vindication of Stanfield's speech and his basic stand. I had no qualms about supporting the new, less Draconian, measure. My Island colleague David MacDonald, a most admirable man, stood out against this new measure although he had voted for the tougher War Measures Act.

Looking back on those disturbing times I see few heroes. Certainly I wasn't one. Tommy Douglas and those members of the NDP caucus who joined him in voting against the War Measures Act earned the laurels that day. Although it has done me no good, I have spent a long time in repenting my own apostasy.

The public opinion polls in the aftermath of the FLQ 'apprehended insurrection' revealed the Liberals soaring. The public applauded the 'no deals, no compromise' stand of their valiant prime minister. Few noticed that, in fact, deals had been made and that the members of one of the cells of the iniquitous group had been allowed to go to Cuba. I believed that the life of Mr Cross was worth such compromises. There was not much public solicitude for the hundreds of people imprisoned without being charged.

In March 1988, the diary of one of Trudeau's brightest and best ministers confirmed what many of us in the opposition suspected at the time. According to Don Jamieson, the government had had no evidence of an apprehended insurrection when it invoked the War Measures Act on 16 October 1970.

Eventually this distressing episode came to an end and Canadian politics returned to something like normalcy. Robert Stanfield was not likely to outglamorize Pierre Trudeau at this stage in their respective careers, so he concentrated on more fundamental aspects of the nation's governance. He told an Ottawa press conference that the Trudeau government had substituted style for content and that the country was in 'a world of illusion where policies are not made but simply talked about.' He also had a sound appraisal of that style describing it as 'one of arrogance in the realm of power, illusion in the field of action and incoherence in the domain of policy.'

It was quite an acute appraisal of what he and the rest of the Tories were up against in the peak of the Trudeau era. Through much of this period there were serious economic problems in the country. Economic indices that should be up were down and vice versa. In my economics courses in university days, we were taught that unemployment and inflation were cyclical phenomena. But under the Trudeau Liberal regime they seemed to come together and remain interminably. In the far-off days of the Diefenbaker government, a 92.5-cent Canadian dollar (in terms of the U.S. dollar) was a major political issue on which the PCs probably lost many votes. But in the Trudeau years a 92-cent Canadian dollar would have been strong indeed. I used to get a good audience reaction when I told of the Canadian in New York whose hotel room was burglarized. Everything was stolen except his supply of Canadian dollars!

Stanfield was an outstandingly able man on economic questions. There was no one in our caucus who could touch him in comprehension or appreciation of the various complex budgets and other public finance bills. I used to marvel at his understanding of highly involved measures brought in by the government. At a time when, in bread-and-butter terms, the country was being poorly administered, his ability was precious indeed. It was on that level that he laboured in the years after 1968. He conducted a nationwide tour studying the problems of unemployment. He had task forces on housing and a wide range of issues of deep concern to the average Canadian. It took a long time but eventually there developed in the country a quiet confidence that the cool, calm, steady Stanfield might just be the man to give the country less exciting but much more competent and sensitive government. He might be weaker on the frills and fantasies but stronger on the fundamentals. The old Chambers cartoon in the *Halifax Chronicle Herald* showing Stanfield as the tortoise to Trudeau's hare was becoming more relevant.

In Ottawa, as he had in Halifax, Stanfield gave high priority to policy. One of his best appointments was that of Thomas Symons as chairman of a committee devoted to the development of policy themes. Symons, the founding president of Trent University, devoted endless hours to his responsibilities, made excellent contacts with experts and leaders of opinion outside the party, and became a popular figure within PC ranks, especially with the YPC and student groups. He organized an impressive conference at Niagara Falls in the fall of 1969. This helped the party consider modern issues in a contemporary way. The conference delegates looked at everything from more liberal laws on marijuana to a guaranteed annual income program. As the chairman of the caucus committee on communications I presided over a panel comprising the head of the Canadian Radio-Television Commission (CRTC) and the chiefs of the CBC and the CTV television networks. Whether anything was resolved or not we had a wide-ranging discussion.

Parties in opposition go for thinkers' conferences. When the party is in government they apparently aren't necessary. From the Port Hope gathering of 1942 on, the Conservative assemblies were useful. As a Red Tory before the expression was in vogue, I was less than enthusiastic about some of the recommendations but had to remember the second part of our name. PCs could hardly be expected to come down on the progressive side all the time.

Along with his ceaseless efforts in stumping the country, Stanfield did some international travel. In 1970 he took an extended trip to Europe, visiting both sides of the Iron Curtain. The next year he went to China and Japan. When he advised caucus that he was giving thought to the Far East trip there were suggestions that he could more profitably use his time at home. I expressed the contrary view – that a man we were presenting as a future prime minister should develop some international recognition and prestige. For once I seemed to be on the majority side.

Stanfield's toils and travels in the period 1968–72 were paying political dividends. In the House of Commons, Pierre Elliott Trudeau might, and often did, treat him with condescension, but the Canadian people were looking at him more earnestly than ever before. He was getting better crowds and doing a better job from the platform. He seemed to like his job more and to an ever-widening group of people his wonderful sense of humour was being revealed. The big problem was that ancient anxiety for Conservatives – what to do about Quebec. The Faribault strategy had been a flop in 1968. Nor did there seem to be any potential strong man among Quebec PCs, either in or out of the House of Commons.

Over a period of many months I had heard rumours that the master strategy was to crown a new Quebec lieutenant. This time it would be a provincial judge and former minister in the Quebec Liberal government of Jean Lesage, Claude Wagner. I had never seen him but had heard a good deal about him, mostly in connection with his hard-line views. He had been minister of justice on the occasion of Queen Elizabeth's visit to Quebec City in 1964, at which law and order was most certainly maintained on the streets of that capital city. Some of his detractors described him by that ancient cliché 'the hanging judge.' From this less-than-ample information I had no reason to believe he would be a Port Hope–type of Tory but our party at its best has been an ecumenical cathedral. And if we could draw to our side a major public figure in Quebec, who would quibble over ideological points?

The rumours circulated for a long time, and eventually Stanfield told caucus about it. I don't recall any strong protests. We didn't have much alternative in Quebec, of course. The thing I recall most vividly in Stanfield's giving us an account of a public opinion poll which the party had commissioned. It showed Wagner more popular than a host of leading Quebec politicians including Trudeau. At the time I wondered whether a man of Stanfield's intelligence could really give credence to such a reading. But it was apparently good enough to set in motion a heavy process of persuasion. According to long-time Quebec Tory Heward Grafftey, the chief suitors were Peter White, Conrad Black, and Brian Mulroney in Quebec along with other Tory giants in Toronto. It was reported that the Wagners were dinner guests at the opposition leader's house, Stornoway, and that Stanfield called on Wagner in his Montreal home. There were reports that a trust fund of $300,000 had been arranged to ease Wagner's way into the Conservative camp. Everything seemed in place and the former provincial Liberal minister entered the fray two days before the 1972 election was called.

Although one would be foolish to attempt to predict election outcomes, I did have a feeling that things were much better in 1972 than in 1968. Stanfield was becoming better known. So also was Trudeau and both these factors were helpful. The PC leader may not have had the personality to turn people on, as did the Liberal leader. On the other hand, people did not take a dislike to him. While Trudeaumania was still abroad in the land, there was also a distinctly different feeling which might be called Trudeauphobia. His cavalier attitude, his biting ripostes, his arrogance were resented by many Canadians. In western Canada resentment was too mild a word for the feelings held by many of the voters. Nor were the westerners alone. It seemed a good omen that the election date, 30 October, was the anniversary of Stanfield's great breakthrough in Nova Scotia in 1956.

In any case, we Tories started off on a stronger foot than in 1968 although the public opinion polls weren't pointing the way to victory. In Hillsborough I had another new opponent. The Reverend Ian Glass was minister of St Mark's Presbyterian Church in Sherwood, an up-and-coming suburb of Charlottetown. He was good-looking, personable, and had good connections in youth work and community activities. He was a formidable candidate but his campaign was not as vigorous as that of Jack MacAndrew in 1968. I felt then and still believe that the PC campaign in Hillsborough was superior to our opponent's. There were excellent, experienced people in our ranks and we always tried to augment our team with new people. With the local effort and the national trend, my majority increased from 1956 to 3437 which, in PEI terms, was a veritable landslide. My colleagues David MacDonald and Angus MacLean in Egmont and Malpeque also had substantially increased majorities. In Cardigan, alas, the story was different. The incumbent, Mel McQuaid, chose not to reoffer and the seat was won by Daniel MacDonald, a popular provincial minister who went on to become a federal cabinet minister. After the election my friend Art Wright kidded me with an amusing question. 'How is it that you've been in Ottawa for 15 years and never made it to the Cabinet? Dan MacDonald is there for fifteen minutes and becomes a minister, and you were supposed to be the smart one of the Island team!'

After our own local celebrations on 30 October, our campaign group and spouses again settled in before television sets in room 411 of the Charlottetown Hotel. But it was a different night from our depressing vigil of four years earlier. In fact it was one of the most exciting election nights I could remember. For hours the outcome see-sawed as we went west from time zone to time zone. At times the PCS were a nose ahead; at times it was a tie. When it was all over, the Liberals had lost in every province and every territory except Quebec. After recounts the total was 109 seats for the Liberals, 107 for the PCS. Some of the Liberal seats were won by fewer than five votes. By such a narrow margin did Canada miss the opportunity of having Robert Stanfield as its prime minister. The near miss must have disappointed him. But the greatest loser of all was the country. One of our sanest clichés is that Stanfield was the best prime minister Canada never had.

But is was a tremendous leap from the 1968 results. The results in Ontario had been most encouraging. An important factor there was the new premier, William Davis, who had taken control of the province in March 1971. Davis came to Ottawa and met with the federal caucus. He told us that he would go all out for Bob Stanfield and that is just what he did in the 1972 election. It had not been the custom for Ontario Conservative premiers to give the type of support which Stanfield, as Nova Scotia premier, had always extended to the federal cause. Leslie Frost had given John Diefenbaker some in 1957 but there was a good deal of standing benevolently aloof at other elections.

It was Quebec which brought gloom to the 'morning after' quarterbacks. In that province the PC party's strategy had been a fiasco. We actually dropped two seats, falling to a grand total of two: Claude Wagner and veteran Heward Grafftey. The Liberals won fifty-six and the Social Credit fifteen. An embittered Grafftey believed that it was the party's 'cynical Quebec strategy' which had denied the PCS a federal victory. He thought that, had local candidates been encouraged and assisted before and during the election, enough would have been elected to put Stanfield into office. Grafftey further observed: 'Instead the party leadership decided, with the help of a suitcase full of money, to metamorphose a "rouge" [liberal] into a "bleu" [conservative]. On election day, the people of Quebec responded to this insult by overwhelmingly rejecting us at the polls.'[2] Even as a Quebec outsider I believe that it was unrealistic to expect the Wagner ploy to have a profound effect upon the political orientation of the province. It would have taken a veritable political superman to bring about a favourable outcome for the Tories with a last-minute entry like Wagner's.

There were the usual post-mortems. Some Island Tories said that had Mel McQuaid run in Cardigan he would have won the seat and that would have meant that Stanfield would have won the government. Others across the land noted that two or three more PC voters in the populous ridings of Ontario would have turned the tide. Despite all the ifs, ands, and buts, it was a heartening result. Surely we were on the way up. Trudeau was no longer deemed invulnerable. By the same token (or the same election) Stanfield had gained his laurels as the 'the man with the winning way.' Considering the fluidity of the parliamentary situation it was only a matter of time until the PCs would be back in office.

It was to take a good deal longer than many Tories thought and even an electoral rematch was not soon in coming. The NDP caucus of thirty-one members had no disposition to defeat the Liberals in a confidence vote and thus precipitate a new election. They feared that in such a run-off they might be ground down between the two parties or, as in the 1958 election, badly beaten by the winner. In that year the NDP's predecessor, the CCF, saved only eight of the twenty-five seats it had won in 1957. It was more openly said by NDP people that, by maintaining the Liberals in office, they thought they could secure the passage of 'good' legislation acceptable to them. But David Lewis and his colleagues should have known both Trudeau and Stanfield well enough in 1972 to know which would be more likely to bring forward socially helpful legislation. In the period after the 1972 election I was amazed at the fidelity of the NDP to the Trudeau government. They refused to support PC non-confidence motions couched in the very terms which the NDP itself had used in the previous Parliament. By sustaining the Liberals in the House of Commons, the NDP were powerful roadblocks to Stanfield's assumption of the prime ministry. Had they accelerated rather than frustrated such a development, they might have made their noblest and wisest contribution to the country. In this connection the only thing I found more deplorable than their voting record was the depiction of Robert Stanfield as a power-hungry politician.

I remember feeling that time was not on our side and that the best thing for us would be another election as soon as decently possible. Public opinion polls were not all that encouraging. In fact we were behind in the popular vote in the 1972 election. Although the PCs had carried nine provinces they had won a bare 21 per cent of the popular vote in Quebec. It is hard to top the national poll with such a handicap in the second largest province. As for gaining support in Quebec there was no magic formula around. Wagner was a PC front-bencher in the House of Commons, but his magnetism for the Quebec electorate had been vastly overrated. There were no other glittering novas in the Tory firmament in Quebec, even if the party should seek once again to return to the strategy which had failed in 1968 and 1972. As Stanfield put it, he had lost any illusions about 'an easy way to win Quebec.' Stanfield, who had done wonders in mastering the French language, went often to the province and sought to draw credible candidates to the PC standard. Roch Lasalle, after a stint as an independent, returned to the Tory caucus. Marcel Masse, former minister in the Union Nationale government of Daniel Johnson, was welcomed. There was a good deal of consideration being given to establishing a provincial Progressive Conservative party in Quebec. On this, as on other matters, there was a disagreement within the small coterie of committed PCs in the province.

Stanfield seemed to be moving to a position favourable to a more decentralized Canada. Premiers of the smaller have-not provinces were generally found among those who advocated a strong central government. If Trudeau was seen as overly assertive of the federal power, perhaps some solicitude for the rights and aspirations of the provinces might be politically popular, especially in Quebec.

But many were convinced that the major strategy for winning the next election was the program to control prices and incomes. Continuing high inflation was revealed by a host of public opinion polls as the number one issue for a vast number of Canadians. Indeed polls weren't needed. A visit to any supermarket was enough to hear the public bitching about the high price of food. If a party can be seen as having a program which could lick the country's worst economic scourge, should not that party win votes from a grateful electorate? So many Conservatives believed, and wage and price controls, as the program was usually dubbed, became the clincher for victory in the next election. I can still hear the ringing oratory of PC members at caucus meetings urging some definite policies. This has been an old cri de coeur among many PCs. To hear some of them, the PC party should really have a great compendium of precise policy statements on everything from Arctic char to zinc mining. Zealots for policy elaboration tend to forget their history, as zealots often do. The party had often been stung badly by overreaching itself on this very question. One of John Diefenbaker's first acts after assuming the leadership in 1956 was to discard and indeed destroy the elaborate policy statement worked out so assiduously at the 1956 convention. But perhaps every political generation has to invent its own wheel, or fashion its own cross.

On 8 May 1974 the Trudeau government fell when the NDP joined the PCs in voting against the budget of Finance Minister John Turner. The most recent Gallup polls had shown the PCs slightly behind the Liberals, 34 per cent to 39 per cent, but a good campaign or a good issue could easily overcome that difference. Many Conservatives felt that they had both. Perhaps we paid insufficient attention to a poll on leader as distinct from party popularity. This showed Trudeau leading Stanfield 46 per cent to 22 per cent with the Quebec figures even further apart at 49 per cent to 16 per cent.

So it was that we Tory candidates hit the campaign trail in 1974 with a prices and incomes policy as the sharpest arrow in our electoral quiver. In Hillsborough we used the national logo and party literature, inviting the voters to finish the job they had almost accomplished in 1972. And once again I had an excellent campaign committee, as well as a highly credible candidate against me. George Chandler, a Charlottetown businessman and community leader had lots of friends in Charlottetown. He and I had attended Prince of Wales College in the long ago. The years had been kinder to him insofar as appearance was concerned and he would look well on television. He was a man for whom I had a good deal of respect but I did not anticipate that he would be particularly adept in the intricacies of political campaigning. He was certainly not as tough a competitor as Jack MacAndrew and he would not be as good at communications as Ian Glass. But George Chandler was a very hard worker and no one in my campaign headquarters was taking anything for granted.

As it turned out, it was to be a tougher campaign than the previous two in Hillsborough or most of the five contests in Queens. But I think it can be said fairly that this situation did not come about because of any grave weakness in the PC organization in Hillsborough or the exceptional strength of the Liberal campaign in the constituency. Nor was the major problem one of the electors' views on the two national leaders. Stanfield remained popular with Islanders. Mr. Trudeau had done nothing to become more popular with them than in 1972. No, the real problem was that we PCs were handicapped with a policy enormously difficult to explain and seemingly impossible to popularize. Every second voter seemed to have a question about wage controls. To begin with we had constantly to assure the people that controls stopped at the farm gate. The farmers, already anxious about markets and prices, were to be exempt. Even more difficult to comment upon was the ninety-day freeze which was designed to set up the proper prelude for the program. I remember having a challenging question after a meeting in York, a rich farming area and the location of an internationally known seed house. I was asked what prices should be put in the seed company's catalogues considering that printing and production of the catalogue would require more than ninety days. I think it was after that incident that my perceptive wife made a very pertinent comment: 'Your people don't understand the prices and incomes program. Are you sure you do?' I don't know that I did, but I do know that by the time I finished my 'explanations' the election was over and I had lost hundreds of votes.

When the Hillsborough ballots were counted on 8 July, I carried the constituency with a majority of 1340 votes over George Chandler. In 1972 I had had 3437 votes more than Ian Glass. My majority over Jack MacAndrew in 1968 had been 1956. These figures might indicate some problem in Hillsborough, perhaps its Tory candidate, but in the other Island seats a similar trend was evident. Angus MacLean's majority of 1262 in 1972 was about halved to 674 in 1974. In Egmont, David MacDonald had a majority of 2187 in 1972. In 1974 it was 1161. In Cardigan the Liberal candidate, Dan MacDonald, increased his 1972 majority of 417 to 1529 in 1974. Across the country the PC total fell from 107 to 95 seats.

It might be said that it was a tribute to Stanfield that the PCS didn't do worse with such an albatross about their necks as the prices and incomes policy proved to be. Generally speaking, at election time it is the supporters of the government who are expected to be on the defensive. One of the goals of the opposition is to keep them in that stance. In 1974, however, we of the opposition were constantly being called upon to justify not our actions but our intentions. Pierre Trudeau was at his theatrical best as he mocked Stanfield on the price freeze. He would list a variety of items after which he would say, 'zap, you're frozen!' David Lewis was effective in disparaging Stanfield's explanation of the ninety-day freeze as being a psychological weapon. Lewis used to say: 'Mr Stanfield is a fine man but Sigmund Freud he is not.' The Liberals and the NDP did a pretty thorough job on the program which Stanfield and the earnest band of Tories had thought to be their trump card. Before the campaign ended, they had bamboozled or frightened enough voters to put *finis* to Stanfield's hopes of becoming the resident of 24 Sussex Drive.

In my own campaign in Hillsborough I always preferred to talk about something else and was pleased when the voters found something else more interesting. In some constituencies Progressive Conservative candidates did their best to dissociate themselves from the program but such a ploy was far from easy. Before the campaign was over a substantial number of Tories believed the program should be jettisoned. This kind of about-face could not be sold to the public.

John Diefenbaker, speaking in PEI, thought it would be better to apply controls to prices but not wages. His suggestion was seized on by Grit spokesmen as another example of Conservative indecision and division. As well as livening up the discussion on prices and incomes, the former leader made some waves on Prince Edward Island. He had accepted a request to come into Malpeque to speak on behalf of Angus McLean but there were some conditions attached. I recall the provincial campaign chairman, Norman Carruthers, coming to my Hillsborough headquarters to outline the restrictions. The Chief obviously didn't want any of his magic to rub off on the termites, David MacDonald and me. But he would be landing at Charlottetown airport which was located in Hillsborough. So MacDonald and Macquarrie must not show up at the airport. Also, we must not appear at the meeting in Malpeque. At this stage I asked Norman Carruthers: 'Do we have to leave the Island?' Having been around a while, I was not surprised at the vindictiveness and was not distressed at being barred from the meeting, since I had a long-arranged senior citizens rally in Charlottetown that night. Before leaving the province next day, Diefenbaker went into the Cardigan riding in support of PC candidate Leo Walsh. Presumably he would have to travel through Hillsborough to accomplish this, but I didn't spoil the show by waving a Canadian flag from the side of the highway as he traversed the alien constituency.

There was nevertheless a feeling of sadness as we adjusted to the election results. Knowing the party, we could expect some of its members to call loudly and quickly for Stanfield's departure from the leadership. The first such voices were raised in the Prairies, but soon they were echoed by the hard-liners from other parts of Canada. The complete change of roles was interesting, perhaps even amusing. Those who in 1965 and 1966 seemed to regard the leadership as eternal and unalterable, like the papacy, had found a new script. It had been sacrilege to dare to put Diefenbaker's tenure to question even after five elections. But Stanfield after three elections should be jettisoned forthwith. The aftermath of the 1974 election was a nasty time. Many short in vision became sharp of tongue. A lesser man than Robert Stanfield would have said 'to Hell with it' and buggered off forthwith. But I knew that he would not quit in a huff. Nor would he try to cling to the leadership as John Diefenbaker had done. He would take his departure decently and in good order. He led the ninety-five–member caucus in the first few months of the 30th Parliament and sought to preserve the integrity of the party's policies and the viability of the organization structures.

Shortly after 9:00 a.m. on 10 July 1975, I had a call from what would now be called the chief of staff in the office of the leader of the opposition. I was asked whether my office could be made available about noon that day. My office, Room 367 in the West Block, was spacious and very close to 371, the traditional locale of the PCs' regular Wednesday morning caucus meetings. Naturally I obliged and asked no questions; I knew full well the reason for the request. So it was that I stood outside my office door as a sizeable group of newsmen heard Stanfield announce his resignation and his request to the PC national executive to set a date for a leadership convention. It was all very low-key but it was also all very correct. Some of his comments were classic Stanfield. He wondered how many Gallup Poll points the PC party would gain as a result of his announcement. He also observed: 'I realize I leave a tremendous void. I don't really expect anyone to be able to fill it.' So with dignity, humour, and humility, but without bitterness, repining, or blaming others, the best leader our party ever had took his quiet departure. With my emotional, sentimental nature, I could not forbear a tear. An era of decency and nobility was ending. What lay ahead for the old party?

In the eight years of Stanfield's leadership I had a variety of caucus responsibilities. My first assignment as party spokesman was not External Affairs, for which I had hoped, but Communications, which included the Post Office. Important too was the new area of telecommunications. Canada was in the process of preparing to send up a communications satellite. My interest in and knowledge of scientific technology, astrophysical or otherwise, was minuscule. Before my stint as Communications critic was over, I went with members of the House of Commons transport and communications committee to Vandenburg Air Force Base in California. There we saw the launching of Anik ii, the Canadian communications satellite which was to bring great benefits to our country, especially the northern areas. I was quite overwhelmed and bewildered by the computer technology dutifully explained to me.

But the visceral part of my 'shadow' portfolio was the operation of the Post Office. It was not at all difficult to find opportunities for criticising the service given to the Canadian public. I spent a good deal of time denouncing the introduction of the five-day week and the imposition of a mail-less Saturday. I felt that this would slow up the delivery of mail for the whole week. If mail put in the box Friday afternoon was not touched until Monday and was not really on stream until Tuesday because of the extra volume, the result was predictable. I have no doubt that this 'reform' was a major contributor to the decline in Canada's postal service.

Sometimes, between minister and critic, a good and perhaps cordial relationship develops. There was none of that between Eric Kierans and me. In the House of Commons, if a member is not satisfied with a minister's reply, he may request a mini-debate later. The latter happened after the close of scheduled business at 10:00 p.m. Under the rules the dissatisfied MP can speak for seven minutes while the minister or his parliamentary secretary reply for three. I seemed rarely to be satisfied with Mr Kierans' replies and, since he had no parliamentary secretary, he himself had to do the replying at what was called the 'Late Show.'

Needless to say, Kierans was less than delighted with this lengthening of his parliamentary day. It was once reported to me that he had said: 'I see the red-faced little bugger has me on the Late Show again tonight.' When I was told this I took exception, pointing out that since I weighed over 190 pounds the word 'little' was unfair. Kierans had a fairly extensive vocabulary and he came up with some colourful names for me. Two I remember are 'the fluttering Falstaff of the Conservative party' and 'the merry monk of Hillsborough.' Being of gentler texture I tried not to call my opposite member nasty names. I did think, however, that as a postmaster general he might make a fairly good economist.

After a stint in Communications, I was given External Affairs in the next shuffle. Of course I liked it better and felt it closer to my interest and training. On the other hand, it had its difficulties. When one is called upon to speak for the party, as is the case after a minister makes a statement in the House, a critic must do just that. He should not presume to relay merely his own opinions. So when I had to reply to Mitchell Sharp, often on very short notice, I used to ask myself what my most right-wing colleagues might think. Then I had to make a blend of my opinions and theirs. I wouldn't presume that my spoken views were universally acceptable in my caucus, but I don't recall getting into any trouble on account of my statements on foreign affairs. Tempering the wind to the shorn lamb was not a problem when I was in Communications. None of my colleagues thought the Post Office was above reproach and none of my criticism of Kierans was ever dubbed as too harsh.

Ever since coming to Ottawa I had had close contacts with many of the embassies. I had also travelled a good deal and found it helpful to my understanding of the vast and complex area which was my official purview as party spokesman for External Affairs. It was also a field which seemed to invoke a great many speaking engagements. All of this was highly enjoyable but none the less demanding of time and energy. Perhaps it was the nature of the field or of the man, but I found my relationship with Mitchell Sharp a good deal more pleasant than that with Kierans.

There is always great interest in who gets what in the list of party spokesmen. At times there is considerable competition and occasionally dissatisfaction. Although the expression is not so widely used as in Britain, the group is often described as a shadow cabinet. Over the years I noted that those who are in it are quite prepared to use this expression; leaders, however, are not given to using it. Presumably they do not wish to give the shadow members any notions about being automatically members of a real cabinet. Nor do they wish to diminish the ambitions and loyalty of those not in the spokesmen coterie. It also seemed to be conventional wisdom to make changes in the personnel of the shadow cabinet from time to time. Whether to diminish any growth of priority rights or just to burnish the collective image, shuffles were fairly frequent. Perhaps the opposition was influenced by prime ministers' tendencies for cabinet shakeups. These are usually undertaken to the accompaniment of press comment about new blood, strengthening this or that, or adding God-knows-what virtues to a government. Prime ministers find it almost mandatory to have a cabinet shuffle before an election. One of Pierre Trudeau's shuffles was likened to rearranging the deck-chairs on the Titanic. Some years later I myself came out with a smart-ass analogy which my then leader, Joe Clark, found sufficiently droll to use in his campaign speeches. It was to the effect that I had never known a change of pallbearers to revive a corpse. I was never much impressed by the idea of mobility for cabinet ministers. Mackenzie King wisely left people like Ernest Lapointe, James Gardiner, and C.D. Howe in place.

As well as responding to ministerial statements, caucus spokesmen are expected to involve themselves in the daily question period on issues in their assigned field. So they must scan the horizon for subjects of national or partisan importance. If there is a really big issue, it goes to the leader to draw the maximum media coverage. In the long ago, before I entered the House of Commons, I was told by Walter Dinsdale that, if one read the *Globe and Mail*, he could predict the highlights of that day's question period. It was that way in my time and it is still that way.

After Claude Wagner entered caucus in 1972, I was made spokesman for National Health and Welfare, which put me opposite the great mover and shaker of the government, Marc Lalonde. I found National Health and Welfare a challenging responsibility. It was not always easy to win support from some of my colleagues for highly popular measures introduced by La-londe. It also fell to me to be our party's spokesman for his great piece of nationalist legislation protecting Canadian football against the hazards of the World Football League.

There were people in our caucus who were outstanding ath-letes. Indeed any of my colleagues had more expertise on this bill that I. In truth I knew as much about football as I did about Sanskrit. But I thought it was my responsibility since I was 'shad-owing' Lalonde. As it turned out, my speech on 18 April 1974 gained me more coverage than any of my utterances on foreign policy, constitutionalism, or political history. In a front page ar-ticle in the *Globe and Mail* that most excellent journalist William Johnston gave my remarks appreciative attention. 'Macquarrie used equal measures of wit, historical allusion, mockery and scorn to vent his disapproval. The minister has obviously decided that he is going to bring down a gridiron curtain at the 49th Parallel.' Johnston also reproduced my comment: 'It is an endless prospect of prohibitions, and I have never liked prohibition very much.' It was the first time that I ever derived any enjoyment out of football. Before my House of Commons career was over, I was offered yet another shadow ministry, Secretary of State. That I declined.

In 1972, on the Sunday before the election, my son Iain asked what cabinet post I thought I would get if Stanfield won. I gave him all the usual cautions about being presumptuous or over-confident. Then my sharp-witted wife remarked: 'Well, by the state of your father's campaign budget I trust it won't be Finance.'

The eight Stanfield years, 1967–75, were, for me, the most pleas-ant of my twenty-two in the House of Commons. His dealings with his party colleagues were vastly different from those of his predecessor. Perhaps the strongest recollection of Stanfield I have is that of a listener. Hour after weary hour in caucus I recall him sitting there, often with his head in his hand, hearing out the flood of opinions. If ever a party leader had a consultative dis-position he did. He invariably attended the weekly caucus meet-ing and remained to the end. On one exceptional day he asked to make his remarks early and then begged to be excused. As he put it: 'Today I'm busier than a whore working two beds.' It was such a relief not to have the diatribes, tirades, and castigations which were so much of Diefenbaker's traditional performance. With his usual candour, Douglas Harkness in his book referred to Dief's 'ranting and raving.' Sometimes, as I listened to Diefenbaker in the caucus room, I thought we could be witnessing some high-strung actor in rehearsal – perhaps doing King Lear on the moors. Stanfield with his calm, cool logic and his gentlemanly demeanour was especially adept at keeping our disparate and sometimes discouraged group on track. He didn't follow the simple but scarcely adequate rule that, if the Liberals proposed it, we Tories must automatically and vehemently oppose it. He was ever alert to the dangers of following the route of momentary satisfaction at the long-range cost to the party or the nation. Canadian voters had not given our caucus a strong Quebec voice but, when Robert Stanfield was at the helm, Quebec's interests and aspirations were never overlooked or discounted.

He would be more than human if he did not have his preferences among his colleagues. But never did he encourage any grouping of buddies or ultra-loyalists about him. I was never aware of special cliques or cronies. Although I felt it the path of duty to give him the full candour of my views when asked, and occasionally when not asked, I would never presume to trade upon my friendship or past support.

But Old Hickory, as we sometimes called him, could inspire loyalty and affection in his understated way. When Marc Lalonde came out with a bill providing for a substantial increase in family allowances, I called a meeting of the caucus health and welfare committee prior to responding to his statement in the House that afternoon. It was a well-attended meeting and a long one. A number of my colleagues deplored this further example of increasing welfarism. Also present at the meeting was the party's national director, Geoff Molyneaux, who was unable to stay to the end because of an appointment with Stanfield. I implored my colleagues to support the measure. To be against it would put us almost literally against motherhood, and would be the very kind of political suicide the Liberals would like us to walk into. Before we wound up our meeting one of my colleagues said: 'Of course we think you're wrong but we'll all support you.' They were basically good fellows and doubtless planned to agree with me all along but wished to express their views. Shortly after they left I had a call from Stanfield, who had heard the report of the committee members' disagreement from Molyneaux. He said simply: 'Heath, I understand your committee doesn't support your views; I would like you to know that your leader does.' Happily I was able to reassure him and I proceeded with my statement on behalf of the party.

Another call from Stanfield which endeared him to me demonstrated his sense of humour. On the eve of one of our annual meetings I wrote an op-ed article for the *Globe and Mail* dealing with the Conservative party's history from 1854, when John A. Macdonald decreed it as a progressive Conservative party and not a hidebound reactionary grouping. I endeavoured to point out how Stanfield was consistent with these worthy traditions. I was delighted that the *Globe and Mail* had used it in toto and included some good photographs. Almost immediately after arriving at the office at 8:30 a.m., I had a telephone call. 'Heath, this is Bob Stanfield and I want to tell you I'm God-damned annoyed at that article in the *Globe and Mail* this morning.' Long pause. 'Yes. Three times you said Macdonald and Stanfield instead of Stanfield and Macdonald.' Then he went on to commend me for my views and also for expressing them at that particular time. He is really quite a man.

Although even to this day some people are incredulous when you tell them Robert Stanfield was a great humourist, it is nevertheless the case. He specialized in droll understatement and often indulged in self-deprecation. The annual press gallery gathering is a highly competitive occasion for after-dinner speeches, usually featuring the governor general, the prime minister, and the leader of the opposition. It was not an easy challenge. Many of us at the gathering, the press and the politician guests, were in varying stages of bibulousness. A sensitivity to mood as well as a carefully thought-out speech was essential. I was at one dinner when both the governor general, Ed Schreyer, and Erik Nielsen, the representative of the leader of the opposition, were pelted with buns and sugar cubes. But in all the dinners I attended – and I was at all but one during my twenty-two years in the Lower House – I never heard a better performer than Stanfield. He regularly out-scored Trudeau, who was no slouch himself. I vividly recall Stan-field's first press gallery performance when he opened up with a crack at Governor General Roland Michener, one of our great physical fitness exemplars. 'I've been meaning to tell you, Your Excellency, that every morning as I come in to work, and pass Rideau Hall, I see some nut running around in his pyjamas.' And that was just for openers.

My *alma mater*, United College, had the custom of honouring a graduate twenty-five years after his or her graduation. I was designated in 1972 and stayed over to attend a banquet of the Manitoba Conservative Party. At the head table I was explaining to Robert Stanfield my presence in Winnipeg. His laconic com-ment was vintage Stanfield: 'My God, it took them a long time to catch on to your virtues.'

During much of the Trudeau era, as I have mentioned, the national economy was in bad shape. The monthly unemployment figures from the Bureau of Statistics were favourite talking points for opposition parties. Then, when the statisticians came up with the device of seasonally adjusting the jobless figures, we Tories had to adjust our lines a bit. I used to enjoy defining seasonal adjustment to partisan audiences. I explained that it was really a sophisticated way of saying it's not as bad as it could be. But as usual the best line was my leader's: 'If they could seasonally adjust the thermometer they could abolish winter.'

Another good one-liner was first heard by John Laschinger, then national director of the party. After giving Stanfield one of his regular run-downs on the less-than-rosy party situation, Laschinger was given a laconic farewell. 'Ok John, keep on bailing.'

Stanfield's forbearance must have been sorely tried by John Diefenbaker. Despite Stanfield's regular and powerful assistance as premier of Nova Scotia to Diefenbaker, the old man's heart was not filled with gratitude. Instead he seemed to relish belittling his successor to those people in the press and caucus who were still in Dief's good books. It was a cross Stanfield had to bear for all his years as leader. Not until the leadership convention of 1986 did Stanfield take public note of Diefenbaker's years of unhelpful attitudes and utterances. On the first night of the convention Diefenbaker had been the theme speaker and in the course of his remarks actually found words of praise for his successor. On the second night Stanfield made the major speech and in his opening words of gratitude said, 'I want to thank John Diefenbaker for his very kind remarks' and after a noticeable pause 'last night.' It may not have been revenge and certainly not a sufficient quid pro quo but I greatly enjoyed hearing it. Some time later, Stanfield in a public statement sharply rebuked Diefenbaker for knifing the new leader, Joe Clark.

In their retirement years, the differences between Stanfield and Diefenbaker became even more apparent. The old Chief could never really let go, while Stanfield's departure was clean and definite. After his announcement in July 1975 many Canadians looking over the field thought the best man available was Stanfield himself. I remember an impressive letter from A.R.M. Lower insisting that on the crucial issue of national unity Stanfield was the man, and urging me to do everything possible to dissuade him from going. This sound judgment of my old professor was vitiated by another suggestion that, if Stanfield had to go, I should seek the nomination. I immediately sent all of Lower's letter to Stanfield except the reference to myself, telling him of my high regard for the great historian. Replying with one of his compact handwritten letters Stanfield said that while he shared my admiration for Lower he was not in a position to reconsider.

I believe that Robert Stanfield in retirement has become our first elder statesman since Sir Robert Borden. Arthur Meighen was too controversial; R.B. Bennett left the country; Mackenzie King practically died in office; St Laurent withdrew almost completely; Lester Pearson died too soon; Diefenbaker never left the active arena. Stanfield, withdrawn but caring, non-intrusive but supportive, has been of help to both his successors. His splendid effort after the ill-starred proposal to move the Canadian embassy from Tel Aviv to Jerusalem was statesmanship of a high order. His words on the Meech Lake Accord were wise and relevant. The country is the better for his past and continuing contributions. With his character, sense, and personality he would have made a truly great governor general. He would have helped us all by being a symbol of the saving grace of humour, as well as of decency and humility in high office. Of course had the high office been offered to him he might well have been too modest to accept. Pity.

9

Idealist Abroad

At the Quaker-sponsored parliamentarians' conference in Switzerland in 1958 Paul Martin sometimes reminisced about his political career. The year 1958 was not a buoyant time for Liberals and this was reflected in Paul's comments. He said that in all his twenty-three years in Parliament his contacts and activities in international relations gave him the most satisfying memories. Today as I look back over my own thirty-four year stint on the Hill I feel the same way.

When I entered the House of Commons, my first preference for standing committee memberships was on the external affairs committee. I was happy to serve on the delegation to the United Nations General Assembly in 1957 and several assemblies in following years. When John Diefenbaker telephoned me in June 1962 offering me an appointment as parliamentary secretary to Howard Green in External Affairs, I was delighted. Later I appreciated the opportunity to serve as caucus External Affairs spokesman under Robert Stanfield's leadership.

Today, international affairs is a popular pursuit for rising politicians. In the 1950s and 1960s, this was not the case. It seemed that only a few academics or other esoteric types went in for the rarefied atmosphere of foreign policy. I was somewhat amused when Claude Wagner joined our ranks and was listed as having been given the 'prestigious' assignment of caucus spokesman for

External Affairs. I had filled the post for three years or more, and, while I generally had a good press, I couldn't recall anyone describing my role as prestigious.

UNITED NATIONS – WITH ALL ITS FLAWS A POWER FOR GOOD

Although like many Maritimers, I knew Boston well and had visited Washington, DC, and some Midwestern states, I had never been in New York before going to the 12th UN General Assembly in September 1957. I found the United Nations itself a fascinating place. Its meeting rooms and corridors were a crossroads of the world. The delegates' lounge was an exceptionally agreeable place to catch the atmosphere of the world body and its barmen were expert in providing the best in liquid spirits. The dining-room provided an international cuisine and a highly cosmopolitan personnel.

As a parliamentary observer on the Canadian delegation in 1957, I had an opportunity to get a valuable overview of the UN. In the next two assemblies I was Canadian representative on the Fourth Committee which deals with trusteeship (including non-self-governing territories). Considering the great advance of freedom and independence, especially in Africa, this was an exciting committee. In the 17th General Assembly, as parliamentary secretary, I was heavily involved in work of the delegation. After becoming a senator in 1979 I returned once again to the UN as a parliamentary observer. I have never lost my interest in this great international institution.

During the 12th General Assembly, and more so in later ones, I had an opportunity to meet or see and hear some of the world's great political and diplomatic leaders. The brilliant Dag Hammarskjöld, the secretary-general, was at the height of his prestige. Two future holders of the office, Kurt Waldheim of Austria and U Thant of Burma, were members of their country's delegation. In those pre-détente days, there was obvious tension between the two superpowers. Old stone face Andrei Gromyko, the Soviet foreign minister, was a UN veteran. His opposite U.S. number, John Foster Dulles, was often on hand, although Ambassador Henry

Cabot Lodge, the affluent Bostonian, normally chaired the u.s. delegation. It was interesting to see Lodge in so prominent a role in the United Nations; his grandfather, Senator Henry Cabot Lodge, had been largely instrumental in keeping the United States out of the League of Nations. When I first saw John Foster Dulles in action, I thought of Cassius's comment on Julius Caesar: 'He doth bestride the narrow world like a Colossus.' In the Eisenhower era, the UN was an important factor in u.s. policy. With an effort they could, on many issues, get their way in votes in the eighty-one–member General Assembly.

I always seem to find the Irish an impressive group. In their small delegation I recall at least four outstanding people. One was the foreign minister, Frank Aiken. Another was the representative Fred Boland, who chaired the Fourth Committee and later was president of the General Assembly. Conor Cruise O'Brien is still a redoubtable figure in Irish public life. Eamonn Kennedy, their representative on the Fourth Committee, was both brilliant and charming.

Although in my more mature years I overcame my distaste for the fruit of the vine and of the cane, I never thought that cocktail parties were one of the greatest human inventions. Mostly, they are given to too much talk and too much smoking. Whatever wit is dispensed is usually totally overborne by someone else's chatter. Often the bar is hard to reach and standing idly about is tiring. At the UN, a conscientious delegate goes to an enormous number of these modern tortures, sometimes three a night. But there occasionally comes along a party with a difference. I remember a luncheon party thrown in 1958 by Prince Aly Khan, Pakistan's permanent representative to the UN. When he was appointed some wiseacres dubbed it another playboy role. But the highly intelligent young man, in a post–Rita Hayworth era, took his job seriously and was an astute and able UN ambassador as well as a great host. As I made my way back from his apartment to a heavy Fourth Committee meeting, I was filled with admiration and respect for the manner in which he had turned a luncheon into a warm and successful event, in a place where entertaining was too often a routine ritual rather than a gracious art.

In the field of entertainment, our own delegation was first-class. Many UN delegates would drop obvious hints to get invited to the annual Canadian party. As should be the case, we had earned a reputation for easy, informal hospitality. I was enormously pleased to add an element to the Canadian party of 1959. My eleven-year-old niece, Brenda, was an excellent piper and she and her father came down to open our jollification. Along with the moose stew (or ragout) and much conviviality we had a jolly time.

I did a good deal of official entertaining and was particularly delighted to tender a luncheon to the representatives of Trinidad and Tobago and Jamaica, Elias Clarke and Hugh Shearer. It was on the day these countries had joined the UN. Mr Shearer later became prime minister of Jamaica and received me when I made my first visit to his country in 1976.

It wasn't all geniality however. I recall a little dust-up between General Assembly president Sir Leslie Munro of New Zealand and Krishna Menon of India. The enormously self-important Menon sought to raise a point of order. Without hearing it, big burly Sir Leslie trumpeted: 'There is no point of order.' Menon was not amused. On another occasion, Munro raised the ire of an ebullient Labour party senator from Australia. Clearly mistaking Munro's accent, Senator Hendrickson said, 'You must be from Australia.' 'Don't insult me.' replied Munro. The cordial tête-à-tête ended with the Senator's, 'and you can go to buggery, mate, and I'll go and talk to someone decent.'

With such a host of people, some unlovable types are bound to show up. Once at a meeting of Commonwealth delegates I was much embarrassed by the tone and stance of the British representative. When a gentleman from Sierra Leone made a sensible procedural intervention His Nibs said: 'Mr Siaka, I am the chairman and I will decide.' Colonel Blimp couldn't have done it better.

Currents of hostility flowed freely at the UN. One of the conventions of the place is that a delegate's first speech begins with the usual courteous congratulations to the chairman, the vice-chairman, and the rapporteur of the committee. On the Fourth or Trusteeship Committee, on which I served during the 13 and 14th assemblies, all the Arab delegates and many third-world countries invariably extended the courtesies to the chairman and vice-chairman. Then followed a noticeable pause. Not for them any congratulations to the rapporteur, Arieh Eilan of Israel. He was an extremely bright and pleasant man. Recalling my Presbyterian upbringing with its strong emphasis on the Old Testament, I used to call him my pre-Calvinist friend. Mrs Golda Meir, his foreign minister, spent a good deal of time at UN sessions. Even more impressive than Golda Meir was Abba Eban. I met him several times since, at the UN, in Israel, and in Canada. He is the most eloquent platform speaker I have ever heard. It is sad that the vicissitudes of national politics have removed this skilled public servant from a position of power in his own country.

All Arab spokesmen gave an oratorical drubbing to the Israelis. In their camp a most loquacious but colourful man was Ahmad Shuqairi, a Palestinian-born lawyer from Brooklyn who was then serving as the Saudi Arabian representative to the UN. He did not go in for the twenty-minute or half-hour orations. His loquacity was as famous as his asperity. But Shuqairi was not a dull man nor was he a fool. Although in my early days at the UN I did not develop close contacts with Arab delegates, I became quite interested in the reports of the Commissioner of the United Nations Relief and Works agency (UNRWA) and began to see the vastness of the problems of the Palestinians.

In that period, of course, an even more denigrated pariah of the UN was South Africa. The first debate in which I participated on the Fourth Committee was about South West Africa, a perennial item on the Fourth Committee's agenda. That issue has finally been resolved and I had the honour of saluting the independent state of Namibia in the Canadian Senate on 20 March 1990.

From the beginning of the United Nations in 1945, Canada was an active and serious member. Our delegates were significant players in the important and sensible partition plan for Palestine. Lester B. Pearson, a major UN figure, was elected president of the 17th General Assembly in 1952. His leadership during the Suez

Crisis earned him the Nobel Peace prize in 1957. So when I arrived at the UN there was an aura of goodwill and appreciation around the Canadian delegation.

I recall the many able people I met at our first delegation meeting in the Beekman Tower Hotel where the mission and the individual delegates were then housed. The under-secretary, Jules Leger, was naturally very active. Others whom I first met in a UN context were John Holmes, William Barton, Ben Rogers, General E.L.M. Burns, John Halstead, Neil Currie, John Hadwin, Charles Ritchie, and many other luminaries.

Although he was not a professional diplomat, the minister, Sidney Smith, was a star. He was devoted to his duties and, while the intricacies of his new political job may have troubled him a bit, he loved the UN, was devoted to its ideals, and relished the new contacts he was making. Sidney Smith had an avuncular charm which endeared him to many. I was amazed when at his delegation party he had invited everyone and knew the name of all the guests, delegates, officials, stenos, and guards. All were made warmly welcome. Early in the session our then representative, Robert Mackay, invited the delegates to a reception in his spacious apartment. So recent was the change of government that Mackay still had on the grand piano a signed photo of Lester Pearson. When he spied this replica of an earlier age, Sidney Smith didn't pretend not to see it nor did he show disapproval. He merely said: 'My, Dr Mackay, I admire your taste in photography.' A quite delightful moment.

In many committees the delegate is a non-professional advised by one or more departmental experts. One of our delegates, Josie Quart (later senator), Canadian representative on the Third (social, humanitarian, and cultural) Committee, told her adviser that while she would appreciate background material she didn't wish any speeches written for her. 'I prefer my own phraseology,' she said. Although Josie said it first, I always took the same attitude. It is important that the representative be well aware of Canadian policy on the matter discussed but External Affairs memoranda don't often make for sparkling oratory.

In 1957 there was a bit of tension between the political and the professional people. Some Tories thought the pros regarded a PC government as something like a fluke. Although I am as suspicious as the next person, I really didn't feel this. Almost without exception, I found the External Affairs people able, dedicated, and helpful.

I found plenty of interesting attractions in the Big Apple, and was thrilled when I first saw Times Square and walked the Great White Way. The Empire State Building was still the tallest in the world; the Statue of Liberty was an imposing sight. I delighted in all the wonders of New York City and enjoyed its restaurants, off-Broadway shows, and the noisy hustle and bustle of a giant metropolis.

As I was to say in many other parts of the world, New York was a long way from Victoria, PEI, but one of our most pleasant experiences had a Victoria inspiration. My next-door neighbour and former pupil, Donalda MacLeod, had gone to New York as a Saks model. She later married Joe Burda, a good-looking, dashing young businessman. Shortly after the 1957 UN General Assembly opened, we were invited out by this elegant young couple. All was handled with great aplomb. When the maître d' at the famed Luchow's restaurant escorted us to our table, the string ensemble played 'O Canada!' Later the maestro came to the table and asked for a request. I chose the 'Radetzky March' which the group played beautifully. After this our hosts took us to the famous Stork Club where Broadway notables gathered. All in all a wonderful evening!

But it was not only on such occasions that beautiful Prince Edward Island was on my mind. In all the many months I was a Canadian delegate to the United Nations I was also a member of the House of Commons for the constituency of Queens. Deeply concerned about international issues and fascinated by the ambience at the UN, I never for a moment forgot the priority of my parliamentary responsibilities. I did not wish to have any constituents feel cut off from their MP because of my being at the UN. So I was on the telephone to my Ottawa office at least once a day. I kept the stenographers at the Canadian mission busy with my heavy correspondence. I also wrote articles for the *Charlottetown Guardian*. The UN radio service was very proficient and I used it often. I did regular broadcasts for CFRA, an up-and-coming Ottawa station, and also sent reports to CFCY Charlottetown. This gave me an opportunity to publicize the UN, as well as Macquarrie, through interviews with prominent figures from other delegations. I recall having Mr Ifeagwu, a representative of Nigeria, as a guest in 1960 when his country entered the UN. He politely but firmly took me to task for not pronouncing his name properly. I apologized and didn't try to exculpate myself by noting that in Victoria and PEI generally I had not run across many Nigerian names.

Despite my unrelenting zeal on behalf of my constituents, even though I was dwelling in the canyons of Manhattan, some of my political friends in PEI were apprehensive. It had not been a custom for Queens MPs to have a high internationalist profile. A few of my PC people thought it might encourage a high-hat, big-shot image which would be hurtful in the next election. Gerald Foster was one who told me not to worry. 'Wherever you are you are always interested in your own people and accessible to them.' Another political friend, Andrew MacRae, took an even stronger line. When some local Grits taunted him about Macquarrie's serving at the UN and NATO instead of Queens, he replied: 'You should be proud that an Island MP is making it in the broader circles; the fellows you people used to elect were never wanted anywhere else.'

Although it was over thirty years ago, my UN period remains vivid in my memory. As the weeks went by, the glamour eroded and the routine of ever-lengthening committee debates became a bit debilitating. Some of the negotiations over the wording of resolutions were time-consuming. I took a keen interest in these exercises and became increasingly appreciative of the skill of our External Affairs people. Both Sidney Smith and Howard Green were enthusiasts for the UN and gave our delegation strong and devoted leadership. At our morning meetings we had serious discussions on the issues confronting the Assembly. At the UN plenary and committee sessions we were active in consultation with other delegations. The general Canadian effort was on the side of compromise and moderation. Some members seemed casual in their voting patterns, but Canada has always been concerned about consistency. We did not support resolutions which would not be carried out. On occasion we had to abstain from resolutions or parts of them because the subject matter came within provincial jurisdiction rather than federal.

In a speech in the House of Commons on 24 January 1963, I appraised the Canadian role and performance abroad. It made its way into the *Dictionary of Canadian Quotations and Phrases*. Because it is my only entry in that prestigious publication I supinely yield to the temptation to reproduce it.

United Nations
There is something extremely humbling to be at an international organization and note on every hand the high respect in which Canadians are held. I think it is humbling because it is quite a challenge to measure up to the tremendous responsibility constantly put upon Canadians, especially in the UN context.[1]

When I was active at the UN I had not yet been to Africa, but it was with matters affecting the continent that I was most involved. The Fourth Committee of the General Assembly was assigned responsibility for UN Trust territories. These were those parts of the former European empires for which the League of Nations had held a mandate. The League had not been very successful in leading the mandates in Africa towards independence. In the UN it was a high priority and much good work was done. The 13th General Assembly (1958) was called the African Assembly in recognition of the UN-aided birth of several new independent African states. When I first studied the map of Africa in my geography classes it bore the same colours as Europe. The red areas were British, the purple French, the green Italian, and so on. It seemed that but a tiny part belonged to the Africans. Today more than fifty of the UN members are from that vast area. I was privileged and thrilled to see at close range the UN's splendid efforts in assisting a host of African peoples to make their way from the inadequacies and frustrations of colonialism to a new and nobler realization of their yearnings for self-fulfilment and sovereignty. As with all worthwhile achievements it did not come about by the mere reading of proclamations. There were interminable debates, constant procedural arguments, long hearings from petitioners, on the spot committees of investigation, and UN-supervised plebiscites.

As I found my way in the Fourth Committee I became increasingly impressed by what it was doing. I sought to inform myself of the intricacies of the issues involved and not to be a mere figurehead leaving the basic operation to my departmental adviser. I also interested myself in developing relations with other delegates. In the political or special committees where explosive superpower rivalries were always at the surface, the attitudes and positions of delegates were readily predictable. In some of the less contentious committees, like the Fourth, more scope and authority seemed to surround the delegates. I discovered that some well-informed veterans, like the Mexican, the Yugoslav, and the Filipino delegates on the Fourth Committee, were extremely important people because of themselves, rather than the countries they represented.

One remarkable person on the Fourth Committee was Marian Anderson. Perhaps there was a touch of tokenism in having an American black of celebrity status as the American delegate. Certainly this gifted artist made a profound impression on all of us despite her generally low profile. Not surprisingly the U.S. often seemed a bit unenthusiastic about the decline of the old order in the former colonial areas. One day during the tense South West Africa debate, Ms Anderson read a prepared statement by no means in accord with the spirit generally prevailing in the committee. Before the sitting adjourned, she asked for the floor and gave her own views; they were quite different from the official U.S. line. She was enthusiastically applauded. Along with a great musical talent the wonderful lady had compassion and courage in abundance.

Although Marian Anderson and I had equal credentials as our countries' representatives to the Fourth Committee of the UN General Assembly, I could not bring myself to regard her as just another UN colleague. For years I had been thrilled by her glorious contralto voice and deeply moved by her dignified response to the affronts which a then blatantly racist society heaped upon her. During my Winnipeg days I recall the Reverend Dr Crossley Hunter declaiming about a *Time* magazine article. It noted that she had received seven curtain calls at Carnegie Hall but still had to go to Harlem to find a hotel room. So I stood in reverential admiration of this great lady.

It was against this background that I received a request from Henry Best, Sidney Smith's executive assistant. (Today he would bear the more grandiloquent title chief of staff.) Of all the people at the UN Henry most desired to meet Marian Anderson and asked my assistance. There had been courteous and somewhat routine greetings at the committee. I had attended a small reception she had tendered at her Manhattan apartment but I felt a bit reluctant to impose upon Marian Anderson for another appointment. But I had a high regard for Henry Best. Sidney Smith was one of my favourite Canadians and, as my super realist father would have said, 'the worst she can do is say no.' So I girded up my loins with strength and asked my illustrious Fourth Committee colleague if she would join me and the minister's executive assistant for tea. Without demur and with quintessential charm, she accepted for the upcoming Friday.

That little tea party in the Delegates' Lounge was one of the most pleasant occasions in my life. Henry and I were uplifted. But we soon fell to earth with a clunk. When we left the UN building to flag a taxi to take us to LaGuardia airport we had our comeuppance. In the Friday rush hour the most polite answer any driver gave us was, 'are you kidding Mac?' The minister and many of the delegates were at the airport in a Viscount headed for Ottawa and a well-deserved break from a busy week. Henry and I, futilely trying to get to the airport, hoped they would leave without us and we could get a later flight. But it was as difficult to contact our Canadian aircraft as it was to get a cab. A worry-filled two hours later we reached LaGuardia and found the Canadian plane waiting for us. Sidney Smith, the diplomat of diplomats, acted as if it was anything but an outrageous desecration on his time. Henry and I knew that a conversation with Marian

Anderson was worth many a travel delay for us but what about the others who yearned to get home to Canada for a weekend?

There were nasty days during the brittle East-West Cold War when the UN's global mandate for good was tragically diminished. The Russians were eternally capable of mischief, but in later years sometimes the rightist U.S. Republicans could also be major inhibitors of the goal of the world organization. One of the most shocking items I've ever seen on a television public affairs show was a 1983 cut of Charles Lichenstein, deputy leader of the American UN delegation. In a statement as callous as it was smartass he told the UN to go away.

If in the judicious determination of the members of the United Nations, they feel that they are not welcome and that they are not being treated with the hostly consideration that is their due, then the United States strongly encourages such member states seriously to consider removing themselves and this organization from the soil of the United States. We will put no impediment in your way. The members of the US mission to the United Nations will be down at dockside waving you a fond farewell as you sail into the sunset.

In an earlier day there was a strong self-righteous isolationist attitude among many American politicians. In the 1980s an even nastier attitude was manifest in some quarters. President Reagan apparently admired the movie character Rambo, who personified an overarmed swashbuckling privateer who would make America safe and great regardless of who was mowed down in the process. Shutting up or starving out the UN with its immoral majority was viewed by some Ramboites as the smart thing to do. I find no record of Ambassador Lichenstein being reproved or rebuked by any official in the American administration.

During my UN years the Cold War rivalry gravely inhibited the institution's effectiveness. Glasnost ushered in a new era in the 1980s and a diminution of tension in many world trouble spots followed. The 1990 Iraqi invasion of Kuwait brought about a voting pattern of almost unanimity under the leadership of the U.S., whose spokesmen had once wished to see the world organization depart American shores. It was an ironic turn of events. Watching George Bush draw the UN flag over himself made me think of Lichenstein's crude comments. Psalm 118 has a nice expression' 'The stone which the builders rejected has become the cornerstone of the temple.'

CUBA – MISSILE CRISIS, 1962, AND SUBSEQUENT VISITS

On the evening of 22 October 1962, I was hosting a dinner in the parliamentary restaurant for a visiting British MP. For the first and only time in my life I brought a radio into the parliamentary restaurant. This was because of President Kennedy's response to the installation of Soviet missiles in Cuba. We all listened with fearful attention to every word he uttered. I wondered how close we were to universal tragedy. I admired his sound and measured indication of strength but I was deeply troubled and apprehensive. On 24 October I heard the following exchange while I was sitting quietly in my seat in the House of Commons:

Mr. Martin (Essex East): Mr Speaker ... In view of the fact that the Secretary of State for External Affairs, for reasons best known to himself, has decided that at this time he should not be at the United Nations, does he not think that in view of all the circumstances it is in the national interest that at least his parliamentary secretary, at any rate, should be present at the United Nations in New York at this time?

Mr. Green: Mr. Speaker, the parliamentary secretary was at the United Nations last Thursday and Friday, and he may be going back in a day or two. He may even go back this evening. However, I can assure the hon. member that my one interest in this present crisis is to do the very best I can for Canada and for peace in the world and I really do not need any prompting from him as to what is my duty.

I had not been in my West Block office for ten minutes after question period when I had a call from my minister, Howard Green. He said: 'Heath, you heard Paul's question. I think you'd better go down right away.' I caught the next plane to New York.

Everyone likes to feel wanted and I appreciated the opportunity to go to the centre of world action at a crisis time. But there were some primitive emotions in my breast. Foremost was plain unadorned fear. When I kissed my wife good-bye at Uplands Airport I wondered whether I would ever see her again.

The Cuban Missile Crisis was not primarily a UN matter but much of the superpower confrontation took place there. On the day after my arrival, I sat in the Security Council chamber and heard the dramatic clash between Adlai Stevenson and Vladimir Zorin. When Stevenson sharply questioned the Russian on what was going on in Cuba, the latter tried to stonewall. Stevenson caustically advised him to answer since he was prepared to sit there until Hell froze over until he did. Adlai Stevenson was well known and appreciated as an articulate and witty man but, in those grim days of the Cuban crisis, he revealed a stern capacity to slug it out with his Soviet counterpart.

UN Ambassador Tremblay and I went to the American Mission every morning for a briefing by Stevenson. I cannot recall exactly who comprised this group but it was essentially NATO countries and Japan. Each day he took us candidly and carefully through the summit exchanges between the leaders of the two nuclear superpowers. The messages passing between Moscow and Washington were impressive and revealing. Eventually it seemed that these two highly dissimilar men, Kennedy and Khrushchev, the products of two sharply contrasting social systems, did eventually find some common purpose. It was as if, in coming close to the edge of a fearsome abyss, they found the strength of restraint and averted a mega-tragedy. I recall some passages in Khrushchev's second letter which revealed the rough old comrade as deeply troubled about the dangers inherent in rashness.

In about a week I returned from New York deeply thankful that the world had missed the ultimate folly of a thermonuclear holocaust. It was my feeling, too, that President Kennedy had displayed statesmanlike qualities throughout the crisis. His handling of the Bay of Pigs invasion had been a fiasco. At the Vienna summit with Khrushchev he had achieved nothing higher than a draw. But he came out of the Cuban missile crisis evincing strength and steadiness. John Holmes, one of Canada's most brilliant diplomats, described Kennedy's unilateral action as 'one of the most remarkable diplomatic moves in history.'

While, mercifully, we avoided nuclear fallout, there were painful political repercussions from the crisis. Relations between Diefenbaker and Kennedy were anything but cordial before; they were worse after. Diefenbaker resented Kennedy's attempts to interfere with Canada's sale of wheat to China. There had been other set-tos over defence and certain Canadian votes at the UN. Two hours before the Kennedy speech on the Russian missiles, Diefenbaker was visited by the American ambassador to Canada, Livingston Merchant, who carried a copy of the Kennedy text and photographs of the missiles in place in Cuba. This was not totally satisfactory to the Canadian prime minister. He, not surprisingly, felt that there was a big difference between being consulted and being informed. The NORAD agreement had been posited on something more than information. Cuba is in North America. But Merchant after the meeting thought that Diefenbaker was mollified and saw no need to make a statement before the following day. So the American administration was surprised and not delighted to learn that at 8:00 p.m., one hour after Kennedy's speech, Diefenbaker had addressed the House of Commons. I was in my seat and heard him suggest that the UN make 'an on-site inspection in Cuba to ascertain what the facts are.' He also declared that 'the only sure way that the world can secure the facts [about the presence of offensive weapons] would be through an independent inspection.'

John Diefenbaker was a touchy, prickly man and his attitude in 1962 may in part be explained by the personal animosity he felt towards Kennedy, which is shown in his autobiography *One Canada*. 'I considered that he was perfectly capable of taking the world to the brink of thermonuclear destruction to prove himself the man for our times, a courageous champion of Western democracy.'[2] But it was more than a personal vendetta. He often railed in caucus about 'the Americans pushing Canada around.'

On the general question of Cuba, I thought Canada had shown far more sensitivity and realism than the United States. I am always at a loss to explain why a great country with such a noble revolutionary tradition can adopt such adamantine stands in favour of the status quo in other countries. I was interested in the Cuban revolution from the beginning and discovered nothing to indicate to me that Fidel Castro was a blood-thirsty, red-eyed Communist. With its vast power in the hemisphere and its powerful economy, the United States could have helped assure a cooperative Cuba. Long ago Woodrow Wilson had declared that the United States must teach those Latin Americans to elect good governments. If this goal was not achieved through the years, it was not for lack of American intervention. So often their efforts seemed to be exerted on behalf of the most outrageously corrupt leaders, far different from the governments for which Wilson had yearned. I remember a series of loathsome Cuban leaders. One of the worst was Fulgencio Batista, the crude dictator whom Castro ousted. To those political friends who over the years have accused me of being soft on Castro, I asked: 'Do you think Batista's rule was a good thing? Don't you see any improvements in the lot of the Cuban people under Castro?'

I thought it was against our tradition and our interests to follow the brittle pattern of u.s. diplomacy. I also believed that we should not only keep our diplomatic and commercial lines open with Cuba but should try for meaningful relations. In 1972 I was instrumental in arranging for a parliamentary delegation to visit Cuba, the first such visit since the revolution. Ralph Stewart, Liberal MP for Cochrane, and Andrew Brewin, NDP member for Greenwood, both had a strong interest in international affairs. The Cuban ambassador, José Fernandez de Cossio, a young man of great charm and savvy, inspired the invitation, which included the three wives. It was a very useful and pleasant visit. We were treated well and had an opportunity to see some interesting aspects of their society. I sometimes felt that the traditional élan of the Latin American was somehow dampened by the heavy emphasis on revolutionary values. But I saw none of the grinding poverty I encountered in many other areas of Latin America and the Caribbean.

I made two more trips to Cuba. On the third one I addressed

their professional service institute at a symposium at the University of Havana. I was somewhat flattered and amazed when I was interrupted by a standing ovation when I referred to the Canadian official response to their revolution, when we kept communication lines open.

Many years after the Cuban crisis, one of Diefenbaker's ministers said something to a parliamentary colleague which I was surprised to hear. Recalling Canada's stance he said: 'I never gave much thought to the issue until I heard young Macquarrie's appeal in caucus.' (The adjective 'young' underlines how long ago it was.) While I'm sure my arguments weren't decisive it was flattering to know that someone followed them. Our critics often suggest that politicians are better at talking than listening.

COMMONWEALTH CARIBBEAN – OLD AND CLOSE FRIENDS

People from Atlantic Canada have traditionally been fond of the Caribbean area. In our commercial heyday, sailors from our ports made many trips to the West Indies. To our people molasses was a staple diet item. We still have a fondness for the stronger by-product of the cane; rum is the favourite booze in all four provinces.

As with a lot of things, Maritimers yearn a bit for the days when we had regular passenger and freight services with the West Indies. My cousin Earl Lord was for many years an officer on one of the Lady boats and he loved the lush and beautiful islands of the Spanish Main. But beyond nostalgia there are compelling reasons for Canadian interest in the Commonwealth Caribbean. We speak the same language and share similar parliamentary institutions. As early as 1855 John A. Macdonald appointed Francis Hincks as his special adviser on West Indian affairs. Since 1911 there have been several meetings of political leaders at a high level. We Canadians have a stake in the political stability and economic prosperity of the people of the region. As the colonies moved from colonialism to independence I, like many Canadians, hoped the Federation of the West Indies might have survived. But I had no difficulty understanding why some of the islands wished to go it alone. Outside experts can wax eloquent on the virtues of Maritime union of the three old Canadian seaside provinces. I never gave the suggestion the time of day. As I once told John Turner, we are not overburdened with luxuries in the Maritimes and would like to retain provincial self-government as one of the few.

It was not until 1971 that I made my first visit to the Commonwealth Caribbean and naturally fell in love with the islands and the islanders. While it was a personal trip, I had made contacts with the branches of the Commonwealth Parliamentary Association (CPA) in the area and I was warmly received. In Trinidad and Tobago I talked with a former councillor at their Ottawa high commission who was in Prime Minister Eric Williams's cabinet. I was also invited to the home of Arthur Robinson, a former minister in temporary limbo who in 1991 is now prime minister. While there are problems and some aberrations on the political side, the parliamentary institutions in the Commonwealth Caribbean are a splendid tribute to strengths of the system from which they and we draw our precedents. To see these tiny islands maintain the full panoply of the Westminster tradition is absolutely remarkable. In some of their newer constitutions they have added some quite interesting features. The second chambers in Jamaica and Trinidad and Tobago are appointed by the president. A certain number he appoints on the advice of the prime minister, a smaller group on the advice of the leader of the opposition. A third group he appoints without advice from either party leader.

In the early seventies I was chairman of a Canada–Commonwealth Caribbean committee of the CPA. An encouraging number of my colleagues from both houses were keenly interested and we had frequent meetings and kept in close contact with all the high commissioners from the region. Because of my committee chairmanship I had a visit in 1975 from the Honourable Liam McGuire, a member of the Legislative Council of the Turks and Caicos Islands. I was delighted to set up a luncheon and intrigued by the purpose of his mission. The Turks and Caicos, although ready to shed the status of crown colony, were not interested in independence. Nor did they wish to unite with another West

Indian state. According to Liam McGuire, his fellow councillors and the people of the islands sought economic and political union with Canada. This was music to my ears! Here was a chance for our prosperous and developed country to do something for a small community which needed help. The British had been there a long time but were not leaving the islanders too well endowed. Canada had all sorts of expertise in areas of their economy which were crying out for development: airport construction, harbour improvement; upgrading of fisheries technology, tourism. As with Newfoundland, our social welfare and health programs would be a boon to their people. With a population of only about six thousand we could take them in without too much strain on our economy.

Liam McGuire told me they wanted to use our dollar as their unit of currency. Considering how many Canadians vacationed in the Caribbean, even in 1975 there were advantages in having our own dollar area in the south. There was sufficient interest within the Commonwealth Parliamentary Association to result in the decision to send a delegation to the Turks and Caicos with myself as chairman. Others in the group were my PC colleague Bill Knowles, Liberals Maurice Dupras and Jacques Trudel, and NDP Max Saltsman from Waterloo-Cambridge.

Upon returning to Canada after a week in the Turks and Caicos, I strongly supported union in the House of Commons, on the media, and in speaking engagements. Some few Canadians were hostile fearing that it would be a drain on Canada. Some even feared a possible burst of immigration. But the most difficult reaction was laughter. So many people thought it all so very funny. Eventually Mitchell Sharp announced the government's reaction. It was totally negative.

There were several other trips to the beautiful Caribbean. One especially poignant visit was to Grenada on the third anniversary of the revolution which overthrew Eric Gairy. A crowded amphitheatre heard Grenada Prime Minister Maurice Bishop, Prime Minister Michael Manley of Jamaica, and Daniel Ortega of Nicaragua extol their socialist ideals. Later I had an extremely interesting and pleasant talk with Bishop. I thought him one of the

Caribbean's most dynamic and sensible leaders. Grenada is a gem of an island and Bishop and his New Jewel Movement seemed a progressive and reasonable group. The gruesome putsch which overthrew him was a frightful action. I regretted the subsequent wholesale intrusion by u.s. forces. It smacked of the high-handed filibustering of the days of Theodore Roosevelt.

In 1970 the Foreign Affairs Committee of the Senate published an insightful and valuable report on Canada-Commonwealth Caribbean relationships. In my talks with leaders in the area I find many still familiar with this study. When I was summoned to the Senate in 1979 I continued my interest in the Caribbean and introduced motions identical to those I had put forward in the Lower House. On one such occasion, in May 1980, I was able to have the Caribbean high commissioners in the gallery and, afterwards, invited senatorial colleagues to join them in my office for a drink of rum. The Senate Hansard for 16 July 1980 indicates the theme of my speech:

(a) subsidization of ocean transport between Canada and the Commonwealth Caribbean area;
(b) assistance in the upgrading of the seaports of Atlantic Canada;
(c) tariff changes to facilitate the exchange of commodities between the two areas;
(d) greater exchange of students between the two areas;
(e) assistance to encourage meetings of political, business and educational leaders of the two areas with a view to stimulating a mutually advantageous North-South exchange of goods, people, services and technology.

OAS – FINALLY WE ARE A MEMBER

In 1949 in my MA thesis, I advocated that Canada join the Organization of American States (OAS). I was delighted that both Sidney Smith and Howard Green favoured membership. My UN experience gave me opportunities to meet many Latin American politicians and diplomats. When in September 1961 Mr Green's special assistant Ross Campbell phoned to ask if I would like to accompany the Honourable Pierre Sévigny on a goodwill visit to Latin America, I accepted readily.

We called at Puerto Rico and at Rio de Janeiro, which I thought one of the world's most beautiful cities. We also went to the then new Brazilian capital, Brasilia, where Sévigny raised the Canadian flag over our new embassy site. There was also a visit to Buenos Aires after which we attended the OAS conference at Punta del Este in Uruguay. Canada was given the first place among the block of Observers. It was a useful meeting but the presence of swash-buckling Ché Guevara tended to overshadow mundane things like discussion of the agenda. In our three weeks in Latin America, Isabel and I found the Sévignys charming and considerate. The visit also gave an opportunity for many good conversations with Yvan Beaulne of External Affairs, one of Canada's leading experts on Latin America. Jim Weld from our embassy in Brazil was the organizer for the Punta del Este delegation. We found him and his wife eternally helpful, well informed, and very pleasant.

Although disappointed in the way in which the OAS handled the Cuban issue I retained my view on Canadian membership in the organization. When in late 1989 there was widespread spec-ulation that Canada would join the OAS, I wrote the prime minister urging such a course. In January 1990 we finally took the long vacant chair. Some critics say we have not done much since as-suming membership. I believe this is unfair and certainly a bit premature. Some have said that the move into the OAS was a further sign of our prime minister's toadying to Washington. Despite some indication of too much deference to Washington on other occa-sions, our joining the hemispheric organization had long been sought by the Latin Americans as well as the United States.

BIAFRA — FAR-OFF MISERY STIRS CANADIANS CONSCIENCE

As I have already noted, my UN experience stimulated a new and deep interest in Africa. In the late 1960s, I became heavily in-volved in parliamentary and public discussions about a grave issue in that continent. On 30 May 1967 Colonel Ojukwu of eastern Nigeria proclaimed its independence as the new state of Biafra.

Like a number of my House of Commons colleagues I was horrified by the repressive measures used by the Lagos government to cow the rebels into submission.

I don't regard myself as strong on partisanship but my contribution to the throne speech debate on 23 September 1968 doesn't sound all that moderate. Suggesting that I reflected the Canadian attitude better than the minister, Mitchell Sharp, I said: 'I am ashamed, I am embarrassed, I am disappointed, I am dejected by the reaction which this government has shown to one of the most shocking crises in humanity.' In my aroused ardour I said: 'Forsake your fears, discard your technical niceties, throw off your protective colouration of protocol and assist the people of Biafra whose suffering is indescribable.'

I became an early Biafrist because of the influence of one of the great internationalists of the Presbyterian Church in Canada, the Reverend Dr E.H. (Ted) Johnston. He knew Nigeria better than anyone in External Affairs. He was an early activist in trying to persuade the Canadian government to be more sensitive to the sufferings of the people of besieged Biafra. Under his inspiration four members of the House of Commons made perilous flights into the war torn area. He successfully urged the church to rally popular humanitarian support for the Biafran cause. It seems that Canadian politicians, except on the issue of abortion, pay little attention to the views of our churches. But on Biafra the churches rallied magnificently to a humanitarian cause. I remember attending a big meeting in an Ottawa church at which Stanley Burke, the handsome, articulate, and popular CBC national newscaster, spoke. He had given up his job to stimulate support for Biafra. He told the audience that he was a church drop-out but might become a church drop-in because of the stirred conscience of Canadian church people.

The pro-Biafra campaign was absorbing and difficult. The Trudeau government had an obsessive wariness about anything that looked like secession. But Mitchell Sharp was sufficiently sensitive to rising Canadian public opinion that he announced an altered Canadian policy which was still somewhat neutral but leaning towards the Biafran cause. More humanitarian aid was promised. As it happened, Colonel Ojukwu threw in the sponge before the Canadian government's new and more sympathetic program could be implemented. The sensitivity and concern of a great many Canadians was the positive aspect of the whole affair. After all the death and carnage, nothing had been gained. As in most wars the old question arose: 'What was all the fighting for?'

THE BIRTH OF BANGLADESH — TRAGEDY, TRIUMPH, TRAVAIL

It was also a secessionist movement which brought about my involvement in another gripping human tragedy. In December 1970 a national election in Pakistan saw the Awami League make an almost clean sweep of all the seats in East Pakistan, whose population was essentially Bengali. Following the election, the dynamic Awami League leader, Sheik Mujibur Rahman, called for the independence of his region from Pakistan. As tension increased, the authorities at Islamabad outlawed the League, jailed Mujibur, and sent in armed forces to quell the disturbances. There followed a mass exodus of East Pakistan refugees who crossed into neighbouring India in the millions.

Reports of the suffering of the fleeing victims and of repressive measures by Pakistani military forces stirred many people in Canada and the western world generally. I was well acquainted with Ashok Bhadkamkar, the Indian high commissioner in Ottawa, and he and some of his officers suggested my going to look at the refugee situation. I became more and more disturbed by what I heard from the region and discussed with Mr Stanfield and our whip Tom Bell the possibility of structuring a small delegation. Andrew Brewin, the NDP critic on foreign affairs, was interested and willing. So also was Georges Lachance, Liberal MP from Lafontaine, who was acting chairman of the External Affairs committee.

We would have been happy had the Canadian government sponsored our trip. They didn't, and we went over via Air India as guests of the Indian government. I had never undertaken such a long air trip in my life, and I didn't look forward to the July temperatures we would find in India. One of our charming Indian stewardesses became quite a favourite medical adviser. She was constantly proferring champagne, declaring it to be good for the circulation. I'm not sure she was wrong. One of my last visitors before heading for Delhi was that indefatigable humanitarian Dr Lotta Hitschmanova, founder of the Unitarian Service Committee. She asked us if we would each take a bottle of a thousand pills and give them to one of her Indian co-workers, a monk whom she described as a Buddhist saint. Doubtless she had fast-talked a pharmaceutical house into donating the antibiotics. A tremendous woman!

After many hours and many time zones we finally arrived in Bombay, and then on to Delhi where our high commissioner, Jim George, took us under his wing. He was helpful throughout, advising us on health and dietary cautions and being eternally accommodating and generous with his obviously good contacts with the Indian authorities. We soon found that our travels would be even longer than we anticipated. The Pakistani high commissioner in New Delhi asked Jim George to arrange a meeting with the three of us. The upshot was that we accepted an invitation to go to Pakistan. Because of restrictions on overflights this meant we had to go around the Indian peninsula.

That the trip was to be a trying ordeal was clear from the outset. There were many people to see. The heat was oppressive and the sight of a seemingly endless stream of refugees or vast encampments of them tried the soul. On the faces of these unfortunate people one sensed fear and bewilderment. At one camp I was much startled and taken aback when an old lady prostrated herself wailing at my feet. Apparently she had thought the zoom lens of a photographer near me was a gun. My interpreter said: 'She has asked to be dispatched now and thereby end her suffering.' The Indian authorities were, I thought, doing an excellent job in coping with this influx of people from a neighbouring country. We had no doubts about the reality of the problem, although I thought at times both Indian and Pakistani officials were somewhat propagandistic. I was generally impressed by the quiet passivity displayed by the refugees.

There is a widespread and erroneous idea that parliamentary visits are mere junkets by good-time Charlies. I never found this to be the case. Our Indian trip was no light or casual affair. The one break our hosts urged upon us was a visit to Agra, where we saw the Taj Mahal both in sunlight and moonlight. Although I had seen thousands of pictures of this architectural gem I was still not ready for its exquisite beauty.

On the way to Agra we were talking about the unfortunate space mishap in which three Soviet astronauts perished. A young officer of the Indian foreign service observed that we seemed much more concerned about the death of three Russians than the three hundred of his people who had perished in a flood the day before. I pondered his comment.

In Calcutta we were put up at the Raj Prajan, the former residence of the British governors. But I remember Calcutta less for our accommodation than for the thousands who seemed to have none at all. In a morning drive to the airport we saw the homeless camping out in alleys, on streets, clad in the rags of poverty and deprivation. From scenes like these and the myriad of horror stories we were told came deep feelings of sorrow and depression. The human problems were so overwhelming, the possibility of correcting them so remote, that it was difficult to retain hope and optimism.

We were nearly three weeks in the area. We met with Mitchell Sharp on 19 July, the day after our return, and presented him with some unanimous recommendations for greatly increased aid to India in its refugee program and Canadian assistance in providing shipping and needed supplies. We lauded India's handling of the refugees, urged international action on the problem and sought to avoid name-calling and assignment of blame. I much appreciated Sharp's reaction to our recommendations. In my experience governments and ministers are not noted for accepting advice from back-benchers. Mr Sharp did and that gave some uplift to us after our bone-wearying and heart-rending visit to far-off India.

Although we were careful in our report, we were basically sympathetic to the aspirations of the people of East Pakistan and we returned home with one of the first Bangladesh flags. Later, after the Indians found it necessary to invade and free East Pakistan, the new state of Bangladesh was set up.

When in 1973 Mr Brewin and I, along with our wives, were invited by the new state of Bangladesh to visit, we rejoiced in its independence. In Pakistan in 1971 we had not been able to see the imprisoned Sheik Mujibur. On our second visit he received us in the presidential mansion at Dacca. I thought him a dynamic and interesting man of great leadership capacity. Tragically, he was assassinated on 15 August 1975. A sad finale to a chapter in the history of Bangladesh.

USSR – FROM COLD WAR TO GLASNOST

When I entered the House of Commons and began my UN experience, the Cold War was a painful fact of life. It was painful because of the heavy-handed performance of the Russians, but disturbing too was the response of the United States. Watergate was an ignoble episode in American politics, but McCarthyism was far worse, showing weakness, paranoia, and spiritual rot in high places.

Believing that a sensible accommodation between East and West was valuable, I was pleased to be able to visit the Soviet Union in 1966. I learned a great deal. We were well treated but it didn't require exceptional perception to realize we were in a highly authoritarian society. There was also, especially in Moscow, a depressing drabness. But it was exciting to be in Red Square drinking hot grape juice and watching the Soviet military might parade by in celebration of the October Revolution of 1917. It was cold that day in Red Square. I was the only Canadian who packed a pair of ear muffs and despite Russia's winter cold such 'luxuries' weren't in vogue in Moscow. But as chilly hour followed chilly hour I didn't mind my sartorial uniqueness! In Leningrad, the once proud St Petersburg, we found more beauty. The Hermitage is one of the great art galleries of the world. Other reminders of Czarist days proliferate. While the Soviet regime began with a bloody break with the past, I'm glad they have retained so much of the history of the old Imperial Russia. Perhaps there is some significance in this. Many of the ills and iniquities of which extreme anti-Communists complain are a part of the Russian tradition and not creations of Lenin. In reading the letters of my most distinguished ancestor, Major-General Lachlan Macquarie, I was particularly interested in his account of a trip to Russia in 1810. He was impressed by the country, liked the people, but was driven to distraction by the eternal red tape and petty bureaucracy. So what's new and what's old? Siberia was not discovered by Lenin and followers as a place of exile. The autocratic Czars used it for stashing away their enemies or critics.

While it is appropriate to recall and study a nation's history, it is not always prudent to seek to repeat it. I find it difficult to be enthusiastic about the idea of Leningrad again becoming St Petersburg. The toppling of statues, even if they are ugly and numerous, is still not a productive pursuit. Sometimes the good old days' were not really all that good. I think often about Imperial Russia as I hear the accounts of today's economic and social problems in the Soviet Union. The opening to capitalism and the free market is exciting. It is wonderful to have a wide range of exotic consumer goods but, if only a minuscule portion of the population can afford them, have we achieved the just society. Even in the grim days of the Czars there was a minority who lived very well.

Indeed, as I view the weakening Soviet superpower I feel both happiness and anxiety. As Robert Burns put it in his sweet, sad poem 'To a Mouse,' 'And forward tho' I canna see I guess and fear.' The vast Soviet federation is likely to fall apart or explode under powerful centrifugal forces within its borders. What kind of uncertainty and decline lies ahead is hard to predict. People of good will must hope that out of today's turmoil and upheaval may come a kind of social democracy which never really flourished in the land of the Czars and the Communists. But chaos is not necessarily the fertile soil for freedom. Another of my Manitoba professors, Noel Fieldhouse, often quoted Benito Mussolini on his own establishment of the Fascist regime. 'Power was on the floor. It required only a strong hand to pick it up.' I hope the affluent west will not be too slow or too insensitive to the desperate economic needs of the USSR. The smug preachments about it not being the time for a blank cheque were not reassuring in this regard, but Prime Minister Mulroney's address to Stanford University on 30 September 1991 was one of the best statements I have heard on the matter. In it he stressed the need to move with dispatch and concern to assist the Soviet government and people in these traumatic times.

Not long after my Russian visit I became acquainted with Alexander Yakovlev, the USSR ambassador who stayed in Canada so long that he became the dean of the diplomatic corps in Ottawa. Yakovlev, a Columbia University graduate and a distinguished hero of the Russian Army, was extremely astute, greatly interested in Canada, and, to me at least, splendidly candid. We often entertained each other. I was delighted to put on a luncheon for him in Charlottetown when he came from Montreal on the Soviet ship *Pushkin*. I was totally delighted when I learned that Mikhail Gorbachev had raised him to a powerful place in the Kremlin hierarchy. That was a good omen for the West or more importantly for peace. He is a man of sense and sensitivity and his elevation was an indication of Gorbachev's sound judgment and good intentions. Regrettably he is no longer in Gorbachev's inner circle.

In 1988, I was active in trying to inaugurate a Canada-USSR Parliamentary Association. In this endeavour people like Robert Corbett and Pauline Jewett of the House of Commons, and my senatorial colleagues Bud Olson, Michel Cogger, Gildas Molgat, and Hazen Argue were among the proponents. Senate Speaker Guy Charbonneau, a good internationalist, was supportive. But alas the project failed. Doubtless it was shot down from on high, most unfortunately I thought. There are many useful and important areas for cooperation between Canada and our trans-Arctic neighbour the Soviet Union.

For some time after the beginning of the Gorbachev era I was troubled by the seeming tepidity of the response of the Canadian government. But in one of his best public statements, Joe Clark on 3 May 1989 revealed to the Canadian Club of Toronto a new awareness and sensitivity towards the profound changes in the

Soviet Union. He rightly referred to 'what can only be called a revolution sweeping Soviet society.' He described Mr Gorbachev's effort as 'one of almost unimaginable proportions for any leader anywhere.'

I am old enough to remember a world in which that cruel and brutal Stalin was a major figure. I recall, too, his generally un-inspiring, if less iniquitous, successors. To see a man like Gorbachev at the helm in one of the superpowers was a development as exciting as it was portentous. There are elections with choice in the USSR; there is an openness undreamed of a few years ago. There is reasonableness and compromise on the international front. The UN began to accomplish something meaningful again as it always can if the two superpowers are in some measure of accord. The age of glasnost and perestroika was a truly wonderful time.

People of peace and goodwill everywhere rejoiced in the thaw in the Cold War, the crumbling of the Berlin Wall and ancient barriers to freedom. Sadly, in his own country Gorbachev is having trouble. It would not be in our interest should Gorbachev fall from power. World peace and harmony would suffer grievously.

EUROPE AND NATO — VALUABLE LINKS

Some of my international visits, like the three weeks spent among the pitiful refugees in India, were saddening. I spent an equal amount of time in South Africa where the beauteous natural grandeur contrasted strikingly with the grim aspects of the political and social structure. But now in South Africa under the far-sighted and sensitive leadership of President de Klerk there is new hope. I was a senior citizen before I visited Australia and found it as exciting and beautiful as the tourist literature claimed it to be.

But my interest has not been centred only on the far-distant and exotic parts of the world. The Scottish Highlands and Islands stirred my blood and touched my heart deeply. I have never been to Europe without being emotionally stimulated. Of course Europe is a bright spot for any internationalist. The ancient enmity between Germany and France has been replaced by the cooper-ation and good will so eloquently symbolized by Strasbourg, where the European Parliament is located. Further economic coordination will make Europe one of the great trading blocs of the world. Our trade with the area is not increasing as fast as I would like, and in my view we may be concentrating too much on the Canada–U.S. Free Trade Agreement.

Although no more hawkish then than I am now, I hailed the establishment of NATO and was proud of the role played by Canada's greatest statesman, Lester Pearson. At the signing ceremony he made a prophetic comment:

This treaty born out of fear and frustration, must, however, lead to positive social, economic and political achievements which will extend beyond the time of emergency which gave it birth, or the geographic area which it now includes.[3]

Pearson's successor, Pierre Trudeau, was not a NATO enthusiast. In his early years he seemed bent on taking Canada out of the alliance as an effective partner. Later on it might be said that he took us half-way out by cutting our contribution. The NDP has often revealed an anti-NATO stance. I think that they are wrong on this point. Canadians are not notoriously keen about foreign policy issues but there has been a strong, positive feeling about NATO.

My enthusiasm for the alliance, is not because it brings us closer to the United States. That sort of incentive we don't need. Rather it is the opportunity for ongoing consultation and cooperation with European countries which moves me. While the end of the Cold War is one of the blessings of our age, the withering away of the Soviet empire and the decline of Soviet power may not be totally good. Although the American style of government and quality of life is far superior to that of the Soviet Union, it may not be beneficial to live in a world completely dominated by the United States.

I have the uneasy feeling that unwholesome trends have developed in the Great Republic to the south of us. One senses a diminution of compassion and an increase in hard-line views on many social issues. George Bush's presidential campaign in 1988 was a nasty exercise and I fear that the Canadian political system will be affected by the virus. As I heard and watched Bush performing during the Gulf War crisis, I thought how far removed he was from Franklin Roosevelt.

At my daughter Flora's graduation from Harvard in 1975, President Derek Bok made a splendid address. His most stirring moment came as he quoted the *New York Times*: 'The cloud of non-leadership hangs over the nation's key activities like polluted air.' Then President Bok went on to say:

In this centennial year, others ask why a little country of three million people could produce a Jefferson, a Washington, a Franklin, a Madison, a Hamilton and more while a nation of 200 million can point to scarcely a single figure of comparable stature.

Tis sad but true that the scene is no better now.

That cerebral Canadian, Pierre Trudeau, often talked of the value of countervailing forces. On the international stage today there seem to be no stars but the Americans. At a Canada-Europe parliamentary conference in Banff a few years ago, I said that when American politicians went to Europe they acted as if they had taken their microphones with them but left their earphones at home. During the final days before the Gulf War President Mitterrand of France might have been onto a formula to accomplish the Iraqi withdrawal from Kuwait without a bloodbath. But his efforts received short shrift.

There is great wisdom and experience in the chancelleries of Europe. Perhaps a stronger, more unified Europe may some day develop not hostility to the United States but a greater sense of balance and proportion in the management of international affairs. In a reversion of George Canning's statement, the Old World might yet redress the imbalance of the New.

MIDDLE EAST — MUCH BEGAN HERE, MUCH COULD END ALSO

Lester Pearson once said that in his Sunday school days he could name all the towns from Dan to Beersheba but not all from Victoria to Halifax. I, too, have been captivated by the Holy Land since my boyhood days. My first non–Sunday school recollections were of the troubles in mandated Palestine and the Arab/Jewish bloodshed of the late thirties. Like most Canadians, I was then highly sympathetic to the Jewish yearning to establish a state. For a while, I even thought the Israelis were the underdog in the Middle East strife. Their smashing victory over Arab military units in 1967 and the enormous acquisition of Arab territory prompted me to re-examine my judgments.

In early 1970 Isabel and I attended a dinner put on by Speaker Lucien Lamoureux and his wife. I was much taken by the genial personality and impressive presence of the ambassador of Lebanon, Alif Gébara. Although I don't usually go in for serious and heavy discussions at receptions and dinners, Gébara and I did have a good exchange on the Middle East situation. The next day I was surprised to get a phone call from Ambassador Choucri of the United Arab Republic asking whether I would like to attend a conference of parliamentarians on the Middle East crisis to be held in Cairo on 2 to 5 February. Some years later, I visited Dr Gébara in Beirut and he somewhat puckishly claimed credit for arousing my deep devotion to Middle East causes. He was certainly not exaggerating. In his person he demonstrated that an ambassador does not have to represent a large country to make a significant impact.

Choucri was a somewhat more restrained man but did a splendid job of arranging Isabel's and my trip to the Cairo meeting along with Liberal MPs Ralph Stewart and his lovely wife Suzanne and Marcel Prud'homme. Choucri and his wife visited us in PEI and I regard him as one of Egypt's finest diplomats.

My first visit to the Middle East was, for a variety of reasons, one of the most exciting events of my life. We flew KLM to Rome and spent a few days in the Eternal City before joining our parliamentary colleagues to go by Egypt Air to Cairo. Ralph Stewart, a devout Catholic and former seminarian, had arranged for us to meet the Pope. His Holiness gave us his prayers for the success of the Cairo meeting. Like many people, I had been carried away by the charming Pope John XXIII but was surprised to find his successor, Pope Paul VI, so benevolent and warm. Ralph had also arranged a meeting with Cardinal Bellini, the Vatican secretary of state. As I expected, he was extremely well informed on Middle East affairs. He was an ideal person to meet prior to going to the conference. After that we spent some time in the Sistine Chapel, St Peter's, and the other glories at the heart and centre of the Roman Catholic Church. I'm sure my stern Presbyterian father would never have envisaged one of his bairns relishing such a visit in the domain of the Pope at Rome.

I was much impressed by the people in our embassy in Cairo. The ambassador, Tom Carter, was clearly an extremely perceptive man. He had an astute group of officers with him. One of these, J.M. Touchette, was especially helpful to us. On Sunday I wished to go to church and hoped I could find not just a Protestant church but preferably a Presbyterian one. Touchette knew exactly where I should go. It was a small but beautiful Church of Scotland hidden in a courtyard in the heart of Cairo.

Gamal Abdel Nasser was one of the leading statesmen of the fifties and sixties whether we like it or not, and I think his initiative in focusing attention on the Palestine problem was most astute. I was a little surprised when I met him to find myself thinking of John Diefenbaker. Their eyes were of a different colour but that laser-like piercing quality was there. Certainly they were commanding personalities and both had a physical twitchiness that was a bit unnerving.

But the man who impressed me most at the 1970 conference was Tusif Sayegh, the tall, lath-thin, well-dressed, and bearded spokesman of the Palestinians. Dr Sayegh, son of a Presbyterian minister, obviously had inherited his father's elocution. He began by saying: 'There is no Middle East problem; there is only a Palestine problem.' He went on to say that no one else can speak for the Palestinians, they must speak for themselves. This simple truth hit me like a sharp arrow and, in the years since, I am more than ever convinced of the compelling truth of his opening remarks. When will the Palestinians be allowed to be their own spokesmen and when will the rest of the world listen?

In its closing communiqué the conference appealed to parliaments to support peace in the Middle East, the withdrawal of Israeli forces from the occupied territories, and the implementation of UN Resolution 242. This Security Council resolution, adopted on 27 November 1967, called for the withdrawal of Israeli occupation forces, the termination of belligerency, and the right to peace and security within secure and recognized boundaries.

When, after the close of the Cairo conference, I visited Jordan, I had an experience which made me appreciate the poignancy of Dr Sayegh's eloquent appeal. The Jordanians who, like all the Arabs on our tour, were wonderful hosts, took us to the Baqa'a refugee camp a few miles outside the beautiful and historic city of Amman (the ancient Philadelphia). There, for the first time, I saw the human dimension of the Middle East crisis. I shall never forget the tragic countenances of the denizens of this squalid camp. Only a person of stone could be unmoved by the hopelessness and bewilderment of the children who had never known a real home. The adults, driven from their ancestral lands in Palestine, still looked hurt and broken in spirit. What did these poor unfortunates do to deserve being expelled? They had not inspired the Holocaust. Their leaders had not been consulted by Balfour when he agreed to give Palestinian land to the Jews.

One of the most impressive Jordanians I met was a charming gentleman, Ahmed Toucon, a former prime minister. He immediately commented on an article I had written for the *Ottawa Citizen*, 'Palestine Is Our Problem Too.' I did not know that either the *Citizen* or I were so famous so far from home. In my article I sought to point out that Canada as a member of the UN had responsibility for its 1948 decision to set up two states in Palestine, one Arab, one Jewish. Canadians were prominent in having the partition plan adopted. Canada, like other UN members, has a continuing moral responsibility to see that the Arab state not languish under cruel Israeli occupation, but have sovereignty over the area which the UN had designated for the Palestinians. It was hard for them to give up their land in the area ceded to Israel. To have the rest taken by force was another and more bitter pill.

The treatment of the Palestinians since 1947 is a blot upon a decent world. Pushed out of their ancestral homes and harried and attacked in the dwellings which they temporarily acquired, they have been brutalized, denigrated, and, at best, ignored. Why have these people been forced into a dreary diaspora in a world in which concern for human rights is supposed to be a watchword?

After seeing the tragedy of the Palestinian refugees, I was never the same again. I had had my academic and rational responses to the current situation. But after Baqa'a it was of the heart. My deepest emotions were touched and I became dedicated to the cause of these victimized people.

These homeless, hopeless, hapless people had been languishing in the camps for twenty years when I visited them. Now, over twenty years later, they are still there. And sadly, so few governments or people seem to care. The Palestinians are the victims of a new Diaspora. Even now, when they have agreed to accept the return of less than half the homeland in which they lived for centuries, their rights and their nationhood are still being denied.

My dedication to the cause of these cruelly dispossessed people has never diminished since 1970 when I first gazed upon them through the pensive eyes of pity. Indeed, as year follows year, I find myself more and more concerned about the Palestinians.

After 1970, I made a dozen more trips to the Middle East, anxious as I was to increase my knowledge of the area and my acquaintance with its leaders. I have talked with King Hussein of Jordan and his royal brother, Crown Prince Hassan. I have been received by President Anwar Sadat of Egypt, and later his successor, President Mubarak. I have had useful discussions with President Assad of Syria, two Saudi kings, and leaders of several other Arab states. I have also visited Israel three times, meeting such people as David Ben-Gurion, Menachem Begin, Shimon Peres, Yitzhak Shamir, and Abba Eban, the most impressive of all. Twice I have had sustained conversations with Commander Yasser Arafat, of the Palestine Liberation Organization (PLO). From the beginning I was deeply impressed by the immensity of the task he faced in trying to lead a scattered and deprived people. Denied the normal attributes and institutions of statehood and the benefit of basic human rights, land, dignity, freedom, and security, Arafat and his people have survived. It is a great and splendid example of the triumph of will and the strength of hope.

I have wept for the wrongs inflicted on the Palestinian people and have been indignant and frustrated at the long denial of justice for them. For years as I sought to champion the Palestinian cause, I have been puzzled by the selective compassion which I see in my own land and often among my political associates and fellow churchmen. People who would readily talk about the denial of human rights in the USSR, South Africa, or anywhere else on the globe seemed unable to interact when I mentioned the Palestinian diaspora. Some feel a strong urge to talk about domestic matters or even about the weather.

While naturally I notice this, I try not to be hypercritical. The pro-Israel lobby, backed by the rich and the powerful, is the strongest and most highly organized lobby in the land. To parade your anxiety about justice for the Palestinians is not a popular cause. I have been described by the *Canadian Jewish News* as being an ignoramus or an Arab agent. I have had the hate literature and the crank telephone calls in the middle of the night. I have been publicly dubbed as a pal of the PLO terrorists. None of this is agreeable. But we must never forsake the conviction that the Palestinians are people too, and, although they may not have many friends in the seats of the mighty, they do have a cause.

Sometimes I've been frustrated by the actions of the Palestinian leaders. For years I counselled moderation in vain. Sometimes I winced as the PLO did things which brought delighted satisfaction to their enemies.

Over the years my views on the Middle East have been made clear in multitudinous speeches and articles. In 1980 I undertook a Canadian Club tour in which I declared that the beginning of a solution should be founded on an act of mutual recognition. The Palestinians must recognize the State of Israel, and Israelis must recognize the Palestinians and their right to a state. I urged the fulfilment of Resolution 242 although I fully understood the Palestinians' lack of enthusiasm for it.

But after the long season of anguish things were better for a while. Arafat, whose capacity for constructive statesmanship I never doubted, gave convincing, strong leadership to his people, especially at the significant meeting of the Palestinian National Council in November 1988. He realized that the West, which was largely responsible for the ills of the Palestinians, is the only source of redress. His pragmatic moderation offers new vistas of hope. More Canadians, Americans, and Israelis seem to see this than ever before. Joe Clark showed an appreciation of current realities, especially in his candid address to the Canada-Israel committee in March 1988 for which he was booed for his pains. Our increased contacts with the PLO augered well. It was my hope that Clark would not be restrained from giving the kind of leadership which would allow Canada to play a major role in the pursuit of peace in that ancient and gloried part of the world in which Armageddon is geographically located.

Alas for Palestinians the blue patch in the sky was not visible for long. The hard-line Likud government in Israel did not respond to the PLO's renunciation of violence and recognition of Israel's legitimate borders. Refusing to meet with any representative of the PLO, the group which Palestinians accept as their bargaining agent, is paramount to declaring that there will be no peace negotiations with the Palestinians. The mass immigration from the Soviet Union and the stern repressive measures in the West Bank and Gaza now make it difficult for Palestinians to feel hopeful.

Regrettably, as the Gulf War crisis developed in 1990, the Palestinians made a grave error in coming out for Saddam Hussein. Prior to this juncture, he had never displayed any special interest or support for the Palestinian cause. The obvious and proper stance for the Palestinians was to abstain from taking sides as the Arab states lined up for the expected bloody conflict. By choosing Saddam they have lost massive financial support from Saudi Arabia, Kuwait, and other Gulf emirates.

I am saddened by this error in judgment and strategy, but I think I can understand the disappointment and desperation which brought it about. It was enormously difficult for Arafat and his people to accept what many of his hard-liners regard as a diminished Palestinian state, namely the West Bank and Gaza strip. To find that this painful gesture was scorned by the other side caused many to question the value of moderation.

The Persian Gulf War brought serious troubles for the Palestinians but there are far deeper reasons for misgivings. Until the final days before the outbreak of war on 15 January 1991, I had not forsaken my view that armed conflict would be averted. With all the great changes in the world, including the ending of the bitter Cold War, the advancing freedom in Eastern Europe, the chance of settlement of racial conflict in South Africa, I had hopes for a greater measure of peace and justice. The UN was capable of working more effectively than ever before.

I asked if we were incapable of finding a peaceful solution of the crisis triggered by Saddam Hussein's brutal invasion of Kuwait. The support for sanctions among UN members was impressive and heartening. When I spoke in the Senate on 20 November 1990 I urged that sanctions not be forsaken prematurely. I agreed with the view of Director William Webster of the U.S. Central Intelligence Agency that sanctions would have devastating effects within seven to nine months. Regrettably other views prevailed and the awful bloodletting of war followed. It seemed to me that the mighty array of power against a third world state of 17 million people was overwhelming. The side with the great power and the vast resources of the world, in command of both the sea and the air, could afford to wait longer than the beseiged Iraqis. Yet, somehow, a number of people allowed themselves to be convinced that the power of Saddam's war machine would increase more than that of the massive coalition of the richest and most technologically advanced part of the world.

Both in my speech and in newspaper articles I embraced Benjamin Franklin's dictum that there never was a bad peace or a good war. Did the Americans become too impatient? It was essentially an American exercise. In the weeks prior to 15 January 1991 it was not the UN secretary general who was conducting the diplomacy but the American administration. One read of Secretary of State James Baker going to international capitals to 'brief' various leaders. The verb is significant. How much real discussion or conferring really took place? In the *Ottawa Citizen* of 15 January there were two notable headlines. One read, 'US Rebuffs French Peace Plan'; the other, 'Bush Would Notify Key Allies Before Attacking, But The Decision Is His *Alone*' (italics mine).

The weeks preceding the outbreak of the war were interesting. The rhetoric of the leaders in the United States was a throwback to World War II, but many anxious people remembered Vietnam instead. In Canada there was surprisingly little debate. Perhaps we were preoccupied with the recession, the goods and services tax, and constitutional problems. As the U.S. goal gradually moved from a defensive one to an all-out offence, we followed. Strangely enough, there was not a free vote in Parliament. On issues such as capital punishment and abortion, free votes are held. It might be thought that one would be almost more appropriate in a situation involving possible mass killing of thousands of people.

Those days preceding war's outbreak seemed unreal. I felt that we were drifting towards something awful but no one seemed to be able to slow or stop the oncoming clash. In a CBC talk on 'Commentary' on 14 January, the day before the deadline, Professor John Sigler of Carleton University, one of our leading Middle East experts, noting the argument of U.S. Democratic Senators and Congressmen in favour of continuing sanctions said:

But the pressures of patriotism, of rallying around the leader in times of crisis, give President Bush a narrow margin to justify a decision to go to war. In that case, we will not have broken the cycle that violence begets. Saddam Hussein will have then succeeded in setting in motion another wave of violence whose full dimensions are impossible to calculate.

For a while it seemed that there might be a quid pro quo for Saddam Hussein's withdrawal from Kuwait. That was the agreement to convene an international conference to deal with the Middle East matters including the Palestinian problems. That was President Mitterand's suggestion. Prime Minister Mulroney's letter to the secretary-general of the UN, Javier Perez de Cuellar, on 9

January also referred to 'a firm commitment in principle to a process to resolve other issues in the Middle East.'

But it became conventional wisdom that there should be no linkage. Former U.S. President Jimmy Carter sagely observed: 'Linked or not there is no way to separate the crisis in the Persian Gulf from the Israeli-Palestinian question.' In an article in the *Halifax Chronicle-Herald*, I wrote that Carter's advocacy of an international conference was 'likely to be a better solution than unleashing the dogs of war.'

The adamant refusal even to entertain the idea of linkage has distressed many Arabs, especially the Palestinians. The war was often sold as being for the integrity of the United Nations. But, the Palestinians ask, what about the vast pile of UN resolutions condemning Israel for its armed occupation of the West Bank and Gaza, the Golan Heights, and parts of Lebanon? Can the UN, which indeed created an Arab and a Jewish state in Palestine, sanction the use of force against Iraq and at the same time pass over Israel's non-compliance with the resolutions of the international body?

I had hoped that Canada might have found a role other than full belligerence. Neither our NORAD or NATO treaty agreements were involved, and Security Council Resolution 678 (29 November 1990) authorized members to use force but did not make force mandatory. Over the past thirty-five years we have won a special status as peacekeepers and must not lose that role.

I had no doubt that Iraq would lose the war ignominiously. How could a third world country cope with the power and might of the world's greatest superpower and its first world allies?

In the aftermath of the conflict which brought few casualties on the coalition side but many among the Iraqis (the ratio was about a thousand to one), conditions within Iraq and the Middle East cause one to ask that old question, did we win the war but lose the peace? At the time of writing I hear suggestions out of Washington that military force will be sent to Saudi Arabia to take action against Iraq again. Will a second war be embarked upon to topple a tinpot dictator? I hope and pray not.

Another hope I have is that Joe Clark, who rendered magnificent service in his role as minister in charge of constitutional matters, will be returned to his original portfolio. He was one of our best external affairs ministers. In these tense and difficult times I would feel better with him at the helm in the realm of foreign policy.

10

Red Tory, Red Chamber

While Robert Stanfield was announcing his resignation on 17 July 1975 in my office, I stepped out into the corridor. I didn't realize that there was portentous symbolism in my withdrawal and that in less than three years I would be announcing my own exit from the House of Commons. In the meantime, my parliamentary activities were not diminished. I continued to give top priority to my constituents. My speaking engagements were still numerous. But as I now reflect upon those years I must have been moving towards an emeritus role. Perhaps this was revealed most in my attitude to the leadership convention set for 19 to 22 February 1976.

For years I had thought that the PCs must find their way into the confidence of the Quebec voters. To do that we had to have a leader who literally and spiritually spoke the language of the vast majority of the people of that province. Although I had heard the rumours of financial arrangements which brought it about, I welcomed Claude Wagner's entry into our party in 1972. It seemed to me that his accretion to our ranks was worth a good deal of money.

Not long after Wagner's move to the PC party, I arranged that he come to Charlottetown to address the annual meeting of the Hillsborough constituency. He made a good impression on the people at the meeting and others he met in the province. That he would be able to deliver a host of Quebec seats to the PCS became an impossible dream. The popular vote in 1972 was 1,289,139 for the Liberals to 457,418 for the PCS. In 1968, in the very heyday of Trudeaumania, the Conservatives carried four seats and the popular vote was Liberal 1,170,610, PC 466,259.

By the time the 1976 convention had been called I was no longer so enthusiastic about the possibility of Wagner's succession to the leadership. Our party's poor showing in Quebec was not the major reason. How could we expect much against a dynamic native son like Trudeau? I had come to the conclusion that, despite many attractive qualities, Wagner was not the person to lead the party.

For a brief time there was a move on Parliament Hill to urge Alberta Premier Peter Lougheed to go federal. I remember a meeting of PC members and senators in the Railway Committee Room at which the possibility of drafting him was discussed. Recalling the Diefenbaker days, Senator Allister Grosart advised making sure we knew how to pronounce Lougheed's name. I somehow became the acting chairman of a pro-Lougheed group. I'm sure I was not coopted because of my good looks, profound wisdom, or intensity of interest. But because much of the strong support for Lougheed came from the Prairies, a figure from another region was thought to be useful. There were suggestions that I go to Calgary and with some western MPs wait upon the premier. I recall telegrams from Harvie Andre and others about such a meeting. For once I was prudent and stayed in the East. A few days later there was great excitement in my office when the premier of Alberta came on the line to tell me he was not planning any move into federal politics at that time. It was the first time I had ever spoken to the man. I appreciated his decisiveness in ending such momentum as had built up. He was probably not an ideal candidate for national leadership in any case.

In the 1967 convention my choice had been easily made. It was Stanfield all the way. In 1976 an entirely different situation prevailed. I could not imagine voting for Jack Horner or Paul Hellyer. I liked Flora MacDonald, admired Pat Nowlan's courage and colour, and had respect and affection for John Fraser. But there was still that urgency of making an impact on Quebec and Heward Grafftey could not win us that province. This, plus the importuning of many Island Tories, prompted me to look favourably on Brian Mulroney. I had known him as a charming, engaging, and sharp leader in our youth and university party organization. I was also resentful of the much-touted notion that, since he had no caucus support, Mulroney was somewhat outside the pale. I could do my part by giving him my support. As it turned out he had only three MPs in his corner: Jack Marshall, Jim McGrath, and myself.

The Mulroney organization was impressive. I did what I could to be helpful. I had one special moment of satisfaction. As Mulroney moved from hotel to hotel, from luncheon group to luncheon group, I was asked to introduce him at the Skyline Hotel. The eager young man in charge was Charlie McMillan, the son of my great friend Dr Joe. With heavy seriousness he laid down the ground rules that my introduction must be absolutely not a second longer than four minutes. I replied: 'Charlie, do you think a man as busy as I am can devote four minutes? I'll have it done in two.' And I did. Once in a while old-timers must get their innings! During the convention I was often in the Mulroney section of the Civic Centre in Ottawa, along with Marshall, McGrath, Paul Godfrey, Alan Eagleson, and other strong supporters. From time to time we were asked to change our seats. As one of the young PR experts put it, this was to alter the 'shape' of the box. Mulroney made a strong showing on the first ballot, coming second only to Wagner. It seemed hard for him to make a real breakthrough in subsequent ballots. One of the problems was Wagner's strength in Quebec, which would normally be an area of expansion for Mulroney. When Joe Clark received the support of Sinclair Stevens, a Clark-Wagner contest became apparent.

Oddly enough, on the convention floor I was able to do more to help Joe Clark than I could for my number one choice, Mulroney. Typical of this was Duncan Jessiman of Winnipeg, a prominent Tory and one-time student of mine. After the third ballot he said: 'You know these two men, I don't know either of them. Who shall I vote for?' I gave the proper reply; I demurred from telling him what he should do but readily informed him that I was supporting Clark. 'That's good enough for me,' was his reply.

It was a close vote. Wagner's concession speech was of a high quality as were all his performances. Flora did a grand job but was deeply hurt when her first ballot strength failed to match the commitments she had received from delegates. I thought of Wellington MacNeill after a PEI election in which he ran in 4th Queens, the home area of Angus MacLean. Like Flora, he counted on people who didn't mark their ballots as he expected. As he later told my colleague, 'There are a lot of two-faced buggers in that district of yours, MacLean.' I knew the 4th Queens people very well and didn't find them deceitful. But then again I hadn't tasted the bitterness of electoral defeat which affects one's judgment.

The 1976 convention was like none other in the party's history. R.B. Bennett's victory in 1927 was no great surprise. In 1938, Manion was the predicted winner. Bracken's 1942 success had long been orchestrated before the delegates settled into the Winnipeg Auditorium. Drew's victory in 1948 and Diefenbaker's in 1956 were foregone conclusions. The only doubt in 1967 was whether it would be Roblin or Stanfield, with the latter having a slight advantage. But in 1976 a dark horse had won. On the morrow of the convention vote a new buzz-word went into our political lexicon. The thin young man from High River, Alberta, a surprising and perhaps surprised winner, was dubbed 'Joe Who?'

The high-profile, highly popular Flora MacDonald, who stood sixth on the first ballot trailing Hellyer and Horner, also gave her name to convention terminology. Ever after 1976 any candidate whose pledged support fails to hold up in the actual balloting is dubbed a victim of the Flora MacDonald Syndrome.

After the convention Brian Mulroney returned to Montreal and success in the world of business. He once invited McGrath, Marshall, and me for a small luncheon and I had the occasional phone call from him.

Claude Wagner, magnanimous in defeat on the convention floor, seemed to evince considerable bitterness and resentment in the post-convention period. In 1977, I was on a PC delegation with him to the Middle East. He made a good impression and performed his duties with charm and thoughtfulness. But his attitude to the newly chosen leader was not notable for appreciation. On 21 April 1978 he was appointed to the Senate by Pierre Trudeau. Tragically, on 11 July 1979, he died at the early age of fifty-four.

Paul Hellyer, after a strange campaign in which for a time he was prepared to read the Red Tories out of the party, finally found his way back to the Grits and made an unsuccessful bid to win the party's nomination in a Toronto riding, St Paul's, in 1988. Jack Horner joined the Liberal party and was Trudeau's minister of transport for a time. He was defeated in the 1979 election. Heward Grafftey, persistent winner in Brome-Missisquoi, lost in the election of 1980. Others went on to impressive roles in the Clark administration and in a post-Clark period. Flora MacDonald and Sinclair Stevens served in both the Clark and Mulroney governments. Pat Nowlan is still a colourful member of the House of Commons.

Clark spent a good deal of time in efforts to strengthen the efficiency of the caucus and gave high priority to the formulation of positive party policy. There were a number of task forces, study groups, and subcommittees. In April 1977, I was sent to Washington as chairman of a small group to hold discussions with U.S. politicians and officials. There was a view in our caucus, and to a degree in the country, that Trudeau was not handling Canada-U.S. relations very well. The committee included George Whittaker, MP from British Columbia, Arnold Malone of Alberta, and Perrin Beatty of Wellington-Grey-Dufferin-Simcoe in Ontario. Even then he was a young man who took himself and his duties with a high degree of seriousness.

That, with the visit to the Middle East, acknowledged my continuing interest in international affairs. It also demonstrated astuteness on Clark's part. To keep your followers busy doing things they like and deem important is good leadership. At the convention, Dalton Camp had told me that Joe was one candidate who had capacity for growth. I think this was borne out in the period between the convention and the election. After an inauspicious start and with friction within caucus he did a good job of consolidation. An increasing number of Canadians began to envisage the defeat of Pierre Trudeau. Slowly more and more of them saw the unexpected winner of the Tory convention as the person who could bring this about.

But before the next election I had some personal decisions to make. Although I loved politics I didn't wish to go on forever. So it was that after the twentieth anniversary of my election and eight successful campaigns, I was thinking about withdrawing decently and in good order, as the old book of Presbyterian discipline put it.

The day 10 June 1957 was a mountain-top experience for me. Only a very few Canadians are chosen to represent their constituency in the House of Commons. I never ceased to feel gratitude for the honour and the opportunity. When, twenty years later, my friends in Hillsborough undertook to stage a roast recognizing my two decades in Parliament I was much moved. Under the leadership of constituency president David Jenkins, the planning committee gave much time and thought to arranging an absolutely top-notch affair. I was closely consulted throughout, and my suggestions acceded to with good grace, often with the kind of cryptic comment some of my party friends enjoyed directing my way. Everything seemed to work out well. Everyone invited to be a roaster accepted and it was a galaxy of talent. Tommy Douglas for the NDP, that most articulate Liberal Don Jamieson, and party president Michael Meighen, one of my favourite YPC leaders over the years, were a prestigious trio. Geoff Scott of the press gallery and a noted impersonator also accepted. Jack MacAndrew of the CBC's theatrical department and my hardest opponent in Hillsborough was a brilliant master of ceremonies. Charlottetown's own Nancy White, a popular CBC singing star and satirist, was a real attraction. Easily the most eloquent man in Ottawa's diplomatic corps, Dr Bobbie Moore of Guyana, was also on the roasters list. I have been privileged to remain on Parliament Hill in another chamber for a twenty-fifth anniversay and even a thirtieth. Sometimes it has been suggested that these later occasions should be celebrated. While naturally touched by such gestures I declined the honour. It's never wise to fiddle with perfection. I'm sure that no later celebration could equal the unforgettable success and sparkle of the 1977 evening.

Roasts were not so common then as they are now. They are essentially entertainment with tribute to the roastee played in a low key. The incomparable Tommy Douglas set a fitting tone at the outset. After thanking the chairman he confessed: 'But I shouldn't be here at all. My father told me if you can't say something good about anyone say nothing. So I have travelled all this way just to sit in silence at Heath Macquarrie's dinner.' Of course he didn't sit in silence but wowed them with his wit. He was the only roaster to receive a standing ovation. Considering that 1464 votes was a good showing for an NDP in Hillsborough, their strongest Island riding, it was a warm personal tribute to Tommy.

Taking a jibe at my interest in the Arab world, External Affairs Minister Don Jamieson referred to me as the Honourable Member for Cairo Centre. He said I sometimes came into the House looking like a cross between an Arab sheik and a Highland chieftain. Michael Meighen had fun stressing that his grandfather and I had been friends. Robert Stanfield wasn't really there, but Geoff Scott took him off to a T as he did with some other notables. Premier Alex Campbell, a very able young man and shrewd politician, twitted me about my publicity techniques. 'Yes, it says right here in yesterday's edition, Heath Macquarrie had lunch at Room 327 of the Château Laurier at 12:15 yesterday.' His closing was one of the best I've ever seen at such a function. In a very serious tone he came out with lavish praise and declaration of respect and affection – then, looking at my wife, closed the tribute with the word 'Isabel.'

Early in her career I recognized Nancy White as one of our brightest musical entertainers. Her song, especially written for the occasion, also dwelt on my assiduous care for my constituents. One verse told of the Charlottetown woman who went to a leading gynaecologist, Dr Irwin, for a pregnancy test. When he later phoned her with the good news that it was positive, she thanked him but said: 'I've already had my congratulatory letter from Heath Macquarrie!'

Joe Clark, who is more humorous than many people readily detect, sent a witty telegram. He noted my political science background and said that my idea of Senate reform was 'to get yourself appointed to it.' That was funny but not fictitious! Tommy Douglas, at the time and more than once later, expressed great satisfaction that my roast was not a party fund-raising event. Proceeds were designated for the United Appeal.

That wonderful day will long remain a golden memory. Friends and colleagues joined us in the celebration. I was touched to see Mike Forrestall, Pat Nowlan, and Ralph Stewart, Liberal MP for Cochrane, among the diners. My wife Isabel had a virulent case of flu that night but, as usual, she rose to the occasion. I was glad that our daughters Heather and Flora were with us although we missed our son Iain. At all elections and between elections, my family has been totally helpful. Isabel doubtless did more canvassing than I did. For those politicians who had indifference or hostility from their family, I always felt great sorrow. Early in the afternoon, CBC Charlottetown had me as guest on a program on which I chose three of my favourite musical numbers. They were a portion of Mozart's *Jupiter* Symphony, one of my favourite campaign offerings, the 'Radetzky March' by Johann Strauss, Sr, and a beautiful rendition of some Burns songs. My heart still glows in the memory of that public but intensely personal evening.

When, in early February 1978, the Charlottetown media carried the story of my announced retirement, one of them played excerpts from my remarks at the roast. With it was the editorial comment that no one at that function thought of the retirement of the 'veteran member.' And indeed it was not as a grand finale that I saw the roast festivities. But there was no traumatic event between 10 June 1977 and 2 February 1978 which triggered the withdrawal I announced that day, to take place when this Parliament was dissolved.

I thought it proper that I finish out the parliamentary term to which I had been elected. Thus a by-election would be avoided. On the other hand it would be inconsiderate to hang on to the last minute before the next general election. The Hillsborough constituency association was entitled to ample time to select a successor as the party's standard-bearer. Having these things in mind I felt that an early February date was just about right. But, because under our system election dates are hard to predict, my departure was painfully protracted. Instead of a 1978 election we had one in 1979. At least one Hillsborough constituent thought there should be a by-election. I also found myself embarrassed by how many times some of my Ottawa friends bade me goodbye!

Naturally I kept my constituency president informed and advised Joe Clark of my intentions. I sent him by hand a draft copy of my official press release which contained one item on national policy. This was an expression of concern about our party's attitude to what used to be called Dominion-provincial relations. I thought a strong central government absolutely essential to a strong social justice program for the people of Canada in all the provinces, the poor as well as the rich.

Clark called me over to his office and showed concern over this part of my statement. He would, he said, be more comfortable had I been running once again. Naturally all leaders are concerned about the security of constituencies they hold. He was seemingly well satisfied with my assurances regarding a successor. But he did ask me to consider not making a reference to my concern with the party's developing policy on federal-provincial relations. I liked the manner and tone of his handling of the whole thing and said I would certainly give thought to his request. When I returned to my West Block office I immediately told my secretary to delete the comments on constitutional development and release the shortened statement. I suppose I could have told Joe Clark in his office that I would do that. Sometimes the old contrariness of the Highland Scot operates a bit in my personality.

Even though my retirement did not involve an abrupt change in my way of life but was an announced phased withdrawal, it was still somewhat traumatic. While my day-to-day duties and routine changed very little, there was certainly an altered perspective. I didn't think so many people beyond Hillsborough or Parliament Hill would have taken notice. I had made no firm arrangements for the future but had hoped for some sort of alternate employment rather than total retirement. Not long after my announcement, while I was gathering with some friends at the Charlottetown Officers' Club I was called to the telephone. It was Bill Crawford, president of Mount Allison University, responding to interest I had expressed in spending a stint on their faculty. I was, naturally, positive in my reply having a high regard for both Bill Crawford and the institution he headed. Arrangements were made for me to visit Mount A to go on display, as it were. In short order I was 'signed up' to join Mount Allison's faculty. A most happy experience it turned out to be.

I had an inquiry from the Canadian Institute of International Affairs (CIIA) but I did not find it possible to pick up their suggestion. I was agreeably surprised to hear from two leading book publishers about memoirs. I didn't proceed on that matter as expeditiously as on the job opportunity offered by Mount Allison.

Parliament Hill has its nastiness but it is also a place where considerable grace abounds. I received many expressions of good wishes. External Affairs Minister Don Jamieson paid a most generous tribute. The chairman of the House of Commons standing committee on external affairs and national defence, Marcel Prud'homme, was laudatory in his remarks at a committee meeting. On Diplomatic Row I was tendered farewell luncheons and dinners. Soviet Ambassador Yakovlev, whom I knew well, put on a dinner at his Lisgar Road residence. As it is courteous custom, he asked me to suggest some fellow guests. It was one of many delightful affairs. In an earlier day Communist diplomats didn't put on black tie dinners. In those post-announcement days I almost felt like someone fortunate enough to be able to read his own obituary.

One special event was a gathering in my own office. I had expected it to be an Atlantic caucus 'do,' since I had been for a long time its chairman. But they had broadened it to take in the whole caucus and a heart-warming number attended. With his usual wit Bob Stanfield said: 'Heath's departure presents some problems. One is how to cope with the Jewish vote.' In a more serious vein he went on to praise me for helping many in the caucus to look upon the Palestinian cause in a different way. Joe Clark was also humorous but I remember best his serious parts.

He was kind enough to laud me for my long and valuable service on the Hill and he hoped to be in a position to bring me back to the Hill in another role.

On my home turf there may have been a few who thought I should have stayed in harness for at least one more time. There may have been some who thought it was nearly time the old bugger quit. One of my friends had once told me in highly amiable terms: 'You know with all these elections, Heath, I'm getting a little tired of voting for you.'

The 1974 election had been held on 8 July and a new appeal to the voters in the spring, summer, or early fall of 1978 would have been the natural thing for a majority government. But the Liberals had been badly mauled in a series of by-elections. Like his predecessor, R.B. Bennett, Trudeau didn't seem in a hurry to face the wrath of the voters. So it was not until 22 May 1979 that our national chieftain was available for electoral appraisal. As it turned out, the Trudeau timidity was a stance well taken. Joe Clark's Tories won 136 seats to 114 for his charismatic rival. The lean young man from High River, who unpredictably had won the leadership of his party, now had the keys to 24 Sussex Drive in his pocket.

Needless to say I was surprised, but totally delighted, with the outcome of the election. While I could respect without liking Mackenzie King and had both affection and regard for L.B. Pearson, I had never felt that Pierre Elliott Trudeau was a good thing for my country. He had colour, courage, candour, and an enduring ability to mesmerize the media. But his haughty attitude towards the provinces, his sneering disregard for Parliament and parliamentarians, his failed economic policies, richly deserved the repudiation of the Canadian electorate in May 1979.

Lest I get carried away with a diatribe on Canadian politics and national affairs, I must return to the cherished realm of the personal. Being a new guy on the faculty at Mount Allison University – few except Bill Crawford and Gareth Greenslade remembered my summer school teaching in 1948 and 1954 – I was excused from the orientation period and didn't have to show up until classes commenced. This was of some importance because, with the delayed election call, I was still a parliamentarian as well as a full-time professor. Whether I liked it or not, I was moonlighting. Luckily the delightful little town of Sackville was only thirty-three miles from Cape Tormentine, the mainland terminal for the PEI ferry. The Moncton airport was about the same distance so I had a good deal of travelling to do. As one critic wrote to the *Guardian*, I could have resigned my Commons seat. But with the impending general election any thoughtful observer would have realized that no by-election would have been called, so my departure would have deprived Hillsborough of any parliamentary representative.

Therefore, for much of my time at Mount Allison I was under double duty. I attended the House of Commons as often as possible. I had my subscriptions to Island newspapers sent to Sackville. I listened to Charlottetown radio stations. But I was a full-time faculty member of a university which I had long admired. Its president and the head of my department were splendid people. My students, who on the whole were excellent types, merited and received my conscientious attention.

I loved Mount Allison and tried to make the fullest contribution I could. I brought to my classes and to the university generally some very interesting people. As well as several distinguished guest lecturers my daughter Heather was even able to attend some of my lectures. She was much impressed. (What alternative did she have?) As a new member of the faculty, I received a good number of invitations to give speeches and present papers in service club and academic gatherings. I accepted nearly all of them since such contact with the wider community is an expected part of a professor's job. All in all it was a grand work-filled but productive and pleasing experience at Sackville. While I exulted in my recrudescence as a university professor and enjoyed as well the continuing participation in Parliament I was, nevertheless, delighted when on 26 March Allan MacEachen told the House of Commons that Mr Trudeau had dissolved Parliament. My moonlighting days were over.

I had spent a good deal of time on airline flights to and from Ottawa as I strove to maximize my time in the groves of academe and in the halls of Parliament. Fortunately, thanks to the generous sensitivity of Liberal governments, MPS now enjoyed reasonable amenities: once a week flights to and from Ottawa and the constituency, long distance telephone service, an office and secretary in the constituency, a three-person staff in the Ottawa office. I made full use of these services. It was somewhat ironic that in my gradual retirement from the House of Commons I found not an easing of schedule but one of the most active and demanding years of my life.

During these months I was a frequent traveller on the Cape Tormentine-Borden ferry run. I was delighted when Tom McMillan received the Hillsborough PC nomination. I thought that this bright young son of Dr Joe would be a top-notch candidate and member, and we maintained close and cordial contact. One morning when High Commissioner Bobbie Moore of Guyana was visiting us in Sackville a telephone call came in from Tom in Charlottetown. After it was finished I told Bobbie: 'That was my brilliant and most excellent young successor on the phone.' Never deficient in vocabulary he replied: 'Ah yes, I thought it might be; your tone was avuncular but not didactic.'

I spoke on the Island during the 1979 campaign, did some radio spots for Tom, and was on hand for his victory celebration on election night. I felt good about leaving the constituency in his hands. I rejoiced with Hillsborough friends over the downfall of the Trudeau government. We Tories hadn't won an election in seventeen years, and the long period of setbacks made the victory all the sweeter.

And it was a major triumph for the underdog Joe Clark. From 95 seats in 1974 the PC total had risen to 136. The Liberals fell from 141 to 114. Only in Quebec did the Liberals run strong; there they added seven seats. West of Ontario they won only 3 seats, 2 in Manitoba and 1 in BC. Of Ontario's 95 seats the PCS won 57 to 32 for the Liberals and 6 for the NDP. In the Maritimes the Conservatives gained a seat by defeating the very popular veterans affairs minister, Dan MacDonald, in the Island constituency of Cardigan. Once again a good showing in Quebec was the one thing lacking for substantial Tory majority government.

In that province we elected only 2 MPs. Many experts scorn the favourite son syndrome as an explanation of Quebec's political preferences, but all contests under the Trudeau leadership of the Liberals would seem to give considerable support to the theory.

There comes a time when even the most charismatic prime minister must take on some of the responsibility for the grievances which the public hold against the administration he heads. In 1978–9 there were a good many reasons for concern. What was going on in Quebec? Was the basic federal structure in danger? Were our sources of energy in jeopardy? There was great anxiety about housing shortages. The heroic Trudeau had promised to wrestle inflation to the ground. He hadn't. In the four western provinces, which under the new Redistribution Act had more seats than Quebec, Trudeau had become anathema. Not even the gunslinger image, cultivated by his PR handlers, could make the prime minister a beloved figure in the West. As important as anti-Trudeauism was a general feeling that the Liberals had been there long enough. The Conservatives made good use of that old-fashioned slogan, 'It's time for a change.'

As usual it is difficult to sort out the reasons for the 1979 result. The delay in holding the election added to the difficulty in assessing it. As Charles Lynch put it, it was the first time an election had been called in the fifty-third week of the campaign. While the writ had not been issued, the contest was really under way in 1978. The twelve by-elections of that year were a sort of little election. The Tories had won handsomely but had doubtless lost some momentum as the Liberals held off dissolution.

Although the Liberals hadn't used their time to create a set of promises that were particularly appealing to the electorate, they gave high priority to denigrating Joe Clark. They naturally made much of the Conservative promise to cut government expenditures while offering a cornucopia of goodies to the voters. Trudeau often referred to Clark as the '7-Billion-Dollar Man.' Clark's commitment to a stimulative deficit was a further source of Liberal platform mirth. Clark's views on federal-provincial relations were seen as 'soft on separatism' and he was depicted as a head waiter to the Tory provincial premiers. There was a great deal of Clarkbashing in the 1979 campaign. Many in the media who had seemed supine and fearful of Trudeau's rude hauteur were hypercritical of Joe Clark whose demeanour with them was much more polite and restrained.

A major factor that hurt Joe Clark's public image and honed the sharp knives of the press was his international fact-finding trip in January 1979. The *Canadian Annual Review* described it simply as 'a public relations disaster.' While he was in Japan, India, Jordan, and Israel Clark was depicted in the media back home as awkward, uninformed, pompous, or ridiculous. When most airline travellers discover their baggage missing at their destination, they blame the carriers. Canadians heard that Joe Clark had 'lost' his luggage. The bright and balanced Geoffrey Stevens made a succinct comment on the trip in the *Globe and Mail*, 16 January 1979. 'Mr. Clark's woes seem to arise in equal parts from bad luck, inferior staff work, lack of money, and the churlishness of accompanying journalists for whom no speck of lint is too small to pick.'

In the campaign Joe Clark had to live with the bad press and 'wimp' image which stemmed from his foreign trip. He also had some difficulties with discordant notes from caucus colleagues. His promises to abolish Petro-Canada and move the Canadian embassy from Tel Aviv to Jerusalem were widely criticized. Considering all that was going against him the marvel of 1979 was not that Joe Clark didn't win a majority (as some later declared), but that under such handicaps he won the government at all.

On 4 June 1979 Joe Clark became, at thirty-nine, Canada's youngest prime minister. In the immediate aftermath of the election, the country seemed to wish him and the new government well. The press was generally favourable. The new cabinet was a most impressive group, perhaps potentially one of the ablest in many, many years.

Unfortunately the honeymoon did not last long. The government showed a refreshing vigour in many areas, but some problems and faulty decisions took the sheen off the new administration. Although a fine sounding piece of bravado, Clark's oft-proclaimed promise to govern 'as if we have a majority' was not practical politics. The six-member Créditiste group did not have a bright future and might not have exacted a heavy quid pro quo for a reasonable degree of parliamentary cooperation. In later days I heard much grumbling from Tory MPs about the folly of this go-it-alone stance. But I remember many of the latter-day critics applauding loudly when Clark proclaimed his intention at a caucus meeting.

I thought then, and still think, that it was a misreading of public opinion to believe that Canadians wanted the crown corporation Petro-Canada abolished. Voters have not traditionally welcomed tax increases and the eighteen-cent levy on gasoline received the expected reaction.

It was unfortunate, too, that the promise to move the Canadian embassy from Tel Aviv to Jerusalem could not have been dropped. In the United States, despite similar election promises, the actual move had been avoided. But, at his first news conference as prime minister, Clark declared that the decision had been made and it was up to the Department of External Affairs to carry out the modalities. The furore over this policy did much damage to the government's reputation. Arab nations and their Ottawa diplomats were deeply concerned. In the Department of External Affairs there was much anxiety. I was not surprised by these sentiments but did not expect so much criticism from Canadian business. For years I had tried to encourage closer cultural and commercial ties with the populous Arab world. I had not detected any great support among our business people, but there was plenty of interest in the proposed embassy move. Even from my own small province, from which potatoes and dairy products are exported, came strong negative feelings.

In the Jerusalem caper, as some irreverent press people later called it, I was much more than academically involved. A day or two after the press conference I had a telephone call from a key member of the Arab diplomatic corps, asking me whether I would go to Ottawa to act as their adviser/consultant on the matter. This request put me into a situation of great delicacy and intellectual conflict of interest. I had for years been intensely concerned about the long-suffering Palestinians. It had also always been my view that it was in Canada's interest, as well as in the interest of peace, to have a more balanced attitude to the Middle-East confrontation. Not being without vanity, I was flattered by the confidence the Arab diplomats were placing in me. On the other hand, I could not with equanimity contemplate a situation where, on a touchy public issue, I would be seen as being in opposition to the government newly formed by the political party to which I had for so long been devoted. And so without asking for further time for reflection I declined the special role but gave assurances I would do everything possible behind the scenes to ameliorate the growing storm. Needless to say, I tried to be helpful and made every useful contact I could think of. Interestingly enough, it was from my diplomatic contacts that I first had word about the possible involvement of Robert Stanfield.

At the time of my announced retirement from the House of Commons I talked with Joe Clark about my interest in the Senate. This hardly took him by surprise since I had long held a high regard for the Red Chamber and an ever greater fondness for finding a place there myself. From long ago I recall a bull session in my office with some caucus colleagues. When I ventured some criticism of John Diefenbaker's government, one member said: 'Okay Macquarrie, what would you do if you were PM?' My reply was: 'My first move would be to appoint myself to the Senate.'

With the PCs back in office and a Senate vacancy existing in PEI, my interest in a place in the Upper House became a quest rather than an academic pursuit. I early communicated my continuing interest to the new prime minister. My eight successive entries into the House of Commons required enormous effort and continuing activity. I was to find that in some ways it was harder to make it to the Upper House. For a good many years it was traditional that the Island quartet of senators be equally split between Catholics and Protestants. When PC Senator J.J. Macdonald, a Roman Catholic, had been succeeded by Dr Lorne Bonnell, a Protestant, it left only one Roman Catholic Island senator. The vacancy I sought to fill was as successor to the late Senator Kickham, also a Catholic. If a Protestant succeeded Kickham there would be no RC from PEI in the Senate. Needless to say there was no shortage of Island Catholics willing and eager to succeed Senator Kickham. The most prominent of these was Leo Rossiter, veteran provincial politician and PEI minister of fisheries. He had the support of many people, including Premier Angus MacLean and the Roman Catholic bishop of Charlottetown. For those who thought the denominational issue was a thing of the past, the 'contest' for the senatorship was a disabusing experience. I had never paid all that much attention to the particular church people attended, and had not much use for bigots of any kind. Not regarding myself as a major pillar of my own denomination or a saint of the bigger fold, I was a little unprepared for the great emphasis upon my religious preferences. Nor did I find much success in noting that I had been succeeded by a Roman Catholic in the House of Commons where it had traditionally been one Roman Catholic to three Protestants. It is likely that the religious issue was more ostensible than fundamental, but it added tension to a war of nerves which went on for a good many weeks.

On 17 September 1979 Isabel came home from a morning in Charlottetown and immediately asked whether there had been any news. I suggested she go to the back kitchen for the answer. There sat a bottle of champagne in a bucket of ice. She then knew that 'the call' had come through. Joe Clark, who apparently had been phoning a number of would-be senators, opened up the conversation by saying: 'I guess we don't need to spend much time on the consent aspect.' He was right.

It was a day of great joy but I could not divulge my good fortune and had to keep the happy news to myself. Sometimes there were items in the local press suggesting that Mr Rossiter was the front runner. I kept a careful ear to the radio news and was disappointed when other senatorial appointments were announced. At a delightful dinner party at the home of our close friends Lloyd and Helen MacPhail I had a chat with PEI Chief Justice Jack Nicholson who in his political days had been an active and astute Liberal tactician. He gave me a lucid analysis of why Rossiter would get the appointment. I couldn't even hint that I had the appointment 'in my pocket.'

Eventually my appointment was officially announced and we

had a little celebration to which we invited some Victoria neighbours. Later, other Islanders came, the media called, and I had a great many congratulatory telephone calls. It was a most wonderful day and a consummation for which I had long yearned. It ended a long summer of uncertainty in a glorious way. I knew it had not been all that easy for Joe Clark to make such an appointment and I shall always remember his strength and consideration.

At the New Year's levée held by the mayor of Charlottetown, I met Chief Justice Nicholson. He greeted me with warm congratulations and said: 'They can say what they like about Joe Clark but anyone who had the guts and the perception to give you that Senate seat is not all bad.' Only in a special place like PEI would a chief justice make such a statement in public.

An appointment to the Senate was perhaps the only thing which would have taken me away from Mount Allison. But we had always found Ottawa a lovely city. Having already sold our pleasant little house in Alta Vista we moved into a downtown apartment, a fitting locale for those of maturer years.

Joe Clark's tenure in the leadership of his party was marked by ill fortune and ill will. Much of the latter came from people bearing the same party label as he wore. He had many able ministers, one of the best being David MacDonald. The government had a positive program. Its way of dealing with the provinces was far more conciliatory. Unlike the new Pearson government in 1963, the Clark government avoided rushing prematurely into a parliamentary session. Had the Clark government remained longer in office, it would surely have regained public support after slumping in the polls during the fall of 1979. Mr Trudeau, not caring for the job of opposition leader, had announced his departure on 21 November. He obviously didn't foresee an early collapse of the new Tory government.

For sure I didn't. Isabel and I were dinner guests of Ambassador and Mrs Tash at the Jordan embassy residence on the night of 13 December. When the vote on John Crosbie's budget was called, another guest, Bob Coates MP, left for the Commons. As we watched the television coverage of the House proceedings, I told the host and others that there would be enough absentees from the opposition parties to preclude a government defeat at this particular time. By 10:30 I knew with a shock how wrong I had been. On the following day, Parliament was dissolved and an election set for 18 February 1980. It was an inglorious exercise on the part of the parliamentary opposition. Elementary decency would have given the government a chance to get its major legislation through. It was unfair and improper not to give the public a chance to make a judgment on the kind of program the recently chosen government had in store for them.

Following this ignoble move came another. The man who had made his farewell was persuaded to retain the mantle of leadership of the Liberal party. The 1980 election would have been a great opportunity for Canadian voters to rebuke those who toppled the new government so prematurely. It would have been heart-warming to be able to record that the electorate, with more compassion and fairness than their professional political leaders, decreed that the government be given a chance. I hoped for this result but I didn't expect it. Although I was dismally wrong in predicting the House vote, I was quite prepared for the reverse at the hands of the electorate. The press, the polls, the morale of our own party foretold a gloomy result. The Trudeauvian characteristics which turned away so many people in 1978 and 1979 seemed to be forgotten. Joe Clark's blunders on his world tour and alleged instances of ineptitude seemed to be magnified. There was no great surge of hearty support from Conservative provincial leaders and parties. And, of course, it's not hard for voting citizens to be against tax increases.

The 1980 election brought the Liberals back, under the returned leader. Their seat total rose from 114 to 147, the PCs fell from 136 to 103. We took 1 seat in Quebec, and 38 in Ontario as against 57 in 1979. The Liberals gained in Atlantic Canada, taking 2 seats on PEI. In the West they bombed as usual but the NDP took some Tory seats.

It was bad enough to have Pierre Trudeau restored, but the 1980 election results brought on a period of intense bitterness and internecine conflict in the Progressive Conservative party. Many MPs who lost their seats were ready to blame the leader for their defeat. Some who won were sore because they had not been put in the cabinet. Some who made it to the cabinet resented not having made it to the inner cabinet. Add to this the bewilderment of the party faithful in the constituencies who wondered what had happened. In the outpouring of despondency, regret, and finger-pointing, there seemed to be no one to give Joe Clark a word of credit for winning in 1979, but muttering multitudes to damn him for the defeat of 1980.

In the last days of the Diefenbaker leadership, there were some unlovely caucus meetings. There had been painful days in the Stanfield era. But I can't recall such a continuing unpleasantness as that of the post-1980 caucus. I heard Joe Clark subjected to sharp and stinging criticism. He was told how poorly he walked. He was once told by one member that one more turkey joke in the media and he was through. The grapevine carried the word of the ABC (Anybody But Clark) group in caucus. Bitching in the ranks is not uncommon after an electoral defeat, but this time there was a new vehicle for expressing the anti-leader sentiment. This was the agenda item at the party's annual meeting known as the leadership review.

Early in the Stanfield years I had been asked to head a constitution committee with a view to enhancing the role and functions of the general membership. We were to report to the annual meeting set for 1969. Other committee members included Jed Baldwin, Flora MacDonald, and Roger Régimbal. I spent long hours on the project eliciting the views of every member of our caucus, officers of the association, and many others. Not all recipients answered my letter by any means, but I did get a sulphuric reply from John Diefenbaker who declared that all save one of the committee were Camp people (Régimbal presumably was the exception). On the first day of the 1969 annual meeting, Dalton Camp, in a dinner speech to the YPC, lauded the report of the Macquarrie committee. In a long and nasty session the next night I found out that some in the party had quite different views. Many of our forward-looking proposals, like the discontinuing of delegates-at-large, were voted down, and in general our attempted reforms were emasculated. I said the next day that I felt like a voodoo doll into which pins had been stuck to wound Dalton Camp as well as me. I also discovered that some of our hitherto 'solid' support melted away in the heat of adverse reception from those out to wreck our new constitution.

But even out of that setback came a form of leadership review, and the idea was refined at subsequent meetings. So, after his defeat in 1980, Joe Clark faced a party ballot in which delegates expressed their support or otherwise of his leadership. In practice, this ballot was found to be a highly imperfect instrument, since it put the incumbent leader against no one or against everyone. All groups desiring a new leader could vote 'no' to open the way for a convention. A better system might have been to have a write-in ballot which would put any challengers against the incumbent and each other. This would turn every annual meeting into an *ipso facto* leadership convention. But the party hadn't thought that far and may never do so.

Another grey area was the interpretation of the vote. Would 50 percent plus one be enough, or would a special majority be required? On the face of it, if a leader could command the support of only a bare majority of his party's leading people, he was not in any strong position to make a great impact on the electorate as a whole.

An the annual meeting of 1981 Clark won 66.7 per cent of the vote. Having been in the fractious party for so long, I thought it would be more than satisfactory to find two out of three Tories approving their leader. But mine was, once again, anything but a general view. Disaffection with Clark was not quietened by the 1981 vote. At the annual meeting in 1983 in Winnipeg he won 66.9 per cent. He had hoped to do better. I also had thought he would, considering that a general election was near at hand. While many of his delegates were dancing in celebration of the expected good showing, Clark was consulting with close advisers as to the best response to the actual count. He then came out to announce, in a sober tone, that the vote was not good enough and that he was requesting the national executive to call a leadership convention. At that convention he would be a candidate. The words I was hearing from the podium chilled my heart. Had my opinion been sought (and there was no reason why it should have been), I would have said unhesitatingly: 'Thank them heartily for their continued support and draw a bead on the next encounter with the Grits!'

Instead we were to have another convention. I didn't have to ponder my own course. I was wholeheartedly for Joe Clark. My motivation was not primarily as a result of his appointing me to the Senate, although gratitude is surely a worthy sentiment. I had seen Clark at close range over a good many years. He was a sharp parliamentarian, a diligent worker, had a sound appreciation of national goals, and most of all was a man of decency and honour. He had developed new skills and new depth since he first became our leader. He deserved a chance to do more for the country. I was on the Clark committee, attended meetings regularly, and did all I could during the days of the leadership convention, 8 to 11 June 1983.

Perhaps it was the heat, the crowds, the many concrete steps in the Ottawa Civic Centre, or perhaps it was my own antiquity, but I found the 1983 convention exhausting. Clark led from the first ballot, but there seemed little prospect for growth. The ABC formula seemed in place. It was a little strange when the representatives of the third-place John Crosbie approached Clark suggesting Clark come to Crosbie. The chosen emissary, Newfoundland Premier Brian Peckford, was not sufficiently close to Clark to make him the ideal carrier of such a proposal. In the fourth ballot Brian Mulroney won a clear-cut victory. Joe Clark decent and noble in defeat, pledged support and subsequently demonstrated the integrity of his convention platform commitment.

Naturally there were many explanations for Mulroney's victory at the 1983 convention. Some ascribed it to his superior organization; others attributed it to the ABC syndrome. Still others affirmed that had John Crosbie not been exposed as so nakedly unilingual he might have won. There were also dark hints that dirty tricks in the delegate selection phase had a big part to play. There may well have been something in these contentions but I think there was a stronger reason.

For years, indeed for generations, Conservatives have failed to achieve power in Canada because they couldn't make even a creditable showing in those areas of the country where the prevailing language was French. If, before the ballots were counted, it was realism to write off nearly all Quebec seats and twenty or more in francophone areas in other parts of the country, enormous momentum was required to break through nationally. Such a situation was ruinous for our party and hurtful to the country. Mulroney presented this argument with consistency and credibility. He was totally at home and idiomatically at ease in the French language. He was not only from Quebec but of Quebec. People like Clark and Stanfield had opened the party to Quebec and to a belief in a greater harmony and ecumenism between the two linguistic groups. In 1983 it was the right time for Mulroney, and he was the right person for the newer, better, wiser, more sensitive political era which had been nurtured in the party by his two predecessors. Once the pre-convention bitterness receded in our memories, and before the highly favourable polls started to come in, I felt good about the coming 1984 campaign. It seemed that we were really in the process of broadening the base of our party as the founder John A. Macdonald so long ago set out as our aim.

In a little pamphlet I wrote for PC party headquarters some years ago, I made this comment on the new party leader. I would not change a word today.

Mulroney's central theme when he sought the party leadership was a call for a dynamic reassertion of the value of the amiable and positive association of Franco-Canadians and Anglo-Canadians within the bosom of the national party. John A. Macdonald had never ceased to recognize the fundamental and essential need of cooperative goodwill between the two peoples. But, through the lean years his party had lost support and understanding in Quebec. Stanfield and Clark had sought to bridge the chasm of this understanding. Mulroney made rapprochement the very cornerstone of his campaign for the party's support.

Before the 1984 election the new national leader's convictions were sternly tested over an issue concerning French language rights in Manitoba, whose premier, Sterling Lyon, was a Conservative. Mulroney went into the province and took a stand against that of the provincial government and of many people in the Manitoba party. His courage helped him in the election, and even Manitobans elected PCs in nine out of fourteen ridings.

The political highlights of 1984 are doubtless fresh in the minds of many Canadians and need to be but briefly recalled here. The Liberals had a divisive convention rather than a quasi-coronation. John Turner, the heir apparent or at least presumptive for so long, won narrowly. The folksy Jean Chrétien, in the words of party president Iona Campagnola, was first in the delegates' hearts if not in their votes. Turner, bearing the heavy burden of the unpopularity of Trudeau, was soundly beaten by Mulroney in the televised debate. Stuck with his predecessor's lengthy list of patronage appointments to major posts, Turner was left intellectually naked and shaken. On the campaign trail the returnee from Bay Street was not the eager, alert young man so many Liberals remembered. Although it may be a denial of the laws of physics, John Turner seemed both rusty and wooden. He obviously made an error in moving so quickly from the convention win to an appeal to the electorate. He had hardly found the bridge before ordering the ship to the high seas. The Liberal ship of state foundered with a vengeance on 4 September 1984. The unfortunate Turner joined Sir Charles Tupper as one of our most short-lived prime ministers. Had he held off the election he might have been able to separate himself from the perceived sins of the Trudeau years.

Out of 282 seats the PCs won a staggering 211. The once great Liberal caucus was reduced to 40, just 10 above Ed Broadbent's NDP. The new government took over on 17 September 1984. Isabel and I were at the victory party at the National Arts Centre that evening. Without question it was the best and smartest social event I had ever attended under the national party's auspices. It was a gala affair and I was delighted to see many long-time stalwarts who had come to Ottawa to join in the jubilation.

Before long, the new government had its problems. There were scandals and hints of scandal. Some ministers left the cabinet. The Gallup Poll wavered and the lustre of victory was tarnished. There was an outcry against proposed moves which would in effect diminish the financial assistance given to the senior citizens of Canada. The prime minister, prudently in my judgment, backed off from this form of fiscal belt-tightening. But steadily the economy of the country was strengthened. Those economic indices which should be high were rising. Unemployment figures fell. So did inflation. Our trade figures were good. Clearly the government was doing a great many of the right things. Whether it was getting credit for this or not was much less certain.

Public opinion polls measuring the percentage of support the different parties had were not all that comforting as a likely election date approached. Through 1988 they fluctuated widely.

	Liberal	PC	NDP
14 January	36	30	31
11 February	41	27	31
10 March	37	28	33
14 April	38	31	30
11 May	39	28	31
9 June	39	31	29
14 July	37	35	27
15 September	33	37	27

In the 1984 campaign Brian Mulroney had been against free trade with the United States. But he subsequently became a strong advocate of such a move. After protracted negotiations a far-reaching Free Trade Agreement (FTA) was drafted. It became the main issue in the 1988 election, many would say the only issue. Both opposition parties took positions strongly against the agreement. There were furious debates in Parliament and in the country. In the television debate in the 1988 campaign Mr Turner was judged the winner. In the immediate aftermath of that galvanic confrontation the Liberals shot up in the polls. Advocates of free trade seemed to go on the defensive.

During the 1988 election campaign itself, there was also amazing fluctuation in the public opinion polls. It was as if the people of Canada couldn't make up their minds, or perhaps they agreed with the last person who tried to cajole or frighten them. The invective was often ignoble and invariably exaggerated. No parliamentary nonsense about honourable or worthy opponents in this campaign! It was too often a discussion of traitors, sleaze bags, people without faith, and similar expletives not helpful to parliamentary democracy at its best. Spokesmen for the Liberals and the NDP were accused of scaring the senior citizens and others about how their financial security would be diminished as a result of free trade. On the other hand there were serious allegations of the none-too-gentle persuasion tactics used by big business employer groups who threatened their workers that without free trade jobs would be lost. Far too often the 1988 campaign revealed some of the roughness and crassness of the sometimes shocking presidential contests in the great republic to the south. I was glad when on 21 November the rough and tumble was over.

Having been in Australia the first two weeks after the election call on 1 October, I missed the first quieter fortnight of our campaign. In that period the PCs had a commanding lead in the polls. After the television debate, a tougher, rougher approach was taken despite the fact that the easy-does-it stance had served well early in the campaign. It will long be argued as to whether the gloves-off tactics were our party's salvation in 1988. Certainly in the last days of the campaign there was a return to the less pugnacious style.

A one-issue election campaign presents certain difficulties to voters. Having chosen Robert Borden for my PHD thesis topic, I was not philosophically a free trader and could not discard some of the verities the Conservative party respected in the 1911 election. At that time big business was also against free trade. (In Borden's time the word was 'reciprocity.') But I had many other reasons for not desiring a return of the Liberals to the corridors of power. There must have been other Progressive Conservatives with similar priorities. And there surely were Liberals who were in favour of the Free Trade Agreement. My colleague Senator George Van Roggen, one of the best informed Canadians on the subject, was one of these. He resigned his chairmanship of the Senate foreign affairs committee in order to support the measure openly.

The 1988 vote gave the Mulroney government a mandate for free trade. When the House of Commons met after the election the two opposition parties began a foolish and futile course of obstruction. The government's eventual use of closure seemed justified. All Canadians can now hope that the measure will generally be beneficial. But sadly I am inclined to believe that it won't be as helpful as its proponents declared it would be.

So refined are our modern polling techniques that a young ministerial executive assistant forecast the result for me in my office on the Thursday before the election. Based on knowledge of last-minute polling, he assured me there would be a majority government but that the likely result in PEI would be a Grit sweep. As I said to Isabel that night: 'Monday's great national effort is almost an anticlimax.'

Even before this astute tip I had heard worrisome predictions about PEI. Naturally I hoped for the best. At such a volatile time I didn't expect Conservative wins in the two seats where the incumbents weren't running, Malpeque and Egmont. But Pat Binns, reoffering in Cardigan, was as close to the ideal MP as one can get. In Hillsborough, Tom McMillan was a credit to any constituency or any government. He was active, intelligent, personable, and, though young, highly experienced in politics. Even after a lifetime in politics I was shaken by the loss of Pat Binns and Tom McMillan. At a dinner at the Australian high commissioner's residence on the Friday before the election, I was asked why PEI seemed to be so strongly against free trade. Although it was a difficult question I welcomed it, since it forced me to organize my thoughts on what motivated my own people.

Certainly it was not because of any demerits in our candidates. Nor was there any strong preference for John Turner as leader. Our provincial premier was actively supporting the Liberals, but in other provinces the views and efforts of the premier seemed not so significant. In my own early days in politics, many of our old people were fearful about voting PC lest their pensions be endangered. Some Liberal activists were both expert and active in sowing seeds of anxiety. In 1988 there were reflections of old-time scare tactics. Also it must be noted that in PEI, as in the Atlantic region generally, there are few big business establishments to mount the opposite type of pressures which were felt in more industrial areas.

But there were other reasons for PEI taking such a strong and contrary stand against the general trend in the country. Behind the Free Trade Agreement, with its stress on the value of great trading blocs, economies of scale, mergers, integration, and the like, there stands the suggestion that bigness of itself is a virtue or even a necessity in the modern world. In PEI we have to believe that small can be beautiful. If economic rationalization is the be-all and the end-all, our continuing existence as a province might someday be ruled counterproductive. When our ancestors, often with reluctance, joined others to form a Dominion, north-south trade with the United States was not considered the big thing. Rather were they sold on the great east-west economic movements which would build a great nation. Many Maritimers to this day have a small feeling of having sacrificed a good deal to join Confederation. This was somewhat relieved by aid from the central government, subsidies, grants, regional expansion funds, and a host of other compensations. If the vitality and clout of the federal government were to be diminished in a supranational trade bloc, what capacity would a Canadian government retain to redress some of the regional imbalances which so heavily burden the Maritime economies?

To a substantial degree it was careful reflection, vague anxiety, and a degree of independent thought which prompted PEI's election performance on 21 November 1988.

Not surprisingly, in the months after the 1988 election I gave much thought to the effect of the Free Trade Agreement upon the Canadian people. Because of the procedures by which the measure was dealt with in the Senate prior to the election, I was never faced with the decision of being for or against it on a recorded vote. After the 1988 election the Liberal majority properly decided to cease their opposition to the FTA. Considering the result of the election and believing that the Senate should not oppose the legislation of a newly elected government, I had no difficulty in voting for the measure on 30 December 1988.

But there was more to it than the terms of the Free Trade Agreement. It seems to me that the present PC government has forgotten that an essential part of Canadian nationalism has been founded on a belief that mere imitation of the American way of life was an insufficient and erroneous way of expressing our national identity. To a large degree we share a great continent with the Americans. We are like them, but we are different. John A. Macdonald knew that. So did Robert Borden. Bennett, as he said at the Charlottetown meeting in 1935, most certainly did. John Diefenbaker did not wish to subsume our way of life under Americanism. I have an uneasy feeling that our present leader Brian Mulroney has no pulse beat for this kind of classic Canadianism.

I had this worry as I saw the cosy relationship developing between President Ronald Reagan and Prime Minister Mulroney. The Shamrock Summit of 1985 may have been good theatre, but it was not a great moment for Canadian nationalists. I used to be proud of Canada's role in the world. We carved out a role for ourselves as a trusted peacekeeper. We were the voice of moderation at the UN and other international assemblies. John Diefenbaker refused to go along with the Americans regarding Cuba, in the early Castro days. Lester Pearson, even in the United States, called for a cessation of the bombing of North Vietnam.

But on the Gulf crisis of 1990-1 it would take a very sharp detective to see much difference between the views and utterances of Washington and those of Ottawa.

I am troubled not only in the field of foreign policy. I fear that a highly casual attitude pervades the present governing party when it comes to serious issues of Canadian nationalism. John A. Macdonald and his colleagues believed that a strong central government was necessary to counterbalance the enormous power of the nation to the south of us. The transcontinental railway for Macdonald was essential to our burgeoning nationhood. Borden opposed reciprocity which he saw as closely equivalent to commercial union which would precede political union. Another

Conservative, R.B. Bennett, sensed that we must control our air-lines and our airways. One of his greatest initiatives was the creation of the Canadian Radio Broadcasting Corporation (CRBC), the predecessor of the CBC. A prince of capitalism, he nevertheless saw the need for state involvement in the media. His enunciation of the media's mandate in the House of Commons on 18 May 1932 reads well to this day.

First of all, this country must be assured of complete control of broadcasting from Canadian sources, free from foreign interference or influence. Without such control radio broadcasting can never become a great agency for communication of matters of national concern and for the diffusion of national thought and ideals, and without such control it can never be the agency by which national consciousness may be fostered and sustained and national unity still further strengthened ...

The cruel slashes of 1990 in the spending of the CBC seem a far cry from the Bennett years. Even in the depths of a Depression profoundly more miserable than today's recession, Bennett found sufficient moneys for the CRBC. In those days the total government budget was a mere fraction of today's vast expenditure.

From the first day I entered the PC caucus in 1957 I heard a heavy strain of hostility to the CBC. Personally I thought that the CBC had done great things for the development of the Canadian intellectual and artistic community. When a CBC outlet was established in Prince Edward Island, the political awareness of all the media was uplifted, and coverage of public affairs increased on all the outlets. The cutbacks announced in late 1990 were hurtful to the CBC. Some of these were particularly difficult to justify. What kind of reasoning would put Windsor in the forefront for closure? Some funny things happen in the world of politics. I had the feeling throughout the debates on the Free Trade Agreement, the 1988 election, and the Meech Lake Accord that the CBC's 'neutrality' had a noticeable and consistent slant to the PCs. I also thought it a remarkable coincidence that, amid the swirling criticism of station closures and 1100 job cuts at the CBC, its president,

Gérard Veilleux, should be given the country's highest public service award.

During the Mulroney years, there was also widespread criticism about the drastic cuts in the Via Rail service and the closure of many post offices in small Canadian communities, both in the name of restraint. Actually the nation's rail passenger service was under the gun long before 1985. Railway abandonment was a complaint during the Trudeau years. Sometimes railway service was first downgraded and then withdrawn because the public weren't using the service. It may be that this did happen, but there seemed to be a widespread deploring of the loss of our railways by many Canadians who, while they may have loved railways, didn't use them. Once upon a time Canadians accepted the view that there were many services which were provided to the citizenry whether or not they were profitable. Today we have accepted too readily a user-pay mentality. We never would have built the country we have if such a view had prevailed in the great years of national Canadian development and growth.

But as I reflect on my party's stewardship, my concerns go beyond a few seemingly besieged national institutions. When I was Mr Stanfield's spokesman on Health and Welfare, my credo was that a government should help most those citizens who most need help. A country rich enough to be among the big seven economic giants should not have the poverty and need that is regularly revealed by the reports of the National Council of Welfare. In its report for 1989 the council was distressed by the range and depth of poverty. In all the provinces there are great numbers of Canadians eking out an existence well below the poverty line. In recent years, sadly, food banks have become a way of life in many cities and towns across Canada. In far too many parts of the country the soup kitchen has reappeared. Surely such a situation should sear our souls.

A few years ago one heard complaints about too much paternalism in government. Reaganism and Thatcherism were in vogue; now some of the devotees of these rigid doctrines are less sure. Perhaps there is room for benevolence and greater compassion. The abrupt ouster of Margaret Thatcher demonstrated a great sensitivity to the changing mood of the public on the part of that highly pragmatic institution, the British Conservative party. Whether dropping the Iron Lady will deflect from the party the public wrath which was coming remains to be seen. There is already considerable evidence that the hard-line policies of the right were not as efficacious as proclaimed. When Ronald Reagan assumed the presidency, the United States was a great creditor nation. Eight years later, it was a leading debtor nation.

Prime Minister Mulroney and his government have fallen far lower in public opinion polls than Thatcher or Reagan ever did. Any thoughtful Progressive Conservative must be deeply concerned about this. Is our lowly estate attributable to the personality of the party leader, the perception and performance of the government, or to some fundamental errors in judgment?

In these days of heady leader dominance, nearly all the blame or credit accrues to the man at the top. Certainly a great many Canadians have intensely hostile feelings about their prime minister. Pierre Trudeau also had many detractors but, in his case, there always seemed to be a large following of die-hard devotees. Unfortunately, I don't see such a group supporting Mulroney. On occasion his maladroit utterances are hard to understand and still harder to defend. After all the travail, pain, and anxiety over Meech Lake, his seemingly boastful utterance about 'rolling the dice' must have taken a great toll in public esteem.

Although I was troubled by the salesmanship of the Meech Lake Accord, I never had any reservations about the value of such a realistic agreement – indeed its necessity. In 1982 I voted against the constitutional accord the Trudeau government had carried through. It was not easy to vote contrary to my national leader, Joe Clark. But I thought a nine-province constitution not good enough for a ten-province country. I was also distressed by a too great emphasis on charters, the exaltation of the judiciary, and the downgrading of the role of legislatures in our political and social structure.

Five years later on Meech Lake I had no reservations. Through all the agony and acrimony of the succeeding months I never wavered in my support. We Canadians would have saved ourselves a good deal of strain had Meech been accepted. On 5 May 1987, the very day it was presented to the Senate by our leader, Lowell Murray, I made a brief, impromptu speech expressing my complete support.

Recalling my 1982 anxieties, I said:

If I felt then that the inclusion of Quebec was the *sine qua non* of my support, how can I now take the view that the inclusion of Quebec is not the most important thing? I suppose that I would fall into Senator Flynn's category. I hope that I am not an extreme centralist, but I am a centralist. I believe that the whole is more important than the parts or the sum of the parts.

Honourable senators, I do not rejoice in what I call 'growing provincialism,' but I do know what our representatives, both provincial and federal, could have done the other day except what they did – that is to complete, to make whole our Constitution –

Senator Frith: They could have said no!

Senator Macquarrie: – from which develops the wholeness and completeness of the country. Therefore, I salute those people.

If we have misgivings, if we have forebodings – and I have some – whoever said that the life of a nation, any more than the life of an individual, was to be devoid of concern and anxiety? Of course there are problems ahead, but I think that the first essential is the viewpoint, the attitude, what Montesquieu used to call 'the spirit of laws.' And the spirit the other day, whether we worry about the details or not, was noble and strong. I want to join those who congratulate our two senatorial colleagues. I was honoured, as a senator, that Senator Murray was given such very important, onerous responsibilities in the Government of Canada. He had discharged them, in such a way that we may all be proud and honoured. I am delighted to speak to this subject today.

Hon. Senators: Hear, Hear!

Some months later, during the Liberal senators' filibuster against the goods and services tax (GST), Mulroney was taken to task by the *Toronto Star* for stereotyping senior citizens in his remark:

'They should be in bed, at 71 years of age, having milk and cookies.' No matter what he thinks of old people, a prudent politician will not alienate them, because both they and their loved ones have votes.

One of my favourite writers on political science, Viscount Bryce, stressed the educative role of political parties. It would seem that the Mulroney government is not adept at stimulating public understanding and approval of its policies. It was a mistake to present the Meech Lake Accord as a 'seamless web' which had to remain intact. Many Canadians resented the suggestion that nothing in the accord could be altered one iota. Such an approach made discussion seem futile.

No Canadian government has ever done so much polling of public opinion as the Mulroney government. Yet it seems so often to be running counter to the overwhelming public attitude. Mackenzie King appeared to be able to read and sometimes anticipate public reaction without any sophisticated polling devices. Recently in Canada we have sometimes seen the unelected chamber, the Senate, as a better reflector of public opinion than the elected House of Commons, or the government which dominates that chamber.

It wasn't a great time to be a Conservative when I was first stimulated by the political game. We went into the wilderness in 1935 and remained there for twenty-two years. But as unloveable as he was and in the throes of a terrible Depression, Bennett won 29.6 per cent in the polls, and in the York North by-election held in December 1990 our vote didn't quite make 10 per cent.

I am sometimes distressed by the attitude of certain Progressive Conservatives as they view the dreary tundra of public opinion polls. They tend to point to the election victory of 1988 as a great example of turning around public opinion. In my youth I often thought that a foot-slogging pessimism diminished our party's chances. Might it not be that an overreliance on a repeat of 1988 might be even more hurtful? The attitude that there is nothing the electorate can do until the next election is not warmly greeted by the voters. I wish, too, that our spin doctors would refer less to a five-year term. Bennett, elected in July 1930, deferred the election until October 1935. Not surprisingly, Canadians tended to see the prolongation as the act of a man already written off. Today's Canadian voters are not likely to be assured by the thought that their views will have no consequence until 1993. It's a long time to be dissatisfied!

It's always dangerous to forecast elections. In Walter Scott's poem *The Lady of the Lake*, King James described public opinion as a 'many-headed monster-thing.' Pollsters tell us that the Canadian electorate is highly volatile. While the PCs are certainly not the darlings of the electorate, the other parties have their troubles too. Many Liberals are today regretting that they didn't choose the able, young, and personable Paul Martin instead of the once-popular but currently uninspiring Jean Chrétien. Despite its popularity – likely to be sustained – in Alberta, it is doubtful that the strangely named Reform Party will do much better outside Alberta than did Social Credit, except as 'spoiler' in a number of constituencies. I would be astounded if the Manning party does as well as the genuine populist reform group, the Progressives, who in 1921 won 65 out of 235 seats in the House of Commons. Lucien Bouchard, Mulroney's erstwhile Quebec lieutenant, may do well in Quebec but will certainly not sweep the province. Unless she has a run of bad luck or makes some egregious blunders, Audrey McLaughlin may do reasonably well outside Quebec. Because of the NDP strength it is imperative that the PCs develop an appeal to Canadians now flirting with the NDP. It may be pleasing to bask in the support of the corporate élite. But to win elections, Bay Street is not enough. There must be support on Main Street and among the ranks of ordinary Canadians, including the impoverished and the depressed. Surely it is of the essence that the PCs today must broaden their base as the founder of our party, John A. Macdonald, so wisely advised in 1854.

It is apparent that some of our spin doctors are advising the PCs to challenge the Reform Party for the hard-line, right-wing vote. But, if such a course should help to push many Canadian voters into the arms of the Liberal party and the NDP, what would be accomplished? Despite the hearty hostility of the corporate élite, NDP Premier Bob Rae of Ontario may not be a lost cause. There is evidence too that the followers of Tommy Douglas and J.S. Woodsworth are making new friends and gaining new support in various parts of Canada. Even in Nova Scotia, the long-time third party may be moving closer to wider acceptance in the broad electorate.

Predicting elections is a fun pastime but foolish exercise. The long-sustained low regard for the Tories in public opinion polls would prompt one to forecast an ignominious defeat for them. Party faithful taught to worship at the shrine of the great 1988 victory have glowing visions of another triumph. They note correctly that Prime Minister Mulroney is a far better campaigner than Chrétien or McLaughlin. He is also more sensitive to political realities than most of his right-wing lieutenants. At this juncture, a PC victory seems a long shot, but the ineptitude of their opponents might bring about a third government for the Tories.

SOBER SECOND THOUGHTS

In the fall of 1990 I was depressed, downhearted, and disillusioned. My country was drifting into a war which didn't appear to lead to a better peace afterwards. At the same time, the Senate, an institution dear to me, descended to shocking depths of nastiness.

As a political scientist and a keen student of Canadian political history, I had long known the value of a second chamber in a federal state. I also knew that one of the essential bargains at Confederation was equality of representation for Ontario and Quebec. As George Brown put it, without that agreement, Confederation would not have advanced a single step. As a member of the Lower House from 1957 to 1979, I knew many senators and realized the falsity of the charges that they were just a bunch of old fuddy-duddies and mostly rich bagmen. In joint parliamentary committees, the senators often outclassed their Commons colleagues. They also did splendid work in Senate standing committees. Many public servants have told me how much more thorough Senate committees were in their examination of government legislation and in their questioning of senior bureaucrats.

In their long-range investigations of important issues, Senate committees have produced some excellent reports. It is invidious to be selective, but I'll take the risk in naming some of the best senatorial inquiries. The foreign affairs committee's study of Canada-Commonwealth Caribbean relations was a splendid exercise. On a tour of several of our Commonwealth neighbours in the south in the early 1970s, I discovered that nearly all Caribbean statesmen had a copy of the Senate Committee report on hand, indeed in their bookcase, and recognized the Canadian Senate committee's view as insightful and helpful.

The late senator, David Croll, was long an acknowledged champion of the rights of the aged and impoverished in our midst. The agriculture committee under Senator Sparrow produced a report entitled *Soil at Risk*, which is widely regarded as an excellent document on environmental protection. Before my elevation to the Senate, its foreign affairs committee had come out with a thoughtful and forward-looking report on the importance of closer Canadian relations with Europe. I was the vice-chairman of that committee when it produced another perceptive report on Canada's relationship with the Middle East. As far as I know, no other legislative body conducted such a careful inquiry of that most sensitive area.

While never an enthusiast for free trade, I must record that the same committee, after a long, exhaustive (and exhausting) study period, pioneered in coming out for free trade between Canada and its big southern neighbour.

For these, as for a broad array of careful studies, the Senate committees were ideally suited. They were not so sensitive to tomorrow's headlines as their colleagues in the Lower House. They had the time for a serious look at serious issues. Although most senators came from a political background, their partisanship was somewhat subcutaneous. Not every issue was dominated by the question: 'What's in it for my party?' Senators had the luxury of not being vote-driven.

In my maiden speech in the Senate, on 16 October 1979, I

expressed the joy of finding myself a Red Tory in the Red Chamber. I noted that the Senate had on paper very great powers. Indeed, I declared it to be one of the most powerful second chambers in the world. I attributed the continuance of this situation to the fact that over the years the Canadian Senate had the wisdom not to abuse its powers. And so it was for my first ten years in Canada's senior house.

But all this changed drastically as the decade of the 1980s came to a close. Senator Allan J. MacEachen, whom I first met in 1955, was a most brilliant parliamentary tactician. He served as House leader with great distinction in the Trudeau minority government. He was and is a highly partisan man. With MacEachen in place as the leader of the Liberal majority in the Senate facing a raft of highly unpopular government bills, a confrontational situation loomed.

With its untrammelled powers, and facing a variety of government measures resisted by the Canadian electorate, a collision was inevitable. MacEachen was a master strategist. Some of the government's front-liners like Harvie Andre were about as graceful as an elephant dancing the gavotte, and so there were many hold-ups and delays. The British, much wiser in these things, had long ago limited the powers of the Upper House. The peers of the realm could hold up legislation for a year except in the case of a money bill, on which their power of suspension was limited to one month. There was a clear-cut formula for the designation of a money bill.

Without this sensible safeguard, the Canadian Parliament found itself in a series of confrontations between the two houses, with the Senate having the more skilled tacticians at the helm. On the hated goods and services tax, the unelected Senate Liberals were in tune with Canadian public opinion, the elected Conservatives in the Lower House were running counter to the popular view.

So far, this is a political scientist's description of a conflict between a government out of touch with public opinion or indifferent to it and an unelected house with potent constitutional powers. But in the fall session of 1990, the Liberals in the Senate embraced tactics which were totally unprecedented and, in a word, shameless. I sat in the Senate, silent but horrified, at the behaviour of colleagues whom I had once honoured and respected. What had been a dignified and praiseworthy legislative body became a jungle. Senators screamed uncouth remarks at their opposite numbers. Reasoned debate was replaced by roaring interruptions, noise-makers, the ringing of cow bells, and other disgraceful exhibitions. All of them made me wonder what had happened to this chamber of sober second thought which I had long held in high regard.

It was not easy to support the GST. This was especially the case when it was so ineptly sold to the Canadian people. For some weird reason, the minister of finance chose to dub the new imposition as 'revenue neutral'! The public might have accepted the new 7 per cent levy if they believed that it was designed to cut the overwhelming national deficit. They might have accepted it if it had been presented as a health or welfare tax designed to help erect a safety net for our good social purposes. But who would be stirred to support an obvious increase in taxes if it was merely revenue neutral. From the beginning, I wondered about the wisdom of the spin doctors sitting on the advisory boards of the Mulroney government. Did none of them think that a hidden tax, even the 13.5 per cent manufacturer's tax, was likely to be more palatable than an open tax, over which you grimace every time the cash register rings?

The country will survive the GST. Whether the government will or not will eventually be determined. But I fear the Senate will require a long period to recover from the excesses of the GST debate. During the weeks of the awful filibuster I said to my wise colleague, John M. Macdonald, that it would take a long while for the Senate to return to the agreeable ambience of earlier days. He replied 'It will never be the same again.' I profoundly hope that my sage old colleague will be proven a pessimist. But so far the evidence does not disprove his forecast.

Almost since it was first structured in 1867, the Senate has been the object of criticism. Senate reform has been like the weather, a subject which, as Mark Twain said, many talk about but no one does anything about. Prior to the ignominious collapse of the

Meech Lake Accord, the favourite nostrum for reforming the long-criticized Senate was the Triple-E solution. Another of Alberta's political theories, this formula sought an Upper House which would be elected, equal, and effective. The idea won great favour in right-wing Alberta and in the West generally. Others in a mood of accommodation to the alienated westerners expressed support for the idea. Prime Minister Mulroney actually appointed a Reform senator who had been elected under what appeared to be a highly unconstitutional piece of provincial legislation.

But in all the ballyhoo about a Triple-E Senate some basic questions were ignored. Under our present parliamentary structure the House of Commons is the chamber of confidence. A government to survive must retain the confidence of the elected chamber. Under the present rigours of party discipline, which makes loyal party members virtual rubber stamps, this formula is not all that meaningful. To posit a situation in which the Upper House is also elected and, as some Triple-E advocates would have it, by a bigger constituency than the House of Commons, what then? Could an elected Senate be expected to bow its head in deference to the men and women in the Green Chamber? Or would both houses have the right to dispose of a government? Before the Triple-E formula is adopted, the members of the House of Commons may awaken to the threat it would present to their role in the nation's Parliament.

Although interested in the Triple-E advocacy, and sometimes bemused by the support my unelected colleagues express for it, I never expected the Triple-E formula to survive. In the last gasps of the Meech Lake discussions, when I never knew whether to laugh or cry at our first ministers' performance on national television, we saw something of an extravaganza on Senate reform.

The since-defeated David Peterson of Ontario offered to cede six Senate seats. On the same auction block, the premiers of New Brunswick and Nova Scotia offered to give up two seats each. This I found mildly amusing since both of their provinces had been diddled at Confederation. At that time, only the PEI delegation argued for equality of provincial representation in the Senate.

New Brunswick and Nova Scotia settled for half the representation given to the new provinces of Quebec and Ontario. Silent in this give-away was the premier of Quebec. In a speech in the Senate on 14 June 1990 in which I showed no enthusiasm for Triple-E, I observed that the distinct society has no desire to become the diminished society in terms of Senate representation. As long as we wish to have Quebec as a part of Confederation – and I hope that is a long time – the Triple-E scheme is a reform solution which will not fly.

I have long been an enthusiast for the Canadian Senate. I made countless speeches stressing its importance in the parliamentary structure. I have written a substantial treatise on the Canadian Senate which I hope to polish for publication in the near future. But the Liberal shenanigans of the fall of 1990 affected me deeply. I had often been asked by the Senate information coordinator to speak to youth groups visiting the Senate. But for five months after the mayhem of autumn 1990, I found it impossible to speak on the merits of the Canadian Senate.

The sad events of the anti-GST filibuster for a while augmented the body of opinion which feels that the only worthwhile reform of the Senate is its total abolition.

The NDP had long been consistent in its advocacy of such a drastic solution. It was therefore interesting to note a discussion paper by an action group of the NDP caucus discussing Senate reform as well as its abolition.

The equal part of Triple-E never had much chance. Nor was the effective part of the trio ever a strong survivor. Governments are not keen on having a second powerful house nor do most premiers really want an upper house of the national parliament enshrined as the spokesman for provincial rights. Premiers themselves feel that is their role. Shrewd observers have argued that it was never in the cards to have a Triple-E Senate. It is unlikely that this move will make a profound difference in our constitutional structure.

I often think that if Canadians had really wanted deep and meaningful alterations in the Senate, such would have been achieved long ago. Perhaps there is much in the popular wisdom. It is hard to be convinced that tinkering with the structure of the Senate is Canada's most profound problem.

In the summer of 1991, it appeared that the constitutional committee of the Mulroney cabinet was committed to an elected Senate. Having arrived at my riper years, I have no personal anxieties over the Senate becoming elected. But as I recall that the worst period of my Senate membership came when partisanship was rife, I wonder. At its best, the Senate kept its partisanship under control. Will not the process of electioneering and campaigning under party labels vitiate much of the value and virtue of the ancient chamber of sober second thought?

Except for those traumatic days of late 1990, I much enjoyed my time in the Canadian Senate. I liked the House of Commons, but found the Senate a more effective and compatible place. The speeches were better, the committee work more productive, the ambience much more agreeable. I fear that an elected Senate might become nothing more than a smaller version of the House of Commons. Such a development would not have been worth the effort.

Notes

1 W. Menzies Whitelaw, *The Maritimes and Canada before Confederation* (Toronto: Oxford University Press 1934), 28
2 *Report of the Royal Commission on Maritime Claims*, Sir Andrew Rae Duncan, chairman (Ottawa 1927); *Report of the Royal Commission On Financial Arrangements between the Dominion and the Maritime Provinces*, Sir Thomas White, chairman (Ottawa 1935)
3 R.B. Bennett, *The Premier Speaks to the People: The First Address* (Ottawa: Dominion Conservative Headquarters 1935), 11
4 A.R.M. Lower, *Colony to Nation: A History of Canada* (Toronto: Longmans, Green & Company 1946), 515

1 J.L. Granatstein, *The Politics of Survival: The Conservative Party of Canada, 1939–1945* (Toronto: University of Toronto Press 1967), 112
2 John R. Williams, *The Conservative Party of Canada, 1920–1949* (Durham: Duke University Press 1956), 231
3 *Convention Documents*, 'Text Statement Issued to the Press by the Right Honourable Arthur Meighen, P.C., K.C.,' 23 September 1942
4 National Archives of Canada (NA), Arthur Meighen Papers, Meighen to Bennett, 16 December 1942

5 Ruth Bell, 'Conservative Party National Conventions, 1972–1956: Organization and Procedure' (MA thesis, Carleton University 1966), 35
6 NA, Macdonald Papers, Sir John A. Macdonald to Captain James McGill Strachan, 9 February 1854
7 John Bracken, *The Party – Its Future: Address at the Second Annual Meeting of the Progressive Conservative Party of Canada: Ottawa, March 3, 1944* (Ottawa: Progressive Conservative Party 1944)
8 J. Murray Beck, *Pendulum of Power: Canada's Federal Elections* (Scarborough: Prentice-Hall 1968), 273, quoting Halifax *Chronicle-Herald*, 29 June 1949

3 PROFESSOR TO POLITICIAN

1 Beck, *Pendulum of Power,* 276

5 IN WITH DIEF

1 *Preliminary Report of the Royal Commission on Canada's Economic Prospects*, Walter L. Gordon, chairman (Ottawa: December 1956), 99–100
2 Dalton Camp, *Gentlemen, Players and Politicians* (Toronto: McClelland & Stewart 1970), 321
3 Jack W. Pickersgill, *The Road Back* (Toronto: University of Toronto Press 1986), 17
4 Ibid., 19

6 OUT WITH DIEF

1 *Canadian Annual Review for 1962* (Toronto: University of Toronto Press 1963), 27–8
2 *Canadian Annual Review for 1963,* 287
3 Eddie Goodman, *The Life of the Party* (Toronto: Key Porter Books 1988), 117
4 Beck, *Pendulum of Power,* 374
5 Peter C. Newman, *The Distemper of Our Times: Canadian Politics in Transition: 1963–68* (Toronto: McClelland & Stewart 1968), 132
6 John G. Diefenbaker, *One Canada: Memoirs of the Right Honourable*

John G. Diefenbaker: The Tumultuous Years, 1962–1967 (Toronto: Macmillan 1977), 302

7 NOBLEST ROMAN OF THEM ALL

1 Geoffrey Stevens, *Stanfield* (Toronto: McClelland & Stewart 1973), 12
2 Ibid., 157

8 THE BEST PRIME MINISTER WE ALMOST HAD

1 Stevens, *Stanfield*, 228
2 Heward Grafftey, *Lessons from the Past: From Dief to Mulroney* (Montreal: Eden Press 1987), 17

9 IDEALIST ABROAD

1 *Dictionary of Canadian Quotations and Phrases* (Toronto: McClelland & Stewart 1979), 917
2 Diefenbaker, *One Canada*, 80
3 *Ottawa Journal*, 4 April 1949

10 RED TORY, RED CHAMBER

1 Heath Macquarrie, *A Brief History of the Progressive Conservative Party of Canada* (Ottawa: The Progressive Conservative Party of Canada 1986), 21

Index